LANGUAGE:
AN ENQUIRY INTO ITS
MEANING AND FUNCTION

SCIENCE OF CULTURE SERIES

Planned and Edited by

RUTH NANDA ANSHEN

LANGUAGE:

AN ENQUIRY INTO ITS

MEANING AND FUNCTION

KENNIKAT PRESS
Port Washington, N. Y./London

LANGUAGE

Copyright, 1957, Harper & Brothers
Reissued in 1971 by Kennikat Press by
arrangement with Harper & Row Publishers, Inc.
Library of Congress Catalog Card No: 75-91040
ISBN 0-8046-1396-6

Manufactured by Taylor Publishing Company   Dallas, Texas

ESSAY AND GENERAL LITERATURE INDEX REPRINT SERIES

TO SUZANNE

I WOULD LIKE TO RECORD MY WARM APPRECIA-TION TO DR. KURT GOLDSTEIN WHOSE VALUABLE SUGGESTIONS HAVE GREATLY ENRICHED THE PREP-ARATION OF THIS VOLUME.

RUTH NANDA ANSHEN

CONTENTS

SCIENCE OF CULTURE SERIES   xii

Part One.   The Principle

    I.   LANGUAGE AS IDEA   3
Ruth Nanda Anshen

   II.   THE NATURE OF LANGUAGE   18
Kurt Goldstein

  III.   THE ORIGIN OF LANGUAGE   41
N. H. Tur-Sinai

  IV.   AUM: THE WORD OF WORDS   80
Swami Nikhilananda

   V.   LANGUAGE AND THE THEORY
OF SIGN   86
Jacques Maritain

  VI.   SYMBOLS AND HISTORY   102
George Boas

  VII.   THE WORD OF GOD   122
Paul Tillich

VIII.   THE LANGUAGE OF SILENCE   134
Richard P. Blackmur

Part Two.   The Application

  IX.   THE CARDINAL DICHOTOMY
IN LANGUAGE   155
Roman Jakobson

X.   SQUARES AND OBLONGS   174
      W. H. Auden

XI.   MYSTICISM AND ITS LANGUAGE   179
      Charles W. Morris

XII. SYMBOLIC LANGUAGE OF DREAMS   188
      Erich Fromm

XIII. LANGUAGE OF POETRY   201
      Leo Spitzer

XIV. LANGUAGE OF JURISPRUDENCE   232
      Huntington Cairns

XV.   LANGUAGE OF POLITICS   270
      Harold D. Lasswell

XVI. LANGUAGE OF THE THEATER   285
      Francis Fergusson

XVII. ART AS SYMBOLIC SPEECH   296
      Margaret Naumburg

XVIII. A PHILOSOPHY OF TRANSLATION   321
      Jean P. de Menasce

XIX. LANGUAGE AS COMMUNICATION   341
      Ruth Nanda Anshen

      BIOGRAPHICAL NOTE   356

      INDEX   357

"Man Is Man By Virtue Of Language"

Wilhelm von Humboldt

SCIENCE OF CULTURE SERIES

Man alone, during his brief existence on this earth, is free to examine, to know, to criticize, and to create. In this freedom lies his superiority over the forces that pervade his outward life. He is that unique organism in terms of matter and energy, space and time which is urged to conscious purpose. Reason is his characteristic and distinguishing principle. But man is only man—and only free when he considers himself as a total being in whom "the unmediated whole of feeling and thought" is not severed and who impugns any form of atomization as artificial, mischievous, and predatory.

Nevertheless, the persistent interrelationship of the processes of the human mind has been, for the most part, so ignored as to create serious distortions in the understanding of man. These distortions are often so great, the specialists so unable to grasp the inner synthesis and organic unity of life, that there are still those who cling to that ancient tenet: "Blessed is he who shall not reveal what has been revealed unto him."

The mutual unintelligibility among contemporary thinkers, their apparent inability to communicate the meaning and purpose of their ideas to those of differing schools of thought, the paucity of their knowledge of the subjects and researches of others —all this has grown to be as profound as it is ominous. And the possibility of clarifying the confusion and of overcoming the distortions often seems remote. The subdivision, specialization, even atomization characteristic of religious, philosophic, and scientific ideas, of political events and social movements during the last three centuries have proved to be an almost invincible impediment to an adequate correlation of these very ideas and movements, which, in truth, are in perpetual interplay. The postulates, categories, dialectical promptings, fecund analogies, or decisive doctrines which first appear in one eminent province of human thought may, and frequently do, penetrate into a diversity of other realms; and to be cognizant of only one of them is to misunderstand the character, kinship, logic, and operation of the entire organism and to obscure the illuminating interrelations.

Human thought and knowledge have never before been so abundant, so vast, and yet at the same time so diffused, so inchoate, so seemingly directionless. And alongside this knowledge exist anxiety, restlessness, despair, frustration, and the dark loneliness of man, who gazes on the universe and finds that it is indifferent to human aspiration. There has been little recognition of the importance of an organic clarification of modern knowledge and of the affinity of ideas, a kind of encyclopedic synthesis, indispensable if human affairs are to be handled with hopeful freshness. All great changes are preceded by a vigorous intellectual reorganization and nothing new can be attempted in collective human thought and action without a reinterpretation of the fundamental principles by which man lives and has his being.

Is there no hope for man to live a well-ordered life, to be able to depend upon the help of his fellow beings, especially upon those who by their ideas direct and interpret the course of his existence? Is the knowledge which man most requires, namely, the knowledge of himself, to be found only in terms of Delphic ambiguity or in erroneous understanding? The modern world imagined itself on the threshold of Utopia but awakened to find itself on the edge of an abyss.

The triumphant advance of science, culminating in new realities concerning the subatomic world and overthrowing the traditional assumptions of causality and uniformity, have almost succeeded in enfeebling man's faith in his spiritual and moral worth and in his own significance in the cosmic scheme.

Out of such considerations as these the *Science of Culture Series* had its genesis. A regard for the integrity of the intellectual life, its moral and spiritual meaning, inspired the plan to bring about a correlation of those contemporary ideas which are concerned not only with sense data and logical universals but with the status of values, the bearing of these values on conduct, and the meaning of man in relation to himself, his fellow man, and the universe. Those leaders of the mind and spirit in the various branches of scholarly enquiry, among them the contributors to this volume, with whom this plan was discussed seemed to be deeply aware of the principal ailment of mankind: the disjunction of empirical approach from theory, of methods of observation from speculative doctrine, and the grave lacunae existent in the study of the nature of man. They seemed to know that values are eternally present, to question how these values might be discovered, to wonder why they are confused, and to be anxious to determine in what sense they are present even when they are not recognized.

It was deemed desirable to establish a series of books, each devoted to the discussion, from diverse and important contemporary points of view, of a single, well-defined question, the object being, first, to make clear how much agreement there is, and on what specific points pertinent to the question; and second, to make as explicit as possible the points of disagreement and their real grounds. This Series (of which this is the eighth volume) is doing much to clarify the present situation with respect to the questions defined, and such clarification should be an aid toward eventual agreement. A cooperative effort to accomplish this, to exhibit with all possible clarity where representatives of different schools of thought agree and precisely where and precisely why they disagree, and to do this fairly concisely is, we venture to say, of the utmost importance. It is hoped that a new vision of man has been articulated. For a doctrine of man has been lacking in our epoch, that doctrine which might permit the virtues of the human race to exist concurrently, in spite of human cupidity and human wilfullness, and which might be nurtured in such a manner as to fulfill that prevision of man of which Dante sang.

A further aim of this Series is to explore the implications of modern natural science and its limitations. At one time in man's history an idea could be suppressed by showing that it was in opposition to religion. In this way theology was often the greatest source of fallacies. In our own epoch, when human thought can be discredited by branding it as unscientific, the power previously exercised by theology has passed over to science. It would appear that the time has come to restrain the abuses of the scientific method both in the interest of other human ideals which are threatened and also in the interest of science itself which is menaced by self-destruction unless it can be attuned to the wider and deeper range of human thought and human experience. The very tendency in natural science to accept the results of its methodology as the ultimate reality rather than recognizing these results as the product of the method itself, is indeed cause for concern. Our purpose is to question whether men are able to pursue their moral ideals within a conceptual framework (scientific) which denies reality to them; to point to the false standard of detached objectivity and to the compulsion in man exercised by it; and finally to demonstrate in what way there is an inherent independence of mental growth which though conditioned by circumstances is never determined by circumstances.

The *Science of Culture Series,* because of the enlargement of the conceptual framework of knowledge, endeavors to restore order within the respective branches of man's consciousness and to disclose analogies in man's position regarding the analysis and synthesis of experience in apparently separated domains of knowledge suggesting the possibility of an ever more embracing objective description of the meaning of life.

One of the values of such a correlation of ideas can be the formulation of a cultural directory for the guidance of mankind, the creation of a systematic circumspection compatible with the principles of liberty and justice, the discernment of possible alternatives in a social crisis, leading to a genuine experience of universality and individuality, dynamics and form, freedom and destiny of the human person, and establishing a genuine social democracy in which collective intelligence is so developed as to make individuality not only possible but effective.

The material necessities of existence and the spiritual values of the contemporary world, which coexist in the same complex social totality, are functionally interdependent and must be coordinated to assure the stability of the civilizations of the world. This Series has been undertaken in the hope that it will manifest and cherish the spirit of *scientia,* which has not been emptied of *sapientia* and which therefore makes the science of culture possible in the conduct of human affairs; that it will be a laboratory for the discussion of important contemporary problems—with an end to directing the thought and action of mankind; that by gathering, in an organic crucible, knowledge pertaining to values it may in part bring back into human society that humanity which has been so rudely eliminated; and that, finally, it may portray the way in which spirit is immanent in nature and nature intimately woven into the fabric of society.

* * *

The problem of this volume, a problem of the greatest antiquity, is one of singular importance. It draws attention to the mystery, the miracle, and the magic of language.

The authors, from their respective disciplines, attempt to define a philosophy of language, to point to the nature, meaning, and function of language, and finally to articulate the unitive principle which justifies and purifies and under which may be subsumed both language and word, *la langue* and *la parole,* the former constituting the universal and the latter the temporal or individual process of the experience of language in the human race. Language is thus conceived as that depository of the accumulated body of experience to which all the former ages have contributed their part and which is the inheritance of all that is yet to come.

The questions treated here possess a certain homogeneity within their multiplicity. The emphasis placed upon the reality that language is not exclusively an exogamic process, not a mere social and historical phenomenon, shows that it is endowed with a metaphysical nature. This metaphysical character of language may not be denied by the atomistic thinking of logical positivism which blends the old empiricism with the new logistic and is enslaved by a theory of tautology based on an illegitimate ignoring of intentional meaning.

The authors attempt herein to analyze the metaphysical hypothesis of language elucidating not only the individual differences in the linguistic structures of human societies and the general rules which must be employed as a means of communication among all the members of the speaking community, pointing to the ways of achieving a genuine communication. They also commit themselves to the clarification of the limitations of common speech. They endeavor to show that the uncritical dialectic is indeed a fallacious tool, that any linguistic discussion is an instrument but not a source, that the word is but a phonic symbol of language, the word which in itself is imperfect and by its nature incomplete and fragmentary.

The reader will observe that there is a conspicuous absence of a chapter devoted to the problem of semantics. The omission is intentional. For any analysis of this question would, in the light of the fundamental postulate of this volume, constitute a critical evaluation. Semantics, from the point of view of the authors in this book, is accepted as a necessary and even valuable cleansing of the Augean stables of language. However, it is here submitted that an ontology of language can never be derived from the isolated, sign-driven, symbol-omitting premise of semantics.

There is a further effort here to point to the errors to which the philosophic method itself is inevitably subjected when it uncritically places its trust in the principle of empiricism as a basis for an epistemology of language. It is shown that man possesses insights and consciousness beyond those meanings which have already been stabilized in etymology and grammar. In this way the various roles of philosophy, literature, and science are constantly engaged in attempting by an inner movement and inclination of reason to find linguistic expression for meanings as yet unexpressed.

This volume's further purpose is to give a perspective on language, to show what language is, its variability in time and place, its permanence, and its relation to the thought and history of man. Among its aims is the attempt to demonstrate the errors and the ineptitude of the exclusively empirical approach in understanding the problem of language and the fallacy of the assumption that thought is the action of language mechanisms. The authors hope to convey that it is important to comprehend the broader implications of the science of linguistics if one is to be preserved from the sterility and futility which a purely technical treatment of the question would inevitably impose. For the significance of language in relation to art, psychology, or law, to mention only three of the multiple aspects here treated, reveals that a philosophy of language, linguistic forms, and historical processes is indispensable for values and diagnosis in the profoundly difficult questions presented by the curious and gathering power which the protean life of the spirit possesses.

It was Euripides who defined in poetic form the basic philosophic problem of man. He uttered the primordial cry, as poignant now as then, the cry of the mystery and the miracle of the *Word:* "Zeus, whether thou are Compulsion of Nature or Intelligence of Mankind, to thee I pray."

It is hoped finally that we have succeeded in avowing that idea and expression are indivisible, and that the power within us greater than any other than ourselves resembles the force of the sublime which transports and transfigures. We have sought that

reality which presses language into word and which compels us to
accept, as Heraclitus did, the last injunction of the spirit: "Do not
listen to me," he declared, "but to the *Word* and confess that all
things are one."

Ruth Nanda Anshen

New York City
1957

Part One

THE PRINCIPLE

Chapter I

RUTH NANDA ANSHEN

LANGUAGE AS IDEA

Language gives evidence of its reality through three categories of human experience. The first may be considered as the meaning of words; the second, as those meanings enshrined in grammatical forms; and the third and, in the view of this author, the most significant, as those meanings which lie beyond grammatical forms, those meanings mysteriously and miraculously revealed to man. It is with the last category that this chapter will endeavor to deal, for its thesis is that thought itself must be accompanied by a critical understanding of the relation of linguistic expression to the deepest and most persistent intuitions of man. An effort will further be made to show that language becomes imperfect and inadequate when it depends exclusively upon mere words and forms and when there is an uncritical trust in the adequacy of these words and forms as constituting the ultimate content and extent of language. For man is that being on earth who does not have language. Man *is* language.

It is by virtue of the procreative power of language, which grasps, shakes, and transforms, that man is man. For nothing really human can be so without this meaning, whether the language be uttered or silent. In this way, language as the power of universals is given to man in order that he may transcend his environment, in order that he may have a world. It is the law of language to create the world, and it is therefore as futile to search for the origin of language as it is to search for the origin of reason. Both are given with man; both are part of his essential, his ontological reality.

Words themselves are ideas—although not all words. This means that man does not create ideas. He assembles them. In this way he is thrust into a state of universal mobility since he attaches the swift and restless force of his individual existence to the retarded

3

and more massive power of his language. And for this there is only one source of help—Spirit. If words issued from an origin other than Spirit, from one's native land, one's country, for example, they would be born and they would die with it. Thus we would be deceived, tricked into an illusion. It is fortunate that the reasons whereby it is generally proved that language cannot have been invented by man are irrefutable. With the infallibility of the intuitive faculty and with the implacability of logic we must concede that if language does not come from empiric man, it must come from Spirit or God. For God created language even as He created man. And it may further be added that man can no more do without language than he can order or direct it. He can only bestow on it his faith, accord it his confidence, endeavoring by all the spiritual and moral means at his disposal and by the depths and seriousness of his individual experience not to violate it. And thus it might be said that in this very law of our thought is contained the proof of the existence of God.

The problem of this wondrous gift which enables man to communicate with his fellows, to reveal to others the hidden secrets of his being, to raise to God his desires in invocations, his sorrows in grief, or his despair in entreaty, this unique instrument which, entrusted to the written or the spoken tradition, defeats the voracity of time, this is the question concerning us, taxing our minds and our hearts. It is language, full-panoplied and alive, issuing hot and pulsating from the human mouth, it is language severed from all practical, all immediate applicability which here demands our investigation.

Many theories concerning language have been advanced. The fact, however, is that this problem resolves itself into another. Words are the ultimate symbols of ideas. They translate images and desires which when thus articulated acquire consciousness and are rendered operative, enabling man to escape from the loneliness of a closed consciousness, to emerge from the isolation in which he is enveloped and to experience a relationship with one other single being, with many others, with himself, or with God. An association with his fellow men is established whether near or far, living or dead. His soul, by an autochthonous impulse, stretches forth and opens to them as theirs do to him since there is present under the substructure of the formal diversity of the symbol a hidden essence which contains an essential and universal identity. If this essential identity were lacking, if words, however different in sound, did not evoke the identical eternal reality, the result would be sounds, not words.

It has been observed, for example, that mentally disturbed individuals possess no linguistic awareness.[1] They have no language. They have only words. Encrusted within themselves, words have been divested of their power to reveal or to communicate. This is because words then have lost their ontological roots. They no longer flow into action. And this inefficacy of mere words without language unmasks them. The word is obeyed but it is not heard; it is not seen; it has lost its connotations, its matrix. And when it no longer has weight it exposes itself, it reveals itself as nothing but a word, sterile, uncreative, the idea sacrificed, just as for Bergson it was the indeterminacy in the reaction that isolated the image from the world. This is true not only for the abnormal but for the normal individual as well.

Words in such a configuration must be distrusted for it is absurd to trust them. Such words, on which a man may so lightly traverse the space of a thought, may be compared to a fragile bridge thrown across a chasm. They may permit crossing but no stopping. A person in rapid motion can use them and get away. But if he hesitates even slightly, this infinitesimal fraction of time breaks them down, and all are plunged into the abyss. The one who rushes must be acrobatic; he must not dwell heavily, for if he does, he soon finds that the most lucid speech is nothing more than a tissue of obscure terms.

Language and "word" are not synonymous. Because of this, languages may be differentiated morphologically. There are, however, evolutions and mutations of words, words which are learned. But at the same time they constitute the varying symbols of the same living reality which is synonymous with the infinite capacity of the human mind. The expression of this capacity might be exemplified by invariable symbols. Leibnitz once proposed that the Chinese ideograms should be adopted to convey the fundamental concepts of philosophy, thus rendering the philosophic ideas intelligible to each in his own language. That great philosopher never relinquished his dream of a *pasigraphy* comprehensible to all men.

---

[1] Cf. Kurt Goldstein, *Language and Language Disturbances*, Grune and Stratton, New York, 1948.

Words, it can then be said, are the incarnations of ideas, the mysterious and magic nexus between the ideal and the real. And language thus becomes the revelation of being, even as it is the intermediary between man and his work. Because of this the idea of being known must never surrender to the substitute of being loved, though unknown. For he who abandons the idea of making the word an instrument of knowledge is ready to accept, out of the depths of despair, an antirationalistic theory of language. Life is not above and below language, as some, especially empiricistic, deterministic thinkers, have believed. The universal value of reason and language must be recognized. For finally man, uprooted and alone, is able to achieve identity and definition not in relation to the earth but in relation to language. A man must *be*. Being is synonymous with stability and objectivity. The planet *is* because its course is set. This is the explicit lesson of all Kantian philosophy. Language creates the world just as language enriches the world because of its symbolic function.

It was in this way that words were conceived by man as soon as he began to philosophize. In words he found the exquisite instrument, the mysterious, procreative power by which God engendered the world and by which man, in turn, can find the gods. This concept is conspicuously contained in the cosmogony of India, where the ritual formula possessed a thaumaturgic and inexorable quality. For it is to India and China that we may turn in our effort to discover the meaning of language, since in those two lands the problem of the word aroused the deepest interest and was discussed through the centuries in such a way as to reveal that the solutions reached were finally not different from those which Western thought has propounded in the course of its articulate history. There exists a fundamental similarity of speculative inquiry between the East and the West. Both are propelled by the same doubts, both bewildered by the same problems, and all language points to the paradoxical nature of man and life, the inner contradictory character of reality.

In ancient India the Word was considered to be uncreated. It is by means of the Word that the Creator creates. For there is a seminal magic contained in the spoken Word. When God said let this be done or let that be done, lo, the act was accomplished. Thus it is pronounced: "In the beginning was the Word." The primordial mythus avails itself of this intuition and reveals in what way, at the beginning of time, the Creator, God, existed alone and close beside Him was the Word. God embraced the Word and it became pregnant. It emerged from Him and after procreating the creatures returned again within Him. In this manner, and in mythical language, is portrayed the necessity of thought transmuting itself into action through the power of words. This is the essential moment of the actualization, the corporealization, of the idea, whether by this word we wish to convey the pristine manifestation of archetypes in all things or the evidence of the creative power of the imagination in the wavelike movement of poetry. It is the translation of will into command, the clarification and the development of thought in verbal speech.

Language is representation and presentation. It would be impossible for man to know himself without language. The word is not language when it is contained in a merely isolated or sensate continuum. When it is so contained, then the word may lie, whereas language can never lie. The phonic symbol and the idea should never be severed. It was because of this indissoluble union of the idea and the phonic symbol that the ultimate and supreme principle, the *Brahma,* was referred to by some Indian philosophers as the Word-Brahman. Thus a monism was postulated, a monism of words identical with the more universally accepted monism of the soul. It is an equilibrium, born out of the tension of spirit and nature.

St. Augustine beautifully portrayed the transempirical character of language, the warning not to betray the inner law of equality, when he drew an analogy between the word and spirit as it manifests itself in music. "When in music there appears a rest sign on the score and the sound thereby ceases, why is our sense not offended by an (apparent) deficiency if it is not because there is something due to the law of equality, of equilibrium, not in sound, but in the extension of time?"[2]

The implication of this is significant for here we have the appearance in rhythm of the being of non-being. The rest, the absence of audible motion, is itself the object of the time-count and plays its role on the same level as the audible sound. Its absence is counted by the extension of time (*spatium temporis*).

[2] St. Augustine, *De Musica*, 10, 27.

The essential point in the attack of Plotinus against Aristotle's "time-is-the-number-of-movement" theory is that there is something like the totality of the constantly recurring motions which necessitates an intellectual accompaniment of the motion. For without this there would be no unity of the past and the present, no one magnitude to be numbered. And the continuum of the law of immutability in language itself would be broken.

This law of immutability is reflected in Brahmanic thought. "The word and the world are born from Brahma who has neither beginning nor end. This is the inexhaustible reality of words, a reality which manifests itself in the multiplicity of things." Words therefore become the solidification of ideas in time. They become the corporeality of ideas. If the idea remains mere potentiality, it is nothing. It is emptied of life and substituted for life. It is ineffectual and inoperative because it is unknowable. It must become sound; it must be heard for it possesses an ecumenical quality; it must spread and give rise to action or to communication. It is of no significance that words themselves live and die. Like all things in time and space they become victims of mutation, are subject to the vicissitudes of history and consciousness; but though they may fade and change, or though they may be usurped by new words, new sound complexes, the primordial source, the procreative matrix of language which gave them birth subsists immutably in the richness and plenitude of its implications. If it is true that some words are born into existence before others, and if, in small degrees, consciousness and experience enrich the content of the vocabulary, it is because man in his laborious pilgrimage slowly raises other veils and reveals other mysteries. In this way new relations and new laws manifest themselves in the infinite, irrevocable, and irreducible certainty of nature, as well as in the boundless regions of man's mind.

By virtue of language, human energy is in a sense preserved. It is not transmitted in the course of its transformations. Yet man is a creature who acts. The meaning and purpose of language, metaphysics and science, are contained within the orbit of this universe of action. But action demands freedom and freedom in a state of transition becomes amorphous and elusive. Has civilization developed a mistrust of language? Has it impeded its growth? The enlargement of the framework of reference in language may be compared to the enlargement of new areas for the mind's maturity. It is a conquest which requires perpetually renewed effort on the part of man, an effort which marks an ever increasing progress but which at the same time presupposes existence.

The "real" is in no way immediately given to us. What we are given are merely the objects of our consciousness; and among these objects only those constitute the material of knowledge which permit univocal linguistic expression. There is only one way from the objects of consciousness to "reality," namely, the way of conscious or unconscious intellectual construction, which proceeds completely free and arbitrarily. The most elementary concept in everyday thought belonging to the sphere of the "real" is the concept of continually existing objects, like the table in one's room. The table as such, however, is not given to us, but is merely a complex of sensations to which we attribute the name and the concept "table." This is a speculative method based on intuition.

It is this consciousness that postulates existence. Unconsciousness in relation to the one who knows is nonexistence. And knowledge is the revelation of the fact of existence in whose relations the creative element is represented by the ceaseless unsatisfaction and activity of man as a being who thinks. Creation lies in effort, in dissatisfaction, in never-ending movement, in the avid curiosity that makes of man a creature of courage, a vigilant explorer wandering over a boundless world impelled toward a goal he does not know and which perhaps does not even exist. Discovery is his destiny and his privilege. Language captures and obediently marks the discoveries. It actualizes them in their symbols. It communicates and transmits them, enabling them to travel through space and through time making known and manifest to all what until then had been secret and hidden.

What we call Truth, those certainties in which we place our trust, is the primordial light, the *lumen supernaturale,* which radiates from an eternal source, the expansion of a pristine force which has taken form. It is the gradual shaping of an idea in diverse symbols expressing in diverse ways its implications and recondite meanings, varying with the maturity and the capacity of the mind which receives them and is rendered conscious by them. And such ideas will appear now as myths, now consummated in an image, or expressed in the abstraction of a scientific hypothesis. And in each case, language, through its phonic conventions, will determine its multilateral nature and value.

Language is not a mere mechanism, although it is also a mechanism and it is the relation of language as mechanism and language as meaning which must be sought. The hypothesis advanced by some modern linguists who are at the same time positivists and who are committed to the mechanistic theory of language, assuming it to be nothing more than a matter of mechanical stimulus and response, is self-refuting. For this would mean that these responses would reveal some characteristic about the linguists but nothing about language. The mechanistic theory of language has as its purpose a rigid, scientific methodology and therefore appears to employ only direct observations of the communicating persons, forgetting that the observer is also within the mechanism. In reality, however, it inevitably depends upon indirect observations through existing records. We must finally concede that the mechanistic theory of language commits the sin of solipsism, since it is the mechanist himself, an organism like any other, who performs the act of observing and it is impossible to interpret an unknown quantity by itself. Thus language cannot be grasped in all its sacredness, meaning, and power.

For the Word is the Law. It is the means by which, through the agency of God, eternal and immutable values are made known to man. It is the means of communication between the human and the divine. Human societies have not ascribed to man, at his discretion or caprice, the basis of the essential relations between man and man, or man and God. On the contrary, they have almost universally postulated a revelation, an announcement. They have invoked the spoken or written word which is the fountainhead of certainty and on that certainty life is erected. The Word delivers and transmits those commandments and those truths which assure the presence of universal principles that are also fixed points in the life of the mind and in history. .

This consciousness of the indissoluble relationship between the word and an immutable idea was clearly portrayed in Mahayana Buddhism. Reality has a twofold nature. One side of it is irreducible and the other is revealed. Being, apart from which all is illusion and vanity, is encompassed by both. The Law, or Dharma, is the phonic expression of the supreme Being, of the Absolute. Thus, so we are taught by the Mahayana Buddhists, the Word, the Word of the Law, in so far as it descends, after it has been heard, touching the depths of our being in the subconscious mind from which emanate the universal forces of life, transforms itself into the antithesis of subconsciousness and of those drives that cause suffering and impede knowledge of the self and therefore salvation. This Word, precipitated into the darkness and travail of life, issues like an emanation of the supreme truth and cancels the fatal ignorance that accompanies life, and in this way conditions and prepares that ultimate enlightenment which will enable one to pass into another plane, that of Nirvana, into the body of the Buddha.

It may again be said that language which we utter through words is not created by man. For man, moved by the desire to *express* his feelings and his thought, using the vocal chords with which he is endowed, evokes through sound the words, each of which has an independent autonomous existence by virtue of its inner life with language, by virtue of its *belonging* to language. Language exists *ab aeterno,* immutable in its transcendent purity and revealing itself from time to time in the historical existence of mankind.

There are, of course, those logicians who concede that the word, whatever may be the origin of its relationship with the object or the reality it designates—either by divine revelation or by ancient convention—does indeed express a universal and a particular thing, and according to circumstances one or the other acquires importance in discourse, depending upon the stress that he who speaks places on one or the other of its aspects. It was one of the greatest logicians (Vatsyayana, in the fourth to the fifth century) in India who affirmed that, when we wish to insist on the difference between one thing and another and when the notion refers to the destructive characteristics of that same thing, then the person is the predominant factor. But if the person and the difference are not brought into relief and if the notion concerns common and general conceptions, then the prevalent fact will be the universal. Above all, the universal is eternally present in the word, and the universal is a reality, and *ens,* contained in the word and bestowing meaning and value on the word.

At the beginning of the nineteenth century Wilhelm von Humboldt laid the foundations for the *science of language,* seeking to understand its nature in the harmony within man of his spiritual and moral being. He closely approximated the Buddhist conception of the Word by emphasizing the organic interaction of the moral and the spiritual elements of being out of which the nature of language is to be understood since it is but a reflection of the eternal idea in the universe of the presence of the Absolute in the relative. This interrelationship manifests itself in the personality of the individual since we might mistrust his speech but we still hold to the expression of the speaker, who to one of insight can never betray the truth contained in language, although his words may do so when they are emptied of the Absolute inherent within them.

If words are not bound to a situation arising from historical cultures but are themselves eternal, or are the expressions of eternal ideas, then language becomes a magic instrument in the hands of man which enables him to maintain himself in harmony with the eternal. The Word is the mysterious bridge between what is beyond time and what is within time. The Word then acquires a much greater value than that generally attributed to it, the value of an instrument of which we often make arbitrary use, often an inappropriate use, so that words are nibbled away; little by little they decay, are emptied of their meaning, acquire erroneous and unprecedented accents by excess or deficiency of content. For if those assumptions to which we have referred are true, the decay, the disintegration, or the darkening of the word's essential meaning, the fact that *it no longer corresponds to the idea which evoked it,* would mean that we have strayed from the world of our *mothers,* who are the fountainhead and reason of our being and our thought. The corruption of language, its confusion, its lack of precision, the amorphousness of expression, verbal equivocations—these are an insult and injury to truth, not a mere insult and injury to words.

"The first step in knowledge for civilized thought is to give a name." Bosanquet, in uttering these words, realized that to adequate the name and the thing is indeed the prerogative of genius. In fact, the number of terms which are inherited from Plato and Aristotle is the most striking evidence of the immense advance which they have achieved for the human intellect. These two seminal minds defined the world of knowledge in its essential features much as this knowledge exists even in our own time, and bestowed upon its main divisions the names they still retain. And in the East during the last journey Confucius took in the State of Wei in the hope that the prince would confer on him the direction of the State, a scholar enquired of him: "Should the king entrust you with the task of government, what would be the first thing you would start by doing?" "I should restore to each thing," the sage answered, "its true name." "But would that be possible?" the other incredulously insisted. "You miss the mark; what would be the use of this rectification of names?" "How crude you are!" replied the Master. "A wise man takes great care not to say and not to do what he does not know. If names do not correspond to things, the result is confusion in the language. If there is confusion in the language, people do not do their duty; if people do not do their duty, moderation and harmony are neglected: then penalties are no longer proportionate with the faults. If this occurs, the people no longer know how to act. The sage therefore gives to things the names proper to them, and he behaves towards them in conformity with the name given them. Therefore, in the selection of names he is very attentive."

Still another Chinese thinker, Hsün tzu, wrote: "Names have been fixed to denote realities, both to make known what is noble and what is vile, and to distinguish similarities and dissimilarities. Our thought will not run the risk of being misunderstood and in affairs we shall not incur the calamity of their being hindered or ruined."

According to this philosopher, words have not a transcendent basis but an immutable ethical content. They are determined by an identity of reaction in man (as a sentient and thinking being) to the same things, to the same stimuli. And this essential identity of human reactions imparts to them a value: even if the denomination given them is the work of man, it has an inevitable constancy, the moral law, which lies at the basis of all human certainties. The word, thus laden with the experience of ages, becomes an entity which is neither equivocal nor ambiguous and on which rest social and moral relations between men. Hence the rectification of names, the vigilant care to see that each word says neither more nor less than its own implicit meaning, is the surest guaranty of the stability of the human community.

In the conception both of Confucius and of Hsün tzu, the wise, those who govern, those who wish to set an example and to be a guide, must watch to see that words preserve their full and precise meaning.

"When the kings," Hsün tzu further said, "had regulated the names, settled the words (appropriate to the things) and had thus distinguished the several realities, and when the principles they laid down had been applied and their decisions made known, they proposed to unify their subjects (on the basis of the universality of the ethical conscience). Therefore the introduction of inopportune distinctions between words, the creation of new terms, the confusion of the correct expressions for things to arouse doubts in the minds of the subjects and to cause disputes, was considered a very serious iniquity."

This evaluation of language would indeed seem to be necessary in our own epoch since now, as in the time of Confucius, Hsün tzu, or, to mention a Western thinker, Thucydides,[3] words often change their essential meaning and assume that which is arbitrarily imposed; the eternal idea inherent in language is violated, and thus a collapse of the moral conscience takes place. To rectify language, to bestow upon it the full and entire meaning which it is intended to express, would demand a rectification of ideas, a definition of their content in their absolute signification. This would also demand that we must maintain uncorrupted and inviolable all those universals which it is man's very entelechy to make manifest in his speech—and in his deeds—of which he is the depository and the transmitter. Human consciousness and human speech are inseparable since both the conscious human mind and language spring from the common elemental foundation of the universal spirit. Therefore language, properly speaking, cannot be taught, although words may be; it can only be evoked and man can only nourish the conditions and leave it to its own unfolding. To paraphrase Pascal, we could not seek language if we had not already found it. This truth is exquisitely portrayed in children, who may be said never to *learn* a language since we can only learn that which does not belong to us. It can in reality be said that we become acquainted with what we already know, as a kind of spiritual

---

[3] Corcyraean Revolution, Peloponnesian War.

remembering, Plato's *anamnesia.* For how could the learner, merely through the expansion of his own developing consciousness, master the spoken thought if there were not in speaker and hearer the same essence, only differentiated for the sake of individual existence and communion, so that a symbol is refined and yet so personal that the articulate sound is sufficient to relate, as a mediator, both speaker and hearer in a pristine harmony?

Words are the instruments by means of which ideas become acts. Thus it is evident that the responsibility of men in the use they make of words is a heavy one. By means of words man inserts himself in the cosmic order, either as friend or as foe. He may continue the divine creation. He may interpret it and assist it. He is either the executor of the eternal idea or a demiurge who offends and disturbs the natural order of things. The word is power; "the power of life or death lies in the tongue." And it is power precisely because it awakens to life secret and latent forces. Its work is that of evoking powers hitherto hidden or inert but awaiting only that summons to bring them into the light, to reveal them, to foster their entrance into existence and into time. Such was the power that, from the very inception of civilization, man has attributed to the word, to the Verb, to the *Logos.*

The name is the person, the expression of the mysterious essence of things, revealing or controlling the inner reality. That is why the essential name of the person may not be revealed; why he who knows this essential name has indeed power over that person, because of the absolute and necessary nexus between the thing and the name, between word and idea. Man possesses this precious key which can open the jewel case of immutable and eternal ideas. He must guard the key, see that it is not injured or broken, for should it be, he will lose the means of communicating with the ground and reason of his being, of his thought and of his deed. For language possesses a life both deeper and less conscious than its articulate, logical life. Language is a process of liberation from conceptual, logical, discursive reason. Language not only articulates, connects, and infers; it also *envisages,* as the Platonic *intellectus esse* reveals, and the intuitive grasping of language is the primary act and function of that one and single power which is called reason. Language is not only logical but, first and foremost, ontological.

The universe itself is language, the corporealization of thought

that has been born through the medium of *logos*. The word intervenes between the motionless, primordial omnipresence and omni-
potence of the idea and its materialization. This idea of *logos* was
contained in some of the gnostic thinking in India, placing this
conviction at the very beginning of creation, at the very moment
in time when the universe was created, when it was determined in
all its variety, in its spatial essence and its temporal becoming.
The dialogue began, the dialogue between Siva and Parvati, between the universal conscience and the creative, seminal force
of the universe. Parvati, by her creative power, by her questions,
evokes a timeless plenitude of absolute thought, the cosmic unfolding and ripening. The question asked by the goddess, in its
verbal concreteness, causes the birth of the formation of things, a
transition process, the transmutation of thought into reality. This
is obviously a myth. But it is a myth which claims for the word
creative power and which places at the beginning of time the
daily occurrence of the miracle, the miracle of the transmutation
of thought into act through the medium of speech. Action is the
archetype. The word is the phonic sign, expressed or unexpressed,
explicit or implicit. It may even be said that each intellectual
archetype is mated with its phonic archetype. Time itself is
scanned by the rhythm of mental representations and verbal
denominations; it consists in a succession of images and sounds;
it is a complex series of thoughts possessing corresponding phonic
expression in which the universe is actualized in consciousness
arising spontaneously from an initial quivering and moving of
original, motionless, absolute Idea.

Thus language is not only being. It is also becoming, existing
anterior to the split between thinking and thought. But the corporealization of the word presupposes a possible dichotomy in
language. For the rise of duality coincides with the formation of
words, when, so to say, a "sacrifice" of pure thought sets in. According to some schools of philosophy in India, words move on the
plane of *māyā;* they represent and reproduce a scheme of relations
whose basis is the exteriorization of the becoming, of the *ens*.
Words on this level possess a certain inexactitude. The linguist
may then study the "parallelism" of the logical and the grammatical, as if, on the one hand, logic were given in the heaven of ideas
and, on the other, grammar were given on earth. Language thus

would become expression but not experience; it would become anonymous, or dead.

When the archetypes are formed and defined in the cosmic conscience, they enter inevitably into the temporal process. Exteriorized in words they decline into temporal and spatial limitations. Therefore, reintegration into the *ens*, the passage from the temporal to the eternal, may take place when the word, and thereby discriminated thought, comes to a halt. Pure consciousness will then be recovered in a totality beyond all duality, and in the silence of the *ens* multiplicity will be absorbed into Unity. Then silence becomes not a state of privation but a condition of plenitude. The images and experiences that illuminate and beatify us in moments of contemplation and meditation engender a death and a rebirth. George Bückner pointed to the implacable void, the fear of silence which possesses so many, especially in an age when both solitude and self terrify: "Do you not hear," he asked, "the terrible voice that howls around us on the horizon, the voice that is usually called silence?" This voice would extinguish us all. But then we remember the teaching of the Upanishads; we remember that very silence which implies language, that silence which gathers within itself and pervades all of language because it constitutes the totality of knowledge which is non-knowing, because it manifests itself at that point where knowledge is transcended, where the totality of language is silence, where "the blind man has found the jewel, one who has no fingers has gathered it, one who has no neck has adorned himself with it, one who has no voice has sung its praises." Language with this power is the Word of God; it possesses the sound and voice of the divine mystery. For then one hears oneself speaking out of the depths of one's silence, and language as idea is not betrayed.

Chapter II

KURT GOLDSTEIN

THE NATURE OF LANGUAGE

The increasing social and political difficulties in our modern age have led us to believe that there must be something essentially wrong in our organization of life. For this reason the problem of the means of mutual understanding, the basis of all natural and rational organization, has come increasingly into the center of scientific interest. Among them language plays a paramount role. While some means are significant tools in special fields, as, for instance, numbers in mathematics and physics, language is a general basis for all relations between men, and fundamental for every organization of their lives. In those fields of human endeavor in which interrelationship is particularly important, as in philosophy, sociology, psychology, and psychiatry, language at present is much in the foreground. This book constitutes therefore a most timely expression of a general trend.

I believe that I can make some contribution to the discussion of the problem by pointing to material which seems particularly apt in order to afford an insight into the nature and structure of language and which up to this time has not received the attention it deserves. The material is based upon observations of some modifications of language which patients manifest when there is a special damage of the brain cortex, modifications which in the medical field usually are called aphasic disturbances.

As I could demonstrate by a great number of examples, a defect due to a brain cortex lesion cannot be understood or even correctly described as long as one looks at it as an isolated phenomenon. It must be considered from the viewpoint that all human behavior, normal as well as pathological, is governed by a basic motif of organismic life, by the trend of the organism to actualize itself, its capacities, its nature as well as possible under the given circumstances. This self-actualization includes the coming to terms of the human organism with the outer world, especially with its fellow men. Language appears in this aspect as a special means to effectuate this coming to terms in the process of self-actualization. The change of the personality which accompanies some defect of language reveals the close relationship between the self-realization of man and the use of language, and a study of this relationship is thus suited to affording an insight into the nature of human language itself.

The use of pathological material to gain an understanding of normal behavior is indeed open to criticism which I cannot consider here. Concerning this, I would refer to my previous discussions, which brought me to the conclusion that, with careful consideration of the changes of function in the organism by pathology, pathological material not only can be used without running the danger of false conclusions but can also become of significance for understanding any human behavior and thereby also language.[1]

I begin with a simple deviation of language which is frequently observed in aphasic persons. It consists in the more or less outspoken *incapacity to name objects,* even the most familiar. There is no doubt that in these cases the inability to name objects is *not due to disturbance of recognition.* That becomes evident by the normal way the patients use the objects, by their ability to find out in a group of the objects that which was verbally demanded, by the circumlocutions with which the patients react to the request to name an object—for instance, when a patient unable to name a pencil or an umbrella or a glass may say it is something to write with, something for the rain, something to drink out of. Because these individuals seem to show no other mental defects it is often assumed that the defect in naming is due to a circumscribed damage of the cortex deprived of a special capacity, the capacity to evoke word images, residuals of previous experiences. In relation to the point of view that language is a tool acquired by

---

[1] More information concerning details in respect to the problems discussed here, especially in reference to literature, may be found in: Kurt Goldstein, *The Organism, A Holistic Approach to Biology Derived from Biological Data in Man,* American Book Company, New York, 1939, and *Language and Language Disturbances: Aphasic Symptom Complexes and Their Significance for Medicine and Theory of Language,* Grune and Stratton, New York, 1948.

experience, the assumption that it can be lost by damage to the
organism is proximate but is in contradiction to other findings
which show that such a loss of word images does not take place.
The patient, for instance, may utter the words when in conversation reporting a situation in which a particular object he could not
name plays a role, or when reciting a series of words to which the
word demanded as name belongs—for instance, though unable to
name a presented red color, he may react to the demand by reciting all different color names, red, blue, green, etc., without this
recital's helping him then to name the red color. In his circumlocutions he uses without difficulty the words which he cannot find
in the task to name an object. One patient, confronted with an umbrella she was asked to name, said, "I have two umbrellas at home,"
without being able to name the object immediately afterwards.

All these observations prove that the inability of the patient
is *not due to a loss of words.* What, then, makes a patient incapable
of naming objects?

The answer and a general clarification of the nature of naming
derive from a careful consideration of the total behavior of the
patient. In his behavior and thought, the patient is concentrated
to an unusual degree on his own personality and on his relationship to the world. He is a person acting in the world rather than
thinking and speaking about the world. His speech is accompanied
by an excessive use of expressive gestures. Often he seems incapable of expressing himself in words but can do so quite well
with the help of gestures. This general change of behavior is
demonstrated clearly in special tests[2] which were developed in
order to study the attitude with which the patient faces the world.
Some sorting tests prove useful for this purpose. For instance, we
place before the patient a pile of skeins of yarn of different colors,
as in Holmgren's test for color vision. We ask the patient to select
all the red skeins, including the various shades of red. Or we pick
out one skein of, for example, dark red and ask him to find skeins
of the same or a similiar shade. A normal person with good color
sensitivity or, as we say, color efficiency usually selects a great
number of different shades of the same basic color, disregarding

[2] K. Goldstein and M. Scheerer, *Abstract and Concrete Behavior. An Experimental Study with Special Tests,* Psychol. Monographs, American Psychological Association, Inc., Vol. 53, No. 2, 1941.

differences of intensity, purity, brightness, etc. According to the task, the subject's attention is directed to the basic color; he then chooses all skeins which he recognizes as belonging to the given type. When the test is given to a patient the results are different. In fact, several types of behavior are observed. For example, in following the instruction to take all skeins similar to a given one, the patient may choose only skeins of the identical or at least of almost the same shade. Though urged on, he limits himself to a small number because there are only a few actually similar ones in the heap. Another patient matches a given bright shade of red with a blue skein of great brightness. At first, one might think the patient is color blind, but it can be demonstrated beyond doubt by other tests that his color sense is normal and that he is able to make fine distinctions. More precise observations disclose that the choice in any given case is determined by a particular color attribute—for example, brightness. We observe further that the choice may be decided now by one attribute, now by another; by brightness, softness, coldness, warmth, etc. Moreover, surprising as it may seem, the patient who is determined in his procedure by a given attribute may be unable to do the same thing if it is demanded of him by language, i.e., if we ask him to choose all bright skeins. Further, we observe that often he does not carry through with the same procedure. He has chosen, for instance, some bright colors. Suddenly he transfers the selection to another attribute—for instance, coldness. On another occasion, the patient will arrange the skeins as if guided by a scale of brightness. He will begin with a very bright red, then add one less bright and so on to a dull one. But if we ask him to place the skeins in a succession according to their brightness, he again shows himself incapable of the performance, even after it is demonstrated to him.

To understand the behavior of these patients, we compare such procedure with the behavior of normal persons in these tasks. If required to choose all red colors, we group various nuances, even though we see that the colors are not identical. We do so because they belong together in respect to the basic quality. For the moment we ignore all but this; we inhibit or disregard all other attributes which may enter attentive consciousness—for instance, brightness, aesthetic liking or disliking, etc. We are able to do this because we can hold fast to the direction of the procedure once it is initiated, since, as we say, we are able to *abstract* from all those others which may encroach upon us.

There is another approach open to the normal person. If we start with one particular skein and pass it over the heap, passively surrendering ourselves to the impressions emerging as we do so, one of two things will take place. If skeins like our sample are present in all attributes, these immediately cohere in a unitary sensory experience. If, however, they match our sample in some respects but not in all, we experience a characteristic unrest concerning the heap and a rivalry between groupings according to the different attributes. In either case, we see that the coherence or conflict results from the sense data. There is an essential difference between the two kinds of approach. In the first, a definite active ordering principle determines our action; in the second, this principle fails to work and our action is passively determined by the outer impressions. We have designated the two as the abstract and the concrete attitude[3] respectively.

These two attitudes are instances of man's twofold orientation toward the world. In this connection, let me stress that in the abstract attitude we are not directed toward an individual object but toward the category, of which the individual object is but an accidental example and representation. Therefore, we also call this attitude the categorical attitude. In the concrete attitude, we are directed more toward the actual thing in its uniqueness. Two types of behavior correspond to these different orientations. In brief, in the first approach we are mainly thinking about things. Our reaction is determined not by the demands of the given object but by the demands of the category which it represents for us. In the second approach we are manipulating the object more than we are thinking about it, and our thinking and acting are determined by the individual claims of the given object.

The patient's behavior is similar to the concrete approach of the normal person. Because he can act only in this way, we conclude that he is impaired in his abstract attitude and has become a being dominated to an abnormal degree by concrete promptings.

In the abstract attitude, language plays a primary role. We are

[3] See K. Goldstein and A. Gelb, "Ueber Farbennamenamnesie, etc.," *Psycho-Logische Forschung* (1925), 6:127.

able to assume this attitude without language, but language induces us to assume it and to organize the world in a conceptual
way, though indeed not all language, not all words are so employed
—only words when used with meaning: in particular, generic words.
Reference will be made to the distinction between language with
and language without meaning. In contrast to this, in the concrete
attitude language is not of particular significance. Manipulation,
which is here in the foreground, is determined by the claims going
out directly from the sense experience and the recollections of
previous reactions to the same object. Words may not emerge at
all. When they occur they are an indication that the immediate
reaction is disturbed by something. Then we begin to ponder
more or less in the form of language what we are to do. When
words appear in such a situation they merely accompany our
doing and represent a property of the object like color, size, etc.
That is revealed in the kind of words we use in this condition,
for the most part special words adapted to the individual appearance of the object. Thus words like "strawberry red, violet blue,
grass green," etc., are used in contrast to generic words like "red,
blue, green," etc., in the abstract attitude.

What we have said about the relation of language to the concrete attitude would make it comprehensible that the patient
deprived of the abstract attitude would evince a lack of language.
But does this explain why he is impeded particularly in naming
objects? The elucidation of this phenomenon obtains from an
analysis of the normal individual's behavior in naming, which
reveals that real naming takes place in the abstract attitude. When
we name an object such as a table, we do not mean a special table
with all its accidental properties but table in general. The word
is used as representative of the category table; it is a symbol of
the idea of table. The fact that naming becomes impossible if the
abstract attitude is lost reveals particularly the nature of naming.
It is a confirmation of our assumption. The patient, we can say,
cannot use words in naming because he cannot assume the abstract
attitude. Since the patient faces the world with a particular attitude to which speech is not relevant or which we could accompany
only with individual words, the nominal words do not even occur
to him. He cannot even understand what we mean by naming
because that presupposes the abstract attitude, which he cannot

assume. This finds indirect confirmation in the fact that the patient can find words in connection with objects if he has such words which fit the concrete situation. The patient who cannot apply the word red to different nuances of red produces easily words such as "strawberry red" and "sky blue," etc., in relation to corresponding colors. He can do it because he has such individual words at his command.

The fact that naming becomes impossible for these patients reveals the *nature of naming*. It shows that it is not based on a simple association between a sound complex and an object but is an expression bound to the conceptual attitude. Words used as names are not simply tools which may be handled like concrete objects but are means of detaching one from the sense experiences and of helping one to organize the world in a conceptual way. Thus naming becomes an intrinsic characteristic of the attitude of man's nature. The paramount importance of the kind of language which appears in naming becomes evident through other characteristic modifications of the language of the patients which also are comprehensible. They are the result of the impairment of the power of abstraction and are parallel with modifications in the behavior of the patients in general.

The behavior of the patients in everyday life may not be grossly disturbed because much of it can be executed in a concrete way. Nevertheless, whenever a performance presupposes an abstract attitude, the patients show deviation from the norm: they lack initiative, they have difficulty in beginning anything voluntarily, in shifting voluntarily from one aspect of a situation to another, etc.[4] We observe all these failures in their language as well. Communication in general may not be grossly disturbed, but it is reduced because speaking under all the above-mentioned conditions is impeded or is rendered impossible. Language is not only quantitatively diminished. One could say it has changed from an active, spontaneous, productive means for expression of ideas and feelings, etc., to more passive reactions, to the utterance of more stereotyped learned speech automatisms which correspond to definite concrete situations. How rich the language of a patient is in spite of these restrictions depends upon the possession of such automatism which he has acquired previously or by training.

[4] Cf. Goldstein and Scheerer, *op. cit.*, p. 5.

Even these automatisms may be reduced because the use of them is somewhat dependent on the abstract attitude, as we shall see later.

I wish to stress some particularities of the language of the patients which are of special interest in respect to the nature of normal language. First, there may be mentioned the different behavior of the patient in respect to different word categories— for instance, the restriction in the use of the so-called *small words:* the articles, the prepositions, the conjunctions, the pronouns, the adverbs. These words may have become so strange to the patient that he is neither able to speak them nor to read or write them isolatedly. The fact that in a familiar combination they may appear without difficulty shows that they are not lost; they can only not be produced isolatedly because that presupposes abstraction. A patient may not be able to say on demand, "me, you, I, on, up, down, in," and other small words but he can utter these words without hesitation in a sentence or in familiar combination, as when he writes an address on an envelope. That the difficulty is due to lack of abstraction becomes apparent when a patient, unable to write one of the words on dictation, suddenly produces a number of them together, after he has often, by our examination, experienced the fact that these words belong together and has kept them in mind as a group without understanding what they mean. Now asked to write one of them on dictation, he brings his knowledge—consisting of the whole group—to the fore without afterwards being able to write one of them alone on dictation. The words themselves remain as strange to him as before.

That the attitude toward the sound complex is decisive for failure or success is evidenced in the patient's behavior in respect to those words which when spoken are similar but which can have a different meaning if one understands them as concrete or abstract words: for instance, the patient may understand the sound complex "for," which could be grasped as the numeral "four" or the preposition "for." If it is meant as a numeral, the patient understands it and can read and write it, but if it has to be grasped as a preposition, he cannot. Similarly the word "one" may be understood as a number, not the similar sound or the similarly written word "on" used as a preposition. Indeed the latter, when it appears in a sentence like "The book is on the table," immediately becomes a concrete word. This corresponds to the fact, mentioned before, that the patient does utter a word which he cannot find in naming in other speech performances, for instance, in conversation or reciting, i.e., where such words appear as parts of a learned automatism. The patient may utter automatisms even more frequently than do normal persons because they allow him to fulfill, at least to a certain degree, the task set before him. Later we shall discuss these automatisms and their role in normal language. Now we emphasize their presence in these patients to show that *uttering of a word need not be meaningful language.* It is certainly not meaningful for these patients and need not always be so even in normal language.

Although the language of the patient lacks generic words, it sometimes seems as if he employs them. He may, for instance, in a situation where we would say, "Give me the knife (or bread)," say, "Give me that thing." From his whole behavior it is evident that the word "thing" does not refer to a concept. It does not represent the category to which a number of different objects belongs. It is not used with a generic meaning but is a sound complex which comes easily to him owing to the frequent use of it in relation to different objects. It is not a name; it is an aid to obtain something. In this intention the uttering of this sound complex, which can fit each object, does well, particularly if it is combined with a pointing movement, as is usually the case. We must be aware of this possibility, i.e., that a person may use words which for us have generic value in relation to concrete experiences without our recognizing it. This not only is important for a correct interpretation of the behavior of the patient but will permit us to avoid much misunderstanding in the communication of normal persons where a word uttered by a speaker involves a different meaning from the one grasped by the listener.

We are confronted with the same situation as we find in an early state of growth when the child has not yet developed the abstract attitude and correspondingly is not yet cognizant of real objects. He may have the same experience with several "objects" which appear to us totally different. The sound complexes he learns which represent for adults names or other meaningful words are connected with these experiences and his reactions to them. Therefore he can apply the same sound complex to what for us would constitute different objects. And when it is a word which for us has a generic value, then it may seem as if the child's language contains words of this kind. One can easily prove that such is not the case, that the word is related to a concrete experience. Even a little change in the appearance of an object which may not disturb our recognition of it may render it unrecognizable to the child. His words fit only specific individual experiences. They are not names denoting objects. They become names and meaningful words only later in relation to the development of the abstract attitude and to a cognizance of real objects. The fact that with the acquisition of objects the world of the child appears in a new aspect manifests itself in the eagerness with which he now tries to learn the name for each object. One can now say that language appears, *sound complexes become words, and "world" takes form. The child has become a human being.*

Helen Keller's description of the situation when in a certain stage of her training she discovered the world of objects and the nature of names is most enlightening. It reveals so profoundly the enormous significance for man's existence of the capacity for naming that it deserves to be quoted here in detail. First Miss Keller describes the experience of warm sunshine as a *"wordless sensation."* Then she continues:

When we walked down the path to the well . . . someone was drawing water and my teacher placed my hand under the spout. As the cool stream gushed over my hand she spelled into the other the word water first slowly, then rapidly. I stood still, my whole attention fixed upon the motion of her fingers. Suddenly I felt a misty consciousness as of something forgotten—a thrill of returning thought; and somehow the mystery of language was revealed to me. I knew then that water meant the wonderful cool something that was flowing over my hand. That living word awakened my soul, gave it light, hope, joy, set it free. . . . I left the well eager to learn. Everything had a name, and each name gave birth to a new thought. As we returned to the house every object which I touched seemed to quiver with life.

The difference between the *wordless sensation* and the *perception of names and objects* and their relation to an experience of a *new world can scarcely be more adequately described.* This extraordinary experience renders intelligible the astonishment and delight with which Helen Keller perceived it.

A further interesting phenomenon to be observed in our patients is their inability to understand metaphors and to use words in this sense. They resort to words only literally, words which for us have metaphoric meaning. Their inability to understand proverbs is a manifestation of this defect. For instance, the proverb "The apple does not fall far from the tree" was interpreted by an intelligent patient, who had before his illness well understood the metaphoric character of the sentence, as follows: "If the apple is beside the tree, it has naturally fallen down from it."

The analysis of all the modifications of the language of the patients demonstrates that these modifications are the manifestations of the same change in their language; in brief, the evidence is drawn of the impossibility of using sound complexes in an abstract way, i.e., as symbols.

By comparing this loss of the character of symbols in their language with the change of personality and of the world for these patients, we are able to define the word symbol concerning which there is so much dispute. A description of their behavior (which must here be omitted) in different fields of activity would demonstrate that the personality of the patients is changed in a definite way in different fields of performance. What we mentioned before as a result of the examination by means of special tests, i.e., that the patients' behavior is absolutely concrete and that they fail when abstraction is necessary for a correct response, is reflected in the same way in their behavior in everyday life. They have lost initiative, creativity, the capacity for voluntary decisions and for adjustment to the necessities of social life.

If one considers their condition from the aspect of the world in which the patients live, one can say that their world is correspondingly changed. What appear to us as objects in an organized world are for them complex sense experiences of an individual singular character which can be reacted to in a definite way but which are not connected with each other in a systematic unit. One can say that they have no "world." The change manifests itself in the above-mentioned modifications in the patients' language and in the loss of the world, and this indicates that they are *deprived of the essential characteristics of man.*

The observation of these patients reveals a human potentiality enabling man to refrain from his immediate reactions to given sense experiences and to utilize these experiences in constructing a world which permits him to see things in a new light and thereby to actualize an essential part of his nature. It is this capacity which we have in mind when we speak of symbolic power. The words of the patients have lost their symbolic function and with that the ability to work as a mediating agent between sense experiences and the world in which man alone can be man. The change of the patient's personality which excludes him from the normal human community brings the essential significance of the symbolic power to the fore and with that the significance of the symbolic character of language.

We can also say that the language of the patients has lost its meaning while emphasizing that the *essence of human language is meaning.* The term "meaning of words" has been used in different and frequently ambiguous ways. I think everyone would agree that the term refers to a relation between an experience of sound complexes and an experience of objects, thoughts, events, feelings. The sound complex is not a simple repetition of these experiences, even when some words also appear to be similar to the experiences. But for the most part they are not repeated. The sound complex adheres to them. It is a means of remembering them when we hear it. The usefulness of language depends on this adherence. But adherence can be of two essentially different kinds. The one is a simple association between a sound complex and a non-language sense experience. That is the character of the words in early childhood, and of some in our own everyday life, i.e., when we use words fitting only a specific situation. But there is the other use of sound complexes, in which the relation does not consist of a simple association where the sound complex "denotes" the objects, playing the role of a mediator between sense experiences and the special organization of our world with the means of man's capacity for abstraction. *Here the sound complex becomes a word, the sense experience becomes "world."* To say that both forms constitute meaning might produce some confusion. A lack of distinction between the two forms has often produced confusion. Therefore, we should differentiate them sharply by applying different terms to them and reserving the term "meaning" for one form only. For which form? There can be no doubt as to our decision. Again pathology can help us by showing that the two forms play essentially different roles in man's life and that the one based on associations and automatisms is applicable to only a restricted experience, while the other comprises the totality of man's experience. Therefore it is reasonable to reserve the word "meaning" for the latter, the more so since the existence of the meaningful language is the presupposition of the other form. We call the first form *automatic speech behavior.*

Pathology teaches us that language is not a sum total of sound complexes in associative relations to definite objects but a special attitude which bestows upon the sound complexes the character of "symbols." Now they have meaning and can be used as descriptions of the objective world. They can be used in different situations with different connotations, different meanings. Language is not a sum total of tools. It has become this for the patient, and therefore his language is deprived of the richness and flexibility of normal language, which is relevant to different goals.

The language we have considered and which we find disturbed in the patient is the language corresponding to our everyday world and the world of science, the world of security and action. But this is not the only world in which man lives. There is the world of art, of religion and metaphysics, etc., each of them corresponding to a definite capacity of man's nature which seeks actualization. To each belongs a different language. But all these worlds have one thing in common: they are worlds built with the help of the symbolic attitude of which the everyday world is only one expression. In addition, the language which belongs to each has the character of meaning and consists of symbols. We thus come out of our knowledge of pathology to the conclusion that human language is meaning and that words are symbols which refer not simply and directly to sense experiences but to some experience based on the function of a particular human attitude, the abstract attitude.

Pathology teaches us something more in respect to language: the body of language consists of other *sound complexes which have no symbolic value.* Our patients are not entirely without speech. They are able with the help of their limited speech to come to terms to a considerable degree with the demands of the environment. We can communicate with them by the use of language. We have already mentioned that for certain objects the patients are able to find an adequate word. Indeed, it is demonstrated that these words do not refer to the category to which the object belongs but to a particular individual object. The words are "individual" words. They are, we have said, properties of the object as are other properties, such as color, size, usefulness. This becomes apparent from the fact that the patients are able to find those words for objects for which we normally possess such individual words.

Thus, for instance, they are able to designate words like "strawberry red" or "sky blue," but not generic words like "red" or "blue." These individual words represent learned associations between a sound complex and a characteristic object. They are not real names. Therefore, we call them *pseudo-names*. By *pseudo-naming*, the disability of real naming can be concealed, and so we may be deceived concerning the defect of the patient. Particularly is this true if he uses in respect to such objects words which we use as names. We observe that after many examinations the patient may find the right word for many objects, which he was unable to do before. A female patient[5] who could not in the beginning use the definite color words "red," "green," etc., or who was able to employ them only in relation to an individual color and not to other shades of the given color, could appear to do so. She also behaved in the same way in respect to other colors and a number of objects. It seemed that the word now fitted the category to which the different objects belonged. It was as if the patient had regained the capacity of naming in respect to words and objects. Closer examination revealed, however, that nothing had changed and that she was not able to build concepts or use words as names and as symbols. If we asked the patient why she now called the different shades of red with the same word, she answered, "The doctors have told me that all these colors are named red. Therefore, I call them all red." Asked if this was correct, she laughed and said, "Not one of these colors is red, but I am told to call them by this word." She had not used the word as a symbol but had learned to build an association between a diversity of things and one word, a rather meaningless connection which, however, helped her to carry out a task, not in the way of a normal individual but in a way in which the result could appear to be correct. The character of the uttered words was not changed. It had not become normal but could appear to be so.

The same situation could be observed on many other occasions.

5 See Eva Rothmann, *Schweizer Archiv f. Neurologie Psychiatrie* (1933), Vol. 33.

Asked, for instance, to mention the names of some animals, the same patient was at first unable to do so; then suddenly she said, "A polar bear, a brown bear, a lion, a tiger." Asked why she named just these animals, she said, "If we enter the zoological gardens, we come first to the polar bear and then to the other animals." Apparently our question had induced her to visualize the situation in the zoological garden in the town where she once lived, and to recollect the animals as they were located there. The visualization of them had evoked the words associated with the animals. The words were a part of a concrete experience and could be produced only in this situation, only in the sequence presented by the location of the animals. That the words were also "individual" words became apparent by the fact that the patient did not use generic words when asked to name animals but rather specific ones—for instance, not the word "bear" but "polar bear," "brown bear," etc.

One other example may be mentioned in order to illustrate that we were concerned with a general phenomenon. Asked to mention different female names, she said, after some hesitation, "Greta, Paula, Clara." Asked why she had given just these names, she replied, "Those are all G's" (G. was her family name), and continued, "One of my sisters died of a heart attack." This example demonstrates clearly that the patient did not think of names but uttered words belonging to her recollection of her sisters, even emphasizing such a specific situation as the death by a heart attack of one of them.

The following example derived from another patient specifically illustrates the concrete individual character of the only words the patients can use. A patient who could not find the name for a presented knife or fork or similar utensils said immediately, when a knife was presented together with a pencil and she was asked what that was, "A pencil sharpener." The same knife together with an apple was an apple parer; with a piece of bread, a bread knife; and together with a fork, a knife and fork. But she never could utter spontaneously the word "knife" only and when she was asked whether one could not simply say "knife," she replied promptly, "No." Apparently the word "knife" did not at all fit the situation.

This phenomenon of pseudo-names is of interest because it is observed not only in patients but also in normal speech. There is no doubt but that here also more or less frequently, and particularly in definite situations such as in conversation in fluent language, words are uttered which may seem to be names but actually are not. It is impossible to evaluate correctly any utterance on its face without a careful analysis of the attitude in which the word is uttered, in which it is meant by the speaker.

Not only name-words can be used and are used without meaning. The same can take place in all other language forms. A great part of our language consists in sound complexes and combinations of such which occur without our producing them voluntarily. They occur passively in concrete situations with which they have been previously associated, as, for example, some habitual phrases, the words corresponding to the result of a multiplication we know by heart, articles, grammatical forms, etc. We call these learned associations *automatisms* because they are reproduced not voluntarily but in an automatic way. They may be designated as *instrumentalities* of language. The quantity of such instrumentalities which an individual may have at his disposal differs according to the structure of the specific language, the greater or smaller need for them in a particular everyday situation, and the capacity and need of the individual to acquire them in relation to the conditions of his life. They represent learned material. Like all learned automatisms, they are acquired by repetition with the help of the abstract attitude, and this dependence upon the latter is always present. They appear normally within the framework of performances executed with the abstract attitude, or they appear in concrete situations as associations with them, coming passively to the fore—just as we may begin in a definite situation to recite a verse, almost without being aware of what we are doing.

In a state of impairment of abstraction such as we observe in our patients, the automatisms appear as the effect of a concrete situation or as associations with words spoken by others. Their dependence upon abstract language becomes evident when the patient with an impairment of abstraction loses known speech automatisms if they are not again and again induced by a concrete situation. Thus, a patient may lose the learned multiplication table which is automatized language when, as an effect of the impairment of abstraction, he has lost the capacity to grasp the value of numbers and so cannot control the correctness of the results.

The importance of speech automatisms consists in the possibility, with the help of these generally accepted means, to facilitate the expression and communication of ideas. Everyday language is a combination of meaningful words and speech automatisms. In a conversation we may begin with a meaningful word for explaining something. We may then continue with automatisms which we expect the listener to interpret in a concrete or abstract way as it may be necessary to comprehend what we wish to express. In a special situation that form of language is used which best expresses what we wish to communicate at the moment. The usefulness of these speech automatisms as a means of referring to definite objects, events, ideas is derived from their rootedness in a meaningful aspect of the world of the particular individual or a group of people who speak the same language.

The automatisms can become dangerous phrases when this relation is not present. Then they may falsely suggest a meaning which does not exist. That is the case sometimes when a speaker who may not have real insight into the meaning of the important things he is talking about impresses the listener enormously by using phrases which are known to be related to important ideas. Then the listener not only will fail to learn anything valuable but may become bewildered by what he hears. A speaker may even use this means intentionally in order to deceive his listeners. What we observe here is similar to our observations in patients whose capacity for abstraction is impaired and who possess a great number of speech automatisms which the listener may interpret as meaningful speech. The patient may then appear not to be as disturbed or as deficient in meaning as he actually is.

This ambiguous character of speech automatisms becomes apparent in learning a foreign language. We acquire the language mainly in *two ways*. The one is the acquisition of words and phrases in relation to definite situations. We are inclined to consider them as words, in the same way as we do the words of our mother tongue, relating to the meaning of the objects or events, as symbols for categories. But the word of the new language may apply only to the situation in which we have learned it, while the word of our own language belonging to the situation may be applicable to several situations; or if the word of the new language can be used with various meanings, the situations to which it applies may be different from those for which the word of the mother tongue is adequate. As long as we do not know the full meaning of the word in the new language, we may use it correctly when we apply it to a situation which means the same to us as to the people who speak the foreign language as a mother tongue, but we will err if we apply the word to a situation which does not mean the same for them and for us.

These errors occur if we are not aware that a word derives its meaning only as a manifestation of a definite attitude toward the world, and out of a structure of language expressing a definite culture. In different structures of language, words which belong together in some instances may be totally unrelated in others.

Another way in which a foreign language may be learned consists in memorizing vocabularies, i.e., learning words of the new language in relation to words of our mother tongue; that is, it consists in the *translation of single words*. This procedure concerning some words may render possible a correct acquisition of the new language. But not always. Even if the two related words are equally applicable to a number of situations in both languages, the new word will frequently be inadequate for a situation to which the word of the mother tongue is applicable. A situation may mean something different in the totality of the one language as the manifestation of one culture from that in another culture and this different meaning may not be at all expressible by the words associated as vocabularies. Translation is correct only if we relate to each other such language performances as have under all conditions in both languages the same meaning. That will be possible only under certain circumstances. It will be correct only if the translator has full command over the instrumentalities of both languages and is able to evaluate each word, phrase, construction in respect to their meaning in the total structure of both languages. Only then will he be able to communicate to people of another culture what the speaker or the writer means. The problem of translation brings to the fore the whole complexity of human language; it makes evident the fact that *a single speech performance derives its meaning only in the frame of reference* to the totality of the special language and the corresponding culture. The necessity to trespass into another culture and language in translation *presupposes the capactiy of abstraction.* Translation is a representation of things of one world in another world so that they can be grasped in the latter.

This complexity of the relationship between two languages becomes apparent in the language behavior of patients, of so-called polyglots, who, before their illness, spoke two or more languages. The effect of the brain damage can be different in different patients. We cannot discuss the cause of the differences here. There are patients who can use only the mother tongue. One has tried to explain that by the assumption that the language acquired first is preserved alone or better than the language learned later. But this assumption cannot render other phenomena comprehensible. There are patients in whom both languages, the mother tongue and the subsequently acquired language, are equally disturbed. Then the patient may use sometimes one and sometimes the other language. It seems that he uses that language which allows him best to express what he wants to express in the particular situation. Thus, when a patient who has previously spoken German and English is disturbed in respect to both languages, he speaks German in the presence of German-speaking people and is not able to speak English under these circumstances, but is able to do so at once in an environment where English is spoken. A patient may even use under this condition a language which he did not speak well before his illness and is still less able to speak now. Even an imperfect use of the language appears a better means of communication in this condition than the use of the language he knows better. It would be wrong to assume that this behavior is the result of *voluntary* acts. That it is not becomes evident when the same patient is not able on demand to shift from the first to the second language. This shows the close relationship between the choice of the language, even in pathological conditions, and the totality of the situation; it shows the significance of the better usability for communication whether he uses one or the other of the *disturbed* languages.

We observe the same phenomenon when after a long time not having spoken a foreign language we try to speak or understand this language. We may have great difficulty, which, however, often quickly disappears when we are in the country where this language is the mother tongue. Then we feel that this shifting to the other language is not based on a voluntary act but originates passively from the total condition in which we have to live. It originates from our being in an environment to which the language is natural. The same is evident in patients who show shifting in spite of impairment of the abstract attitude, which, according to many other experiences, makes shifting in general impossible. Here the shifting can take place only passively under the determination of the total situation in which the patient tries to communicate.

One patient of mine was of Swedish origin. She came to America as an adult many years ago and learned to speak English fluently. After her brain damage she spoke Swedish for the most part, but she had not lost her English. When somebody addressed her in English she spoke English but not in all situations, for the most part only in connection with simple things, such as everyday events. Her English apparently consisted in speech automatisms. If she had to think what to say, to explain something, then her English was insufficient and she would then prefer Swedish. Apparently the use of symbols was better preserved in Swedish. An explanation would be that the second language was learned only for practical reasons. Sometimes the patient repeated words in Swedish which she had first spoken in English. One could think she translated, but it became evident that we were not dealing with real translation since she was not able to translate on demand. She was not able to *understand* what one meant by translation even if one tried to explain it to her by example. The shifting to the other language was apparently not translation based on real shifting but a passive coming to the fore of learned material.

This case shows clearly that producing words in another language need not necessarily constitute translation. Everybody who learns a foreign language knows that he makes more or less serious errors by using a word which is learned as a translation. We have no real insight into the meaning of the words or phrases in the as yet unknown system of the language corresponding to the unknown world. It is interesting again in respect to the experiences with patients that we may speak sentences without fully understanding all the connotations of the contents, sometimes without the listener's even recognizing this fact. The situation changes after we have acquired a real conception of the structure of the new language in relation to the life of the people who speak it. Then the words become representations of the particular approach with which the surrounding world is considered by the people who speak this language, and we begin genuinely to understand the new language. We no longer translate our language into the words of the new language. We think, as one says, in the new language.

One might say that the language of our patients is somewhat similar to our knowledge of a foreign language before we have reached this state. Each word has a definite reference to one specific experience. But what we can achieve by use of this language is a very poor result, corresponding to a restricted world in which we live in this stage of learning a foreign language, and it is certainly not what we want to achieve. The reason is not that we have not yet acquired enough of the instrumentalities but that we have not yet grasped the meaning of the new language. That goal we can achieve only by living with the people who speak the language. Speaking and understanding a language are ultimately based upon a communion between the speaker and the listener; and this in turn depends upon a *common attitude toward the world,* to which a definite structure of language corresponds. The individual word gets its meaning from this frame of reference. Because the world of the patient and our world are essentially different, the understanding of our language by the patient presents the greatest difficulty. It is not only due to the defect of meaning. There is another fact which plays an important role in understanding normal language which the patient is not able to consider, the fact that the speaker does not express by words all that he wishes to communicate. He omits words, he expresses some things simply by speaking in a definite cadence, in the form of a question or assertion or doubt, and he can do so because he can expect that the listener will add what he has omitted, will understand the character of a question, of an assertion, of doubt, etc. But that is possible only if there exists objectively a common atmosphere in which all these modifications are immediately understood or if the speaker is able to produce this atmosphere and the listener is able to grasp it from what the speaker says. In other words, both have to act under the abstract attitude. Therefore, a patient frequently does not understand us if we are not able to adjust ourselves to his situation and organize our language in a way that will enable him to grasp what we wish to express. What we say about the patient's understanding of the language applies in the same way to our mutual understanding among normal human beings. A consideration of these factors is of the greatest significance for the phenomenon of *communication*.

The goal of *communication* is that something is transmitted from a sender to a receiver in such a way that the receiver obtains correctly as much as possible of what is transmitted. This can occur in two ways. If the sender and receiver belong to the same system of perception and action, the transmitted material (a tone, for example, or a sign of some other kind) is transmitted in such a way that it produces the intended definite effect. It is comprehensible that one tries to organize communication between human beings in this way. One believes that such definiteness is also possible through the use of human language, that it is the goal of human language to perfect itself in this way, a way which precludes misunderstanding. Many criticisms of human language are based on the fact that this perfection is not achieved. One attempts to build a language in which each word or construction has only one definitive meaning, producing definitive ideas or actions. Such a form of communication may be fruitful for special forms of organization of the world and of behavior in circumscribed fields of performance, as in special science or in communication of definite orders which have to be executed. Here automatized relations between words and definite experiences and actions will be successfully used, and the more they are automatized the greater the successful usage. *But this is not communication by means of human language.* This is not communication between two human beings who are able and willing to use human capacities. This is nowhere more manifest than in the futile attempts to communicate in the traditional way with patients. Here communication is possible only if we restrict essentially our human intentions. We should even use another word for transmission by language in this form of communication. We may apply the words *unambiguous transmission.*

I am well aware that my conception of the nature of human language will not meet with agreement on the part of a number of well-known scientists concerned with the problem of language. The principle I have attempted to propound is the assumption that understanding human language is possible only if one considers it from the point of view that language is not a simple tool but an expression of the nature of man and that there exists only one definite aspect of this nature by which language can be understood. In this frame of reference, which has developed from my studies of the behavior' of individuals with brain damage, all the facts, even those stressed by my opponents, can find their place.

It affords me great satisfaction to discern that I am not alone in my conception of the nature of language but that there are those with whom I am in conformity, namely, with Herder, Wilhelm von Humboldt, Carl Bühler, Ernst Cassirer, W. Urban, Roman Jakobson, and Susanne Langer. No matter how different the material they used, our frame of reference is the same. They all stressed the necessity of considering language in relation to the nature of man in general and to the particular form in which man appears under the special conditions in which he lives according to the respective cultures. Language is an expression of man's very nature and his basic capacity. It is an expression of his symbolic power. Animals cannot have language because they lack this capacity. If they had it, they would have language but they would no longer be animals. They would be human beings.

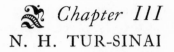

THE ORIGIN OF LANGUAGE

How did language come into being? This question did not exist for ancient man. In his opinion, language as a whole, as it was, was a "gift of God," and each people thought that its language was the correct one and the mother of all other languages, the primeval language used by Adam, in which he gave a name to everything.

As against this, science has established—at least in principle—that language is not a fixed thing, determined by unchanging laws and logical judgments. It was not given or created, but has developed by a long, complicated process, and even today it constantly changes in the mouth of the persons using it. Nor was its genesis governed by preexistent laws; rather, both the words and the structural rules of a language are the outcome of a long evolution. Within it, language arose not by dint of a supreme logic controlling it but in slow progression from "zero" to the most highly developed idiom, capable of rendering the minutest shades of thought.

Generation after generation tried to discover the particular way in which language developed. Generation after generation was baffled by this problem. In the end, science despaired, so much so that it almost became a rule in language research to ignore that question of questions; linguistic problems were dealt with only within the limits of the existing forms of the spoken or written language, which alone one attempted to explain historically; but the question of the distant, nebulous past, the problem of the origin of language, was not tackled any more. Thus science evaded the main question, the question of the emergence of language as such, and confined itself—or so it imagined—to the sphere of the phenomena known to it.

But in fact, it is impossible to explain even the smallest detail of linguistic morphology without a definite idea as to the whole of the vast process by which language has arisen. Let us take, for instance, the limited problem of the etymological relationship of words, viz., the case of the Latin verb *curro*, "to run" and the noun *currus*, "carriage," or of Hebrew *pana(h)*, "to turn," "face," and *panim* "(the) face." The relationship is obvious. But which is older, the verb or the noun? Or have they perhaps both arisen from a third source? Or another example. In all languages we find—as will also be discussed later—"derived" nouns denoting concrete, simple and most elementary things, as "child," "ear,"[1] "earth," "heaven," etc. Are such names of things which a human being perceives before all others, and which are most familiar to him, derived from verbs? Are they, originally, abstract derivatives? Has man chosen abstract names even for the most concrete things known to him through his senses, through sight, hearing, and touch?

How were names given at all? The forms of a language are built in accordance with certain laws; how could these laws, the basis of the forms of the language, have existed before the names, indeed before the very first words in which man began to express his budding thought? This is impossible for the simplest psychological reasons. But if so, where do those laws come from? And how were they able to influence the structure of the words if they arose after them?

Has science in fact succeeded in avoiding a decision of these fundamental questions? It has not. However, instead of forming a well-founded judgment, it has relied—consciously or unconsciously—on prejudices.

A case in point is the above-mentioned question of the relation between such words as *currus* and *curro*. Here we make an absolute distinction between two word categories, noun and verb, as if language had from the outset intended to create two separate words. But who knows: perhaps the logical difference between the two concepts has not from the start also been a linguistic difference. In the case of words such as "man—men," "son—sons," "thing—things" we assume, as a principle, that the singular arose before the plural, because in the mind, in counting or making things, we

[1] Latin *auris* to *audire*, "to hear."

naturally proceed from the one to the many, and not vice versa. But how do we know that words were actually created in this logical order? This view, on which science bases its explanation of the forms of language, is an arbitrary, preconceived one. How did flectional endings, as the plural ending in "son—sons, flower—flowers, fish—fishes" (Latin *ovum—ova, mons—montes, servus—servi*; Hebrew *dag—dagim*), develop grammatical meaning? How did a short additional element come to denote the plural? Is it really an independent word meaning "many"? These and numerous other questions arise.

So we are forced to the conclusion that we must strive anew for a well-founded solution of the problem of the origin of language, a solution which alone can serve as a basis for correct judgments as to the problems of the actual forms of each particular language.

This solution cannot, after all, be very difficult if we but succeed in freeing ourselves from those prejudices which warp our judgment and blind us to the facts. For even in the most primitive tribe we find fully developed languages, rich in forms and nuances. The road followed by the development of language must therefore of necessity have been a simple and primitive one, springing from the very nature of man's mind, from psychical properties common to all the human family.

This attempt is an inductive one, based on facts within languages known to us. Obviously, it has to refer to a system of historically related languages. The one chosen for the purpose is the Semitic language family, which for simplicity's sake is seen as if going back to a single "proto-Semitic" language. Even so, it is impossible to establish the general process by examining the meanings of individual words; for each word is a creature by itself, whose history is different from that of its fellows. Only the history of the forms of a language enables us to trace its development; for the form system of a language—comprising many words, each of which, as it were, wards off changes in the common form—develops slowly; and each little trait in its development is attested by many instances, all of which together show it to be a fundamental and necessary step, determining the process itself, and not a fortuitous happening, occurring in this or the other case for special reasons, and from which no general conclusion can be drawn.

The prime source of human speech is indeed known and agreed

upon. Language arose as an exclamation, an emotional cry, at first not voluntary but reflex, a reaction to external influence. But this reflex cry is not language and is not sufficient to explain linguistic expression except in a small porportion of language phenomena, viz., interjections such as "oh, ah, ha," and onomato-poeia, as "crow, cuckoo, to buzz, to twitter" and the like. There is no recognizable way from it to the other facts of language. And this is just the problem facing us: How did that emotional cry engender a fully developed idiom, capable of expressing the most varied concrete and abstract ideas?

May I first mention here two basic attempts of nineteenth-century scholars to explain the genesis of grammatical forms: the agglutination theory of the Indo-Europeanist F. Bopp and the adaptation theory of A. Ludwig. The former is to this day the prevailing one in the conception of persons who view words in relation to the reality which they express; and it is, therefore, the prevailing one also in linguistics, so much so that we find it difficult to free our minds from it. Thus, for instance, the Latin and Greek words *domi, servis, pessimus,* express the composite ideas "at the house, to the slaves, the worst"; similarly, the Hebrew words *yomam, yamîm, shamarti* express the composite ideas "by day, days, I guarded." The agglutination theory takes the line, natural to an unhistorical mind, that those words are composite, like the ideas they express. They are believed to contain one central, main element, i.e., the root, which expresses the substance of the idea; further, they contain elements of which some produce the special form of the word, the pattern peculiar to it, as, in the Latin and Greek words mentioned, the vowel between the letters of the root and the ending, or, in Hebrew, syllables like *on* or the *ah* and *at* of the feminine, which distinguish words such as *shim-shon* or *shimshah,* as separate words, from the root *shmsh;* and lastly, flectional elements denoting number, case, person, tense, etc. The elements additional to the root, which today represent gram-matical modifications of the word—number, gender, case pro-nominal suffix, etc.—are according to the agglutination theory remnants of words which have been added to the principal word and have subsequently become blurred in pronunciation owing to loss of their independent accent. Thus, for instance *montes* "mounts," is regarded as a compound of two words meaning respectively "mountain" and "many," *lupa* is "wolf" plus "female," etc.

Now the very concept "root" is taken from the grammar of the Semitic languages, especially of Arabic and Hebrew. Precisely in the domain of Semitic languages, however, it is easiest to prove that a thing such as a root did not exist in language from the outset. In the Semitic tongue, the concept which we call "root" is essentially expressed by the consonants of the word. In forms such as *katabh, ketobh, ketabh, kotebh, katubh,* "he wrote, write! writ, writing (participle), written," the root is represented by the consonants *ktbh*, while the specific sense of the derivative and the various grammatical modifications are expressed by the changing vowels of the word. Now it is obvious that such a root, represented only by consonants, never existed in the language. We, and only we, isolate from the various forms of the word family *katabh, ketobh, ketabh, kotebh, katubh,* by logical abstraction, that which is common to them, viz., the consonants *ktbh*; also, from the concepts expressed by these words, we isolate by logical abstraction their common substantial content. This procedure of abstracting a root from the various forms actually existing in the language may be very useful for purposes of practical study, in that it helps to arrange the different forms of the words in a well-conceived system; but it is clear that a Semitic grammar which erects its foundation on such roots, and for which the concepts of the root are the chief aid in viewing linguistic phenomena, places the end of the development at the beginning; it inverts the true process of the history of the language and thereby precludes any historical understanding of the latter's genesis.

Let us now make clear to ourselves that the concept of the Semitic root may be transferred to European languages, e.g., English and German, which will help us to realize the whole absurdity of the view just referred to. English and German verbs, too, make forms by a change of vowel:

a With 2 consonants

    English: to give—gave, to bear—bore—born, to take—took

    German: *gebe—gab, lüge—log, sehe—sah*

b With 3 consonants

    English: to bind—bound, to find—found, to sing—sang—sung, to speak—spoke

German: *singe—sang—gesungen, schlage—schlug, binde,*
   band, gebunden
c With 4 consonants
   English: to stand—stood, to stride—strode
   German: *spreche—sprach—gesprochen*
d With 5 consonants
   English: to spring—sprang—sprung
   German: *springe—sprang—gesprungen*

This phenomenon has been rightly treated in those languages
as *ablaut* (vowel gradation), a regular change in the vowels of the
word—verb or noun—in question. But let us imagine that this
vowel change, as "give—gave, bind—bound," had spread in those
languages, as it did in Semitic, to all verbs and nouns; in that case,
those grammarians who see language from a logical viewpoint
only would have distilled from these forms roots such as *gb, sng,*
sprch, sprng and explained the forms out of them; they would only
have debated, as the students of Semitic do until today, whether
the earliest roots consisted of only two radicals, or of three, four,
or even five. Needless to say, there is no historical basis for such
"roots."

Equally lacking in foundation is the different conception of
roots and stems customarily applied to Indo-European languages.
Out of different forms of a word, as Greek πόνος, πόνον (accusative),
that which is common to them is extracted as the stem: πόνο; and
out of several words appearing to be related to one another, that
which is common to them is extracted as the root (πόν). This root,
too, supposed to be the beginning of the word's history, is in fact
its end, an abstraction born in the brain of grammarians; we
realize that scholars whose gaze was rigidly fixed in the wrong
direction were unable to recognize the course of the historical
development, which went the other way.

Just as one seeks roots for words, one tries to find a first or
basic meaning for families of words. This basic meaning, too, is
necessarily wrong, a philosophical abstraction existing only in the
minds of grammarians, a crooked mirror in which the history of
language appears distorted and upside down.

Essentially wrong, therefore, is the agglutination theory, which
regards living words, since their meaning is composite, as actually
and primarily compounded of shorter words, representing the

parts of that composite meaning—though there are, of course, words which today seem of one piece but which in reality are combinations, no longer distinctly recognizable as such, of several words; these, however, do not represent the basic historical phenomenon which accounts for the forms of words in general.

Now let us consider the adaptation method. It rightly rejects the assumption that grammatical endings and the like, and especially *ablaut*—vowels with a grammatical meaning—are essentially separate words added to roots and stems. According to it, these additions and variations had no separate meaning, but the words, in the course of their history, have adapted themselves morphologically to the purpose of expressing grammatical concepts, such as number, case, and tense.

This theory, too, is unsatisfactory, (1) because it introduces into the explanation of language the notion of purpose: language was not created deliberately and not, therefore, for one purpose or another; (2) because it fails to explain how that adaptation came about—it does not tell us, e.g., why and how the grammatical meanings of case endings developed, and with similar results, in languages far removed from each other, offsprings of absolutely different language families; (3) because the forms which according to it were designed for a certain purpose do not really achieve that purpose; we observe, for instance, how in the further course of the development such forms recede and vanish, apparently because they served no useful purpose in the languages concerned. Thus case endings had developed in Semitic and Indo-European, so that in classical Arabic we have *rabbun* "lord" for the nominative, *rabbin* for the genitive, *rabban* for the accusative, and similarly in Latin *servus* for the nominative, *servi* for the genitive, *servo* for the dative, *servum* for the accusative, etc.; but in colloquial Arabic and in the Romance languages, the daughters of Latin, these different case forms do not exist, and it seems that speakers felt them to be useless, so that colloquial Arabic has *rabb,* and French *fils,* in all cases, while the case meanings are expressed by separate words, prepositions, as French *du (père),* English "of (the father), to (the father)."

So this theory, too, provides no real explanation of the process by which, out of emotional cries, well-ordered and differentiated expressions developed for the concepts of our mind.

To achieve a solution, we shall have to change our approach to linguistic questions. Orthodox linguistics dispense with exploring the genesis of language; but as they are for the most part logically rather than historically oriented, they apply grammatical categories as if these were not concepts born of the evolution of human thought but facts inherent from the start in the nature of language. It is true that fully developed languages indicate every notion of doing or being by a special category of predication word, called *verbum*, "verb," or in German *Tatwort* (action word) or *Zeitwort* (time word), every thing—subject, object, and the like —by a noun, every quality by an adjective, etc. But it is obvious that when man first began to speak linguistic categories and rules did not exist. The earliest specimens of speech, therefore, are of necessity older than categories and rules, which developed only in them and out of them. We should consequently devote particular attention to such specimens as cannot be explained on the basis of the rule. These specimens may be older than the categories and any rule, and we may possibly learn from them how the categories and rules arose and developed. But what does the linguistic science do instead? It proclaims the categories as eternal and tries to impose them on phenomena which refuse to fit into them.

Let us take words meaning "here, there, above, below, within, outside, then, already, still, thus," etc. Such words express essentially a local, temporal, modal relationship. Words such as "here, there, above, below" are locative; "then, still, already" are temporal; others are modal or instrumental, not because of their grammatical form but by dint of their inherent meaning. We therefore ought to examine whether other locative, temporal, modal, and instrumental words were not fashioned after them, in imitation of their sound, and whether the local, temporal, and instrumental case forms did not arise in this manner. But orthodox grammar starts from the full-fledged case and the full-fledged noun; it therefore tries to find a nominal stem and root even in such little words as Greek πρίν, πρό, Latin *prae, pro*, English "(be)fore, (be)hind, (be)low," and debates on how to interpret the ending of such a little word—whether it was originally a locative or an accusative, a dative or an ablative; it thereby blocks to itself the road to a historical explanation of the phenomena concerned.

Words meaning "before" or "behind," "above" or "below," as Greek πρίν, Latin *prim(us)*, German *ehest* (compare "next," *nächst*) —which later became *erst*—Latin *extra, supra, extrem(us)*, and their many counterparts in Semitic languages, are, by virtue of their inherent signification, indicative also of rank: he who comes before others, ahead of others, is also foremost or first in order and rank; he who is behind or late is the last. On the pattern of these words, therefore, language evolved special forms for the ordinal number and the superlative: after *primus* or *extremus*, Latin modeled *maximus, minimus*, "the greatest, the smallest," and in analogy to Hebrew *elyôn*, "above," Accadian *elânu*, "above," *rîshôn, qadmôn*, "foremost, first," some Semitic languages have *shaniânu* etc., "the second." Besides these words, however, there are others, such as the numerous Hebrew words ending in *ôn*, or German words like *Hengst*, "stallion," *Herbst*, "autumn" (harvest), which show that the form in question was not created deliberately as a superlative, and that its superlative sense is not an original one. But what are we to say if a great linguistic scholar, A. Hirt, devotes a special study to the problem of interpreting words like *Hengst* or *Herbst*—by distorting their plain meaning— as superlatives? Such a method obviously cannot lead to a real understanding of the phenomena of language.

If we ask an educated person who has not thoroughly investigated the facts of language what are the first things to which man gave names, he will surely say that they were the concrete things nearest to him. However, an examination of the names of such things shows, surprisingly, that every one of them originally denotes merely a quality of the thing in question.

In Hebrew (where these facts appear more strikingly than in Indo-European languages), the words for egg, white of egg, moon, poplar tree, frankincense, (Mount) Lebanon, milk, fat, originally only mean: white, Hebrew *bēṣah* ("egg") is actually the same word as Arabic *abyaḍ*, fem. *bêḍa(h)*, "white"; *lebhana(h)*, "moon," *libhne(h)*, "(white) poplar tree," *lebhona(h)*, "frankincense," *Lebhanon*, "the snow-covered mountain," Arabic *laban*, "sour milk," are the same as Hebrew *labhan*, "white"; and Hebrew *ḥalab(h)*, Arabic *ḥalîb*, "milk," *ḥelbon*, "white of egg," *ḥelebh*, "fat," represent another word meaning "white." Hebrew *'aleh*, "leaf, leaves" (of a plant) is that which is on (the tree), above (*'al*, 'alê); similarly, German *Obst*, "fruits of a tree," originally meant that which is *oben*, on the tree. Hebrew *hamma(h)*, "sun," is that which is *hamma(h)* "hot"; *shamaim*, like "heaven" in English, actually means "above, high (compare Arabic *sama*, "to be high," etc.); Turkish *kyök*, "sky," really means "blue," and Latin *coelum* means "hollow, vaulted" (compare Greek κοιλόs). Words such as German *Gesicht, Gelenk, Glied*, denoting parts of the body, are derived from *sehen*, "to see," *lenken, leiten*, "to direct, lead." The English names of insects, flea, fly, basically contain the concept "to flee, to fly." "The plate," "the flat" go back to the adjectival concept "flat." German *Spitze*, "pointed tip," is derived from "*spitz*, pointed"; "hill, heaven" from "high," *hoch*; "room," *Raum*, is that which is *geraum*, "spacious," and its synonym *Gemach* is that which is *gemach*, "convenient, comfortable."

How are we to account for all this? We certainly cannot assume that "names" for these concrete things were chosen in reference to this or that quality—there was no deliberate name giving at the beginning of language. Paradoxically enough, the ultimate cause of any change of meaning, in fact of the origination of any meaning, in language is *error*, a misunderstanding between speaker and hearer. Error is the productive factor in language. A person accompanies his gestures with speech, saying, for instance: "Here (is something) flat; here, pointed; here, aloud; here flying, in flight; here, above, below, high, behind, in front," and the hearer understands: "Here is a flat thing, a flat; a point; a bird which cries; a flea or a fly which flies; fruit which is on the tree; the lower part of the human body; a mountain or hill; the buttocks; the face." Prior to names and to any concrete term, language thus had short demonstrative words serving to point out and refer to the simplest relations: here and there, above and below, flat, pointed, and the like. These designations for here and there, above, below, in front and behind, flat and pointed, these linguistic hints, which did not first originate under a scheme of linguistic forms, which are neither masculine nor feminine, neither singular nor plural, are found even today in every language—we call them, in flagrant curtailment of their linguistic function, "adverbs," qualifiers of the verb— and innumerable specimens of them are indeed such ancient words, born prior to any grammatical rule. Even today we can observe adverbs turning, for instance, into nouns: the yes and the no, ifs and ands, the whereabouts, the why and the wherefore, the ups and downs, the ins and outs, the wherewithal, the hereafter, the beyond, or in German: *das Ach, das Weh, das Durcheinander, das Um und Auf, er kennt kein Genug, das Wie, das Wenn, das Aber, das Gestern, das Morgen, den Garaus machen,* and the like. Thus these "ungrammatical" words turn into nouns. It is easy to see how in other cases the same ungrammatical designations were understood—at first by mistake—as verbs. One said, for instance: "here, in front"; when the "in front" of the human body was pointed out, the hearer might understand the reference to be a noun, the front of the human body, the face; in Hebrew *panîm.* But in the same way, one said πρό, "*prae,* fore," *vorn, vor, fort,* when pointing to some person or persons who was or were moving forward, and the hearer understood: "he faces, they face" (in Hebrew *ponîm*), *er fährt, sie führen,* and the like; also, one said: *das förder (vorder),* "that (pron.) further," *das hinter,* "that (pron.) behind," and understood, in German and English: *fördere, hindere,* "further, hinder," as a command to act, an imperative.

We thus realize that etymological relationship of words does not mean a logical connection. Rather, it means that there was at one time a single word, either a late word, built according to the rules of grammar, or a primitive word, older than any rule; this word was erroneously given a new sense and a new application. We have not to do here with the creation of a new word but with a new use of the same word, due to a misunderstanding between speaker and hearer, or sometimes, at a later period, between writer and reader. We know of simple cases of this kind, involving no change in the structure of the language, e.g., Exodus 13:14: "Three times [in Hebrew *regalîm*] thou shalt celebrate unto me in the year." This sentence was naturally understood—without a change in its general purport—to have meant from the outset: "Three *festivals* thou shalt celebrate unto me in the year"; hence the word *regalîm* received the new, substantival, meaning "festivals," the three great festivals of the year.

In the same way, we should understand the etymological relationship between noun and verb, and the like. Let us take the case, already mentioned, of the Hebrew noun *panîm,* "face," and the verb *panah,* "to face." The latter represents a different use of the ancient word meaning "in front" which we found to have been understood as a noun when the speaker pointed to the "in front" of the human body—the face. In the present case it was understood as a verb, "he faces, they face, to the front," when the speaker pointed to some person or persons who was or were moving forward, facing a certain direction. The relationship between the Hebrew noun *'iqqar,* "root of a plant" (and by extension "root of anything"), and the Hebrew verb *'aqar,* "to uproot," is to be understood on similar lines. The speaker used, for instance, a word in order to convey the verbal idea: I see a plant being uprooted; but the hearer in many cases understood a noun: I see the *roots* of a plant, which are being pulled out; so the word came to be both a verb and a noun.

Etymological relationship was thus originally etymological identity. To explain the relation between words which seem akin to each other, we must not content ourselves with discovering a logical connection between the concepts expressed by them. Rather, we should try to reconstruct the circumstances in which one of these words, by a naturally occurring error, was taken to have a different meaning from the one which alone it had until then, this marking the emergence of the other word.

The extent to which this view changes our conception of the interrelation of words and meanings may be demonstrated by a striking example.

The Hebrew word *shet,* plural *shatôt, shetôt,* denotes the buttocks and the foundations of a building. From a logical viewpoint, it has no connection with the verb *shatô, shatôt,* "to drink." We should remember, however, that several words used in a sense close to "drink" originally meant "below," since in order to drink one had to go down to the river. In Hebrew, the word for river itself, *naḥal,* originally meant "below, in the plain," since it is there that the river flows and the water of a spring collects. Arabic *warada,* the equivalent of Hebrew *yarad,* "to go down," means "to go down to drink water"; thus the name *Yarden,* "Jordan," originally meant "(the river which is) below in the wadi." Greek ποταμός is connected with πίπτω "to fall (down)," and probably with similar sounding words meaning "to drink." We now see the natural connection between those words of widely different meaning. *Shet, shatôt* meant "below." In certain cases a person said this word while pointing to the "below" of the body or of a building or the like, and so a noun arose meaning the buttocks or the foundations of a building, as e.g., in Psalm 11:3; in other cases a person said, e.g., "I am going to *shetôt*," meaning "I am going down to the river"—his intention being to drink there. In such cases, it was natural for the hearer to understand *shetôt, shatô* in the sense of the verb "to drink," and so such a verb came into being.

Other verbs originated in the same way. The noun did not arise from the verb, nor the verb from the noun, but noun and verb arose by different understanding of one and the same primitive word, which itself had not arisen under any linguistic category or grammatical rule but by what was basically a misunderstanding, the identification of the "word" with a reality hinted at by a cry. Thus these simple deictic words owed their meaning to a misunderstanding. There is no "basic meaning" in language, neither of a word nor of the grammatical form of a word. The meaning of linguistic phenomena is the outcome of their fate in history. A man cried, for instance, under affect or in imitation of a sound he had heard: "Ha!" pointing at the thing which had aroused his excitement or attention; and "ha" became, for instance, a demonstrative word meaning "here" or "there." In the course of time man came to use this deictic word to point out, in particular, the "here" or "there" which was above or below, in front or behind; the hearer then no longer understood simply "here" or "there," but "above" or "below," "in front" or "behind."

In the same way, a child begins to speak by making meaningless babbling noises. Hunger impels it, when feeding time is near, to move its mouth or lips and thereby to produce, for instance, the sound "mam, mammam, ham, hamham," and we, parents and relatives, mistakenly believe this "hamham" to *mean* "food" or "to eat," and thus give the child the first word of its vocabulary.

Those primitive, meaningless words arose apart from any morphological scheme. It was only by phonetic development that a word like πρίν, *pro*, brought forth different forms, as *porro, prae,* πρός, *primus, prior, praeter.* But each of these forms had a history of its own. As those words were used in relation to all kinds of things and concepts, they immediately, at one and the same time, became concretes and abstracts, nouns and verbs, past, present, and future, singular and plural, accusative and locative, according to the things or concepts whose names they were—erroneously—understood to be. The form of every such primitive word which, by its particular history, became, for instance, a noun or a verb, a nominative or an ablative, was the nucleus which, by analogy, could become the starting point for the development of a special grammatical form for a noun or a verb, a nominative or an ablative, and which in fact became such a special form if it prevailed over other analogies, which worked in other directions.

Man possesses language, and he believes that in language he possesses the universe. Just as in the world of reality there are objects and actions, so—he believes—the facts of language are from the outset symbols, names, of objects and actions. Objects on the one hand and actions and processes on the other are to him the center of the language, and from that center—misconceived from a historical point of view—it seems to him that the primitive words are frozen cases of nouns[2] or infinitives of verbs, formed from the full-fledged noun or verb by inflection, e.g., by the addition of an adverbial ending. A word meaning "morning," *Frühe,* is essentially,[3] in all languages, a phonetic development of an adverb meaning "early, in the morning" and has only become a noun in the course of its history, by way of its different uses in analogy to other words. But the linguistic science proceeds from the full-fledged noun "morning," *Frühe,* and regards the adverb as a frozen form of one or the other grammatical case of that noun. A person speaking and, to an even more misleading extent (by its methodicalness), the linguistic sciences are oriented toward the object of language, viz., reality in its manifold aspects, and not toward the ways of language itself; their gaze is turned toward the purpose of all speech, and not toward the origin of language and its evolution since its beginnings.

However, the fact that language did not come into being as a mirror of reality, by the giving of names to the things of reality, could have been deduced also from the abstract terms, found even

[2] In individual, late instances, of course, it happens that extra-grammatical words, adverbs, arise from full-fledged grammatical expressions, but the main development is in the reverse direction: from the ungrammatical cry to nouns and verbs governed by grammatical rules.

[3] The reference is not to those particular words, but to the concept which is expressed by many words in different languages.

in the most primitive languages, which have no counterpart in reality—terms whose large number would make one think that primitive man, prior to all language, created abstract philosophic concepts, even though he may have had no use for them. But this, too, is an inverted view of the actual development. Just as there arose, in the beginnings of language, certain marker and pointer words—such as "on, under, large, small, much, little"— which in many cases were used in relation to concrete things and which therefore became names of things, so it necessarily seemed to the speaker that other marker words of similar form and used in a similar way, as "(to do) good," i.e., a boon, "kind," a kindness, a favor," as against "(to make) a chair, a house," were likewise names of particular things—nouns. Thus linguistic analogy gave man abstract terms and abstract concepts, which—in my opinion not without damage to his logic—gained control of his thinking.

This misoriented view of language, owing to which the latter appeared as having from the start been a mirror reflecting reality, produced the "fruitful error" of language. However, it prevented the solution of the problem of the origin of language.

Moreover, the evolution of language by way of grammatically formless deictic words of necessity gave rise to certain processes of development which the science of language failed to recognize. As an example of these processes we will outline here the rise of the singular and plural.

How does language indicate the singular as against the plural? And is that indication at all original and natural, that is to say, is it *per se* to be understood as such an indication?

Most frequent and well known is the indication of the plural by the addition of a flexional ending, as Latin (mons) *montes,* (pater) *patres;* English "(horse) horses," and the like. The impression is—and the layman really believes so—that the action of the plural is inherent in the ending of the word. If this impression were correct, we should have to assume that the ending had arisen from a separate word which meant from the outset "many, much, more than one." But in fact it is absolutely impossible to conceive of all the short endings which, in addition to the plural, express also the masculine or the feminine, the nominative or the genitive, etc., as compounds of words and particles which not only meant "many" but were also indications of gender, case, etc.

Another assumption appears, at first sight, more likely. In some of the cases mentioned, the plural forms are fuller, longer than those of the singular, as in Arabic *qātilûna* (plural) as against *qātilun* (singular), or in European languages *mons—montes, pater—patres,* "horse—horses," *Berg—Berge.* It might thus seem that the plural was expressed by a mere extension of the word, or by the increased stress which led to that extension, so that the numerical increase was symbolically expressed by an increase in the length of the word. However, this attempt to explain the plural form is likewise mistaken. In some ancient groups of words and forms the plural form is not fuller but, on the contrary, shorter than the singular (as in the Arabic instances of the pattern *qatl, qitl,* etc., which serve as the plural of a singular of the pattern *qatlat, qitlat,* etc.). In addition, and above all, this whole method of interpretation, like any symbolical interpretation of language, is mistaken for a psychological reason. Let us make clear to ourselves how, in fact, the meaning of a word is changed if we pronounce it more fully, with greater stress—if we say, for instance, "t a b l e" instead of "table," "r e d" instead of "red," "g o !" instead of "go." It is only the concept expressed by the word itself that is thrown into relief by a more emphatic pronunciation: "a table, and not something else," "red, and not green or blue," "be sure and go, do not do anything else." In this way we are able to understand, for instance, the reinforcement expressed by the double consonant in the intensive conjugation of the Hebrew verb (as *kittebh,* from *katabh*), which changes merely the degree of intensity of the action. But even the most emphatic pronunciation of the words "table," "red," or French *"prends!"* can never convey the idea "some or many tables," "several red things," or *"prenez!"* in the plural sense. Symbolic indication by stress is not, therefore, a natural, obvious way of expressing the plural.

A primitive and natural means of expressing the plural was seen by others in reduplication, either of a whole word or of part of a word. Repetition of a word, so they thought, naturally indicates the plural of the concept denoted by it, for a horse and horse are two horses, a person and a person and yet another person are three persons, etc. But this, too, is wrong. In the first place, the facts show that reduplication is not used as an actual means of expressing the plural. It is not a means of building the plural form in either Indo-European or Semitic; we do not say "horse-horse" or *mons-mons* rather than "horses" or *montes,* and the few alleged specimens of a phenomenon of that kind are not actually distinguished from the singular by reduplication alone. This goes also for a language of a different character, such as Sumerian, in which, e.g., *gal-galla* instead of *gal* ("great") is used not only for the plural but also for the singular. Here again, our negative conclusion will be readily understood; linguistic reduplication is not a pictorial "side-by-side," but an acoustic "one-after-the-other." We say, emotionally: "My God, my God, why hast thou forsaken me?" "O earth, earth, earth, hear the word of the Lord," and the like, in order to express again what has been said before, so that the hearer may perceive it more exactly and with increased attention and understanding. But the conditions of the linguistic process make it impossible for "God, God" to be understood as "gods," or "earth, earth, earth" as "earths." Thus, reduplication, too, cannot be regarded as an intrinsically apt mode of primitive plural expression.

We therefore conclude: All the extant linguistic forms indicative of the plural are not obviously and specifically so, and are not, accordingly, original expressions of that concept. If they are nevertheless used in that function, it is only because they have assumed it in the course of the history of words, in the process of language development; and we can only understand and explain them if we succeed in tracing their genesis in the light of the facts.

Now what are the facts? What is it that language designates as plural? A scrutiny of the material from different languages and language families reveals that everywhere the forms in question describe not only the actual plural but also definite singular concepts.

In Semitic, Indo-European, and other language families—in complete parallelism—the plural form frequently indicates

a. Single parts of the body, as: the head (Semitic; Gothic *zi houbitum,* German *zu Häupten,* etc.), the face, the throat (Latin *fauces*), the neck or back (Latin *cervices,* Greek νῶτα, etc.), the chest or waist (Gothic *brusts,* etc.), the heart, the hip(s), the loin(s), etc.

b. Materials, as: water (in Indo-European), νίπτρα "water for washing," fire (Accadian), blood (Hebrew, Accadian), flesh (Hebrew, Accadian), ashes (Latin *cineres*), foam (Latin *spumae*), smoke (Greek κάπνοι), snow (Latin *nives*), oil (Accadian), dirt (Latin *sordes*), residue (Hebrew; Latin *reliquiae*) etc.

c. Notions of place, as: right-hand side (Greek τὰ δέξια), surroundings (Hebrew; English and French "environs"), north (Latin *septemtrionalia*), heaven (Semitic), depth (Hebrew), distance (Hebrew), surface (Hebrew), side (Latin *partes*), ambush (Latin *insidiae*), camp (Latin *castra*), grave (Greek τάφοι and corresponding forms in Hebrew), cradle (Latin *cunae, cunabulae*), house (Latin *aedes,* Greek δώματα), etc.

d. Notions of time, as: morning and evening (Semitic; in Indo-European: Greek δυσμάι, Spanish *buenas tardes, buenas noches*), midnight, noon, and also particular days, as Latin *calendae* (the first of the month), *nonae* (the ninth of the month), *idus* (the thirteenth or fifteenth of the month), *nundinae* (the market day, following an eight-day week); festivals, as Latin *Olympiaca, matronalia, feralia,* German *Ostern, Pfingsten,* French *Pâques,* etc.

e. All kinds of abstract concepts, as: Latin *nuptiae,* "wedding," *exsequiae,* "funeral," *divitiae, opes,* "riches," *grates,* "thank(s)," *indutiae,* "armistice," and many others; Hebrew: life, old age, youth, eternity, betrothal, marriage, divorce, upbringing, blindness, wisdom, perversity, uprightness, fidelity, mercy, sorcery; Accadian: anger, fear, and countless others; regular infinitive forms (especially in Aramaic); etc.

In these and numerous other cases, in part of which the word exists only in the plural form (*plurale tantum*), the concept expressed by the plural form is a singular one. How has this been explained up till now? On the one hand the singular concepts have been explained as basically plural, the contradiction being covered by a term: "hidden, *discrete*" plurals. It has been asserted, for instance, that plurals of location express "the idea of a whole composed of innumerable separate parts or points";[4] ex-

---

[4] "Plurals of local extension . . . denote localities in general, but especially level surfaces (the surface-plural), since in them the idea of a whole composed of innumerable separate parts or points is most evident." Gesenius-Kautzsch, *Hebrew Grammar,* 2nd English ed. by A. E. Cowley, §124b.

pressions of quality or action involve, according to one opinion, "a more or less intensive focusing of the characteristics inherent in the idea of the stem";[5] Greek ἥλιοι "heat of the sun," is said to be plural "because the sun burns again and again";[6] etc., etc.

There is no need to demonstrate in detail the absurdity of these arbitrary explanations; it will be sufficient—for the time being—to show that there is from the start no reason to depart from the plain meaning of the words.

Certain forms which in many cases designate a plural concept are called by us, *a potiori,* plural forms. However, what permits us to assume that this is the function of those forms everywhere and that we must look for it even in cases in which we have a singular meaning before us? Are we not like a man who, having never known any but white people, assumes, when he first sees a Negro, that the latter is also basically white and is only trying fraudulently to conceal the fact?

On the other hand, one has sought to account for the seeming multiplicity of meanings of the plural forms by the theory that language does not from the outset designate the plural as a numerical qualification but expresses—by a special category of words—only the emotive value (*Affektionswert*) attached by it to that concept (*"Die Sprache legt zunächst keinen Wert (!) auf eine deutliche formelle Scheidung jedes einzelnen, sondern begnügt sich damit, diese je nach den Unständen in eine der alten Wertklassen einzureihen. . . ."*—Brockelmann), and that, therefore, for instance, an Arabic "feminine suffix" may also be a plural ending.

This "explanation" not only explains nothing but it is essentially wrong. It is wrong because the facts do not permit us to assume that any form, whether singular or plural, masculine or feminine, expresses from the outset any "value," either "plus" or "minus." The Semitic suffix which, for instance—as what we call the "feminine ending"—designates the *nomen unitatis* (e.g., Arabic *namla(t),* "ant," as against the plural *naml,* "ants"), that is to say, a supposed "minus" value, is also, as shown especially by the masculine numerals for two, three, four, etc., common to all

[5] *Ibid.,* §102a.
[6] *"Weil die Sonne einmal ums andere brennt."* R. Wagner, *Grundzvuege der griech. Grammatik,* p. III.

Semitic languages, an ancient expression of the plural, i.e., of a supposed "plus" value. Instead of the "plus-value" plural form (as German *Männer*), we often find the "minus-value" singular (50 *Mann*); and in many cases of this kind in Semitic languages, the singular form is the only correct one for the expression of the plural. Another reason why that explanation is mistaken is that it quite unjustifiably credits language with a symbolic mode of expression. An emotive "plus value," is expressed by a word reinforced—as shown above by various examples—only the concept represented by the word itself, and not any grammatical relation of that word; no stressing of a word can express the plural concept, any more than it can express the masculine or the feminine, the past or the future. Nor does that explanation really explain anything, because it fails to account for the fact that despite all, in the majority of cases, that obscure dispensation of values designates, precisely and unequivocally, the plural as plural and the singular as singular: *patres, montes* always mean several fathers or mountains, and not only one.

But the very approach to language implied in that explanation is fundamentally wrong. It puts the phenomena of language, as it were, on one and the same plane and tries to reduce all the different and contradictory meanings of the so-called plural to a common denominator, to subsume them logically under one inclusive concept. Such a concept, which would comprise all those contradictory terms, would of necessity be so devoid of character and color that no specific, definite, and recognizable meaning could be derived from it. However, the phenomena of language must be explained, not from their condition in a particular period of the past or present, but from their evolution; not by logical generalization, but psychologically.

That this is possible, that the numeral signification of what we call "plural" is a thing that has evolved, was proved by Johannes Schmidt in 1889 in his book on the plural forms of the Indo-European neuters (*Die Pluralbildung der indogermanischen Neutra*). As instances of such an evolution he mentions, *inter alia,* the German suffixes *lich* and *er* (Old German *ir*, as in *Kälber, kalbir*), which were originally a part of the "root." These elements surely had no primary connection with the plural concept or anything like it, but they nevertheless became, in certain dialects or daughter languages, specific expressions of the plural. The suffix *lich*, in particular, is known also from Yiddish, which has, e.g., *fisch, bein* ("fish, bone") for the singular and *fischelach, beindelach* for the plural. This suffix is an element which is present also in English "like" and German *gleich* (formerly *ge-leich*) and which means "equal"; but we nevertheless observe that by a historical process it has clearly assumed the function of a plural sign. A particular historical process has endowed a linguistic form with a function that it did not by any means possess from the outset.

However, Schmidt did not perceive the wide scope and psychological pattern of this development, which he confines to a single class of words. He rightly refers, for a parallel to the phenomena mentioned, to the forms of the Arabic "broken" plural,[7] which, too, are seemingly singular forms, as *kalb*, "dog," plural *kilâb; himâr*, "donkey," plural *hamîr*. He thinks that these singulars were once used also as abstract nouns and subsequently developed into collective nouns and ultimately into plurals. But this alleged process requires explanation. How could simple, concrete meanings, such as "ox, horse, leaf," come to be replaced at first by abstractions, then by collective concepts, as "herd, stud, foliage," and eventually by concrete, definite plural concepts, as "oxen, horses, leaves"? True, the singular form—as already mentioned—sometimes denotes the plural concept. Expressions such as German *50 Mann* (singular) occur in many languages. Arabic, in fact, has no other way of expressing the plural in such cases than by the singular form. But has this plural meaning developed, by way of abstraction, from the singular? The case of the numerals shows that this is impossible. The numerals *quatuor, quinque, sex, septem*, like their Semitic counterparts, undoubtedly express a plural concept and yet are singular in form. Who will dare to maintain that their basic meaning is singular, i.e., "one," and that only an abstract or collective use is responsible for their plural meaning?

Clearly, this is not so. Rather, the facts show that just as certain plural forms, the *pluralia tantum*, in spite of their form, are used,

[7] The term "broken plural" is used where a noun or adjective has two forms, differing in vocalization, of which one expresses the singular, the other the plural, as *qatl* (singular) and *qutûl, aqtâl* (plural). That this phenomenon is not confined to singular and plural, or to Arabic, and how it arose, has been explained by me, especially in the first volume of my Hebrew book *Ha-Lashon we-ha-Sepher (The Language and the Scripture)*. Essentially it is not different from such *ablaut* forms as English "man—men, mouse—mice," etc.

without any connotation of plural, to express singular concepts, so the form called singular was used, without any singular connotation, to express the plural.

A systematic survey of the above generally known facts will reveal the full scope and direction of the development which led to the emergence of the plural meaning. We have already mentioned that both in Semitic and in Indo-European the plural in place of the singular is used principally in names of materials and abstract concepts, that is to say, in cases in which one cannot actually speak of either singular or plural. We do not speak, in the proper numerical sense, of one or several water(s) or depth(s). In such cases, the singular is not a singular or the plural a plural; but what we call "singular" is the more frequent form, and what we call "plural" the less frequent one, independently of any numerical relation. There is no singular-plural distinction here at all. However, the fact that the plural forms of such words are most prevalent in poetry, which preserves ancient language habits, suggests that in general the plural forms are probably older.

It is only in names of concrete things, which are actually counted, as man—men, table—tables, that the plural is really and regularly a plural and the singular a singular. However, the particular usages of poetry, as well as proper names, which are peculiar to a single thing and not usually countable, reveal, both in Semitic and in Indo-European, an earlier stage of language, in which for concrete concepts, too, the plural was used with a singular meaning: Αἰγοσπόταμοι (the River of the Goats), ᾿Αδῆναι, *Syracusae,* and similar instances in Semitic; French *Bruxelles;* German *Aachen, Baden* (by the side of *Ache, Bad*); *Mauthausen* instead of *Mauthaus,* "customs-house," etc.

It follows that the singular and plural forms of concrete nouns, too, originally had no numerical meaning. It was out of, and in, such forms, which originally imparted no numerical distinction, that a plural expression first arose, mainly by having the older form assume the plural meaning and the younger form the singular meaning.

That this was really so, and how a grammatical expression of number necessarily developed in this way, will be first demonstrated here by the example of the commonest Semitic plural suffix. The plural suffix in the various branches of Semitic is the syllable *âm, ân, êm, ên, aim, ain, îm, în, ûm,* or *ûn,* or its abbreviation, the variously voweled nasal suffix *(tamwîm* or *tanwîn);* the nasal sound being often omitted (originally, e.g., in assimilation to a following consonant), which resulted in the formation of similar plural suffixes without the nasal.

A part of these suffix grades expresses a special case of the plural, viz., the dual. The genesis of the dual meaning is apparent. The oldest group of words which became duals were words without grammatical form and not belonging to any grammatical category—exclamations, originally accompanied by a deictic gesture or facial movement, and later expressing, e.g., relationships of locality, such as: here, there, above, below, beside, in, out, before, behind, etc. In the course of time, these deictic words came to denote a specific "above," "below," or "beside." Thus, e.g., a word used for "above" more and more assumed the meaning "heaven" (compare expressions such as "God above"); Accadian *ishdân* ("below") came to mean the foundations of the house, or the "below" of the human body; Greek πεδίον, perhaps originating in an imitation of the sound of footfalls—pat-pat—came to mean the ground, while a variant phonetic development, ποδέ came to mean the feet. A similar imitation of a tapping sound, *pa'mâm,* took on the meaning "foot, feet" in Canaanitic and Hebrew. Semitic *yadâ(m),* which originally may have meant "(the) aside" or may have accompanied a gesture, was sometimes understood as a verb, *yada* "to throw" (aside), and sometimes as the "by the side" of the human body, i.e., the hand(s).

Now the thing nearest to our senses and thoughts, our body, is built symmetrically. What was called *ishdân* or *pa'mâm* was, in the case of man, a pair of *feet;* the *yadâm* of man were two sides, two hands. These words, therefore, became duals because the objects to which they were applied and for which they served as names were dual. It was in view of these and similar instances that man developed the feeling that the phonetic form of these words was indicative of the dual. Thus, without any morphological or semantic intent, the dual form arose, in Semitic, and similarly, as can easily be proved, in every other language.

The foregoing provides at the same time the explanation of the genesis of any plural expression. In some Semitic languages the above-mentioned dual form is the form of the plural in general.[8]

[8] Compare Accadian *ân(i)* as the ending of both the dual and the plural, Aramaic *ain* in the same double function, the Hebrew *pluralis constructus* such as *harê,* "mountains," etc.

But all other Semitic plural suffixes are likewise merely phonetic variants, characterized by different vowels, of the ending that became the dual sign. Moreover, as explained below, the development of the broken plural is not different from that of the plural indicated by a suffix.

It can be proved that Semitic plural forms of all kinds were at first, in many cases, definite "adverbs," used as such everywhere. The oldest Common Semitic participles denoting place relations of the simplest order—as "on, to, upon, beneath"—show, particularly in connection with pronouns, a plural form which cannot be explained as a real plural, and a host of such "plural" adverbs and particles in Indo-European languages is pointed out by F. K. Brugmann in his *Grundriss der vergleichenden Grammatik der indogermanischen Sprachen.*

All plural forms have developed in the same way as the above-mentioned dual endings. Not only is the dual merely a special case of the plural, but a noun in the dual form denotes, and denoted in the past, e.g., besides the two feet of man, also the four feet of a beast and the many feet of many men or beasts. Conversely, a word meaning "around" ἀμφί in many cases indicated numerous objects or points around the speaker or around a thing referred to, and then by its sense-content represented a plural; but in references to many other objects, as a street, a stick, a tablet, or the symmetrically built human body, the "around" was in the main only the "on two sides" and so Greek ἄμφω and Latin *ambo* assumed the meaning " (on) both (sides)," and what originally described the "around" of the body or the street was in the further course of development understood as "both hands" or "both houses." The Semitic "dual" *shinnaim,* which originally meant "sharp-edged" and then came to be used for the sharp-edged thing(s) in the mouth of man or animal, does not signify "two teeth" but many teeth and, in spite of its dual form, serves as an ordinary plural.

The human body is but one of the things—though the most obvious—in relation to which the plural concept was bound to arise. Among the concrete things which surrounded man, and which he designated at first by referring, e.g., to their location and later, progressively, to other relationships as well, there were many that always appeared to him in numerous specimens. He said, e.g., "above" or "bright," when referring to the many stars which shone in the sky; or he said "behind," when what was behind was a numerous retinue; "green" referred to a large number of vegetables, herbs, or leaves; a child would use a word meaning "great, old" to designate his parents; "above," "high" referred to hills and mountains, while "hard" or "sharp-edged" meant hard and sharp-edged stones. Since certain things and beings, such as stars, trees, shrubs, herbs, and animals, occurred in large numbers, the respective concepts and the words denoting them were plural from the start.

We readily understand how in the same way, at a later period, words such as *Kälber, Räder, fischelich* likewise became plurals; in most cases man saw before him not one calf or wheel or fish, but many calves, wheels, or fishes.

Several of the relations expressed by words were, by logical necessity, in themselves plural concepts. "Together," "near," "equal," "similar," and on the other hand "between," "distant," "separate," "different," necessarily relate to plural terms; one term is not by itself together, near, and similar, or separate, distant, and different, but only in relation to some other term. On the other hand, words whose very meaning is plural, as "much," "several," "all," "some," "more," were likewise plural from the start.

Thus, perforce, a situation arose in which the forms of each such word seemed to be a plural form, necessarily expressing the plural number. The names of the double parts of the body and of symmetrically shaped implements produced, by analogy, the "dual" form; tripartite objects gave rise to another analogical development, which in some languages led to a *trialis* form. But in general the result was the emergence of prototypes for analogical patterns which determined the ancient expression of the plural concept. Thus, the dual and plural often originated before there were singular forms in the cases concerned, and without their developing.

Originally—as in later stages only in the case of proper names and in poetry—the old form designated also single objects. The Semitic plurals or duals *appaim, panîm* designated the "in front" of the human body, the face; Hebrew *ṣohoraim*, "noon"— like Accadian *ṣîru*, Arabic *ẓuhr*—meant the "above," the highest point, the zenith; *(zi) houbitum* and its Semitic analogies were the "above" of the body of a person standing and the "in front" of an animal or of a procession of many people; etc. But gradually the analogy of the plural meaning began to produce a tremendous effect, altering the meaning of the words. Words meaning "thick, thickening," "moving about in large numbers," "creeping," "ramificating," "forest, wood (the material)," *"familia,"* "establishment of servants" came to mean "clouds," "creatures that move about in large numbers," "creeping animals," "branches," "trees," "male and female servants." A similar development occurred in German words like *Schwarm,* "wood" (= German *Wald*), which denotes both a material and a forest of trees. The form of these words was in many cases the same as that of the "plurals" meaning "feet," "hands," "legs," and consequently they, too, became plurals, meaning "clouds," "bees," "branches," "trees," "slaves."

At the same time, by physiological sound changes—such as omission of the final syllable (which in some cases was drawn to the following word) or shortening of vowels in the construct— new, younger word forms emerged. These had not yet undergone the development that might have made them into plurals. Out of these younger, blurred forms an analogical series of singular words developed, which linked up with the plural forms by a fixed method. Where there had been only a plural, a singular was added, and a plural was added where there had been only a singular. As for the ancient plural forms, they increasingly came to be interpreted as real, definite plurals. The Hebrew "dualic" word *moznaim,* related to Arabic *wazn,* "weight," came to mean not a balance but its two beams or pans; *reḥaim* was no longer the mill but the upper and nether millstone, *delataim* was now not the (closing) door, in the sense of Accadian *edêlu,* "to close," but the two leaves of a (folding) door; *yarkataim,* etc., instead of "that which is behind," "the behind" (as Accadian *warka,* "behind"), denoted the two thighs, hips, or loins; ἀντί, instead of "opposite," meant "two ends," *Enden.* But it goes without saying that such a change of meaning was not always possible. Names of materials, such as fire or water, the names of certain parts of the body, as the head and the face, numerals such as two, three, four, five, and especially nouns referring to abstract concepts such as life, pity, old age, marriage, etc., and words which had remained adverbs while showing plural forms, did not denote things consisting of several units. The concepts they expressed were not plural in themselves and could not be split up into two or more equal terms. This is why these words have preserved their original sense-content and have not assumed a plural meaning.

Nor was it possible to split up the meaning of words which had become proper names. Dualic names such as Hebrew *Maḥanaim, Qiryataim* remained designations of a single place—even though legend would interpret them as referring to "two camps" or "two towns." *Naharaim*[9] means a single river (compare Dutch *Vlissingen* or German *Baden* for a single watering place), though everywhere else this form assumed the plural meaning "many rivers" or "many mountains."

It is not true, therefore—what used to pass for a basic fact in the grammatical view of language—that the plural or a collective form arose in addition to an already existing singular form. On the contrary, the form and "comprehensive" meaning of the plural are essentially older than the form and meaning of the singular. It is only as a result of linguistic analogy that we understand the name of the part, which is younger, as a singular base-word, and the real, original base-word as the plural to it. And it is the height of misapprehension if prevailing grammatical theory extends that analogy to words which were never affected by it, viz., abstract nouns. These words are relics of the original state of things and the starting point for any historical explanation of the facts. It is futile to ask what was, e.g., the singular form of the Hebrew *panîm,* whether in the sense of the adverb ("before") or in the sense of "face," or the basic, singular form of *raḥamîm* "pity," "commiseration." Primary actual singular forms of such words have never existed.

Both the structure and the meaning of all linguistic forms in Semitic, Indo-European, and any other language must be derived from the plural. The singular is younger than the plural in both respects, not only occasionally, in cases in which this has sometimes been noticed before, but—in ancient words—essentially and regularly.

[9] The ancient Hebrew dual was used only for a unitary (though divisible) concept, such as "balance," "door," whereas "two rivers" had to be expressed by the numeral.

This insight yields a host of other novel explanations of a great many facts which have hitherto not been explained or have been wrongly explained. In this context we must content ourselves with a few selected instances, but these will probably be sufficient to show that everything points in the direction indicated.

Etymology, the derivation of words and their meanings, must start from the plural form. Let us repeat here that scientific etymology cannot content itself with establishing a logical connection between words by stating, e.g., that the connection between the verb "to share" and the noun "share" consists in the fact that a share is the result of the division of a thing. A scientific, historical-psychological explanation of a change of meaning requires the reconstruction of circumstances in which a certain word could be and was understood in a new sense—as a different word. If we consider accordingly the aforementioned connection between "to share" and "share," it seems obvious that a person who heard sentences meaning "I see a division, a splitting, a halving, a cutting off, a breaking, a sharing" could not but understand: I see some parts, splinters, halves, segments, fragments— at least two, in other cases several or many; for where there is only one part, segment, or fragment no division, cutting off, or breaking can be observed. The *Glieder,* the *Gelenke* together lead *(leiten, lenken)* the body (similar instances in Semitic). When people saw a creeping movement or an undulation, they saw many creeping things or many waves. He who saw a plaiting of hair saw plaits or strands of many hairs. He who saw a hovering, soaring, or flying saw, in most cases, many chicks, fowls, flies, or wings, and not only a single fly, wing, or feather. He who saw a dripping, trickling, or leaking saw drops, and not only one drop. He who watched the action of fishing saw the fishes that were being caught. He who saw or heard a treading, stepping, or striding saw or heard many treads, steps, or strides. He who traced a person's movements saw many traces. He who marked or branded something produced many marks or brands. A sounding, ringing, *Klingen, Rauschen, Hallen, Tönen* consists in most cases of several sounds, noises, *Klänge, Geräusche, Töne.* The wearing-out, Greek φθείρειν, of a fur involves many lice, φθείρες, and not just a single specimen. The bridge between the verb and the concrete noun is the plural. The actual singular forms are *nomina unitatis,* younger than the plural.

For the same reason, the plural is also the bridge between the concrete and the abstract. There are many Semitic abstract or collective words, corresponding to concepts such as Indo-European *familia, Gesinde, Gefolge, Geflügel, Getier, Geäst,* "service, poultry," *Gezweig, Geranke,* which are synonymous with plurals: *famuli, Knechte, Vögel, Begleiter, Tiere, Äste,* "servants, fowls," *Zweige, Ranken.* But the reason for this is not that language philosophically condenses and summarizes the plural in a comprehensive abstract concept, but that the objects expressed by those words are themselves plurals. As it is a fact that what a man bought or acquired was mostly not only one ox or sheep, that a master was mostly served not only by one male or female servant, and that those who followed a leader (*Gefolge*), or who were sent (*Gesinde,* from *senden,* "to send"), were several or many followers or messengers, these "abstract" words became names of general, as it were, pluralic concepts. Such words as *Gefolge, Gezweig,* "following, branching," describe a combination of many men or branches, and therefore express the same idea as the forms *Boten, Zweige, Ranken,* "messengers, branches." They were understood as plural forms, and they developed singular forms, meaning "branch," etc., although a branching necessarily involves more than one branch.

The fact that the development went by way of the plural is clearly apparent wherever the name of a thing indicates a quality particular to the plural. Certain names of animals, e.g., the Hebrew words for big or small cattle, fishes, insects, etc., etymologically mean also "(to be) numerous," and two such words have become actual numerals, meaning "one thousand" (*elef*) and "myriad" (*rebhabha*). The quality of numerousness fits the plural only; one bovine or one fish cannot be numerous.

By the side of words meaning "to copulate, to become double, to accompany each other, to become friends, to become allied, to become joined together," Semitic and Indo-European have words such as "brother, twin," Accadian *mishlu,* "half," Arabic *kifl,* "one of a pair," Latin *par,* "one of a pair" (who is like his fellow), German *Gatte,* English "mate." But where there is only one, there can be no copulation, doubling, accompanying, becoming friendly, joining, or being like. Those words first arose as plurals and originally meant "together, belonging together," while other words for "kind, class" contain the notion of separating, sundering. A German word of like meaning, *Gattungen* (plural), belongs to *(sich) gatten*, "to copulate" and originally meant, approximately, "together"; but since *Gattungen* was necessarily understood as a plural—"the things which are together"—it was supplemented by a singular form, *Gattung*, denoting a part of the "together," any of the classes comprised by it.

It is not surprising, therefore, that alongside the ordinary Semitic word for "man," Arabic *insân*, there is the Arabic verb *anisa*, "to be in company," not, as has been thought, because man is so called from being a social animal—there was no deliberate name giving at the beginning of language—but because, e.g., "we are together" had been understood to mean "we are the persons gathered together," at first perhaps within a "family" of slaves or a band of warriors.

Another case in point is the German word *Gesellen*, "companions." Its ancient form is *Gesäle*, which originally meant "hall." The word for hall was understood to mean the people assembled in the hall, just as we say today "the House of Commons" or "the Chamber of Deputies." The word *camera* underwent a parallel development, so that the terms "comrades," *camarades*, *Kameraden* are used in a similar sense to *Gesellen*. Latin *collega* belongs to *colligere*, "to collect, assemble," and thus originally means "assembly." German *Genossen* once denoted *Geniessen*, *Genuss*, the enjoyment of a common repast; *Gemahl*, "husband," the wedding feast (*Mahl*, "meal"); *Gefährten*, "the journey," *Fahrt*, which was in many cases a joint one. There are many words which originally denoted an action carried out in common, and subsequently, in some way or another, a collective concept; the singular meaning came about by a division of a plural meaning.

In the instances mentioned we observe a peculiar sense-development: Words which essentially expressed plural, dual, or collective concepts were—since they were understood as plural in form—supplemented by singular nouns, which invariably meant "one of the two," "one of the many." In short: Words whose original meaning was plural brought forth singulars meaning *one*.

Even ordinary numerals meaning "one" originated in many cases in words meaning "together"; Hebrew *yahad, (la) 'ahadim*, etc., Accadian *ishtenish*, Latin *una*, German *einige* mean "several together." But as these words were understood as plurals, they were supplemented by singular words: Hebrew *eḥad,* Accadian *ishten,* Latin *unus,* all meaning "one."

Here are some further ways in which the singular was formed. German has an interjection *hurre*—whence the adjective *hurtig,* "quick"—cognate with English "to hurry" and Latin *currere,* "to run, hurry." As a noun in the plural form *currus,* the Latin word was used for "chariot, (fast) carriage." Identical with Latin *currus* are English "horses," German *Rosse.* We understand the development: the word which originally meant "fast," and hence "fast carriage," was understood by some—owing to its form, which in other words had become plural—as "the horses of the carriage." The same development accounts for similar phenomena in Semitic. By the side of Hebrew *maher,* "fast," we have Arabic *muhr,* "young horse, colt." Hebrew ʿagala(h), "carriage," goes back to a word which (as attested by Aramaic and Arabic) means "fast." But as the "fast" car of the peasant in ancient Palestine was usually drawn by young oxen or cows, the word for "carriage," which originally appeared in a plural form, was understood to mean these animals, and thus the word ʿegel, ʿeglah for calf was born.

The ancient Indian word *rati,* "there is," occurs in German as a noun: *Geräte, Rat, Unrat, Hausrat, Vorrat* ("what there is"). But what there is, *rati,* consists of many implements, and therefore the plural form was supplemented by the singular *Gerät,* "implement." The same word is Latin *res,* "what there is, implements, things."

By the side of words meaning "around" or the like there are, in many languages, words meaning "wall." Thus, by the side of *winden, wenden,* "to wind, to turn," German has the word *Wand,* "wall." But one *Wand* is not *gewunden,* "wound, turned." Such words are usually explained by the assumption that the first *"Wand"* was a fabric of twisted, plaited willow twigs. But the name of the Palestinian stone wall, *ḥoma(h),* is related to Arabic *ḥama,* "to surround," and the name of the Babylonian brick wall, *dûru,* is related to *dâru,* "to surround." The reason is that the initial concept was the "around"—*die Wende, Wände*—not one *"Wand,"* but the whole of the wall(s) surrounding the house, room, or city. It was only after such a word had been understood as a plural that a singular word was formed from it for a part of that "around": a single *"Wand,"* wall, which neither in itself was twisted nor surrounded the house or city.

Again, words signifying "round about," when transferred to notions of time, frequently received the meaning "recurrent," for what surrounds us in space reappears before us, again and again, in the course of time. Thus, Latin has *saepe*, "often," by the side of *saepio*, "to surround," *saepes*, "enclosure"; Semitic has Hebrew *dôr dôr, tadîr*, Accadian *dârish*, "always," by the side of *dûr, dâru*, "to go around." Now, words meaning "often" or "always" are likewise modified by being understood as plurals, and "often" and "always" become "many periods of time" and "all periods of time." Thus Accadian *dârish* or *ana dûri dâri* and its Hebrew counterparts developed a plural, *dôrôt, dôrîm*, and along with it a singular, *dôr*, meaning a portion of the "always," a generation. Arabic *târa*, "to go round" (Hebrew *tûr*), developed the singular *târa(t)=une fois*; Arabic *karra*, "to return (again and again)," developed to *karra(t)*, also=*une fois*. By the side of Arabic *raga'a*, "to return," there is Hebrew *rega'im*, originally (as in Job 7:18) "ever and again, always"; after this word had been understood as a plural, it produced a singular, *rega'*, meaning a portion of the "always," a moment. Many more instances could be quoted.

Now what is the position in Indo-European? By the side of the Latin verb *movere*, "to move (on and on)," there is the noun *mo(vi)mentum*, "moment," not, as often suggested, because the moment is the "medium" of any movement, but because an ancient word for "moving on and on, always," had been interpreted as a plural. The moment is, here, too, the singular of the "always." Similarly, Greek ἀεί, "always," has beside it the "singular" αἰών= Latin *aevum* or *aetas*, "period, generation." Latin *diu*, "for a long time, lasting," has a corresponding singular *dies*, "day," just as other languages have the singular *Weile*, "a while" alongside the verb *weilen*, "to last," though one day or "while" does not last long. German *Jahr*, "year," formerly meant also "season," and its Greek and Latin cognates are ὥρα and *hora*, meaning "season" and "hour" respectively; English "hour" is a loan word from Latin. This variety of meaning is due to different splitting-up of the ancient meaning "always." Alongside the Greek and Latin verbs μένω and *maneo*, "to remain, to last (for ever)," there developed, e.g., the expressions *in menses*, "for ever," *per menses*, "permanent"; but *menses* seemed to be a plural form and was therefore understood to refer to the portions of the "permanent" or "always," viz., moons or months—as the plural of *mensis. Annus, anni,* "round about" (compare *anus, anulus,* "ring"), likewise referred to perpetual recurrence and was therefore understood to mean "the years." Further instances abound.

If we consider the above-mentioned words for always, on and on, everywhere, etc., from the point of view of the singular words "generation, place, kind, category," and the like, their final meaning will appear to us as that not of an ordinary plural but of a comprehensive or distributive one: every person, every place, every generation. But the view from the standpoint of the singular concept unjustifiably extends a later notion to the primary stage.

The fact that expressions like Hebrew *(le)dôrôtaw,* etc., denote not an ordinary but a comprehensive or distributive plural—"for all generations, for all time(s)"—should thus not be explained from the singular form and meaning of the words but from their own ancient meaning, "(for) ever." Similarly, Latin *singulatim* (like *semel*) and *gregatim* originally meant "together, combined," and it was only in a later view—after the creation of the singular words—that their form seemed to express collective and distributive variants of singular concepts ("each one separately, each flock—*grex*—by itself").

We now understand that in ancient instances of reduplicative expressions—as Hebrew *dôr dôr,* "always"—it is only the influence of the later singular that makes the reduplication appear as representing a collective or distributive meaning all generations. In fact, here, too, reduplication is not, originally, an expression of either the ordinary or the distributive plural. Rather, the ancient meaning of the word—"together," "always," or the like—was preserved in these cases when elsewhere it developed a singular concept. The same goes for phrases like Hebrew *îsh îsh* ("man, man") for "every man." Here, too, the singular form is not a real singular but has preserved the ancient meaning, which attached also to this form which in other cases came to denote the singular only.

Out of a large number of further relevant phenomena I will mention here only the "correlative" singular. Semitic has words which may denote either of two correlative terms, such as Hebrew *dôd* for either "uncle" or "nephew," *ḥâm,* the usual word for "father-in-law," which in South Arabic means also "son-in-law,"

Arabic *mawla*, which means both "master" and "servant." This phenomenon is due to the splitting-up of the meaning of an apparently pluralic word which referred to a correlation existing between two persons and in which each of them had a different standing.

However, not only the meaning of words but also their form should be explained with reference to the ancient plural words. This concerns, principally, the plural form itself, which as a rule has not developed from the singular form but, on the contrary, is—as in *Kalbir, Kälber* against *Kalb*—older than the latter. In fact, in many cases a derivation of the plural form from the singular is not even phonetically possible. A detailed discussion of this subject does not, however, come within the scope of the present study but must be undertaken for each language separately.

The development of singular and plural is but one—comparatively simple, instructive—instance of the development of linguistic forms and their meaning. Here are some further important examples of that process, which, though complicated in its particulars, is simple and thoroughly uniform in its general trend.

Man first began to speak by uttering simple syllables, like those produced by an infant. These syllables, when ending the speech, frequently terminated with a nasal sound, as *am, bam, gam, an, ban, gan* (the vowel *a* is the most frequent one in a natural position of the speech organs), and nasal suffixes, therefore, are numerous to this day in most languages. In other cases, when several syllables were joined into one word, and mouth and lips closed only after a group of syllables, the nasal sound produced by the closing of lips and teeth usually occurred only at the end of the group: *abalam, abalan.* The limits of these first words were determined by the rhythm of breath.

These words, in being applied to features of reality, assumed meanings different as to both substance and linguistic category according to the different features of reality to which they were related. The cry of man first beginning to speak might—like that of the infant—be understood in some cases as a singular or plural noun, in others, as a verb or adjective, a past or future, first, second, or third person, active or passive, according to the facts or processes of reality to which it referred. This provides the starting point for the explanation of the genesis of different word forms.

When faced with a group of words all denoting plural concepts, man was led by analogy to conclude that it was the form of these words that expressed the plural. In the case of a plural with the same ending, it was this ending that was understood as a plural sign, and in the case of a broken plural, as *kilâb*, "dogs," by the side of *kalb*, "dog" (compare English "man—men, mouse—mice"), the plural meaning seemed represented by the different voweling. In reality, we have to do here merely with variants of the word in question which, on the analogy of certain patterns, were applied to singular and plural, respectively. The same holds, *mutatis mutandis*, for grammatical modifications of the verb, such as past, present, and future. Indeed, orthodox linguistics, on perceiving that not always does the past form denote the past, or the future form the future, tries, in its usual manner, to find new names, which would cover all possible meanings of these forms. The form used mostly for the past is called, e.g., "perfect" (or "aorist") and the form usually denoting the future "imperfect," as if language had intended first of all to indicate the completeness or incompleteness of an action rather than the simple relations of past, present, or future. Orthodox linguistics is unaware that there can be no name covering all the facts. We have not to do here with a static surface for all the points of which a common denominator must be found; language did not intend from the outset to denote either the actual past or future, or completeness or incompleteness of action, but shows the results of a development originating in a period which intended no real grammatical meaning at all—though all such meanings already existed potentially in the relationships of words to features of reality. The past meaning of a particular form is essentially the result of an analogical development starting with those numerous cases in which a past event was referred to by that form, while remnants have survived of a different use thereof, based on different features of reality; and the future meaning is essentially the result of an analogical development starting with those cases in which a future event was referred to, while remnants have survived of the application of the form in question to a present or past event.

Denominatio fit a potiori. Whatever name we choose, it need not and cannot fit the totality of actual uses. The latter are, as stated, the final product of an early period, in which the distinctive use of forms was altogether unknown, and the name we give a form can only be based on the predominant use and will predicate nothing as a reference to some other feature of reality. It is pointless, under these circumstances, to look for a name that would cover all possibilities. Such a name, which would have to comprise different and often contradictory facts, would of necessity be devoid of content and fail to cover even a part of the principal use of the form. It can be proved, for instance, that the morphological difference which in most Semitic languages serves to distinguish the past and the future (viz., the use of a suffix for the former and a prefix for the latter) originally, e.g., in Accadian, served to distinguish the active (transitive) and the passive (intransitive); it is only because another form with suffixes, similar in voweling to the active form, was added by analogy that a "past"—active and transitive—developed in other Semitic languages. However, neither the voice nor the tense nor the mood of the verb was represented from the start by suffixes or prefixes, or by different voweling, but such representation is the result of analogy; on the basis of certain words which showed one or another of these forms, and which were applied to certain features of reality, that form came to be regarded as a specific grammatical form, expressing the grammatical category of past or future, active or passive.

Similar conclusions apply to the distinction between masculine, feminine, and neuter. It is futile to seek for some abstract meaning to explain why words and concepts—not all connected with sex—were "marked" as masculine or feminine (though this linguistic differentiation afterwards led us, for instance, to think of the sun as a man in one language and as a woman in another). There is no point in assuming, as many scholars do, that language at first "intended" merely to establish classes of words (*Wortklassen*) one of which included, *inter alia*, the females of living beings. This, too, is an attempt to determine a feature common to all individual instances with their many differences of sense. Here, too, there was no such feature connected with the grammatical form; the dominant grammatical signification developed in this case on the analogy of that group of words which, in themselves, denoted females of man or animals. These words, similar in meaning, became similar in shape and thereby engendered a specific grammatical form. We now call this form, *a potiori,* the feminine but should be careful not to generalize from here as to the meaning of other words of this form. It is interesting to note, for instance, that the form which in Semitic nouns and adjectives describes mainly the feminine is used for the masculine in Semitic numerals, in continuation of an early use—from before the differentiation of genders—which here has eluded the "pressure of the system" (*Systemzwang*). The system did not extend to either the numerals or the pronouns in which the masculine and feminine were expressed in a different manner—according to other analogies.

What appears today as a suffix has not been a suffix from the start. As stated above, it was mainly the rhythm of breathing that determined the limits of words. An element which occurred only in part of the forms of a word came, in the course of time, to be felt as a suffix, or, if it stood at the beginning of the word, as a prefix. It might happen that the same syllable which in a short word was added at the end, and therefore regarded as a suffix, was, at the end of longer words, for rhythmical reasons, joined to the following word and accordingly regarded as a prefix. Thus, the same short syllables of Semitic which are used as suffixes of nouns and verbs are, in other cases, conjugation-forming prefixes of the verb, as Hebrew *he'ebhîd,* "he caused to serve," and *ne'ebhad,* "he was served," from *'abhad,* "he served." These, too, were from the outset not special grammatical forms, but were created by the endings of words, through the rhythm of breathing, being joined to the following word. The grammatical meaning of the "new" forms is the meaning which was assigned to the earliest products of that process by their relation to features of reality, and which was generalized by analogical extension.

A syllable which in some cases was felt to be a suffix and in others a prefix was in yet others regarded as an independent word and then assumed a special grammatical signification which had no counterpart in reality. The syllable *ma(h),* for instance, which in Hebrew and Arabic became a question word ("what"), or the syllable *im, in,* which introduces a conditional clause ("if"), was formerly the nasal ending of a preceding word which stood between two sentences; in other cases, the same nasal ending (*m, n*) became a prefix-forming noun, such as *mishpaṭim,* "judgment," by the side of the approximately synonymous *shephaṭim*. An ending which in short verbs (less than three "radicals") was part of this verb, as *(lekhall)ot*, "to finish," was in longer verbs (of three or more "radicals"), as *lishmor (oto)*, "to guard (him, it)," considered a separate word, and thus the particle *et, ot* arose as a word indicating the (accusative) object—not by virtue of any inherent meaning but owing to the fact that it arose between the verb and the object, the latter of which usually stands immediately after the verb.

Now just a word or two more about the endings which in certain Semitic as well as in Indo-European languages indicate different case relations, viz., the nominative, genitive, dative, etc.

To the layman and the classical grammarian it seems that every noun came into being as a nominative, by way of name giving, just as it seems to them that most nouns came into being as singulars. Forms such as Latin *mane*, "early, in the morning," *domi*, "inside (the house)," *extra*, "outside," *supra*, "above," are thus believed to have been from the outset inflected cases, derived from the nominative of a noun or adjective. But, as we said before, the concepts associated with these words, viz., "morning, interior, exterior, upper region," have no other content or recognizable quality than being "early," or "inside, outside, above." These words did not first occur in the nominative but in what seems to us to be an "inflected" form and was really a primitive, pre-grammatical "adverb." The grammatical cases of other words are basically due to analogy with such primordial words, which had the meaning of the case as part of their essential, inherent meaning. In explaining the cases, we must—in principle, if not in every instance—regard those primeval specimens as the starting point of the development, and not as a result thereof, as suggested by traditional linguistics, which is focused on features of reality and centered round the full-fledged noun and the full-fledged verb.

In this way, as I have shown for the Semitic languages, the problem of the origin of language as a grammatical system may, in principle, be simply and easily solved. We must only rid ourselves of the preconceived notion that language has from the start been a mirror of empiric reality. Science must comprehend that basically simple process, also in order to understand the actual facts of language, often interpreted in contradiction to the true sequence of their development.

It is indeed possible—for age-long experience has shown how difficult it is for man to renounce an opinion even if proved wrong —that one voice among so many will not at once change the inherited views as to the relation of linguistic phenomena to reality. This will require a radically new approach to the facts of language and an ability to disregard notions which for practical reasons we must go on applying when discussing language matters from a logical viewpoint. The adherents of traditional linguistics cannot claim, however, that they stand on the firm ground of fact, and that it is unnecessary to seek for a method to explain the genesis of language. Even they, who profess to keep strictly to the "facts," base themselves on a certain theory—the mistaken theory that the grammatical categories, such as noun and verb, singular and plural, are immutable data in language as in logic, to be taken for granted for every time and place. They postulate the root and the stem, which never have nor ever could have existed. With this theory they stand—and will someday fall. For the linguistic categories are the final result of an evolution, which has left its mark on every language to this day.

AUM: THE WORD OF WORDS

St. John begins the Fourth Gospel with the statement: "In the beginning was the Word, and the Word was with
God, and the Word was God."

The most sacred word in the Vedas, containing the essence of
the Vedic wisdom, is Aum, often written Om. This word is regarded by the Hindus as the holiest symbol of Ultimate Reality,
designated by them as Brahman, the knowledge of which bestows
upon man freedom and bliss. "The goal which all the Vedas de-
clare, which all austerities aim at, and which men desire when
they lead the life of continence, I will tell you briefly: it is Aum.
This syllable Aum is indeed Brahman; this syllable is the Highest.
Whosoever knows this syllable obtains all that he desires. This is
the best support; this is the highest support. Whosoever knows this
support is adored in the world of Brahmā (the Creator God)."[1]

"Aum, the syllable, is all this (the visible universe)."[2]

"Aum is the signifying word of Iśvara (the Godhead)."[3]

"He who closes all the doors of the senses, confines the mind
within the heart, draws the prāna (life breath) into the head, and
engages in the practice of yoga (concentration), uttering Aum, the
single syllable denoting Brahman, and meditates on Me (the Godhead)—he who so departs, leaving the body, attains the Supreme
Goal."[4]

We shall try to show in this chapter the relationship between
Aum and the "Word" which St. John describes as being one with
God.

According to Hindu philosophers, especially those belonging to

[1] *Katha Upanishad* I. ii. xv-xvii.
[2] *Māndukya Upanishad* I.
[3] *Yoga Sutras*, by Patanjali, I. xxvii.
[4] Bhagavad Gitā VIII. xii-xiii.

the non-dualistic schools of Vedānta, Reality, or Brahman, is Consciousness—indivisible, non-dual, timeless, spaceless, and causeless. Brahman alone exists; it is non-different from the individual soul and the universe. The subject is one with the object. If a man sees anything other than Brahman, he is seeing an illusion.

This Brahman, without any compulsion from outside, and through a power called māyā inherent in itself, appears as the universe. The appearance, however, is unreal, like the water in a mirage. How Brahman appears as the universe will ever remain unknown to the finite mind, for the mind itself is a part of the appearance.

There are two characteristics of an appearance: first, it cannot affect the reality even in the slightest degree, just as the water of the mirage cannot moisten the sands of the desert; second, as long as the illusion lasts, the appearance is taken to be real. This is why the manifested universe appears real to the average individual, as the dream world to the dreamer.

The conditions for the manifestation of the universe are name and form (nāma and rupa); and they may exist in a gross, subtle, or causal state. Devoid of names and forms, the universe is Brahman; it is these that distinguish it from Brahman. Māyā is nothing but name and form. To the enlightened sage, however, name and form are, in essence, identical with Brahman, like the waves and the ocean. Apart from the ocean the waves are unreal; so also, apart from Brahman the universe of name and form has no reality.

The form is the outer crust of which the name is the inner essence or kernel. The name is inseparable from a word or sound.

The universe perceived by the five senses is the form behind which stands the Word or Sound, or what was called by the Greeks the Logos. Since the universe, relatively speaking, is without beginning or end, the Word is also beginningless and endless. This eternal Word, the material of all ideas and names, is the power through which Brahman manifests the universe; nay, Reality first becomes conditioned as the Logos or Word, through its own māyā, and then evolves the concrete and sense-perceived universe. According to Hinduism, Aum is the symbol of this Logos or Word.

Since a word is inseparable from the idea it represents, Aum and the eternal Word are inseparable. That is why the eternal

Aum, mother or source of all names and forms, is the holiest of all holy words. Therefore one sees the appositeness of the statement: "In the beginning was the Word." The word *beginning* is to be understood as meaning "prior to the manifestation of names and forms through māyā."

What is the connection between an idea or thought and a word or sound? It is true that a thought must be expressed by a word, but it is not necessary that the same thought requires the same word for its expression. People in twenty different countries may express the same thought by twenty different words. And the sounds, which are non-distinguishable from the words or names, vary in different nations. A Hindu philosopher says: "Although the relation between thought and word is perfectly natural, yet it does not indicate a rigid relationship between a sound and an idea."

Though these sounds vary, yet the relation between sounds and thoughts is a natural one. Only if a sound describes a thought correctly can it be said that the sound establishes a real connection with the thought; only then will that sound be universally used to express that particular thought. That is to say, if a word is to be so used, there must be a natural connection between the word and the thought, the symbol and the thing signified.

There are various words to denote the eternal Logos; but the Hindus contend that Aum is a unique word and uniquely apposite. The Logos is the material or foundation of all sounds or words, which are inseparable from names or ideas; yet it is not any definite, fully formed word. It is the substratum, the common ground of all words or sounds. If all the peculiarities that distinguish one word from another are removed, then what remains will be Aum, the Logos.

Aum is called the Nāda-Brahman, the Sound-Brahman, that is, Reality expressed through sound. The three letters, *A, U,* and *M,* pronounced in combination as Aum (to rhyme with *home*), are the generalized symbol of all possible sounds. *A* is the root sound, the key, pronounced without the tongue's touching any part of the palate; it is the least differentiated of all sounds. Again, all articulate sounds are produced in the space between the root of the tongue and the tip; the throat sound is *A,* and *M* is the last sound produced by the closing of the lips. *U* represents the rolling forward of the impulse that begins at the root of the tongue and ends at the lips. If properly pronounced, Aum represents the whole gamut of sound production as no other word can. Therefore it is the matrix of all sounds, and the fittest symbol of the Logos, the Word "which was at the beginning." As the Logos, being the finer aspect of the manifested universe, is nearest to the Lord, or the Manifester, and is indeed the first manifestation of the divine wisdom, Aum is the most effective symbol of Reality.

It may be asked why the English word *God* cannot be used to denote Ultimate Reality. This word, it may be said in reply, performs only a limited function; and if you go beyond it you have to add adjectives to denote whether God is Personal or Impersonal or Absolute. So with the words that stand for Reality in every language; their significance is limited. The word *Aum* is free from any such limitations. In India Aum has been manipulated to mean all the various ideas about Reality, and retained through all stages of the country's religious growth. Dualists, qualified non-dualists, absolute non-dualists, and all other schools of Hinduism use Aum, one way or another, to denote the Ultimate Reality. Even the Buddhists and Jains, who repudiate the authority of the Vedas and are therefore regarded as heretics by the orthodox Hindus, have accepted the sanctity of Aum. This word, the material of all words, can be used as a sacred symbol for reality by non-Hindus also.

Hindu philosophers have used Aum to denote both the Personal God and Impersonal Reality, or Pure Consciousness. The Personal God has been defined as the Creator, Preserver, and Destroyer of the universe. The three aspects of creation, preservation, and destruction are expressed by the three symbols which are the three letters of Aum, namely, *A, U,* and *M. A* signifies the creative aspect of the Deity because *A* is the beginning of all sounds; no sound can be produced without first uttering *A. U* signifies the preservative aspect of the Deity because the sound that is produced in the throat is preserved, as it were, by *U,* while rolling through the mouth. Finally, *M* is the symbol of the destructive aspect of the Deity because all sounds come to an end when the lips are closed.

There is also an undifferentiated sound which comes at the end of the utterance of Aum and is the symbol of Pure Consciousness, described in Vedānta as Satchidānanda, or Existence-Knowledge-

Bliss Absolute. Both the symbol and the entity signified by it are without parts or relationship; they are indestructible and transcendental. This undifferentiated sound finally merges in silence, which also is the final experience of the mystics.

The three letters of Aum apply to the relative universe: *A* to the gross aspect, *U* to the subtle aspect, *M* to the causal aspect, and the undifferentiated sound applies to Pure Consciousness, which cannot be described in terms of relations but which permeates all states and also transcends them.

Aum is the symbol of Ātman, or the individual soul, in its various aspects. Thus, *A* is the symbol of Ātman experiencing the gross world in the waking state through the gross body; U of Ātman experiencing the subtle or mental world in the dream state through the subtle or the dream body; and *M* of Ātman experiencing the causal world in deep sleep through the causal body when the physical body, the senses, and the mind are at rest. Free from all the experiences of the relative world, Ātman, called Turiya, remains as Pure Consciousness and is signified by the undifferentiated sound that comes after the sounds *A, U,* and *M.*

Ātman is Brahman: "Thou art That." There is no intrinsic difference between microcosm and macrocosm. The sky seen through the skyscrapers of a big city is essentially non-different from the vast, unlimited sky. Whatever difference is seen, is created by names and forms, which are limiting adjuncts. In the case of the Godhead these adjuncts are the acts of creation, preservation, and destruction, and in the case of the individual, these are the states of waking, dream, and deep sleep; but all limitations are falsely superimposed through nescience upon Pure Consciousness, which remains unaffected by them.

The word *Aum* was not invented by any man. It is the primordial and uncreated sound which is heard by mystics absorbed in contemplation, when their minds and senses are withdrawn from the relative world. Through this word is revealed to them the eternal process of creation, preservation, and destruction. Perhaps Pythagoras referred to Aum when he spoke of the music of the spheres.

Ramakrishna, the great mystic of modern India, thus described Aum both in its relative and in its absolute aspect:

I give the illustration of the sound of a gong: "tom," t-o-m. It is the merging of the relative in the Absolute: the gross, the subtle, and the causal; waking, dream, and deep sleep, merge in Turiya (Pure Consciousness) . The striking of the gong is like the falling of a heavy weight into a big ocean. Waves begin to rise: the relative rises from the Absolute; the causal, subtle, and gross bodies appear out of the Great Cause; from Turiya emerge the states of deep sleep, dream, and waking. These waves arising from the Great Ocean merge again in the Great Ocean—from the Absolute to the relative, and from the relative to the Absolute. Therefore I give the illustration of the gong, "t-o-m." I have clearly seen all these things. It has been revealed to me that there exists an Ocean of Consciousness without limit. From it are projected all things of the relative plane and in it they merge again. Millions of universes rise in the Pure Consciousness within the heart of man and merge in it. All this has been revealed to me; I don't know much about what your books say.

Chapter V
JACQUES MARITAIN

LANGUAGE AND THE THEORY OF SIGN

I should like here to take up again some parts of an outline on a general theory of the sign I wrote a number of years ago,[1] and to make use of them to propose some considerations on language. These considerations may be grouped under three headings: language and awareness of the relation of signification; language and the magic sign; language and reverse or inverted signification.

I No problems are more complex or more fundamental to the concerns of man and civilization than those pertaining to the sign. The sign is relevant to the whole extent of knowledge and of human life; it is a universal instrument in the world of human beings, like motion in the world of physical nature.

Signum est quod repraesentat aliud a se potentiae cognoscenti. A sign is something that makes something other than itself present to knowledge. A sign manifests and makes known something for which it stands vicariously and to which it is related as the measured is to the measure.

The ancients drew a distinction between the natural sign (*signum naturale*) and the conventional sign (*signum ad placitum*). In their view, a sign is what it is by virtue of its specific and characteristic function of making known some other thing. The relation of the sign to what it manifests is a real relation, i.e., is founded in reality in the case of a natural sign, since a natural sign is better known than that which it manifests, and since the

---

[1] Cf. "Sign and Symbol," in *Journal of the Warburg Institute* (1937-1938), Vol. 1. Also cf., with considerable additions, my book *Ransoming the Time,* Charles Scribner's Sons, New York, 1941.

property of being more knowable, and this in relation to something else that is thereby made knowable, is a real property, not a purely ideal relation (*relatio rationis*) existing as such in thought only. The fact that smoke gives us knowledge of fire rather than of water, and that tracks of oxen give us knowledge of the ox rather than of man, and the concept of a horse of the horse rather than of stone—all this is based on a real intrinsic proportion between these signs and the things they signify. This realistic notion of the natural sign rests, in short, on a metaphysics for which intelligibility and being are consubstantial (*verum et ens convertuntur*.)

This real relation is not one of efficient causality. Sign strictly keeps to the order of "objective causality" or of the formal causality of knowledge, not of efficient or productive causality. When a sign produces an effect it is never by virtue of being a sign. The sign is not even the efficient cause of the knowledge of the thing signified; it makes it known only by standing in lieu of the object within the cognitive faculty to which it brings the presence of the object, thus functioning in the same line of causality as the object itself (formal causality).

Not every image is a sign, and not every sign is an image. For the image (which "proceeds from another as from its principle and in the likeness of that other") may be of the same nature and have the same ontological status as that of which it is an image (the son is the image, not the sign, of his father). And many signs are not images (smoke is not the image of fire, nor is a cry the image of pain). We might define a symbol as a *sign-image* (both *Bild* and *Bedeutung*), a sensible thing *signifying* an object by reason of a presupposed relation of *analogy*.

Signs have to do with all types of knowledge. They are of considerable importance in the psychic life of nonrational animals, and here I think we should interpret the data concerning conditioned reflexes from the point of view of psychology, not merely of physiology.

The external senses make use of signs (I see Socrates when I see his statue; my eye sees him in it), for the use of signs does not necessarily imply discourse. Thus the thing signified has a kind of presence—the presence of knowability—in the sign; it is there *in alio esse*.

The birth of ideas and thus of intellectual life in us seems bound up with the discovery of the signifying value of signs. Animals make use of signs without perceiving the relation of signification. To perceive the relation of signification is to have an *idea,* i.e., a spiritual sign. Nothing throws more light on this subject than the miracle of the first dawning of intelligence in people who are deaf and dumb and blind (like Marie Heurtin, Helen Keller, Lydwine Lachance). It depends essentially on the discovery of the relation of signification between a gesture and the object of a desire. The keystone of the life of the mind is the sign.

In the realm of social life, the part played by signs is no less important: they give rise to social as well as to individual consciousness. It is through its symbols that a city, a class, or a nation becomes conscious of what it is.

Only in God does the life of the intellect make no use of signs. He knows Himself and all things by His essence. That is the privilege of the pure Act.

At this point I should like to submit my first remarks about language. I just alluded to the first awakening of intelligence in blind deaf-mutes. Let us look a little more closely into the case.

For the first stirring of the idea as distinct from images, the intervention of a sensible sign is necessary. Normally in the development of a child it is necessary that the idea be "enacted" by the senses and lived through before it is born as an idea; it is necessary that the relationship of signification should first be actively *exercised* in a gesture, a cry, in a sensory sign bound up with the desire that is to be expressed. *Knowing* this relationship of signification will come later, and this will be to have the *idea,* even if it is merely implicit, of that which is signified. Animals and children make use of this signification; they do not perceive it. When the child begins to perceive it (then he exploits it, he toys with it, even in the absence of the real need to which it corresponds)—at that moment the idea has emerged.

But in "imprisoned souls," among blind deaf-mutes, the first stirring of an idea cannot spontaneously arise for lack of natural sensory signs. These require the convergence of all the senses; a cry which is not heard, a gesture which is not seen—how can these poor walled-in souls actively make use of such to express a desire? With them there can be no natural and spontaneous exercise of a relationship of signification, preceding the knowledge thereof, and hence preceding the birth of the idea.

In order to *exert* the first relationship of signification of which they are to make use, they must *know* this relationship; the idea, the very knowledge of signification must needs come to life at the same time as its first practical use! That is why some external help is indispensable. The miracle of awakening to the life of thought will come to pass precisely when—owing to the patiently repeated attempts of the teacher, who denies a desire and then suggests a sign, an *artificial, conventional* sign, intended to procure the satisfaction of the desire he has denied—the child suddenly *discovers* by some sort of sudden eruption of the idea the signification of this conventional sign (for example, of some gesture or other, in the language of the deaf), and from that moment on progresses with astonishing rapidity. A Marie Heurtin, a Helen Keller achieved the higher levels of intellectual life.

Now it seems to me that the way in which ideas are born to blind deaf-mutes can help us to picture how the discovery of language may have taken place.

The discovery of language, then, coincides with the discovery of the relation of signification, and this would explain why, as a matter of fact, the invention of language and the birth of ideas, the first release of the intellect's power, probably took place at the same time.

It is conceivable, I think, that a genuine language of *natural* sensory signs may have preceded language strictly so called (made up of conventional sensory signs), and that the latter may have developed out of the former. The "miracle" would have happened at the moment when man, beyond the fact of using natural gestures to express hunger, anger, or fear, would also have grasped the notion that this gesture was possessed of the virtue of signifying. By the same stroke a field of infinite possibilities would have opened. Then, once the relation of signification was discovered, the process of arbitrarily selecting or inventing other gestures and of using them as *conventional* signs no doubt developed quite rapidly.

Did a language made up of simple natural signs ever actually exist? Did, on the other hand, a language made up of conventional signs which were only gestures ever actually exist? It is not within my province to discuss such hypotheses. Moreover, my private opinion is rather that things took place according to an altogether different pattern. But as a philosopher I wish to point out that such hypotheses are logically conceivable. I do so in order to emphasize that what defines language is not precisely the use of words, or even of conventional signs; it is the use of any sign what-soever *as involving the knowledge or awareness of the relation of signification,* and therefore a potential infinity; it is the use of signs *in so far as it manifests that the mind has grasped and brought out the relation of signification.*

Granted the imaginary possibility that a language of gestures ever existed, we might also imagine that later some kinds of vocal gestures or wordless singsongs led to articulate language. In any case, the invention of those particular conventional signs which are words, the creation of a system of signs made up of "phonemes" and "morphemes" was in itself a second "miracle," a further dis-covery of human intelligence, no less characteristic of man, but less essential than, and by nature not prior to, the discovery of the relation of signification.

So far we have spoken of genuine language. Let us point out that the word "language," when referring to animals, is equivocal. Animals possess a variety of means of communication but no genuine language. I have observed that animals use signs. But, as I also pointed out, no animal knows the relation of signification or uses signs as involving and manifesting an awareness of this relation.

The full import of this is best realized in connection with the use of conventional signs by animals. Karl von Frisch's admirable studies[2] have shown that bees use conventional signs: he has ob-served that a scouting bee performs two types of dance (a round dance and a wagging dance) to indicate to the other members of the hive in what direction and at what distance the source of food it has visited is to be found. Yet, as Professor Benveniste rightly points out,[3] such conventional signs do not truly constitute a lan-guage in the genuine sense of this word.

[2] Karl von Frisch, *Bees, Their Vision, Chemical Senses, and Language,* Cornell University Press, Ithaca, N.Y., 1950.
[3] Emile Benveniste, "Animal Communication and Human Language," in *Diogenes* (1952), No. 1.

The bee's message does not call for any reply from those to whom it is addressed, except that it evokes a particular behaviour which is not strictly an answer. This means that the language of the bees lacks the dialogue which is distinctive of human speech. . . . Moreover, the bee's message cannot be reproduced by another bee which has not seen for itself what the first bee has announced. . . . The bee does not construe a message from another message. Each bee, once advised by the scouting bee's dance, flies out and feeds at the spot indicated, reproducing the same information on its return, not with reference to the first message but with reference to the fact it has just verified itself. Now the characteristic of language is to produce a substitute for experience which can be passed on *ad infinitum* in time and space. This is the nature of our symbolism and the basis of linguistic tradition. If we now consider the content of the message it is easy to see that it always concerns only one fact, viz., food, and that the only variations of this theme concern the question of space. The contrast with the boundless possibilities of human language is obvious. Furthermore, the behaviour which expresses the bee's message is a special form of symbolism. It consists in tracing off an objective situation of fact, the only situation which can be translated into a message, without any possibility of variation or transposition. In human language, on the contrary, the symbol as such does not trace out the facts of experience in the sense that there is no necessary relationship between the objective reference and the linguistic form. . . . The essential difference between the method of communication discovered among bees and our human language . . . can be stated summarily in one phrase which seems to give the most appropriate definition of the manner of communication used by the bees: it is not a language but a signal code. All the characteristics of a code are present: the fixity of the subject matter, the invariability of the message, the relation to a single set of circumstances, the impossibility of separating the components of the message, and its unilateral transmission."[4]

All this means, in the last analysis, that the relation of signification remains unknown to the bees. They use signs—and they do not know that there are signs. By what process the dance of the bees developed as a conventional sign is a great mystery of biology and animal psychology. But in itself it no more implies language, in the genuine sense of the word, than the fact of a dog's barking when he sees a stranger, or of his crouching down or sitting up when his master utters certain words. The whole thing belongs to the realm of conditioned reflexes, whereas language pertains to the realm of the intellect, with its concepts and universal notions.

[4] *Ibid.*, pp. 5, 6, 7.

A particularly important place in a general theory of 2 sign should be given, I think, to the distinction between *logic* and *magic* signs.

By a *logic* sign, I mean a sign operating under certain functional conditions through which it is a sign *for the intellect* (whether speculative or practical), that is, when the predominance of the intellect defines a particular psychological or cultural regime. Under such conditions the sign, be it in itself sensible or intellectual, speaks ultimately to the intellect and refers ultimately to a psychic regime ruled by the intellect.

I call *magic* a sign operating under a different functional regime, where it speaks primarily to the imagination, regarded as the supreme and ruling standard of the psychic or cultural life as a whole. The sign, be it in itself sensible or intellectual, ultimately speaks to the imaginative faculties and refers ultimately to a psychic regime immersed in the vitalizing depths of the imagination.

My working hypothesis is here the new notion of "functional conditions" or "states,"[5] and I am pointing to a fundamental distinction between the state of our developed cultures and another state, in which for the psychic and cultural life as a whole the last word rests with the imagination as the supreme and final law. No doubt the intellect is present, but, in a way, it is not free. That is the kind of "state" I am calling the "magic" regime of psychic and cultural life.

May I add that this working hypothesis was lucky enough to reconcile opposed points of view in a particularly controversial field. Some time before his death, Professor Lucien Lévy-Bruhl was so kind as to write me of his agreement on this point. "As you put it quite rightly," he said, " 'primitive' mentality is a *state* of human mentality, and I can accept the characteristics through which you define it."[6]

As we have seen above, animals make use of signs. They live in a kind of magical world; biologically united to nature, they use signs belonging to a psychic regime which is entirely imaginative.

Intellect in primitive man is of the same kind as ours: it may even be more alive in him than in some more civilized people.

[5] I am using the word "state" here in a sense similar to that intended by chemists when they speak of the solid, liquid, and gaseous "states" of matter, or by theologians when they speak of the "state of pure nature," the "state of innocence," etc.
[6] From a letter dated May 8, 1938, and published in *Revue Thomiste*, July, 1938.

But the question here is that of its "state" and of the existential conditions under which it operates. The whole mental regime of primitive man is under the authority of the imagination. In him the intellect is in every way involved with and dependent on the imagination and its savage world. This kind of mental regime is one where acquaintance with nature is experienced and lived through with an intensity and to an extent we cannot easily picture.

This is a state of inferiority, but it is by no means despicable. It is a human state, the state of mankind in its infancy, a fertile state through which we have had to pass. Under this regime humanity enriched itself with many vital truths, a number of which were perhaps lost when it passed on to an adult state. These truths were known by way of dream or instinct and by actual participation in the thing known—just as if we imagined that in the knowledge a bee has of the world of flowers a light which the bee does not possess, the light of reason or of the intellect, were present in a diffused, undifferentiated state, before becoming condensed into stars and solar systems separating daylight from darkness.

Here we meet with a difficulty analogous to that which we find when we try to penetrate the mental life of animals. Whatever *we* picture to ourselves is bathed in intelligence, and in intelligence which is free. We have great trouble in depicting to ourselves what another mental regime can be like. (And if we are Cartesians, it is impossible for us to do so.)

Let me say in brief that in our logical state, sensations, images, and ideas are *solar,* bound up with the luminous and regular life of the intellect and its laws of gravitation.

In the magic state they were *nocturnal,* bound up with the fluid and twilight mental life of the imagination and of an experience which was astonishingly powerful but entirely lived through and dreamed.

The same is true of the sign, and of the relation of sign to thing signified.

Since truth is a relation of the cognitive faculty to the thing and belongs only to the judgment of the intellect which grasps it as such, it should be said that in primitive man this relation is experienced but is not winnowed out for its own sake. It is known, of course, because the intellect is present, but it is known in a nocturnal manner, since intelligence is in this case immersed in the powers of the imagination.

When we consider primitive man we may say that in him the relation of the mind to the thing is ambivalent: the same relation is "false" (in the eyes of our evolved consciousness) to the extent that it asserts, for instance, the existence of composite tribal ancestors (like duck-men or kangaroo-men). It is "true" to the same extent that it affirms the vital union of man and nature of which this myth is the symbol. But for primitive man a distinction of this kind has no meaning. This is because his very adhesion to truth is not ours, since for him the idea of truth has not been winnowed out for itself.

He adheres *en bloc,* at the same time and indistinctly, to the symbol and the symbolized: here is for him, in indivisible fashion, an image or a likeness of truth, an equivalent, an *als ob* of truth, without his having winnowed out the idea of truth for its own sake. In similar fashion a child believes in a story, in the adventures of Alice in Wonderland; awaken the child, withdraw him from the world of the imagination and he knows very well that a little girl cannot enter a rabbit hole. But primitive man does not wake up; he is not yet withdrawn from the motherly bosom of the imagination, which makes him familiar with the whole of nature and without which he could not face the relentless severity of his existence as a cave dweller at war with the beasts. He lives in the world of *make-believe.*

Bergson has admirably shown that what is to be found at the source and basis of magic as a primordial element is the relationship of causality.

> . . . [Man] realized at once that the limits of his normal influence over the outside world were soon reached, and he could not resign himself to going no further. So he carried on the movement, and since the movement could not by itself secure the desired result, nature must needs take the task in hand. . . . [Things] will then be more or less charged with submissiveness and potency: they will hold at our disposal a power which yields to the desires of man, and of which man may avail himself. . . . [The workings of Magic] begin the act which men cannot finish. They go through the motions which alone could not produce the desired effect, but which will achieve it if the man concerned knows how to prevail upon the goodwill of things.

Magic is then innate in man, being but the outward projection of a desire which fills the heart.[7]

That which I believe to be lacking in Bergson's theory is that it does not take into account the indispensable instrument of magical activity—the *practical sign*. It is surely true that magic implies an appeal to some cosmic power which brings the desire of man to a happy outcome, an appeal which itself presupposes some sympathy, some compliance in things. But it must be added that magic makes use of signs. Here the relationship proper to the sign, and to the practical sign, necessarily intervenes. Man does not merely outline some causal action; he *makes a sign* (to semi-personal cosmic elements). It is needful that we insist upon the mental characteristics of these practical signs, subject as they are to the nocturnal regime of the imagination.

1. First of all, in my opinion, we here find ourselves confronted with a refraction in the world of imagination, or with a nocturnal deformation, of the practical sign in its quality as sign, or considered in the order of the *relationship itself of signification,* that is to say, in the order of *formal* causality, wherein the sign is, by its essence, the vicar of the object. Let us not forget that this relationship of sign to signified is, in its own order, singularly close. The motion toward the sign or the image, says St. Thomas after Aristotle, is identical with the motion toward the object itself. *"Sic enim est unus et idem motus in imaginem cum illo qui est in rem."*[8] In the formal-objective order the sign is thus something most astonishing, whereat the routine of culture alone prevents our wonder. And this marvelous function of containing the object —with respect to the mind—of having present in itself the thing itself *in alio esse,* is fully exercised in primitive man. Words are not anemic or colorless, they are overflowing with life—with their life as signs—for primitive man. But that in itself sets a snare for his imagination. Thanks to the condition of experienced and lived participation wherein is established his whole mental life, the presence as to knowledge of the signified in the sign becomes for him a presence as to reality, a physical interchangeability, a physical fusion, and a physical equivalence of the sign and the signified (invocation of mythical names; magic objects, spells,

[7] H. Bergson, *Les Deux Sources de la Morale et de la Religion,* Alcan, Paris, 7ᵉ ed., 1932, pp. 175-177; *The Two Sources of Morality and Religion* (tr. by R. A. Audra and C. Brereton), Henry Holt, New York, 1935, pp. 155-157.
[8] *Summa* Theologica, III, 25, 3.

idolatry). Primitive man is intoxicated with the excellence of the sign; yet the sign never altogether loses its genuine relationship of signification (to some *other* thing). The idol is god and yet is never altogether god.

2. Then again a slurring takes place from formal-objective causality to *efficient causality*. The creation of signs is a mark of the preeminence of the mind, and the instinct of the intelligence quickly informed man that symbols make him enter into the heart of things—in order to know them: at once, in a psychic regime wherein the imagination is dominant, this slurring will take place, man will think that symbols make us enter into the heart of things in order to act physically upon them and in order to make them physically subject to us and in order to effect for us a real and physical union with them. Moreover, are not the signs in question first and foremost practical signs? At once the imagination will take a sign directive toward an operation as an operating sign. And why should we be astonished that the imagination of primitive man cannot distinguish between formal causality and efficient causality, when the intelligence of philosophers so often confuses them?

The sign, then, not only makes men know, it makes things be; it is an efficient cause in itself. Hence all the procedures of sympathetic magic. In order to make rain, the sorcerer waters the ground. In order to obtain abundant tubers, he buries in the ground at seed time magical stones of the same shape as the desired tubers, which shall "teach" the yams and the taro to grow big, to reach the same size as the stones. The stones make them a sign, they are pattern symbols. The theory of *mana* among the Melanesians (*avenda* among the Iroquois, *wakonda* among the Sioux), the theory of a force spread throughout nature wherein all things participate in various degrees, seems to be the fruit of a later reflection upon this use of the sign. To the extent that reflection will be intensified, the idea of this semi-physical, semi-moral environment will become more materialized.

3. But the sign, in spite of everything, remains a sign. Inevitably there will take place a return of the order of causality to which it belongs, that is, of formal causality and of the relationship of signification—which with primitive man becomes a relationship of fusion and of physical equivalence—upon the relationship of

efficient causality and of operation. And the imagination will oscillate from one way of thinking the sign to the other. In the perspective of efficient causality (as well as in the perspective of the relationship of signification understood in accordance with its true nature) there is a *distinction*, a difference, between the cause and the effect (as well as between the sign and the signified). In the perspective of formal causality denatured by the imagination, and of that intoxication with the sign induced in primitive man by the relationship of signification, there is a physical *interpenetration* and fusion of the sign and the signified.

Since we are by hypothesis dealing with the nocturnal regime of the imagination, and since for the imagination as such (as dreams bear witness) the principle of identity does not exist; and then again, since the intelligence is still present, bound up with and clothed in the imagination, it is easy to understand that for primitive man the identity of things is constantly unmade and made again. It is altogether too hasty for us to say that with him there is simply an identity between the sign and the signified. No, there is an oscillation, there is a going and coming from distinction to identification. When children play by building sand castles, these castles are truly castles for them. If you trample them, the children will cry with rage and indignation. But once their play is at an end, what were castles are only sand. Primitive man believes to be identical (through the living power of the imagination) that which he obscurely knows to be different (through his intelligence, bound up in the imagination). It is impossible to understand anything about his thought if it be conceived from the point of view of the logical or daylight state of the intelligence, taken as the rule and measure of all thought. It is the thought of an awakened dreamer, wherein the role of *play* (and the allowance of *play*) is tremendously great.

If the above remarks are true, we may conclude that language began in mankind in the form of "magical" language. To the mind of the primitive man the word does not signify a concept, and, through the concept, a thing; it directly signifies a thing; and the word and the thing it signifies are both distinct and one, for the word, in so far as it remains a sign (formal causality), is not physically the thing, and in so far as it is a magical sign (confusion between formal and efficient causality), is physically the thing or causes it to exist. Nothing is more natural for primitive mentality than to make the name into a real equivalent of the thing named, and to have a patient as confident in swallowing the prescription as in swallowing the medicine itself. Under cover of the deceit and illusion of magical thought, at least the dignity and sacred mystery of the words were felt and recognized (even though over-rated).

Once the mind and the society have passed under the solar regime of intelligence, the sense of this dignity and sacred mystery —now purified of its magical connotations—remains essential to human civilization. When civilization decays, the sense in question dissipates itself and is finally lost. Then, in order to recover it, poetry may possibly be tempted to return to magic and to crave for *the power of words,*[9] as can be seen in Mallarmé and many other modern poets. There is a curious—and tragic—phenomenon, where something great and invaluable is looked for, and missed (namely, the genuine dignity of words, which refers to truth, not to power), and where by dint of refinement the civilized mind retrogresses to that magical notion of the sign which was normal in the childlike state of mankind, yet is for mankind in its adult state but a pathological symptom.

3   As appears with particular clarity in the consideration of works of art, a final distinction must be made, namely, between the *direct* sign (which denotes an object) and what might be called the *reverse* or *inverted* sign (which manifests the subject). All the signs which we have been considering in this study are direct signs. The letter *A* signifies the sound *A*, mourning weeds signify death. But the sign can also act in the inverse way. While manifesting an object it can by a kind of inverted or retroverted signification also denote the subject itself which is using the sign and its states, its dispositions, and its secrets which it does not admit to itself, the subject being in that case taken as object by some observer. This is the sense in which Freud and his disciples understand the word *"symbol"*; they no longer think of its direct but only of its reverse or inverted

[9] Cf. Allen Tate, "Poe and the Power of Words," in *Kenyon Review*, Summer, 1952. (Reprinted in *The Forlorn Demon*, Henry Regnery, Chicago, 1953, under the title "The Angelic Imagination: Poe as God.")

signification. The Freudian symbol is a conscious content caused by the unconscious states of which it is the symptom. The birth of Minerva from the forehead of Jupiter is no longer the symbol of the divine origin of wisdom; it is the "symbol" of the idea of physiological birth *ex utero* which has been thrust back into the unconscious, and the idea of the divine origin of wisdom becomes itself the "symbol" of this unconscious representation. As has been pointed out by Roland Dalbiez,[10] it would be better in this case to say "psychic expression," a notion that is valid especially for the products of "dereistic" thought (dreams, hallucinations, neurotic symptoms).

But even in normal thought the signs which man uses to signify things (direct signs) signify man himself (reverse signs). Every work of art is a confession, but it is by discovering the secrets of being (guessed at by dint of suffering the things of this world) that it makes confession of the poet's secret.

As far as language is concerned, the part played by the *reverse* or *inverted* sign appears in an arresting way in those kinds of slang which are not simply spontaneous appropriations of speech to a special (and especially trying) human task or a closed (though possibly large) environment, divided from the society, manners, and speech of "cultivated" people, but which are, in actual fact, discriminating languages, typical for groups which segregate themselves from the community, either because they are composed of derelict, potentially delinquent, or criminal people at war with society or because they are composed of highbrow people who consider themselves privileged, as happens with young persons who have been selected to be trained in certain prominent institutions especially devoted to the formation of a vocational or intellectual elite.

The phenomenon is particularly interesting in this latter case, and it seems to be linked, as a rule, with those rites of initiation which are called *brimades* in French, and which correspond roughly to "hazing." As an instance among thousands, I would refer to the book in which Romain Rolland tells us of his recollections as a student in the École Normale Supérieure of Paris, a highbrow school for future intellectuals; he gives us a curious lexicon of the slang that was used there at that

[10] Cf. Roland Dalbiez, *La méthode psychoanalytique et la doctrine freudienne.*

time. For example, with reference to the Director of the School (Georges Perrot), to some professors (La Coulouche, Chantavoine, and Fortunat Strowski), and to a general in charge of military instruction (General Jeanningros), *faire un Perrot* meant to make a blunder; *faire un Coulouche,* to play the phrasemonger; *faire un Chantavoine,* to play the euphuist; *faire un Tunat,* to make a bad pun; *faire un Jeanningros,* to utter a stupidity.[11]

Slang, as a rule, not only signifies concepts and things but also, and first of all, the subjective behavior, the feelings, habits, oddities, jokes, tricks, collusions, experiences, and resentments which are peculiar to the group and differentiate it from any other; it alludes to the secret life of the group and strengthens this collective life. It affords a particular delight because only the man who belongs to the group can understand it, and because in using it he immerses himself in this incommunicable hermetic life. Each time he uses the slang of the group, he affirms and reinforces his communion with the group and, in one sense, the giving up of his own personality to the group. The word becomes a kind of magic and operative sign of the unity of the group, and of its difference from ordinary mankind. Then, indivisibly from its function as direct sign, the word is essentially a reverse or inverted sign of the subjectivity, self-love, and pride of the group.

That is why slang cannot really be translated into ordinary language without losing its meaning and flavor. More than an object of thought, it means the overtones that accompany this object in terms of human and social subjectivity. The human despair and abjection with which certain abject writers have to saturate the world of things could not be expressed except in their slang.

Now, if it is true that the essence of language is to manifest thought and objects of thought, it is difficult not to conclude that the various slangs of which I spoke involve a kind of perversion of the function of language.

Finally, the question I would like to raise in this connection no longer deals with slang. It is whether, since the event of Babel, all tongues of the earth—though they are in no way slang but genuine types of language—do not run the risk of being tinged with some admixture of a similar impurity. For peoples divided from each

[11] Romain Rolland, *Le Cloître de la rue d'Ulm,* Albin Michel, Paris, 1952, pp. 18-19.

other by their languages, and walled up in their own particular means of intelligible communication, there is an inherent temptation to yield to an inner spiritual trend toward cherishing over and above all the closed subjectivity of the group its difference from the rest of mankind.

No doubt an element of reverse or inverted signification is inseparable from the direct signification of the words. But genuine language, while expressive of the group's subjectivity, gives unquestionable prevalence to objectivity, and direct sign, and to the universality of direct, intellectual meaning; and then the secondary function of language, i.e., the intention of expressing subjectivity, remains itself *open,* it is oriented toward a *communication* of the collective self, which tends to make itself sincerely known to others. The risk of impurity of which I am speaking materializes when this intention of expressing subjectivity becomes oriented toward the *self-assertion* of the group in a *closed,* aristocratic, or resentful manner, and as against all other groups.

The primary and the secondary functions of language are both human. Language attains complete freedom, and the excellence of its own nature, when these two functions are perfectly fused. The subjective function, however, is, as I have said, secondary. Furthermore it remains, as a rule, in an inchoate and unsatisfactory condition, because our words are primarily destined to designate material and external things. As a result, in their secondary function itself they signify the subjectivity of the social group rather than that of the individual person, and they do so in a more or less awkward and rough manner, which depends on the particular history and accidental experiences of the group. Let me say, therefore, that if Angels used words, it is only in the language of Angels that the two functions of which I am speaking would be really and perfectly fused. It is only in the tongue of Angels that language could attain complete freedom and the excellence of its own nature.

But Angels use no words.

Poets, in mankind, desperately endeavor to achieve a certain similarity of the language of Angels, or of perfect language, capable of expressing things and the self together in one and the same breath. Thus, what birds realize by music only, man can somewhat realize by poetry, and his music has also an intelligible significance, a spiritual meaning.

❧ Chapter VI
GEORGE BOAS

SYMBOLS AND HISTORY

One of the persistent traits of human beings, at least in the West, has been their desire to escape from time, change, and diversity. One has only to think of our proverbial philosophy, of such slogans as "Human nature does not change," of such catch phrases as "eternal values" or "immortal masterpieces," of such popular beliefs as that in the immortality of the soul, of such pathetic attempts to arrest the course of history as monuments to the dead, the preservation of ancient buildings, last wills and testaments, reconstructions of dead cities such as Williamsburg in Virginia and the ghost towns of Nevada, to see how deeply rooted in our tradition is this denial of one of the most obvious features of the world. And since symbols seem to be the most enduring of our instruments, it is of some interest to disentangle, if possible, that which dies from that which lives in the realm of symbols.

Any symbol, whether word or picture, group of letters or diagram, icon or sign, must perforce, have both a meaning and what Charles Morris has called a sign-vehicle. The simplest illustration of this distinction is to be found in words in which two different sounds may have the same meaning. Thus *chien* and *dog* have the same meaning though the appearance of the two symbols is different. But again, a single symbol may of course have a variety of meanings, as is true of ambiguous words or of such designs as the scallop shell, the cross, or the swastika. One cannot then argue that if two people or two cultures or two ages use the same sign or symbol they must inevitably mean the same thing by it. And conversely, if they use different symbols or signs, one cannot argue that they do not share the same ideas.

It is perhaps unnecessary to point out that the use of symbols is needed not only for thought and for artistry but also for every act which attempts to retain the past or fix the present for use or for simple recall. If we are to utilize the so-called lessons of experience, we must find some way of preserving experience. We cannot store it up as squirrels store up nuts. We have to use surrogates of experience, as we use money instead of barter. Language is the most obvious example of how this practice operates. We can work out even the most practical problems by thinking in words. The word either may stand for the thing or the act or the event which it names, and be known as a substitute for it or may be actually thought of as a part of the thing it names. We know too little about the "primitive mind" to use our partial knowledge dogmatically, but it looks as if the savage actually identified, for instance, a person with his name. There have been religions in which the name of God must not be pronounced, presumably on the ground that it is as holy as that which it names, others in which the head must be bowed when the holy name is pronounced, others in which the name of a god is endowed with magical properties, others in which even a person's name must be changed on certain occasions such as initiation into the tribe or marriage. In all these cases the symbol participates in the nature of that which it symbolizes. This is analogous to the belief which at least we Occidentals have that certain words are in themselves bad or indecent. It need not be that the thing named is itself bad or indecent, for in English, for instance, one may speak of such things and acts in Latin or Greek derivatives but not in Anglo-Saxon. But it is not always a question of indecency; sometimes it is simply a question of avoiding the facts, as when people refuse to say that someone has died but are willing to speak of his passing away. Whether a man passes away or dies does not depend on the brute facts; it depends, I suppose, on his survivors' feelings about the brute facts. Birth, death, sexual relations, digestion, excretion, and the like are all matters which we cannot deny, but we can avoid them by periphrases in speech or by using approved symbols for them rather than disapproved. It is something like the practice in Greek tragedies of having all violence take place off-stage. It apparently is all right for a messenger to rush in and give a vivid description of what has happened; it is all wrong for it to take place in front of the audience. It is therefore important to admit in any discussion of the role of symbols in life not only that they stand for things but also that each is likely to have an affective coefficient attached to it. This becomes important since the emotional co-efficient may determine in part what the meaning of a symbol is. And since the emotional coefficient may—and usually does—have a history, one cannot argue that the persistence of the sign-vehicle is proof of the eternality of the meaning. Thus the cross may indeed be the key symbol of Christianity, but there have been Christian sects which have not used it. One never finds it, for instance, as the finial of old New England Protestant steeples and indeed it does not appear in Christian painting until several centuries after the Crucifixion.

I do not propose in these remarks to make any distinction between signs, symbols, signals, or icons, except incidentally, but shall use the word "symbol" throughout. For what I shall have to say will apply, I think, to all types of sign or symbol or icon or signal. The first trait then of symbols in general is the presence of an emotional coefficient, the aura of feeling, good or bad, of approbation or disapprobation, which attaches to them. The question which must first be raised is whether this aura persists unchanged throughout history. Clearly it does not. The most obvious case is that of words, which, as has been suggested, actually shift their emotional tone from pleasant to unpleasant or from unpleasant to pleasant. I do not say that this always occurs, for no one knows whether it does or not; I simply say that it does occur. Thus words which once were decent become indecent and words which were once indecent become decent. So much would be granted by any student of historical semantics. Sometimes this happens because the things or events or practices named change their value, probably when people discover that what they once thought was ignoble or funny or strange is actually worth while.

Professions such as surgery or dentistry or commerce or warfare or craftsmanship have in themselves changed only in that new tools or new scientific knowledge has made their practitioners more expert. But the value which we are likely to attach to them has changed not because of the knowledge required to exercise them, for most of us know nothing of that except from hearsay, but because of the benefits which they confer on us. There may still be people who think that it is nobler to be a good general than a good surgeon, but on the whole there is no stigma attached to being a surgeon. We still in university circles are likely to think that it is better to be a pure scientist than an applied scientist, a mathematical physicist than an engineer, and the word "engineer" may still be used with a curl of the lip in these quarters. If such usage is general, then we have a good case of words which in themselves carry an emotional charge though what they name is not valued because of benefits conferred, utility to society, inherent beauty, or anything of the sort. Presumably the faint stigma attached to the profession of engineering in the subsocial groups in question may be attributed to the old prejudice against working with the hands. But modern engineers do not work with their hands but with their brains and seldom have to touch anything more degrading than the same pencil and paper which pure physicists touch. If that is so, then one of the things which a student of the role of symbols in history has to reflect upon is the survival of obsolete attitudes.

But once again we are in the realm of conjecture. We know that many ancient practices have survived in Western society long after their original significance has been lost. We see a good illustration of this in superstitious practices and in social etiquette. We probably see it also in many of our games. A good argument may be made for seeing it also in our fine arts. Thus we have forgotten why people originally greeted each other by shaking hands, why they originally baptized their children or circumcised their sons, why they have a king, queen, bishop, castle, and knight in chess, why they play music in church. But one can at least guess. Whatever the original reason, it is not the present reason for preserving these vestigial practices. What is of interest is that they are preserved and that their primitive significance has been lost —or at any rate is known to only a few specialists. The analogy to memory in the individual is irresistible, for in memory too we retain the past—though what we remember is still a matter of debate. Yet it may be admitted that if we did not remember we could not learn, and if we did not learn, each moment of time would be a completely problematic situation which we could never solve. For clearly the absolute novelty is the absolute problem and learning is in part due to the recognition of the old in the new.

In social memory, if that is not too fanciful a term to apply to

custom and tradition, a definite and overt effort is made to retain
the past. Here there is little if any automatic retention of what is
obsolete. For no argument is needed to show that human beings
begin life as helpless creatures who are educated by people who
have already established habits which in turn were handed down
to them through the efforts of their elders and so on back through
the centuries. Whatever the man from Mars would do on this
earth, we are not men from Mars. We philosophers seem to forget
that we start life without having much to say about what we shall
approve of or disapprove of. We inherit or absorb our standards
from others. Nor is there any way of escaping this. But if this is
so, then it is also true that we inherit and absorb our symbols
from the groups who educate us and along with our symbols the
emotional coefficients which are attached to them.

If one asks what is the utility of custom, one can at least answer
that it gives society a kind of stability which memory gives to the
individual. The use of the first personal pronoun in the past tense
would be impossible without memory, and indeed one of the few
justifications for believing in personal identity is memory and the
repetition of habitual acts. Whether we project ourselves into
society and think of it in personal terms, or whether we interpret
ourselves in social terms, or whether we utilize our perception of
the visual and tactile physical object as a model for both ourselves
and society, I have no way of knowing. Nor, I suspect, does anyone
else. But the fact remains that for some reason or other we talk
about the most fluid of beings, consciousness, as if it were a *thing,*
a thing to whose nature time is indifferent, a thing which floats
along a stream of time like a stick of wood on a quiet river. Being
bound by the inertia of custom to do this we transfer the characteristics of our symbol to what it symbolizes. We know that we are
not today what we were ten years ago or what we will be ten years
hence. Yet we say with complete seriousness that ten years ago
we did this or that and that ten years from now we shall be such
and such. The antecedent of the pronoun is supposed to be the
same in all three cases, though what is the same is minimal and
the only reason we have to believe that anything is the same is
memory. But similarly we write the history of a family or a nation
or even a civilization as if there were at least a core of identity
running throughout its length. That core of identity is of course

tradition or custom. But once again, just as memory is never complete—so that countless incidents of our personal lives seem to be forgotten (and indeed our infancy is totally forgotten)—so the identity of nations and groups of people can be constructed only out of the social memory. And just as individual memory is selective, so is tradition.

If at this point we could enlist the help of the psychologist to tell us why we retain certain incidents of the past and forget others, we might transfer the analogy to society to explain why tradition is so selective. But unfortunately there are so many different theories of memory that we are at sea when we turn to them for aid. We may remember only what fortifies our self-esteem, only what we wish to remember, only what our parents and social approbation permit us to remember, only what can be related to our sexual aspirations, only what we make a definite effort to remember, only what is determined to be remembered by the so-called laws of the association of ideas, only what is so frequently repeated in one form or another as to be compulsory, only what is attached to praise and blame, and so on. The probability is that the true explanation is a complex of many of these and other factors. But two things can be admitted without much doubt: (1) that society plays some part in what we remember and what we forget and (2) that we can remember anything only by the help of symbols which we do not invent but take over from others.

That we remember some things vividly because they were associated with shame or with special honor or with fear—which is perhaps not unassociated with shame—or with affection—which is certainly not unassociated with honor—is indubitable. It is not necessary that society determine all our memories for our purpose. If it determines some of them, we can see how history and symbols are related. For if we remember through symbols, verbal, pictorial, or what you will, the symbols themselves are part of our social heritage; they could scarcely be anything else. That they are symbols in the sense of being things that stand for other things cannot be doubted. For we cannot carry along with us in our memories the total experiences which we have undergone for the very reason that these experiences are over and done with. We may remember by means of the names of things and recollect the past by reciting inwardly a whole litany of names and synonyms, scraps of conversation. We may intermingle with these verbal symbols bits of visual data, colors, shapes, or even odors and textures. But in no case is the complete experience present. It is not present even in the present for that matter, for perception too is selective. If we could remember the past in its entirety, there would be no need of learning anything, except in so far as our bodies are incapable in infancy and childhood of doing everything which they will have to do later on. It would be possible for a baby to know everything almost immediately, for everything is taking place about him. All he would have to do is to open up his sense organs and observe. But aside from the inadequacy of his sense organs, he is living with parents and siblings and nurses and then with those highly selective social sense organs, teachers and books and friends, who rigorously determine what he shall perceive and what he shall not perceive. In other words if his circle of experiences is limited, the limitations are due not simply to his own inadequacies but also to the will and desire of others. These others constitute his society. No parent is so foolish as to allow a baby to have all possible experiences. He is protected from harm and of course should be. He is given pleasant perceptions and of course should be. He is given a vocabulary with which to express these experiences. The words and the fragmentary perceptions form a symbolic complex which is his memory. And like everything symbolic, there is always the possibility that values will be attached to it, both good and bad.

It is the symbol then, if we are right, which provides the continuity of life, and not the literal stuff which is being symbolized. The stuff is gone. But that too must be true of history in the larger sense. If tradition retains the past, it is only in the sense that it is preserved there in symbolic form. The main difference in this respect between memory and tradition is that we are not conscious of the principle whereby we select what we shall forget, whereas in tradition the principle is well above the level of consciousness. No one is any longer in doubt why history is always written from the point of view of the nation whose history is being written, why great men are sometimes the center about which history revolves, and why at others economic conditions become that center. We know now that several points of view are possible and that the way the past will be presented will be determined by the point of view. We know also that it is impossible to write about the past without taking some point of view and, though we may differ about the truthfulness of what the point of view gives us, and the relative value of various points of view, we certainly know that no historian can be without some hypotheses concerning what is important and what unimportant in the past. But for our purposes the question is the role which the symbol plays in the writing of history.

To begin with we have the question of what is to be the subject of history. One cannot simply write history; one has to write the history *of* something and that immediately raises the problem of the underlying identity of that whose history we are writing. Suppose, for instance, that we are writing the history of France.' We know that the word "France" has meant a variety of things in the past and that what it denotes today is what was formerly a large group of autonomous regions. Are we then simply to trace the expansion of the denotation of that name to cover Provence, Burgundy, Brittany, parts of Navarre, Picardy, Lorraine, Alsace, and so on? Are we to describe the spread of the Capets' power to regions which formerly were not in their power? Are we to use this verbal symbol to project what it names at present into the past and to discuss the changes in the habits of living of the people who have occupied this territory from the time of the Merovingian kings to the present? Are we to assume that the symbol stands for a *Volksseele,* which is in turn another symbol binding together the aspirations, fears, occupations, ways of living, and so on of such individuals? Any of these things may be legitimate—we shall not argue this point—but they all use a symbol to give unity and persistence to what we know is diversified and changing. The name "France" then is analogous to the personal pronoun, which also glues together into a lump what was diversified and changing from moment to moment. The unity and persistence are conferred upon the variety and mutability by the symbol. The symbol does not and cannot name a genuine persisting identity for there is none. There is nothing other than magic which can turn two people into one. The two people may resemble each other and we may talk about their resemblance rather than their differences. It may also be true that the resemblance is due to the presence of an identical something in both of them, as when we say that two things are red because redness is present in both of them. But there again, redness is found in thought, not in things, and the redness of thought, though possibly a Platonic universal, can be stated to exist in actual spatio-temporal experience only metaphorically, as Plato well knew. Christianity has made us accustomed to mysteries. But to assert that something is a mystery is obviously to avoid explaining it. I do not mean by *mystery* something which is mysterious simply because of our ignorance, but something which like the doctrine of the Trinity cannot be expressed in rational, that is, noncontradictory, terms. Symbols then are a device for escaping from time.

For man is confronted with individual events and things which it is his primary task, as a thinking being, to organize in classes, groups, *kinds* of things. Such simple terms as "cat," "dog," "man" are class terms; they bind together certain individuals through the resemblances which are noted among them, omitting for linguistic purposes all differences. Thus a child grows up to learn the proper word to cover a variety of things and consequently his attention is invariably oriented toward similarity and away from peculiarity. He knows of course that his dog is not just a dog, just a member of a class of animals; that he has traits of his own which no other dog shares and which are probably precisely those traits which endear the creature to the child. Furthermore, if he loves his dog, he can project into this special animal his affection and thus it becomes a lovable dog. But all this is not necessarily true of all dogs. Again, in spite of Aristotle, children do not call all men "papa." But they do soon learn to know that Papa is a man and not a dog, cat, or inanimate object. But no child ever grows up to make his own groupings and to invent his own terms for the groupings which he has made. Indeed whenever a child does attempt such classifications, he is corrected by his loving parents before he goes too far. Even a man may confuse stars and planets, but it does not take much time before the pedagogic desires of his fellows correct him.

Our present classificatory terms are fairly recent. This is well illustrated by such a science as entomology. The very word "insect" has become clear only in the last three hundred years. Aristotle says that he calls insects those beasts which have their bodies cut up, and the Greek word he used, of which "insect" is a Latin translation, means simply things which are sliced. If one reads Renaissance treatises on insects, one sees at once how the ancient term —not direct observation—guided the studies of the entomologist, and even as late as John Ray (1705) insects included spiders, crustaceans, centipedes, and annelida, as well as our hexapods. What all these creatures had in common was their segmented bodies, and as long as that feature of their anatomy was of main interest, they could all be grouped together without inconvenience.[1] My point is that the survival of the verbal symbol determined the course of scientific history, not the observation of any noticeable difference in embryological development or the life cycle. Yet anyone at any time could have observed for himself that a spider is very different from an earthworm. But to observe difference is not in keeping with scientific practice; it requires a kind of mind which is willing to reject the accumulations of tradition and to look for something which one's predecessors have not looked for. The notion of the open scientific mind, as contrasted with the closed theological mind, is contrary to fact. Scientists are as slothful as anyone else in tolerating exceptions to established law. Such tolerance is based on the notion of exceptions which are trivial, too small to count, or eliminable under laboratory conditions. But laboratory conditions are purposely set up to be uniform, not to reproduce nature, and what is too small to count depends on the measures one is using.

We consequently have the notion that our terms stand for essences which are eternal and it makes little difference whether these essences appear embodied in nature or in art. The *genres* which some people seem to think were established by Aristotle— though actually he established only two and those in dramatic literature—may be found pretty well exemplified in Greek peninsular art up to the fourth century B.C. But just as we are likely to assert that, for instance, an insect is *really* "any animal of the sub-phylum . . . *insecta,* a group of small, air-breathing arthropods

---

[1] In fact, the cultural revolution, which seems to have begun in the sixteenth century, shifted men's attention from anatomy to physiology, from structure to function, from geometry to algebra, from the static to the dynamic, and introduced a great emphasis on history, biology, and even music. The older interest of course has never died out and the revolution will perhaps never be complete, but in metaphysics— and indeed physics—the metaphor of *growth,* which is biological, has begun to replace the metaphor of the *thing.* The return to Thomism, or what has been called the Gothic Revival in Philosophy, is a counterrevolution.

characterized by a body clearly divided into three parts: head, thorax, and abdomen, and by having three pairs of legs, and usually two pairs of wings," so we are likely to assert that a tragedy is *really* "an imitation of an action, that is serious and also as having magnitude, complete in itself, etc., etc." The adverb "really" in these phrases would seem to mean that there are somehow and possibly somewhere Platonic insects and tragic essences and that the words in question are names for them. In other words, it appears to be believed that our symbols, which exist obviously in time and which therefore change, are mutable labels for eternal substances. That the definitions in question are descriptions of the way certain human beings use certain labels is believed only by one group of philosophers, far from being in the majority.

The probability is that the labels are less mutable than that for which they stand. This sounds like a paradox until one considers that the objects of our reflection, first, are selected out of the total mass of possible experiences, and second, never can include all the characteristics of such objects. As for the first point, the principle of selection determines what is important and what unimportant. But importance varies sometimes with nothing more profound than the use which one is going to make of one's discoveries, or with the relevance which they have to generalizations previously made, or for the purpose of simplifying the natural scene. Thus such terms as textiles, wood, house, food are all terms which gather together things we wish to use in certain ways in spite of the fact that they can be so used only because of certain "natural" characteristics. On the other hand, in such a science as zoology, certain animals are grouped together for phylogenetic reasons. The zoologist may refuse to call termites "white ants," in spite of popular usage, as the horticulturist refuses to call the *Philadelphus* a syringa. His reason is that the termite does not behave like ants, that the genus has a history different from that of the ants. Hence if the termite were to be classified with the ants, it would be impossible to make generalizations about the compounded group which would fit in with conclusions already established—or accepted, if one will—about those insects. Finally, we can simplify the confusion of experience by overlooking obvious differences and grouping large masses of clearly dissimilar things together under one name. One has only to think of such words as "mammal" or "nation" or "war" or "art" to see this practice in operation. Each of these four terms covers a great variety of observable events and things, yet it is sometimes useful and indeed illuminating to use them, since they do help us to see what is similar in a mass of peculiarities. If we were to see nothing but the peculiarities, no science, no organization of knowledge would be possible.

If the non-linguistic ways of human life had been unchanged in all respects from the beginning of time, it is likely that language would not have changed at all. We can see a sort of corroboration of this in rural life, with its retention of certain older linguistic habits which have disappeared in urban life. Though rural living itself has changed enormously in a country like America, there are still communities where, we are told, people speak seventeenth-century English, and even in less "backward" places old terms are in constant use. City people rarely know the meaning of such apparent subtleties as are involved in the differentiation of colts and fillies, heifers, cows, shoats, gilts, boars, sows, ducks, drakes, geese, and ganders. They must know that there are physiological differences between the various classes of animals named, but they see no reason to differentiate them by name. They are like the Japanese, who have something like forty words for what we call rice and only one for what we call the various meats. But one does not have to resort to rural life to see this. Those activities which have most resemblance to savagery still retain their savage names, and when we are obscene in speech, we do not use scientific terms. There is little in modern warfare which resembles savage warfare except the end results of slaughter, looting, and devastation. But those are sufficient apparently to justify calling both our forms of slaughter and that of the Red Indian by the same name.

The fact that human life has changed is one of the many differentiae of man. It is strange that, whereas other animals seem to go on living according to the same rules as those which obtained when they first appeared on earth, man lives variously not only in different regions of the planet but at different times. We have no recorded history of African and early American and Oceanic people and hence do not know how their manners and customs have changed. But certainly Europe and much of Asia are enough to convince anyone that, whether he believes in progress or degeneration, there has been change. It is even possible that another animal, turned taxonomist, would classify the various human societies under a name which would differentiate them as we differentiate varieties of plants and animals. Varieties of plants and animals can interbreed and produce fertile offspring, but they have certain transmissible characteristics which stabilize their appearance. But tradition does the latter for human beings, and the compulsions of habit determine a sense of responsibility for being true to the social pattern. Whatever such an animal-scientist might do, we insist that human beings, whatever their customs and compulsions, whatever their beliefs, whatever their general culture, are all human and we attempt—usually vainly—to find in the sameness a clue to human nature. I say "vainly" because the generalization usually amounts to nothing more than indicating what human beings are not, rather than what they are. The matter is of no great importance except in disputes about the universality of human traits, a universality which is believed to be evenly distributed in both space and time. If we come down to biological traits, we shall undoubtedly hit upon it. But it is more interesting, one would think, to note that the gratification of even our biological drives is controlled by societies in various ways. No society, except certain religious societies, has ever forbidden the procreation of children, for instance, but all societies have their rules about when, with whom, under what economic conditions, to what extent children should be procreated. These rules differ not only from society to society but also within the same society from period to period. It is the latter peculiarity of human beings which justifies calling them historical animals. So all human beings talk and hence are symbolizing animals. What has been said about procreation can also be fitted to speech.

Even an amateur philosopher of history will notice that people in the Occident both cling to the past and at the same time reject it. Western societies as units have varied in the degree to which they have permitted change. There are some languages spoken today, such as German, which are almost as highly inflected as Greek, and others, such as French and English, in which such inflections are almost lost, as in Chinese. If one were to date a language like German, one would put it earlier than French and later than Latin. But if therefore one were to conclude that the

Germans as a whole were more "backward" than the French, one would be mistaken. The linguistic symbols of this nation may indicate linguistic conservatism. But the *furor teutonicus* of the Man of the Forest goes hand in hand with amazing technological ingenuity which, although it has been put to the service of war and other forms of savagery, has also been put to the service of the various arts of peace.[2] England, again, has a language which has changed rapidly in the last two centuries. But that does not imply that the English as a whole are any less conservative in social matters than the Germans. People in the United States have a language which is constantly shifting its symbols, incorporating slang terms and phrases with a rapidity which at times bewilders people of even a single generation. Yet there has never been a people less eager to accept novelty in the arts or in ideas, whether the ideas be political, religious, social, or economic. Hence one cannot argue from the character of the prevailing symbolic system to the character of the people who use it. A social psychologist might be able to explain the apparent paradoxes, though it should be noted that they are paradoxes only if one presupposes that every group of individuals called by a common name, such as American or English, should be homogeneous. The fact is that no society is all of a piece. There are Americans who are conservative linguistically and Americans who are "radical" linguistically. There are others who accept the latest fads in gadgets and others who disdain them. There are some who are hospitable to fads in medicine—or other forms of applied science—and at the same time hold religious beliefs which are thousands of years old. Nor can one maintain that because a man is a fundamentalist in religion he will speak Old English or even the English of Shakespeare.

In some fields, such as the arts, we can see how the retention of old, if not obsolete, symbols operates to create the illusion of permanence. There may be thirty-eight *Amphitryons,* but all that is identical in them is the names of the characters. Similarly the

[2] I suppose that if one hated the Germans enough one could also argue that the savage also manifests surprising technological ingenuity, for it was the savage who invented the wheel, ways of making fire, baked clay, weaving, and the domestication of animals. And all this without precedent to guide him. But obviously I am not saying that the only trait which differentiates German mores from those of other people or that the only trait that they have in common is technological knowledge.

story of the Widow of Ephesus has gone through perhaps more mutations than that of Amphitryon, as was shown by Frances Newman, and indeed, after Miss Newman's study of the matter appeared, new versions also appeared. But again, the story as told by Christopher Fry is scarcely that of Petronius. Students of folklore have been very ingenious in their sorting out of various plots, such as the Cinderella theme, which appear over and over again in Occidental literature. But no one would say that Trollope's *Miss Mackenzie* was identical in more than a superficial sense with Perrault's famous story. Painting too has its apparently eternal themes, such as the sleeping Ariadne or, to take a less ancient example, the Crucifixion. But any reclining female nude could be exhibited as a sleeping Ariadne, if one wished, without committing the spectator to a belief in Greek mythology, and similarly a Crucifixion by Giotto is hardly identical with one by Bellows. They are clearly alike in some details; if not, the same titles would be puzzling. But the whole spirit and feeling of the two pictures are so different that they constitute two interpretations of the same events. What is significant in both of these examples is that, while ideas and feelings change, the symbol which stands for them may remain the same. There is an analogy in architecture, where details, such as crenelations, which were once useful, remain as ornamentation. The entrance to the College of the City of New York, for instance, is similar to the entrance to a typical fourteenth-century castle with towers, drawbridge, loopholes, and all the other paraphernalia of a fortress, even to an incipient moat. But so far no one has ever been mistaken about the function of such details as might cause confusion to a historian of architecture.

It is thus possible that our desire for permanence can be satisfied by our symbols and our need for change by what they represent. This would be almost certainly true in the history of philosophy, where certain terms are retained while their meanings have changed. The most notorious example of this is the word "God," which in metaphysics seldom, if ever, means what it does in religion. In fact, the conflicts in meaning are sometimes such that a given philosopher frankly admits that he has come up against a mystery. It would be possible of course to confess that one is not talking about the same things when one is referring to the God of religion as when one is referring to the God of metaphysics. But most philosophers seem to think that they are talking about the same thing. Renouvier in a chapter of his *Histoire et Solution des Problèmes Métaphysiques* points out some of these conflicts in so clear a fashion that one would imagine the matter to have been settled once and for all. But that has not prevented philosophers from continuing the traditional usage and I suspect that this applies even to those who have read Renouvier. What block operates to prevent our admitting the existence of ambiguities in symbols is beyond my knowledge. But that such a block does exist cannot be denied. The desire to retain old symbols and thus avoid the conclusion that ideas have changed is strong enough to defy the Law of Contradiction. Indeed in the mind of some philosophers inherent contradictions seem to confer additional value on the symbols in which they inhere.[3]

It has been maintained by some psychiatrists, the early Freud and, I believe, followers of Jung at present, that some symbols are always univalent. Thus Freud in his early work on Leonardo da Vinci was able to interpret dreams of Leonardo on the basis of Egyptian hieroglyphics, and the disciples of Jung have gone even further in their use of the Collective Unconscious. The Collective Unconscious in this case is what is pervasive of human nature and hence has no more history than the human eye or hand. When it expresses itself in art or religion or indeed in science, the outer form of the symbols, the sign-vehicle, is various, but the meaning is always identical. History thus becomes a sort of illusion since it always is found on the level of the symbols, not of their meaning. But even on the symbolic level there is a distinction to be made between such symbols as the cross, the pyramid, the circle, the swastika, which appear in the visual patterns of many cultures— on pottery, in textiles, tattooing, and painted decorations—and those, such as the use of certain colors to indicate mourning or licentiousness or jealousy, which may and usually do vary from culture to culture. In the case of such a symbol as the cross, it obviously could not have the Christian meaning until Christianity appeared in history, though the Crucifixion may itself become interpreted as a symbol of something else which is common to

---

[3] Is it necessary to point out that a symbol, as a sound or shape, cannot be self-contradictory? I am of course simply indicating that contradictions appear when the meaning of the symbol is expanded into sentences.

a variety of cultures. Verbal symbols would be of the latter type. No proof is needed that, even if the varieties of vocabulary and syntax in, let us say, the Indo-European languages can be reduced to relative simplicity through the work of the philologists, there still remains the diversity which initiated the problem. Reduction of diversity to unity of origin does not eliminate the diversity. If it did, one might as well argue that there is no real difference between whales and cows, since both are mammals and thus have a common evolutionary source. Or for that matter between ozone and oxygen. I am not maintaining that such historical studies are valueless; I am simply saying that the genetic unity of empirical diversity does not eliminate the diversity. This surely should be apparent to anyone who speaks two languages and is confronted with the task of translating one into the other. Frequently he finds that he cannot translate a word until he has grasped the context.

The context, or the *Gestalt,* the total configuration in which a symbol appears, shows that a given symbol may mean different things in different lives, whether it be a word or a shape, used deliberately or motivated unconsciously. This may make a great difference not only in our interpretation of other people's ideas and feelings and ceremonies but also in such disciplines as aesthetics. One has only to study the works of Margaret Naumburg on the paintings of neurotics and psychotics to see how impossible it would be to appreciate the symbols involved without a pretty thorough knowledge of the person who created them. In mathematics the context and the personality of the scientist count for next to nothing. But mathematics studies possibility, not actuality. A mathematician can symbolize possible functions and relations; he does not have to worry about facts. Yet the very existence of such a discipline demonstrates that we do not know all there is to be known. And if that is so, then change is real. And if change is real, so is time. The classical tradition in philosophy, as the *scientia scientiarum,* has been to deny time and to assert eternity. It had to face the problem—to which no solution has ever been given—of how the eternal could become temporalized, how the universal could become particularized, how the one could become the many. But if one begins with the temporal, the eternal can be understood as that which does not appear to change, or perhaps as that whose rate of change is so slow that it appears to be negligible. But to repeat a point suggested above, that is precisely characteristic of the symbol.

Symbols, regardless of their meaning or of their emotional charge, do have a kind of persistency in them which excuses people for treating them as the object of knowledge. They happen to be the vehicle of knowledge, the shell of the mollusc, the case of the cicada, the husk not the kernel. It is they which are transmitted from person to person, from generation to generation. The "life" has gone out of them, though each person and each generation puts new life into them. Julien Green in one of his autobiographical books tells how he was taught to salute the United States flag as he passed the embassy in Paris and also how one of his Southern relatives was shocked to see him do so. The physical flag was clearly identical on both occasions, or so nearly identical as to be called identical. Similarly a statue of the Roman Emperor was a symbol of a god to a pagan, of a man to a Christian. If the Emperor was simply a man and a pinch of incense simply a chemical substance, then the Christian was foolish not to burn the incense before the statue. Clearly it was the symbol, not the sign-vehicle, which counted in both cases. The statue stood for a complex of ideas which the Christian could not accept. And for some reason or other, many human beings prefer truth to falsity. That in the case of the early Christians no one knew precisely what these ideas were and indeed could not even formulate them in consistent symbols cannot be denied—though it will be. They could at least accept the same symbols, even if they could not agree on their signification.

For just as there can be no contradiction in things, but only in statements, so the sign-vehicles could all be accepted as harmonious, much as the variety of colors in a painting can seem to form an aesthetic whole. A social group can also speak the same language and yet disagree about its meaning. Communication still presents difficulties even among members of the same profession. But there is no difficulty in transferring the symbols without inquiring into their meaning. This can be witnessed at meetings of learned societies as well as in classrooms. It is the one justification for strict obedience in military establishments. A set of simple signals will do very well and the soldier or sailor of the lower orders never knows much of the overall plan of his commanders. This no doubt sounds like cynicism of the worst type. It is merely common sense. When one drives through a strange city, one has simply to follow the visual signals which indicate the proper route without seeing a complete plan of the city and without understanding the reasons for the signals. Similarly one can do complicated mathematical operations without deriving for oneself all the formulas by means of which one does them.

For all practical purposes the symbols of the sciences and literature have meanings established by convention. But this is by no means true in the arts. There the constancy is found in such symbols as are determined by the unconscious in the same society. In so far as a society is unified in its purposes, in what it approves of and what it disapproves of—and such societies in the West must be rare except in rural communities—the repressions of its members will probably be highly similar and their release will be expressed in determinable ways. But when one reaches the conscious level, all that will be constant is the symbol itself, not its meaning. The changes in the symbolic system will be slight and the illusion of permanence compelling. By steering clear of historical dictionaries, one need never know that any change has occurred. And thus he will talk about "perennial philosophy" with the assurance that he is right. Similarly if one does not study iconography, one will have the illusion that he thoroughly appreciates the most complicated paintings of the Renaissance, which, if he wants to appreciate them in the sense in which their painters wished them to be appreciated, would have to be read, not merely seen. One is permitted to put into such works of art his own meaning, and since all of us seem to have a tendency to set ourselves up as fair samples of the human race, we shall put back into the minds of the artist our own interpretation of their works of art. If, for instance, we have an interest in spatial relations in pictures, we will say that the African sculptor was constructing volumes and masses in spatial relations and not gods or ancestors. And if we are interested in social problems, we will point out that Picasso, Picabia, Matisse, and Braque never got out of their studios, for the subject matter of their paintings is so often merely guitars, newspapers, bottles of wine, fans, and the other odds and ends which littered Bohemia in the early twentieth century. We can read Keats's sonnet on first looking into Chapman's Homer as a complex of metaphors taken from the Greece of the early nineteenth century and medieval feudalism, or as the poetry of a man stricken by tuberculosis whose deepest experience was that of literature, not of "life." (For life is usually not thought of as including that which makes life most enjoyable.)

In all these cases the symbol stands relatively unchanged from year to year. Our craving for unity and permanence is thus satisfied. History becomes an illusion and we escape from our dread of change. We are thus confirmed in our dislike of individuality and difference and justified in our punishment of those who differ from us. By setting up a priesthood, whether of magicians, medicine men, or simply professors and authorities, we are in a position where innovation becomes heresy and conformity to the rule becomes moral and epistemological excellence. It is in order to illuminate this situation that this chapter has been written.

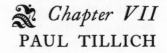

Chapter VII
PAUL TILLICH

THE WORD OF GOD

The term, "Word of God," whether written or spo-
I   ken, should never be used without quotation marks.
This warning is especially needed in such a discussion
of man and his language as this volume contains. For if we leave
out the quotation marks, we may encourage the idea that God
has a language of his own and that the holy writings of religion
are translations of the divine words into the words of a human
dialect. Or if such an absurdity is avoided, it is still possible to
insist that there are circumscribed places in man's oral and written
traditions where the "Word of God" may be found to the exclusion of all other places. An example of this insistence can be
seen in theological fundamentalism and primitive Biblicism where
the sum of words contained between the two covers of a book is
identified with the "Word of God."

Against such literalistic misinterpretations it must be emphat-
ically stated that the term "Word of God," like everything else
man says about God, has symbolic character. Using words, having
language, is a basic function of the human mind. Without exag-
geration it can be said that language makes man man. With his
language are given his reason and his freedom. Through the word
man grasps the structures of reality; through the word he expresses and communicates the hidden depths of his personality.
The word makes community between men possible, and it is only
in community that man creates the word and becomes a man—a
rational and free personality.

A god who did not have the word would be less than man. But
God as the creative ground of man and his world cannot be less
than his creature. He must be the ground of word and reason
and freedom and personality. Therefore, the ancient world, Greek,

Jewish, and Christian, attributed divine character to the *Logos*, the *debar*, the *verbum*, which belongs to God. Man's experience of himself as having the word became the material for the symbol "Word of God." To say that "Word of God" is a symbol does not diminish the truth and the significance of the term. For a genuine symbol, in contrast to a sign, participates in the reality of that which it symbolizes. "Word of God" is reality, but it is not the reality indicated by the literal understanding of the term. God is not a person who speaks to himself and to his creatures in words which grasp an object and reveal a subject. But God manifests himself in ecstatic experiences, and those who have these experiences express them in words which point to the divine self-manifestation. These words, and the divine self-manifestation which they express, are the "Word of God." The ground of our being is not silent, but he does not speak the language of finite beings, even of those who are called his images, namely, men. He does not speak their language, but he speaks to them through their language. He is manifest to them, and they use the word given to them symbolically, in order to grasp and communicate his manifestations. "Word of God" is the necessary and adequate symbol for the self-manifestation of the ground of being to man.

2   The symbolic interpretation of the "Word of God" is supported by the religious and theological tradition and its manifold use of the term. We can distinguish six different ways in which the "Word of God" is applied symbolically to the divine self-manifestation. We can order these six meanings in a hierarchy, starting with the mystery of the divine life, which is the mystery of being itself, and ending with the daily conversation between men, which ordinarily hides but sometimes reveals the mystery of being.

"Word of God" can be and has been understood as the inner word which God speaks to himself, and in which he becomes manifest to himself. Such a statement is highly symbolic, but it can be understood in terms of the Parmenidean sentence that where being is, there is also the *logos* of being, the "word" in which being grasps itself. This is the basis for the Christian doctrine of the Trinity which also describes in symbolic terms the outgoing of God from himself and the reunion of God with himself. It is a description of life in its duality of dynamics and form, and it underlies philosophies like that of Schelling, Whitehead, and Heidegger in their later periods. It means, in most simple terms, that being is not only hidden but also manifest, and that it is first of all manifest to itself. The "Word of God" in this sense is the symbolic expression of that element in the ground of being which breaks its eternal silence and makes life and history possible.

This leads to the second use of the symbol "Word of God." It is the manifestation of God which underlies the existence of a finite universe—the Word of creation. When the Gospel of John says that all things are made through the Logos, who is eternally with God, it points to the transition from God's self-manifestation within himself to his manifestation in the universe. It is the same "Word" which is effective in both manifestations. The world is made by the "Word of God." This symbolic statement means that the structure of the universe is dependent on the divine self-manifestation, on its eternal or primordial form. But the statement that the world is created by the "Word" has still another implication. It points to the spiritual character of the relation of the ground of being to all beings. This relation does not have the character of a natural emanation of the universe out of a divine or demonic substance, or out of both, but it has the character of a spiritual affirmation of the finite by its infinite ground. The symbol "Creation by the Word" guarantees the freedom of the creature from its creative ground, the freedom of man for good and evil, for fall and salvation. It is the basis of the historical thinking of the Christian Occident.

The third use of the term "Word of God" is dependent on this historical interpretation of the universe. The Word by which the world is created appears in history. It appears in two forms: as inspiration and as incarnation. It inspires the prophets, whose words express in human language what they have received from the divine Logos, the divine self-affirmation in human history. Inspiration does not mean divine dictation. It does not mean that those who are inspired receive words under divine authority so that their words are the words of God. But inspiration means the ecstatic experience of the ground of our being breaking into our ordinary consciousness, driving it beyond itself without destroying its natural structure. This experience is what the Old Testament describes as the speaking of Yahweh into the ears of the prophets. The words subsequently spoken and written by the prophets are not inspired words, but words resulting from inspiration.

The other form in which the "Word of God" appears in history is incarnation. In paganism this means the self-manifestation of a divine being in a finite form, subhuman or human. In Christianity it means the unique, divine self-manifestation in the man Jesus of Nazareth, who for this reason is called the Word Incarnate. In contrast to the prophetic experiences of inspiration, his being as such is the divine Word. Not the words of Jesus but he himself is the "Word of God." His words are one of several expressions of his being, which is the bearer of the Word, the principle of the divine self-manifestation. One of the most frequent misinterpretations of Christianity is the identification of its message with the words of Jesus and of the words of Jesus with the "Word of God." But for classical Christianity, Jesus as the Christ *is* the "Word of God," and this includes his actions and sufferings as much as his sayings. Nothing shows the symbolic character of the term "Word of God" more convincingly than its identification with a human being.

3 The three levels of the meaning of "Word of God" which we have discussed constitute a unity. They symbolize the transcendent foundation of what is called "Word of God." There are three other levels of meaning of the term which also constitute a unity. They symbolize divine self-manifestation through the human word. In connection with the discussion of inspiration and incarnation we have already touched these levels from the point of view of the divine self-manifestation. We must now consider them from the standpoint of human reception and expression of the divine self-manifestation. The term "Word of God" is used in Biblical literature for the preaching of the Christian message and for every word and event which can become "Word of God" for someone in a special situation.

In some church services the minister concludes his reading of the Bible with the sentence, "May God bless this reading of His holy Word." For a thoughtful congregation, nothing could be more misleading than this sentence, for it identifies the "Word of God" with the Scripture. It reduces the different meanings of "Word of God" to one, and it blurs the difference between the divine Word given to the prophets and apostles in their state of inspiration and the human words in which they expressed their ecstatic experience. The Biblical words are human words, created by the development of languages under many different influences. The Biblical language is neither a divine language nor a divinely dictated human language. The Biblical language is the human expression of the state of revelatory ecstasy which the Biblical writers have experienced. They express their experience in a human way, each in his own language. And each of these languages is shaped by its history and the innumerable influences which determine every historical reality. God speaks through human words in the books of the Bible. But these words are at the same time "Word of God" in so far as they are received by men as the divine self-manifestation. This is true of both forms of the divine self-manifestation in history—inspiration and incarnation. The Biblical writings are based on the experiences of inspiration of prophets and apostles. The New Testament is based on the "Word Incarnate," to which it is the first and determining witness. It is the document of the appearance of the "Word of God," manifest not in an inspiring experience but in a personal life. This makes the New Testament the "Word of God" in an outstanding sense for all those who accept its message that Jesus is the "Word Incarnate." But even for them it is not divine dictation that makes the Bible the "Word of God" but its content, namely, the witness to the event Jesus the Christ.

It is this message, too, which makes the preacher's words the "Word of God." The minister, when he enters the pulpit, intends to give "Word of God" to the congregation. Taken in this sense, the term can be interpreted objectively and subjectively. It can mean that the preacher, by giving the Christian message, gives the "Word of God," whatever the effect of the sermon may be on the congregation. If he gives the message without distortion, if he is able to express the doctrine purely, wholly, and without deviation, he preaches the "Word of God." In Protestantism it is identical with the message contained in the Bible; in Catholicism, with that contained in the Bible and in tradition. Such an interpretation of the "Word of God preached" is in line with classical orthodoxy. It is completely objectivistic. The other interpretation of the "Word of God preached" is subjective in the sense that the sermon must *become* "Word of God" for someone who listens to it. According to this understanding, the objective content of the sermon does not make it "Word of God." It must speak to the listener as God's self-manifestation to him. It must grasp the listener "existentially" in order to become "Word of God" for him. This means that a sermon or any other expression of the Church *can* become "Word of God" for someone but that this does not necessarily happen.

This subjective interpretation of "Word of God preached" leads to the last step in the whole analysis. If any sermon, independent of its content, can become the "Word of God" for someone, the boundary line between the speaking of the Church and any other speaking has disappeared. Every word, and also every event, can become "Word of God" for someone in a special situation. If it is experienced as divine self-manifestation it *is* "Word of God" for him who experiences it. This makes the whole of nature and culture a possible bearer of the "Word of God." Someone may experience ultimate meaning in a casual conversation, in the encounter with a human being, in a philosophical text, in a piece of art, in a political event. If this happens, he has heard the "Word of God" through these media.

4 In view of this large application of the subjective meaning of "Word of God" we must ask: What is the relationship of this subjective meaning to what was described before as objective meaning—the Word of inspiration and the Word Incarnate, the Biblical Word and the message of the Church? If everything can become the "Word of God" for someone in a special situation, why should there be the objective side at all? One can support this question by pointing to the doctrine of the "inner Word of God"—God can speak to man immediately, directly, and independently of any objective manifestation. In Christianity this was the attitude of the enthusiastic movements of a spiritual and mystical character. In this they followed a wider tradition, namely, of those who understood "Word of God" as the "inner Word," the immediate experience of the divine presence in the innermost center of the soul. They described it in terms similar to the terms used for the external "Word of God," as "Voice," "inspiration," "logos." But they added other terms, such as "seed," "Spirit," "castle," "spark" in the soul. In the Reformation period especially, the struggle between those who emphasized the "inner Word" and those who rejected it was heated and led first to a suppression of the doctrine of the "inner Word" and its adherents. But slowly the situation changed. The "inner Word" of the enthusiasts of the Reformation period was more and more secularized and became the principles of Reason in the Enlightened philosophy and theology of the eighteenth century. According to the teaching of this time, there is an inner "Word of God" in every man: the rational structure of his mind, in the power of which he can know the ultimate principles of being and develop a rational theology, ethics, and logic.

However, since the victory of empiricism and positivism in the nineteenth century, even this secular use of the symbol "Word of God" disappeared. Neither the "outer" nor the inner "Word of God" had any reality for the typical representatives of the nineteenth-century mind. This was not only a terminological change; it was also a progress in secularization beyond the eighteenth and early nineteenth centuries. As long as the logical and ethical principles with which the mind encounters reality were accepted in their validity, they had something of the authority and holiness which was invested in the term "inner Word." But any relation to the "Word of God" disappeared when the immediate validity of those principles was replaced by methods of scientific verification. Now man was completely on his own. Nothing was given to him, nothing was said to him, nothing was invested in him. According to this thinking, man produced by experience and argument the norms of his thinking and acting, which remained tentative and questionable.

It is understandable that in reaction to this attempt to reinterpret the term, "Word of God" became antirational, supranatural, transcendent. This is what happened when, in the 1920's, immediately after the First World War, a theology arose which disregarded or rejected not only modern positivism but, even more, any form of rationalism and, most passionately, the doctrine of the "inner Word." It is the so-called neo-orthodox theology, connected above all with the name of Karl Barth, which made the attempt to create a new theology of the "Word." In contrast to the teachers of the inner "Word," these theologians insisted on the transcendent, supranatural, and unique character of the "Word of God." It comes to us, it speaks against us, it transcends all human possibilities. The place where it is to be found is the Bible, and its content is the message of the Christ. The "Word of God" is again identified with the inspired Word of the Bible, not necessarily with the Biblical words, but with the message of the Bible—Jesus as the Christ. The theologians of this school call their position "theology of the Word." They are suspicious of the theologies of the sacrament; they reject mysticism and humanism. The Word which God speaks is spoken against man. It has no point of contact in man. It must be accepted or rejected. One of the negative consequences of this interpretation of "Word of God" is that in the practice of the Protestant churches, the theology of the Word often becomes a "theology of words." If "Word of God" is identified with the spoken word of the Bible and the Church, instead of being understood as the symbolic expression of all divine self-manifestations, this distortion is almost unavoidable.

5   We must now ask, What is the quality of that which is called "Word of God?" Only on the basis of this consideration can the question connected with the idea of the inner "Word of God" be answered. In the Biblical literature the "Word of God" has a power which no other word has. It penetrates into the depth of the soul, it judges where no human judge can decide, it drives to despair and gives certainty, it threatens and promises, it condemns and saves. Whenever it is heard, the "Word of God" is of ultimate concern to him who hears it. It has been compared with lightning, a sword, a burning fire, an earthquake. It turns ordinary human existence upside down. Nobody can say when and where it will happen. It is not bound to any situation, but it cuts into every situation.

The "Word of God" does not aim to give information, but its aim is to effect a transformation. Of course, like everything spiritual, it has cognitive elements. It reveals something about man and his world, and the relation of man to the ground of his being.

But the word of revelation does not mediate theoretical truth, separated from its shaking and transforming power. The "Word of God" answers existential questions existentially; it does not tolerate theoretical detachment. He who receives a "Word" from God is involved in its truth with his whole existence. And if he rejects it, it is not theoretical rejection on the basis of arguments but an existential rejection, a resistance against or a turning away from the content of the "Word." Theoretical criticism is possible and necessary wherever the cognitive element in the revelatory "Word" is expressed in a doctrinal form. For the doctrinal expression is secondary to the "Word of God" itself.

These considerations provide an answer to the question of the objective criterion of the "Word of God." The answer is both simple and inexhaustible: "Word from God" is always also a word about God. The "of" in "Word of God" can be understood not only as a word coming *from* God but also as a Word *concerning* God. No word about man and his world as such can be a "Word of God." No assertion concerning nature as such, its laws and structure, no assertion concerning history as such, its facts and processes, no assertion concerning man as such, his biological and psychological nature, can be a "Word of God." But assertions about nature, history, and man can be "Word of God" if they relate these realities to ultimate reality. Nature created by God, history directed by God, man judged and saved by God—these are assertions which can appear as "Word of God." Therefore, the "Word of God" never interferes with rational knowledge. Only if it is identified with the human word, through which it expresses itself, such as the words of the Bible, are conflicts unavoidable. The historical and scientific (or prescientific) assertions of a religious text are the material used by those who have received a "Word of God," but they are not parts of the "Word" itself. The "Word of God" speaks out of and into another dimension than that of rational observation and analysis. This excludes, in principle, a conflict between them.

However, a conflict is unavoidable if the claims of different groups or individuals to have received the "Word of God" contradict each other. In this case, the question of the objective criteria of what a "Word of God" is becomes urgent. It is an obvious consequence of the existential character of "Word of God" that such a criterion cannot be taken from outside the revelatory experience. There is no "neutral observer" of the self-manifestation of God. The criteria by which a claim to have "Word of God" is made are parts of the "Word" itself for those who receive it. From this it follows that no religious claim can refute another except by applying criteria which are acknowledged by the other religion too. But if such is the case, then not rejection but union under the common criterion is possible. Christianity believes that it has this universal criterion and that therefore the union of all religions under its criterion, the "Word Incarnate," is possible. This, however, is not a matter of argument and definition but a matter of world-historical developments which the risk of faith can anticipate but not verify.

6 If the "Word of God" necessarily includes a word about God, its linguistic form must be the symbol; for every statement about God is unavoidably symbolic. God, in revealing himself, creates symbols and myths in which he is manifest and through which he can be approached. "Word of God" itself is such a symbol, the central symbol for the way of the divine self-manifestation. The religious symbol is the form of speaking about God. Certainly words about God are only one element in the "Word of God." There are also the words spoken to man which use the nonsymbolic language of commandments, threats, promises. But even in them the symbolic background never disappears. The fact that God is thought of as speaking produces a symbol-laden atmosphere. It is *God* who threatens and promises. This elevates empirical materials such as threats and promises into the sphere of ultimate reality and unconditional concern. And if they are elevated into the sphere of the divine they receive symbolic character. Symbol is the form into which every expression that enters the realm of the holy is transformed. A prophetic word threatens a city with destruction. "Destruction of a city" is an event in ordinary experience. But "destruction of a city" seen in the light of a divine threat is a symbol, because it introduces a special divine causality into the situation, and because the application of the category of causality to God is a symbolic way of speaking.

It is not possible to develop at this point a complete theory of religious symbolism. But since symbol is the religious form of expression and since the "Word of God," if expressed in religious language, has symbolic character, a few points about symbolism must be made.

Symbols are figurative; they point beyond themselves to something for which they stand. In this they are not different from signs. But there is a basic difference between symbols and signs. Symbols participate in the power and meaning of what they symbolize and signs do not. Symbols of the holy themselves have holiness. From this it follows that symbols cannot be replaced arbitrarily or according to expediency, as signs can be. They grow and die but they are not invented or abolished. The symbolic language of religion is an expression of man's actual relation to that which concerns him ultimately. If the character of this relation changes, the symbols also change, and these two processes are often interdependent. Changed symbols express as well as effect a changed relation to the holy.

Symbols, therefore, are safe from criticism by nonsymbolic language. "Stories of the gods" (myths) can be criticized in terms of other myths born out of another relation of man to the divine sphere, but they cannot be criticized because of their miraculous-fantastic character. They cannot be criticized as contradicting natural laws or historical facts. Such criticism is a confusion of language and, since language expresses reality, a confusion of dimensions of reality.

It is the function of symbols to open up levels of being and levels of the soul which symbols alone can open. This is true of all realms in which symbols appear. As an example, let us look at artistic symbolism. It is not the so-called symbolistic school of art to which I refer. This school's productions are questionable. But I refer to the realistic schools of art and affirm that they create symbols in so far as they create art. They express levels of reality which remain hidden in our ordinary encounter with reality. In relation to these levels they are symbolic even if they try to be as naturalistic as possible. The tree in a picture by Ruysdael is symbolic for treehood, but it is not the beautiful copy of a possibly real tree. It is the impression of a level of experience which may be provoked by an actual tree. But the picture does not depict the actual tree. It transforms it into a symbol.

Religious symbols point to ultimate reality, the deepest level of being, the level of "the ground of being" which is not *a* level but the creative ground in all levels. They open up this "level" and they alone can do it. Discursive language (for instance, arguments for the existence of God or similar nonreligious activities) is unable to open up ultimate reality, the level of the holy. And discursive language does not express the ground of the soul in which the holy is experienced.

The religious symbol uses materials of ordinary experience. But it never takes the material in its literal meaning. It says Yes and No to the material it uses. It says Yes to it as a necessary and adequate material. It says No to it if it claims to be more than material. In ancient theology a distinction was made between positive and negative theology. Positive theology says what God is; negative theology shows that he is not that which is said of him. God transcends everything that can be said about him, and therefore it must be denied in the moment in which it is said. Symbolic language unites positive and negative theology. The symbol is the language of religion.

The symbol is true if it expresses adequately the relation of man to God out of which it is born. The symbol is absolutely true if it expresses the relation of man to God in terms which are adequate to the human situation in relation to God universally. It is the claim of Christianity that this is the case with him who is called symbolically the Christ or the "Word of God Incarnate." Whether this claim is true is a matter of daring faith and never-ending experience, for the "Word of God" is not a collection of propositions, but a symbol for the dynamic, ever-changing encounter between man and what concerns him ultimately.

Chapter VIII
R. P. BLACKMUR

THE LANGUAGE OF SILENCE

I Those of us who are lovers of words—to whom a fine phrase brings a blush of response—know that words are merely one medium in which we express our crying-out and our salutation, our discovery and our assent, to what happens to us within and to what happens to us from without. Like all lovers, we add as much as we can to what we love: the particular from within and the general from without. Our compassion is merciless because it is absolute. We have merciless compassion for the dancing bears, the ballet of our best words, because we understand they would if they could have been the moving stars—moving in their own drift and also our own. We are not lovers for nothing, but for life itself. *E pur si muove.*

That is why we blush; it is in the blush that ripeness is all, and it is under the blush, in the honey of its generation, that we know the rest is silence. It is silence that tries to speak, and it is the language of silence which we translate into our words. If we do not hear the silence in our spoken or written words—if we do not hear their voice—we find them dead or vain echo calling on something already disappeared. If we do hear the silence we know that the words are animated by and united with a life not altogether their own, and superior to it; and with the same life we respond; we blush to a blush.

Sometimes the words themselves blush with what they're made on and are burdened with the very cry of silence, the hymn in the throat. There is *King Lear* (II, iv, 56-57):

> O! how this mother swells up toward my heart;
> *Hysterica passio!* down, thou climbing sorrow!
> Thy element's below.

It may be that "mother" is a contraction of "smother." But I have seen, in a comment on this passage (Kenneth Muir's revision of

Craig in the Arden edition) a citation from a contemporary of Shakespeare in which the disorder is defined as "the Mother or the Suffocation of the Mother, because, most commonly, it takes them with choking in the throat; and it is an affect of the mother or wombe." At any rate, something is being translated into words from another language. Whatever that language is it passes through thought into words bringing its rhythm with it, undismayed at the translation. It is amusing to reflect that Sir Walter Scott (in *Rob Roy*) found a mercy for his hero in this compassion when he fell aweeping, deserted of his love in the dusk: "I felt the tightening of the throat and breast, the *hysterica passio* of poor Lear." Sir Walter calls on Lear for the weight in his own voice, but the blush is there just the same.

But if Shakespeare has contracted the smother of the great storm into the inner violence of the "mother," what has Dante done in the words he gives Francesca but to turn all the mother in us into the smothering voice of the throat and breast, that yet comes clear in the words. Here again is the voice of merciless compassion, and it was Dante the Pilgrim, not Dante the author, who fainted with pity and fell as a dead body falls. Here is all the harshness of the love that moves the body in order to move the stars: it is sweet, even, and hoarse, in its fatality. We are saved from the mere ideal (as the ideal is saved from its mere self) by the throaty linkage of the voice of silence, the running rhythm through the other linkage of words and rhymes. It is as if Dante had translated his words back into the language of silence; and it is as if we listened to him to find what we had to say. There is no *tabula rasa* even in the purest expression. We listen to great men in the arts, and imitate their words, to find how our own great skill in the language of silence might break through, as theirs did, not into convention, conformity, compromise, but into the violent incarnation of style. We blush when we recognize our partners in this effort. Sometimes this is called wooing the Muse. We blush both in our inequality to our love and in our rising blood. Did we not wish to equal her, knowing we cannot, and did we not already know her voice, however imperfectly, in ourselves, the Muse would long since have become an unblushing lie. As it is, even her toes are faintly pink.

With so much for exordium (and with the substance of a peroration well in mind) let us first examine a little certain remarks of select ancestors, and then proceed to a sketch of the equivocal nature of present awareness. We shall see, I think, how the insight into inspiration has become a technique of troubles, how the sense of wisdom has become a set of schedules, and yet with nothing lost. After all this, the peroration will seem the mere hebetude of the daily disadvantageous task. But all the toes are pink.

On the ground of tradition, Scripture should come first, and here are the second and third verses from the thirty-ninth Psalm: "I was dumb with silence: I held my peace, even from good, and my sorrow was stirred. My heart was not within me; while I was musing the fire burned: then spake I with my tongue." The combination of loose idiom, basic metaphor, and an accurately stated order of procedure—almost as strict as surgery—is an astonishing witness to the depth of unconscious skill. Or, if that is too much, let us say that it is a complete example of small ritual in inducing inspiration: a ritual to persuade the reasons of the heart to translate themselves into the spoken word. Perhaps it is both; perhaps there is little difference, ultimately, between an order of procedure based on metaphor and a persuasive ritual based on the expectations of faith; between surgery and prayer. In any case, the emphatic clause is: "while I was musing the fire burned." To muse is to be out of one's mind and deeply in one's mind at the same time; musing is like ecstasy without the excess of frills, with only the slight excess of concentration in heat to receive, a ready intensity to find. Of such matters David sang.

But is it not the same, and a paradigm, in our own ordinary experience when in serious conversation we say something grossly short of our meaning? No, no, I say, that is not what I meant at all. Wait! Wait! In just a moment I'll have it; and indeed the heart is so hot it must surely burst into fire with the right musing. Sometimes it does, and we make either a mystery or a cliché. But mostly we wait and writhe, and the Muse will not revisit us, until at last we make a lame issue and hope others will catch from our words the meaning that has all along been half-born between the heart and the mouth. The hope is not very strong.

The language of silence, so near in pressure, is far away in availability. St. Augustine, in his *De Musica,* thought it was fundamental. Perhaps he thought so only because he lived under a collapsing empire where in many aspects there was a sharply diminishing *modus vivendi* between the mind and its languages. Not till the languages had almost entirely replaced the mind (what we used to call the Dark Ages) was anyone content. St. Augustine was profoundly discontented, and some of his discontent was expressed in language appropriate to these notes and to our time. It is curious that he felt what he wrote under this head was less inspired (perhaps not at all inspired) than his doctrinal and other religious works. To us (to myself at least) he was equally inspired; and by the same Muse, or the same inspiration. Let the reader judge.

Judgment will perhaps require preliminary interest. St. Augustine was interested in meters and their relation to rhythm and the relation of the two to the truth of the arts, which in his view are man's increment to God's creation. His discussion of meter is fascinating, but it does not immediately affect us so much as do certain of his remarks on rhythm—the beat in words apart from but transpiring in meter. He thought there were three classes of rhythm, in memory, perception, and sound, with rhythm in perception coming first in experience. The whole matter, to him as to any of us who are interested, was very complex; the frames of discourse do not here adequately represent its subject. The mind moves by flashes and jumps, only now and then resting on the web of words. Thus St. Augustine was not sure of his words, but he could risk appearances. "Apparently," he says, "rhythm existing in silence is freer than rhythm created or extended not only in response to, *ad,* the body, but even in response to, *adversus,* the affects, *passiones,* of the body." ("Extended" is a wonderfully apt term for what happens to a bodily rhythm when it takes hold of a meter.)

The rhythm existing in silence, then, is freer than that related to the body. It is also more, and is itself subject to another thing. "Anything," he says, and I think the idiom, whether Latin or English, is as important as in the Psalms, "anything which the ministry of carnal perception can count, and anything contained in it, cannot be furnished with, or possess, any numerical rhythm in space which can be estimated, unless previously a numerical rhythm in time has preceded in silent movement. Before even that, there comes vital movement, agile with temporal intervals, and it modifies what it finds, serving the Lord of All Things."[1]

"Agile with temporal intervals" is a glorious phrase, full of all the horrors and also the blow of beauty in actual perception. One would think Augustine had read Longinus, and a great regret rises for the loss of his treatise on Beauty. One would also think he had read Pascal in manuscript and meant to admonish him; for here, in these quotations, is adumbrated a rhythm for the language of the reasons of the heart—not the vagaries, but the reasons, of which the mere head knows nothing and is therefore, as La Rochefoucauld says, their continual dupe. There is indeed something French about Augustine when he gets to the arts; his reason shivers a little, and the logic gets a little frantic: but one learns as one shivers. There is after all a predestinate shudder at the end of things. But Augustine was also resident in Italy, and there is a flowering in him few Frenchmen have reached, a special Italian knowledge of how chaos takes form as it must. He knows that thought does not take place in words—though it is administered and partly communicated in words and is by a fiction often present in them, and though, so to speak, it creates them, and creates further what they do to each other. Surely no one ever seriously thought words were autonomous. The story of the tower of Babel should have broken that fiction: every man speaks the language he can, and the angels understand them all. And if Babel is not enough, there is Coleridge, who said, with no arrogance whatever, that he put more meaning into his words than most people. The value we find in the writings of others is the value of the meaning they put in, as it drags out of us and expresses our own meaning; they lodged their meanings, and attract our own, into their words. They jumped from one level of skill, which we all have from the cry spanked out of us at birth to the last rattle, to another, which most of us do not have at all, and about which we deceive ourselves vastly, because we hanker so for the doubtful comfort of hearing a thing said. What oft was thought, but ne'er so well expressed. Pope was at the easy level there: the level which thinks there are words for everything; Joyce was nearer right—he acknowledged the vocabulary but thought the words often wrong. Half the labor of writing is to exclude the wrong meanings from

[1] Quotations from *De Musica. A Synopsis,* by W. F. Jackson Knight, The Orthological Institute, London, n.d.

our words; the other half is to draw on the riches which have already been put into the words of our choice; and neither labor is effective unless the third thing is done, unless we can put into the arrangement, the ordonnance, of our words our own vital movement, "agile with temporal intervals."

St. Augustine was ancestrally right. To be agile is to be supremely responsive to every possibility—both those which can be dealt with in a given language and those which cannot. To be agile is to be inspired; the pink toes of the Muse are in your lap; poets, in any mode of the mind, come dripping from the intimacy of sleep. Hence the positive obscurity of the greatest poetry in the words and hence the terrible clarity under them, pushing through. That is why, as the components of beauty, St. Thomas' *consonantia, claritas, integritas* are not enough. Beauty hits us on both sides of the face, silencing us in the after-silence. St. Thomas left the silence to God; we cannot, even with the aid of Jacques Maritain; for it must be in another way, and much farther afield, with only an alien comfort, our own silence out of which we explode. We are all—if I may be permitted a theological clench— we are all, in the modern world, enthusiasts of direct access, and the wholeness of our minds must be our own—a little tykish, a little rash, and with no rancor of a completed revelation. Our eclecticism is our only revenge upon our orthodoxy.

It would be easy, if we were not using words as our present language, to go into the field of absolute silence of landscape, even into the verging silence of sculpture, or even into the plunging silence—the cresting then the plunge—of the dance; and indeed we are immersed and swimming in the "vital movement, agile with temporal intervals" of these arts. But we use words, and the farthest field we can draw on is the predatory and compassionate distillation of Chinese verbal thought, which to a Western ear is surely the least noisy of all thought, and the least mutually comprehensible in the ordinary babel of human voices. Chinese written words are voiceless pictures drawn with elegance and style: what we would call speaking likenesses when we do not call them ideographs. (There is no better parody of what we mean by the language of silence than the problematic image of a dozen Chinese understanding perfectly each other's written words but unable to converse aloud.) My authority has luckily been recently twice translated into English and has dragged some of the original

Chinese silence into both of the conflicting Englishes; and the meaning is probably as plain as that of Aristotle's *Poetics,* which is all the more appropriate since my Chinese author, Lu Chi, wrote his *Wen Fu* as a kind of *Poetics* or *Art of Letters.* It was written in A.D. 302 and the version I use is that of E. R. Hughes.[2] It is painted in couplets, like Pope, but it is as far from Pope as it is from Aristotle, and is much more like Augustine than either, especially if you listen to the two with the aid of Longinus and look forward to D. H. Lawrence, his screaming dark. He comes at Augustine's position, another way, not from the postulated existence of God, not from the Word, but from the experience of non-being (the kind of nothingness that can be apprehended only from the center of inadequate being) and from a quick of hidden sense and skill that may yet become words. If Lu Chi's position seems precarious by Western standards it is vital and creative (it *makes* something) with or without standards. Our Western standards conform to only a part of our experience, and to only certain aspects of that part. Hence our silent mutiny. Hence in Dostoevsky the *boont:* the stubborn rebellion in the soul against any standard picture of the world. Hence, too, Lear can say: "Aye, every inch a king."

Under the right situation, says Lu Chi, every man is all that kingly inch:

1. What joy there was in all this, the joy worthies and sages have coveted.
2. He was taxing Non-Being to produce Being, calling to the silence importunate for an answer:
3. He was engrossing the great spaces within a span of silk, belching forth torrents [of language] from the inch-space of the heart [*Wen Fu,* I, b].

It should be remembered that by Lu Chi's time writing was done by a brush on silk with soot for ink. Mr. Hughes' commentary says the word translated as "taxing" means also "divining," and that the "inch-space of the heart" has "a connotation of emptiness." This I cite only to point more firmly toward the nature and process of the inspiration wooed in the silence. In further confirmation, here is what Lu Chi says about words without inspiration.

[2] Pantheon Books, New York, 1951.

1. It may be language has been employed in one short strain, one with no traceable sources, a foundling production,
2. which looked close to the Silence but found no friend, looked far to the Void but gained no response [*Wen Fu,* II, g].

Lu Chi evidently had an austere taste and had no use for ornamental verses, at least when he took to writing poetics, except to relate them to what might have been done. One would like to say he understood the potential force of the topical and the immanent abyss in the trivial—which have always been with us—or the more modern possibility that revelation itself may be unseemly, puerile, and offensive. But there is no evidence for it; one doubts if he could have done anything with Smollett's phrase (to which we shall return), "Our satiety is to suppurate." But he could do a great deal with what he had. Here is how he redeems his orphans or foundlings to their lost parents. It is the darkness before the light, then the terrible light.

1. Then comes the blocking of every kind of feeling, the will [to create] gone, the spirit held bound.
2. It is like being the stock of a sapless tree, being empty as a dried up river.
3. Lay hold of the mutinous soul by sounding its secret depths, pay homage to its vital fierceness as you search for the very self:
4. reason screened and obscured begins to creep forth, thought comes screaming, forced out from the womb [*Wen Fu,* II, o].

We are returned to the mother and the hysterica passio in Lear, but in a different construction, which I think compels us to go on to Pascal. Mr. Hughes believes Lu Chi meant poetry to be governed by reason. I would suppose any poet of magnitude to agree; but there are several ways of understanding what the term "reason" means. Meter is one of the reasons governing poetry; rhythm is another; and there is a third which in the cliché taken from Pascal we call the reasons of the heart of which the reasons of the head know nothing, only in the end we manage the public affairs of the heart's reasons with those of the head, especially in poetry and the verbal medium of thought. *L'esprit de finesse* is what gets hurt when the management goes wrong. Pascal gives us a great example in his *pensée* on silence. "Le silence éternal de ces espaces infinis m'effraie." It makes a great difference what the head does with this whether or not you hear the two words *silence éternel* as governing the insight. Mr. Eliot made a good deal of this observation a long time ago with a polemic against sentimentalists in mind. I have no polemic intent; I merely wish to keep the reasons of the heart distinct. The eternal silence is what gives vital movement agile with temporal intervals to the infinite space; as if the heart, with reason, reminded one of the empty spaces in the head, by filling them, under the guise of speech, with speechless knowledge. Erich Heller, in his little book called *The Hazard of Modern Poetry*.[3] goes farther, evidently holding speechless knowledge a special aspect of modern times. "The music of modern Europe is the one and only art in which it surpassed the achievement of former ages. This is no accident of history: it is the speechless triumph of the spirit in a world of words without deeds and deeds without words." In the general current of our citations from Augustine and Lu Chi, one could observe at once that it is when words are filled with the language of silence that they become deeds; or, Aristotle would say, that they become *praxis* or action. But Mr. Heller has more to say a little further on. In trying to define the hazard of modern poetry he cites Hölderlin's question: Why should one write poetry in such spiritless times? Why should one be a poet at all? Mr. Heller goes on: "What was this *dürftige Zeit*, this time poor in spirit but farther than any from the Kingdom of Heaven, that made Hölderlin question the justification of being a poet; this meagre but forceful time that pushed poetry to the very edge of silence, of that 'abyss' that Baudelaire too sensed at the feet of poetry; this hostile time that yet inspired in Hölderlin, and in Baudelaire, and in Rimbaud, poetry truly unheard of before? For in their poetry speechlessness itself seemed to burst into speech without breaking the silence."

It is as if Mr. Heller were giving analogies to the processes of inspiration and creation we found described in Augustine and Lu Chi; and Mr. Heller, too, believes in reason; only, if I follow him correctly, the poets named above, and Rilke also, worked against their inspiration, and in spite of reason. T. S. Eliot, in Mr. Heller's account, almost alone does better: he is a poet of civic virtue. Indeed he is, in the sense that Mr. Heller means so Roman a phrase for so obstinately protestant an Anglican as Eliot. Indeed he is, and he is so by lodging his poetry almost from the begin-

[3] Bowes and Bowes, Cambridge, 1953.

ning in the language of silence. There is not only "Looking into the heart of light, the silence"; there is also "The silent withering of autumn flowers/Dropping their petals and remaining motionless"; and there is, a little later in the same poem ("The Dry Salvages"), this distich:

> There is no end of it, the voiceless wailing,
> No end to the withering of withered flowers.

There is not much manifest civic virtue in these lines, but there is the condition of epiphany from which the several sorts of virtue, including the civic, spring. The silent withering and the voiceless wailing are working together as one explorer's cry. They "burst into speech without breaking the silence." They burst into the virtue which is the declared and sustained allegiance to the nature of things: the mother that will not down the intractable ache of vital movement wherever it may be.

It is by means such as this that poetry avenges itself upon doctrine that has become mere argumentation (become the "mere" ideas which, to redact on Eliot's famous phrase about James, violate most minds); and the revenge is a catharsis, "a tax on Non-being to produce Being, calling to the Silence." The wind is silent; even the winds of doctrine are silent. Even the wind the Lord tempers to the shorn lamb; that wind and that doctrine above all are silent. It is we who hear the wind, ruffling and recommoding both the surface and the marrow of the mind; but we hear it truly only when we have learned how to translate it to voice-learning or speaking forms. Again it is Eliot who says this well—avenging its impudence by transmuting it—in "the inch-space of the heart."

> Words move, music moves
> Only in time; but that which is only living
> Can only die. Words, after speech, reach
> Into the silence. Only by the form, the pattern,
> Can words or music reach
> The stillness, as a Chinese jar still
> Moves perpetually in its stillness.

I do not know that Eliot would admit that there is much thinking in these lines; there was a time when he argued that Dante did his thinking in Aquinas and such like places, and that Shakespeare did not do any thinking at all; but I would say there is a vital movement of thought here, alive with temporal intervals. Only one version of thought takes place in the medium of concepts and only another version originates in the medium of words. The weight of life in these lines is the moving weight, the momentum —the momentum and the buoyancy—of the experience of thought in its primary and final languages, for which concepts and words furnish only concentrates and analogues. The reality that drips from live words is the reality of this thought: the silence that is in them and the silence to which they reach. If this were not so there would be no thought in the other arts. We would not quake at the *thought* of the Medici tombs or at the *thought* in the blue vault, only gradually visible, the gradual apparition of thought *each* time it is seen, in the Empress' tomb at Ravenna, which is the shiver of the thought of the last place, moving "perpetually in its stillness" because it *is* thought, the operation of the mind rendering the substance of its experience its own. This is the permanent task of the imaginative reason, of the rational imagination. But the reason must not be too clear: the cost in perception is too great: perfect clarity is a form of deafness to the human and the nonhuman alike. Hence Lu Chi's conclusion: "reason screened and obscured begins to creep forth, thought comes screaming, forced out from the womb."

George Eliot, in an interesting paragraph in *Middlemarch,* says much the same thing in a less oracular but almost as prophetic language. She is referring to the representative aspect of the horror which has happened to Dorothea Brooke in her sterile marriage: and what she says represents Dorothea's five weeks of silent sobbing during her Roman honeymoon. Dorothea does not know she has company in the next stranger's house—or at least in the next to next. "The element of tragedy which lies in the very fact of frequency, has not yet wrought itself into the coarse emotion of mankind; and perhaps our frames could hardly bear very much of it. If we had a keen vision and feeling of all ordinary human life, it would be like hearing the grass grow and the squirrel's heart beat, and we should die of that roar which lies on the other side of silence." And then, as if to say what a life would be like which heard the roar the other side of silence, and yet did not die, a little down the page she goes on: "Permanent rebellion, the dis-

order of a life without some loving reverent resolve, was not possible for her; but she was now in an interval when the very force of
her nature heightened its confusion." What was this force but that
roaring? Tolstoy would have made the identification absolute; and
it is a pity we do not have the language of his silence available.
But Ivan Ilyitch heard the force roaring; and Dorothea Brooke is
an Anna Karenina, only saved by the machinations of English
novelistic conventions. The reader meditating the possibility does
not require salvation; he requires a further flight of reason; for
it is exactly here that George Eliot refuses a further screening and
obscuring of reason. "Permanent rebellion" without resolve is
one of the regular conditions of life. Reason must find it,
for only reason can deal with it, and reason is not reason unless it
does so; it is mere dead reason, the course of inert ideas and
anesthetized sentiments, the rubbish of lost knowledge. But she
is nevertheless presenting the experience of reason, not only here
but again and again: for instance, when she *shows* us, and then
proves it, how Rosamund Vincy, that blond vampire with no blood
of her own but with a charm that requisitioned blood where she set
her mouth softly, "was particularly forcible by means of that mild
persistence which, as we know, enables a white soft living substance to make its way in spite of opposing rock." Her uncle, Mr.
Bulstrode, is better still; filled with the roaring force, he makes
out of a probable death a possible murder—George Eliot provides
nothing if not *serious* entertainment—and mires his own act in
reasonable prayer. "Early in the morning—about six—Mr. Bulstrode rose and spent some time in prayer. Does anyone suppose
that private prayer is necessarily candid—necessarily goes to the
roots of action! Private prayer is inaudible speech, and speech is
representative; who can represent himself just as he is, even in
his own reflections?"

We do not hear what Mr. Bulstrode says, but we know what
it is—we would have said it ourselves; we too would have wanted
both to make our action total and also to have made ourselves free
of it. Our deepest prayer is to disengage ourselves from our behavior. There is no prayer for justice; we pray for mercy and
for justification; and of this the reasons of the head need constantly to be reminded, if ever they are to be moved, not merely
duped, by the reasons of the heart. It is not for nothing that

the reasons of the head are associated with *l'esprit de géometrie;* they must be able to measure any earth—any inch-space of the heart whatever—else they are mere orts and slarts.

George Eliot, short only of the first magnitude and often grappling with it in a furious dull fervor, could say this with specific reference, in the apprehension of the fingertips on the roughened table-top. Mr. Bulstrode in his downfall is an example. First there are the rat shrieks of his colleagues in "the agony of the terror that fails to kill, and leaves the ears still open to the returning wave of execration. . . . But in that intense being lay the strength of reaction. Through all his bodily infirmity there ran a tenacious nerve of ambitious self-preserving will, which had continually leaped out like a flame, scattering all doctrinal fears, and which, even while he sat an object of compassion to the merciful, was beginning to stir and glow under his ashy paleness." George Eliot's own compassion was merciless; she writes with reason fired, burning in its own ashes, not yet wet. When Mrs. Bulstrode hears of her husband's downfall, the reasons of the heart are horripilated. "There is a forsaking which still sits at the same board and lies on the same couch with the forsaken soul, withering it the more by unloving proximity." That perspective inhabits without tampering with the action Mrs. Bulstrode took; heart and head work together; she dug for strength into her old aspirations, and so did her husband. "She took off all her ornaments and put on a plain black gown" and went in to see him, a Lady Macbeth all milk and mercy. "His confession was silent, and her promise of faithfulness was silent." Something like ninety pages later in the book, George Eliot, moving through both perspectives, reaches her own precarious conclusion: that in looking at all these people we see all at once that great feelings wear the aspect of error, great faith reveals the aspect of illusion. So she hears the roaring the other side of silence.

Dante had a tougher mind and took greater risks; he worked on the double war of the journey and the pity, and was implacable; he depended on the memory that cannot go wrong (*che non erra*): the roaring was not only part of the silence, it instigated reason and told him what to say. This is why one is seldom at home with the uncomforting terrors of Dante's mind. One longs always, as he did himself, for the sweet air. To Dante, feeling is absolute tidings, faith is substance. But I cite Dante only for a post of observation from which to triangulate George Eliot and Joseph Conrad. Think then of Francesca's words, and from that vantage think both of the passages quoted from *Middlemarch* and of the following from *Nostromo*. It is a balcony scene, the abridged privacy, with people all round, both strangers and those eager with gluttonous interest. But the manners that left Martin Decoud alone and exposed with Antonia Avellanos also required of them to make the most of their open chance. It is the essence of the balcony that while you are there everything is at stake. They must talk both of the world and of themselves. It is the situation where you come both on hopeless longing and hope mercilessly free of longing. Here is Conrad. "She was facing him now in the deep recess of the window, very close and motionless. Her lips moved rapidly. Decoud, leaning his back against the wall, listened with crossed arms and lowered eyelids. He drank the tones of her even voice, and watched the agitated life of her throat, as if waves of emotion had run from her heart to pass out into the air in her reasonable words." We do not hear what Antonia said—any more than we hear what Dorothea Brooke heard—in so many words; and perhaps we do not need to, for we have all heard these words and wear them as stigmata or as amulets; we have all heard the sirens and we know they sing sweetest when the heart makes reasonable words out of the language of silence. The sirens are not much given to finding words, except for individuals, and only at the moment when the individuals are themselves brimming with the language of silence into reason.

The sirens, I take it, are earlier forms of the Muses and haunt us more deeply.

Poor Decoud, in *Nostromo,* heard and was haunted, and could not make the words his own. He died alone therefore, killed by the blow of that other silence which, when it is dominant, when the heart is inadequate to its theme, prevents human voice altogether. "The great gulf burst into a glitter all around the boat; and in this glory of merciless solitude the silence appeared again before him, stretched taut like a dark, thin string." It is the silence kills him. He "rolled overboard without having heard the cord of silence snap in the solitude of the Placid Gulf." There is no murderer like your silence, once heard, when there are neither sirens, nor muses, nor the reasons of the heart to give words. What we cannot make human kills us. What we cannot keep human makes us kill ourselves. The rest is silence.

George Eliot had hope of the reforming heart. Conrad seemed to think the nonhuman world bears us up as a race while destroying us as individuals. Dante was implacable to see what lived. All dealt with the wastage of the precious, the erosion of belief by fact. Speaking in the same voice, but with half the register missing, yet with a singularly intimate effect upon our own ears, is E. M. Forster, and especially in *A Passage to India*. No timeless humanist he, but a rancorous doll; but the rancor in our own, the voice of the grudge we bear against what besets us and puts us about whatever tack we bend to. In Forster it is as in Yeats' poem: our creation was an accident. "My dear, my dear, it was an accident!" In Forster, I think, is the sink of energy, with no running out of awareness. Reading Forster, we know what we are aware of at our moments of the conviction of loss or of the bottom of futility: we know the hope which Luther said guaranteed the hopes in Purgatory; and this is another form of the language of silence.

In *A Passage to India*, an old woman more than senile, Mrs. Moore, speaks the language of silence; but it is others who hear it. She *says* nothing; but the young woman, Adela, who was to have become her daughter-in-law heard, not words, but the idea in her heart and made out of it the principal action of her life. What she heard at first was echo, then an idea, then the fledgling of both into words. The old woman fills the younger with the heart's knowledge which, to Forster, is neither reason nor unreason. If a great deal of guilt is built up in this way, it is because Forster wants it so. When the heart, which bites others so often, is bitten back, it winces. The heart's unreasons are the heart's offenses. Hence the guilt.

Later there is a fillip the other way. When Adela has been filled with guilt and emptied of life she has a talk with Fielding, the senior boy scout, or catalyst of the book. When they have said all *they* could say, "there was a moment's silence, such as often follows the triumph of rationalism." In that moment silence speaks *through* rationalism. And when, a little later, they have their last conversation, it is the same the other way round. "She was at the end of her spiritual tether, and so was he." Their tether was very short; a snaffle. "Were there worlds beyond which they

could never touch, or did all that is possible enter their consciousness? They could not tell. They only realized that their outlook
was more or less similar, and found in this a satisfaction. Perhaps
life is a mystery, not a muddle; they could not tell." Here the
voice of silence cries through rationalism to be heard, and neither
the man in the first withering of middle age nor the drying girl
knows how near they come to hearing the voice they do not know
they invoke. All that was left of them—as they *were,* as Forster
could *see* them—was "a friendliness, as of dwarfs shaking hands.
. . . dwarfs talking, shaking hands and assuring each other that
they stood on the same footing of insight." Dwarfs are unattended
sirens.

I know no better sign that a new form of civilization, or culture,
or living social anthropology—call it what you will—is afoot than
such things as Forster's reductive interpretations of the language of
silence. The tower of Babel is falling again, for the voices make
rancor. There is no pain, says the incredible English saint in his
early senility, "but there is cruelty," and he says it, at the very
end of the book, as if it were the sweetest possible thing to say, as
if cruelty were the rod that struck water from the rock and brought
down the light. And indeed in some incipient forms of morality
abroad today, this seems to be so. We have techniques for finding
moral trouble, trouble in the customs of the heart, which we can
only treat with the nearest stroke of cruelty, and we think cruelty
virility, loyalty, predictability, when in another time we would
have thought it was the abuse of these. In applying these remarks
to the novels of E. M. Forster, I know I am invidious; I mean to
be—but no more so than I would be were I applying myself
to Graham Greene or Evelyn Waugh or Henry Green.

What do we have? We have a clatter of lacerating facts to enforce and hold to a false and muddled and calamitous annuncia-
tion and an aborted incarnation. The facts do not acquire order
(reason finding order) but descend into a deep disorder in which
they have no relevant part. One's imagination grows tired, with
the fatigue of any day. At the end of *A Passage to India* the
imagination is tired indeed: the god is invoked in a crash of
shallow waters, in a fusion and muddle of disrelated echoes:
the cobra slithering, the kissing sound of the bats, the rearing
horse, the narrowing path. Rancor becomes the substance of

affection. *La lune ne garde aucune rancune.* Perhaps the moon is still there. But the sky says No, not yet, No, not there. The haunt no longer comes because there is nothing left for it to frighten. There is only the shadowy sub-deity of old Mrs. Moore, who had been filled with senility, and the dried virginity of Adela Quested, who had been emptied of echo. The haunt no longer comes.

Yet the haunts are still there; and if they do not come, then, as Mistress Winifred Jenkins is made to say in Smollett's *Humphrey Clinker*, "our satiety is to suppurate." Mistress Jenkins is one of the great commentators on human experience; she believes in high literacy and reaches higher than she knows, and higher than she could tolerate if she did know it; she is inspired by the possibilities of language itself—not the language of direct perception and momentous thought. But she uses words, and if you do not know what she means, then you do not know what she *also* means. She has the brutality of the Muse, even if she does not always furnish the transport. She deprives every word she uses of its cliché, its clutter of false and degenerate meanings. In short, she has style, in the sense A. N. Whitehead once defined it (*The Aims of Education*): "Style, in its finest sense, is the last acquirement of the educated mind; it is also the most useful. It pervades the whole being. . . . Style is the ultimate morality of mind." Whitehead goes on, that there is something above style and knowledge, which he calls Power, and then he says, "Style is the fashioning of power, the restraining of power," and, lastly, he adds, "Style is always the product of specialist study, the peculiar contribution of specialism to culture." Mistress Jenkins was such a specialist; and her function was to transmit judgments and insights that could not be direct either in the rational or in the lyric modes of language. Mistress Jenkins was a *persona* whom Smollett threw off in that ripeness he thought was old age (and which he knew, rightly, was the onset of death), through which you may hear as many voices as you have ears for. "Our satiety is to suppurate"; our society is to suppurate; our satiety is to separate; our satiety is indeed to suppurate. A *persona* is the invoked being of the muse; a siren audible through a lifetime's wax in the ears; a translation of what we did not know that we knew ourselves: what we partly are.

2 Smollett seems the right author with whom to end a series of citations relating to the language of silence.

He knew nothing of such a language: it was not disengaged in his consciousness, or at any rate not in that part of it which resorted to words for its expression; and he would probably have rejected discussion of it as waste motion, though possibly he might have accepted it as a key to the hypochondria—the desperate health—of his last years. He knew the chaos upon which his reason supervened: which explains both his brutality and his goodheartedness; and he knew how that chaos twisted and impugned his reason: hence his coarseness and compassion. Whether or not he knew how the vitality of the chaos provided the elements of true order to his reason does not matter; it happened so, and it happened by the rhythm of the full mind. In all the best of Smollett you feel the force of St. Augustine's testimony. "A numerical rhythm in time has preceded in silent movement. Before even that there comes vital movement, agile with temporal intervals, and it modifies what it finds, serving the Lord of All Things." About the Lord there may be doubt. The rest is true.

3 The rest is not only true but pertinent to practice or action where truth is only the culminating objective (is pertinent to the Aristotelian notion of *praxis:* how action transpires in the language of the mind). "Our satiety is to suppurate" could never have been written except as a verbal translation of thought which was not verbal. Translation is what verbal language does to the language of silence. If there were no language of silence, there could be no translation from Arabic or French into English; and what is wrong about so many translations is that they pay too little attention to the silence that has got into the words. The poetry of Verlaine, for example—of a haunted sweetness craving light in French—will be empty cliché in direct English; but on the other hand it may seem packed with silence in French merely because it ought to be; we sometimes no more know how little a poet has put into his words in the way of meaning than how much. The *Dies Irae* may crack the psyche in Latin and bring a drowse in English. To say *inshallah!* in Arabic may be to say nothing, but coming out of an English throat it may renew everything that was ever meant by saying "As God wills."

And the children on the street speak a language between that of the parrot and that of the dove. If we regard speech as translation, it will, when it does not leave us tongue-tied, find us the right urgency and a transpiring rhythm; and thus there is something right about James Joyce's reported remark that though there were plenty of words in English they were not the words he wanted. Smollett knew this as well as Joyce. We live in a world of the *mot injuste* out of which the heart may yet create reasonable forms.

We translate most in our own language, and so little of it gets into our words. If there were no gaps between our words—in which silence speaks, and in which we recollect ourselves (by tranquillity Wordsworth must have meant a gap)—we should never find our thoughts or recognize the thoughts of others: the rhythm would not transpire. In verse—the oldest discipline of words we have, older than grammar, and reaching the naked syntax—in verse the silences animate with rhythm the variations of the meter, enlivening the metronome. Rhythm is how we feel and how we translate action in the soul. The action may not be our action, though it is what moves us, but we move it through silence into words and when it is there the words remain alive. As Eliot says, "You are the music while the music lasts," and if poetry is heightened speech it is heightened with silence. Meaning is what silence does when it gets into words.

But here is Baudelaire, in his poem "La Voix," with provisional consolation:

> Mais la Voix me console et dit: "Garde tes songes;
> Les sages n'ont pas d'aussi beaux que les fous!"[4]

[4] "But the voice comforts me and says: 'Cherish your visions; The wise have not more beauty than the fools!'"

Part Two

THE APPLICATION

THE CARDINAL DICHOTOMY
IN LANGUAGE

To Raymond de Saussure.

I   If aphasia is a language disturbance, as the term suggests, then any description and classification of aphasic syndromes must begin with the question of what aspects of language are impaired in the various species of such a disorder. This problem, which was approached long ago by Hughlings Jackson,[1] cannot be solved without the participation of professional linguists, familiar with the patterning and functioning of language. To study any breakdown in communications we must first understand the nature and structure of the mode of communication that has ceased to act.

During the last few years the significance of linguistic analysis of aphasic phenomena has been expressly pointed out by leading psychopathologists, in such fundamental treatises on aphasia as A. R. Luria's *Travmaticheskaja afazija* (Moscow, 1947), Kurt Goldstein's *Language and Language Disturbances* (New York, 1948), and André Ombredane's *L'aphasie et l'élaboration de la pensée explicite* (Paris, 1951). And yet in most cases this valid insistence on the linguists' contribution to the investigation of aphasia is still ignored. For instance, the instructive book by H. Myklebust, *Auditory Disorders in Children* (New York, 1954), which deals to a great extent with the complex and intricate problems of infantile aphasia, calls for coordination of various disciplines and appeals for cooperation to otolaryngologists, pediatricians, audiologists, psychiatrists, and educators; but the science of language is passed over in silence, as if disorders in speech perception had nothing whatever to do with language. This omission is the more deplorable since the author is Director of the Child

[1] *Selected Writings*, II, London, 1932.

Hearing and Aphasia Clinics at Northwestern University, which counts among its linguists Werner F. Leopold, by far the best American expert in child language.

The linguists are also responsible for the delay in undertaking a joint inquiry into aphasia. Nothing comparable to the minute linguistic observations of infants of various countries has been performed with respect to aphasics. Nor has there been any attempt to reinterpret and systematize from the point of view of linguistics the multifarious clinical data on diverse types of aphasia. That this should be true is all the more surprising in view of the fact that on the one hand the amazing progress of structural linguistics has endowed the investigator with efficient tools and devices for the study of verbal regression and on the other the aphasic disintegration of the verbal pattern may provide the linguist with new insights into the general laws of language.

Only a few questions have been raised: the improverishment of the sound pattern was observed and discussed by the phonetician Marguerite Durand together with the psychopathologists Th. Alajouanine and A. Ombredane (see their common work, *Le syndrome de désintégration phonétique dans l'aphasie,* Paris, 1939) and by the present author (the first draft, presented to the International Congress of Linguists in Brussels in 1939, was later developed into an outline, *Kindersprache, Aphasie und allgemeine Lautgesetze,* Uppsala, 1941), and finally, a joint inquiry into certain grammatical disturbances was undertaken at the Bonn University Clinic by a linguist, G. Kandler, and two physicians, F. Panse and A. Leschner (see their report, *Klinische und sprach- wissenschaftliche Untersuchungen zum Agrammatismus,* Stuttgart, 1952).

2   Speech implies a *selection* of certain linguistic entities and their *combination* into linguistic units of a higher degree of complexity. At the lexical level this is readily apparent: the speaker selects words and combines them into sentences according to the syntactic system of the language he is using; sentences are in their turn combined into utterances. But the speaker is by no means a completely free agent in his choice of words: his selection (except for the rare case of actual neology) must be made from the lexical storehouse which he and his addressee possess in common. The communication engineer most properly approaches the essence of the speech event when he assumes that the optimal speaker and listener have at their disposal more or less the same "filing cabinet of *prefabricated* representations": the addressor of a verbal message selects one of these "preconceived possibilities" and the addressee is supposed to make an identical choice from the same assembly of "possibilities already foreseen and provided for."[2] Thus the efficiency of a speech event demands the use of a common *code* by its participants.

" 'Did you say *pig* or *fig*?' said the Cat. 'I said *pig*,' replied Alice." In this peculiar utterance the feline addressee is attempting to recapture a linguistic choice made by his addressor. In the common code of the Cat and Alice, i.e., in spoken English, the difference between a stop and a continuant consonant, other things being equal, may change the meaning of the message. Alice had used the distinctive feature "stop *versus* continuant," rejecting the latter and choosing the former attribute; and in the same act of speech she combined this solution with certain other simultaneous features, using the gravity and the tenseness of [*p*] in contradistinction to the acuteness of [*t*] and to the laxness of [*b*]. Thus all these attributes have been combined into a bundle of distinctive features, the so-called *phoneme*. The phoneme [*p*] was then followed by the phonemes [*i*] and [*g*], themselves bundles of simultaneously produced distinctive features. Thus the *concurrence* of simultaneous entities and the *concatenation* of successive entities are the two ways in which we speakers combine linguistic constituents.

Neither such bundles as [*p*] or [*f*] nor such sequences of bundles as [*pig*] or [*fig*] are invented by the speaker who uses them. Neither the distinctive feature "stop *versus* continuant" nor the phoneme [*p*] can occur out of a context. The stop feature appears in combination with certain other concurrent features, and the repertory of combinations of these features into phonemes such as [*p*], [*b*], [*t*], [*d*], [*k*], [*g*], etc., is limited by the code of the given language. The code sets limitations on the possible combinations of the phoneme [*p*] with other following and/or preceding phonemes; and only a part of the permissible phoneme sequences are actually utilized in the lexical stock of a given language. Even when other combina-

[2] D. M. MacKay, "In Search of Basic Symbols," *Cybernetics,* Transactions of the Eighth Conference, New York, 1952, p. 183.

tions of phonemes are theoretically possible, as a rule, the speaker is only a word user, not a word coiner.

In any language, there exist also coded word groups called *phrase-words*. The meaning of the idiom "how do you do" cannot be derived by adding together the meanings of its lexical constituents; the whole is not equal to the sum of its parts, whereas in the case of individual words we expect them to be coded units. In order to grasp the word "nylon" we must know the meaning assigned to this vocable by the lexical code of modern English. Those word groups which in this respect behave like single words are a common but nonetheless only marginal case. In order to comprehend the overwhelming majority of word groups we must be familiar only with the constituent words and with the syntactical rules of their combination. Within these limitations we are free to set words in new contexts. Of course this freedom is relative, and the pressure of current clichés upon our choice of combinations is considerable. But the freedom to compose quite new contexts is undeniable, despite the relatively low statistical probability of their occurrence.

Thus in the combination of linguistic units there is an ascending scale of freedom. In the combination of distinctive features into phonemes, the freedom of the individual speaker is zero; the code has already established all the possibilities which may be utilized in the given language. Freedom remains small in the combining of phonemes into words; it is limited to the marginal situation of word coinage. In the forming of sentences out of words the speaker is less constrained. And finally, in the combination of sentences into utterances, the action of compulsory syntactical rules ceases and the freedom of any individual speaker to create novel contexts rises substantially, although again the numerous stereotyped utterances are not to be overlooked.

Any linguistic sign involves two modes of arrangement:

1. *Combination.* Any sign is made up of constituent signs and/ or occurs only in combination with other signs. This means that any linguistic unit at the same time serves as context for simpler units and/or finds its own context in a more complex linguistic unit. Hence any actual grouping of linguistic units binds them into a superimposed unit: combination and contexture are two aspects of the same operation.

2. *Selection.* A selection between alternatives implies the pos-

sibility of substituting one for the other, which in some respect is equivalent to the former and in some respect is different from it. Actually, selection and substitution are two aspects of the same operation.

The fundamental role which these two operations play in language was clearly realized by Ferdinand de Saussure. Yet from the two varieties of combination, the concurrence and concatenation, it was only the latter, the temporal sequence, which was recognized by the Geneva linguist. Despite his own insight into the phoneme as a set of concurrent distinctive features (*éléments différentiels des phonèmes*), the scholar succumbed to the traditional belief in the linear character of language *"qui exclut la possibilité de prononcer deux éléments à la fois."*[3]

In order to delimit the two modes of arrangment which we have described as combination and selection, Ferdinand de Saussure states that the former "is *in presentia*: it is based on two or several terms jointly present in an actual series," whereas the latter "connects terms *in absentia* as members of a virtual mnemonic series." That is to say, selection (and, correspondingly, substitution) deals with entities conjoined in the code but not in the given message, whereas in the case of combination the entities are conjoined also or only in the actual message. The addressee perceives that the given utterance (message) is a *combination* of constituent parts (sentences, words, phonemes, etc.) *selected* from the repository of all possible constituent parts (code). The constituents of a context are in a status of *contiguity* while in a substitution set signs are linked by various degrees of *similarity* which fluctuate between the equivalence of synonyms and the common core (*tertium comparationis*) of antonyms.

These two operations provide each linguistic sign with two sets of *interpretants,* to utilize the effective concept introduced by Charles S. Peirce: two references serve to interpret the sign—one to the code, and the other to the context, whether coded or free; and in each of these ways the sign is related to another set of linguistic signs. A given sign may be replaced by other, in part more explicit, signs of the same code, whereby its general meaning is revealed, while its contextual meaning is determined by its connection with other signs within the same sequence.

[3] Cf. p. 68 f. and p. 170 f. of his *Cours de linguistique générale,* Paris, 2nd ed., 1922.

3   It is clear that speech disturbances may affect in varying degrees the individual's capacity for combination and selection of linguistic units, and indeed the question of which of these two operations is chiefly impaired proves to be of far-reaching significance in describing, analyzing, and classifying the diverse forms of aphasia. This dichotomy is perhaps even more suggestive than the classical distinction (not discussed in this study) between *emissive* or *expressive* and *receptive* aphasia, indicating which of the two functions in speech exchange, the encoding or the decoding of verbal messages, is particularly affected.

Head attempted to classify cases of aphasia into definite groups, and to each of these varieties he assigned "a name chosen to signify the most salient defect in the management and comprehension of words and phrases."[4] Following this device, I distinguish two basic types of aphasia—depending on whether the major deficiency lies in selection and substitution, with relative stability of combination and contexture; or, conversely, in combination and contexture, with relative retention of normal selection and substitution. In outlining these two opposite patterns of aphasia, I shall mainly utilize Kurt Goldstein's data.

For aphasics of the first type (selection deficiency), the context is the indispensable and decisive factor. When presented with scraps of words or sentences, such a patient readily completes them. His speech is merely reactive: he easily carries on conversation but has difficulties in starting a dialogue; he is able to reply to a real or imaginary addressor when he is or imagines himself to be the addressee of the message. It is particularly hard for him to perform, or even to understand, such a closed discourse as the monologue. The more his utterances are dependent on the context, the better he copes with his verbal task. He feels unable to utter a sentence which responds neither to the cue of his interlocutor nor to the actual situation. The sentence "It's raining" cannot be produced unless the utterer sees that is actually raining. The deeper the utterance is embedded in the verbal or non-verbalized context, the higher are the chances of its successful performance by this class of patients.

[4] H. Head, *Aphasia and Kindred Disorders of Speech*, New York, 1926, Vol I, p. 412.

Likewise, the more a word is dependent on the other words of the same sentence and the more it refers to the syntactical context, the less it is affected by the speech disturbance. Therefore, words syntactically subordinated by grammatical concord or government are more tenacious, whereas the subordinating agent of the sentence, namely, the subject, tends to be omitted. As long as any start is the main obstacle for the patient, it is obvious that he will fail precisely at the starting point, the cornerstone of the sentence pattern. In this type of language disturbance, sentences are conceived as elliptical sequels to be supplied from antecedent sentences uttered, if not imagined, by the aphasic himself, or apprehended from the other partner of the colloquy, actual if not imaginary. Key words may be dropped or superseded by abstract anaphoric substitutes.[5] A specific noun, as Freud noticed, is replaced by a general one, for instance, *machin, chose* in the speech of French aphasics.[6] In a dialectical German sample of "amnesic aphasia" observed by Goldstein, *Ding,* "thing," or *Stückle,* "piece," were substituted for all inanimate nouns, and *überfahren,* "perform," for verbs which were identifiable from the context or situation and therefore appeared superfluous to the patient.

Words with an inherent reference to the context, like pronouns and pronominal adverbs, and words serving merely to cement the context, such as connectives and auxiliaries, are particularly likely to survive. Thus only the framework, the connecting links of communication, are spared by this kind of aphasia at its critical stage.

In the theory of language since the early Middle Ages, it has repeatedly been asserted that out of context the word has no meaning. The validity of this statement is, however, confined to aphasia, or more exactly to one type of aphasia. In the pathological cases under discussion an isolated word means actually nothing but "blab." As numerous tests have disclosed, for such patients two occurrences of the same word in two different contexts are mere homonyms. Since distinctive vocables carry a higher amount of information than homonyms, some aphasics of this type tend to supplant the contextual variants of one word by different terms, each of them specific for the given environment. Thus Goldstein's

---

[5] Cf. L. Bloomfield, *Language,* New York, 1933, Chap. 15, "Substitution."
[6] S. Freud, *On Aphasia,* London, 1953, p. 22.

patient never uttered the word "knife" alone, but according to its use and surroundings alternately called the knife a pencil sharpener, apple parer, bread knife, knife and fork; so the word "knife" turned out to be changed from a *free form,* capable of occurring alone, into a *bound form.*

"I have a good apartment, entrance hall, bedroom, kitchen," Goldstein's patient says. "There are also big apartments, only in the rear live bachelors." A more explicit form, the word group "unmarried people," could be substituted for "bachelors," but this one-word term has been selected by the speaker. When repeatedly asked what a bachelor was, the patient did not answer and was "apparently in distress." A reply like "A bachelor is an unmarried man" or "An unmarried man is a bachelor" would present an equational predication and thus a projection of a substitution set from the lexical code of the English language into the context of the given message. The equivalent terms become two correlated parts of the sentence and consequently are tied by contiguity. The patient was able to select the appropriate term "bachelor" when it was supported by the context of a customary conversation about "bachelor apartments," but was incapable of utilizing the substitution set "bachelor=unmarried man" as the topic of a sentence, because the ability for autonomous selection and substitution had been affected.

The same difficulty arises when the patient is asked to name an object pointed to or handled by the examiner. The aphasic with a defect in substitution will not supplement the pointing or handling gesture of the examiner with the name of the object pointed to. Instead of saying "This is (called) a pencil," he will merely add an elliptical note about its use: "To write." If one of the synonymic signs is present (as, for instance, the word "bachelor" or the pointing to the pencil), then the other sign (such as the phrase "unmarried man" or the word "pencil") becomes redundant and consequently superfluous. For the aphasic, both are mutually exclusive; if one is performed by the examiner, the patient will avoid its synonym: "I understand everything" will be his typical reaction. Likewise the picture of an object will cause suppression of its name: a verbal sign is supplanted by a pictorial sign, or, to quote Peirce, a *symbol* by an *icon.* When the picture of a compass was presented to a patient of Lotmar's, he responded: "Yes, it's a . . . I know what it belongs to, but I cannot recall the technical expression. . . . Yes . . . direction . . . to show direction . . . a magnet points to the north."[7]

Even simple repetition of a word uttered by the examiner seems to the patient unnecessarily redundant, and despite instructions received he is unable to repeat it. Told to repeat the word "no," Head's patient replied, "No, I don't know how to do it." While spontaneously using the word in the context of his answer ("No, I don't . . ."), he could not produce the purest form of equational predication, the tautology $a=a$: "*No* is *no*."

One of the important contributions of symbolic logic to the science of language is its emphasis on the distinction between *object language* and *metalanguage*. As Carnap states, "In order to speak *about* any *object language,* we need a *metalanguage*."[8] On these two different levels of language the same linguistic stock may be used; thus we may speak in English (as metalanguage) about English (as object language) and interpret English words and sentences by means of English synonyms, circumlocutions, and paraphrases. Obviously such operations, labeled *metalinguistic* by the logicians, are not their invention: far from being confined to the sphere of science, they prove to be an integral part of our customary linguistic activities. The participants in a dialogue often check whether both of them are using the same code. "Do you follow? Do you see what I mean?" the speaker questions, or the listener himself breaks in, "What do you mean?" Then, replacing the questionable sign with another sign from the same linguistic code, or with a whole group of code signs, the sender of the message seeks in this way to make it more accessible to the decoder.

The interpretation of one linguistic sign through another, in some respect homogeneous sign of the same language, is a metalinguistic operation which also plays an essential role in children's language learning. Recent observations have disclosed what a considerable and decisive part talk about language takes in the verbal behavior of preschool children.[9] Recourse to metalanguage is necessary both for the acquisition of language and for its normal functioning. The aphasic defect in the "capacity of naming" is

[7] F. Lotmar, "Zur Pathophysiologie der erschwerten Wortfindung bei Aphasischen," *Schweizer Archiv f. Neurologie u. Psychiatrie* (1933) , *35*:104.

[8] R. Carnap, *Meaning and Necessity,* Chicago, 1947, p. 4.

[9] See the remarkable studies of A. Gvozdev: "Nabljudenija nad jazykom malen'-kikh detej," *Russkij jazyk v sovetskoj shkole* (1929); *Usvoenie rebenkom zvukovoj storony russkogo jazyka,* Moscow, 1948; and *Formirovanie u rebenka grammaticheskogo stroja russkogo jazyka,* I-II, Moscow, 1949.

properly a loss of metalanguage. As a matter of fact, the examples of equational predication sought in vain from the patients cited above are metalinguistic propositions referring to the English language. Their explicit wording would be: "In the code that we use, the name of the indicated object is 'pencil' "; or "In the code we use, the word 'bachelor' and the circumlocution 'unmarried man' are equivalent."

Such an aphasic can neither switch from a word to its synonyms and circumlocutions nor give its *heteronyms*, i.e., equivalent expressions in other languages. Loss of a polyglot ability and confinement to one dialectal variety of a single language is a symptomatic manifestation of this disorder.

According to an old but recurrent bias, a single individual's way of a speaking at a given time, labeled *idiolect*, has been viewed as the only concrete linguistic reality. In the discussion of this concept the following objections were raised:

"Everyone, when speaking to a new person, tries, deliberately or involuntarily, to hit upon a common vocabulary: either to please or simply to be understood or, finally, to bring him out, he uses the terms of his addressee. There is no such thing as private property in language: everything is socialized. Verbal exchange, like any form of intercourse, requires at least two communicators, and idiolect proves to be a somewhat perverse fiction."[10]

This statement demands, however, one reservation: for an aphasic who has lost the capacity of code switching, his "idiolect" does become the sole linguistic reality. As long as he does not regard another's speech as a message addressed to him in his own verbal pattern, he feels, as a patient of Hemphil and Stengel expressed it: "I can hear you dead plain but I cannot get what you say. . . . I hear your voice but not the words. . . . It does not pronounce itself. . . ."[11] He considers the other's utterance to be either gibberish or at least in an unknown language.

As noted above, it is the external relation of contiguity which unites the constituents of a context, and the internal relation of similarity which underlies the substitution set. Hence in aphasia with impaired substitution and intact contexture, operations

[10] R. Jakobson, "Results of the Conference of Anthropologists and Linguists," *International Journal of American Linguistics* (1953), Supplement, *19*:15.

[11] R. E. Hemphil and E. Stengel, "Pure Word Deafness," *Journal of Neurological Psychiatry*, III (1940), p. 251-262.

involving similarity yield to those based on contiguity. It could be predicted that under these conditions any semantic grouping would be guided by spatial or temporal contiguity rather than by similarity. And actually Goldstein's tests justify such an expectation: a female patient of this type, when asked to list a few names of animals, disposed them in the same sequence in which she had seen them in the zoo; similarly, despite instructions to arrange certain objects according to color, size, and shape, she classified them on the basis of their spatial contiguity as home things, office materials, etc., and justified this grouping by a reference to a show window where "it does not matter what the things are," i.e., they do not have to be similar. The same patient was willing to name the primary hues—red, blue, green, and yellow—but declined to extend these names to the transitional varieties, since for her words had no capacity to assume additional meanings associated by similarity with their primary meaning.

One must agree with Goldstein's observation that patients of this type "grasped the words in their literal meaning but could not be brought to understand the metaphorical character of the same words." It would, however, be an unwarranted generalization to assume that figurative speech is altogether incomprehensible to them. From the two polar figures of speech, metaphor and metonymy, the latter, based on contiguity, is widely applied by aphasics whose selective capacities have been affected. "Fork" is substituted for "knife," "table" for "lamp," "smoke" for "pipe," "eat" for "toaster." A typical case is reported by Head: "When he failed to recall the name for 'black,' he described it as 'What you do for the dead'; this he shortened to 'dead.' "

Such metonymies may be characterized as projections from the line of a habitual context onto the line of substitution and selection: a sign (e.g., "fork") which usually occurs together with another sign (e.g., "knife") may be used instead of this sign. Phrases like "knife and fork," "table lamp," "to smoke a pipe," induced the metonymies "fork," "table," "smoke"; the relation between the use of an object (toast) and the means of its production underlies the metonymy *"eat"* for *"toaster."* "When does one wear black?" "When mourning for the dead": in place of naming the color, the cause of its traditional use is designated. The escape from sameness to contiguity is particularly striking in such cases as

Goldstein's patient who would answer with a metonymy when asked simply to repeat a given word and, for instance, would say "glass" for "window" and "heaven" for "God."

When the selective capacity is strongly impaired and the sense for combination at least partly preserved, then *contiguity* determines the patients' whole verbal behavior, and we may designate this type of aphasia *similarity disorder.*

4 Since 1864, the following was repeatedly pointed out in Hughlings Jackson's pioneer contributions to the modern study of language and language disturbances:

"It is not enough to say that speech consists of words. It consists of words referring to one another in a particular manner; and, without a proper interrelation of its parts, a verbal utterance would be a mere succession of names embodying no proposition. . . .

"Loss of speech is the loss of power to propositionize. . . . Speechlessness does not mean entire wordlessness."

The impairment of the ability to *propositionize,* or generally speaking, to combine simpler linguistic entities into more complex units, is actually confined to one type of aphasia, the opposite of the type just discussed. There is no *wordlessness,* since the entity preserved in most such cases is the *word,* which can be defined as the highest among the linguistic units compulsorily coded: i.e., we compose our own sentences and utterances out of the word stock supplied by the code.

This contexture-deficient aphasia, which could be termed *contiguity disorder,* diminishes the extent and variety of sentences. The syntactical rules organizing words into a higher unit are lost; this loss, called *agrammatism,* causes the degeneration of the sentence into a mere "word heap," to use Jackson's image. Word order becomes chaotic; the ties of grammatical coordination and subordination, whether concord or government, are dissolved. As might be expected, words endowed with purely grammatical functions, like conjunctions, prepositions, pronouns, and articles, are the first to disappear, whereas in the first type of aphasia we found them, quite naturally, the most resistant. The less a word depends grammatically on the context, the more likely it is to survive; substantives are the longest lived, then verbs. The first type of aphasia naturally displays the inverse order of destructibility.

The aphasia affecting contexture tends toward infantile, one-word sentences. Only a few longer, stereotyped, "ready-made" sentences manage to survive. In advanced cases of this disease each utterance is reduced to a single one-word sentence. While contexture disintegrates, the selective operation goes on. "To say what a thing is, is to say what it is like," Jackson notes. The patient confined to the substitution set (since contexture is deficient) deals with similarities, and his aproximate identifications are of a metaphorical nature, contrary to the metanymical ones familiar to the opposite type of aphasics. "Spyglass" for "microscope," "fire" for "gaslight," "dig up" for "recollect"—these are typical examples of such *quasi-metaphorical expressions,* as Jackson christened them, since in contradistinction to rhetoric or poetic metaphors they present no deliberate transfer of meaning.

In a normal language pattern, the *word* is at the same time both a constituent part of a superimposed context, the *sentence,* and itself a context superimposed on ever smaller constituents, *morphemes* (minimal units endowed with meaning) and *phonemes.* We have discussed the effect of contiguity disorder on the combination of words into higher units. The relationship between the word and its constituents reflects the same impairment, yet in a somewhat different way. A typical feature of agrammatism is the abolishment of inflection: there appear such *unmarked* categories as the infinitive in place of diverse finite verbal forms, and, in languages with declension, the nominative instead of all the oblique cases. These defects are due partly to the elimination of government and concord, partly to the loss of dissociation into stem and desinence. Finally, a paradigm (in particular a set of grammatical cases such as "he—his—him," or of tenses such as "he votes—he voted") presents the same semantic content from different viewpoints associated with each other by contiguity; so there is one more stimulus for aphasics with a deficiency in contiguity to dismiss such sets.

Also, as a rule, words derived from the same root, such as "grant—grantor—grantee," are semantically related by contiguity. Either the patients under discussion are inclined to drop the derivative words, or the combination of a root with a derivational suffix and even a compound of two words become irresolvable for them. Patients who understood and uttered such compounds as "Thanksgiving" or "Battersea" but were unable to grasp or to say "thanks" and "giving" or "batter" and "sea" have often been cited. As long as the sense of derivation is alive, so that this process is still used for creating innovations in the code, there can be observed a tendency toward oversimplification and automatism: if the derivative word constitutes a semantic unit which cannot be entirely inferred from the meaning of its components, the *Gestalt* is misunderstood. Thus the Russian word *mokr-ica* signifies "woodlouse," but a Russian aphasic interpreted it as "something humid," especially "humid weather," since the root *mokr-* means "humid" and the suffix *-ica* designates a carrier of the given property, as in *nelepica,* "something absurd," *svetlica,* "light room," *temnica,* "dungeon" (dark room).

When, before the Second World War, phonemics was the most controversial area in the science of language, doubts were expressed by some linguists as to whether phonemes really play an autonomous part in our verbal behavior. It was even suggested that the meaningful *(significative)* units of the linguistic code, such as words and perhaps morphemes, are the minimal entities with which we actually deal in a speech event, whereas the merely *distinctive* units, such as phonemes, are an artificial construct to facilitate the scientific description and analysis of a language. This view, which was stigmatized by Sapir as "the reverse of realistic,"[12] remains, however, perfectly valid with respect to a certain pathological case: in one type of aphasia which sometimes was labeled *atactic,* the word is the sole linguistic unit preserved. The patient has only a total, undissociable image of any familiar word, and either all other sound sequences are alien and inscrutable to him or he merges them into familiar words by disregarding their phonetic aberrations. One of Goldstein's patients "perceived some words, but . . . the vowels and consonants of which they consisted were not perceived." A French aphasic recognized, understood, repeated, and spontaneously produced the word *café,* "coffee," or *pavé,* "roadway," but was unable to grasp, discern, or repeat such nonsensical sequences as *féca, faké, kéfa, pafé.* None of these difficulties exists for a normal French-speaking listener as long as the

12 E. Sapir, "The Psychological Reality of Phonemes," *Selected Writings,* Berkeley and Los Angeles, 1949, pp. 46 ff.

sound sequences and their components fit the French phonemic pattern. Such a listener may even apprehend these sequences as words unknown to him but plausibly belonging to the French vocabulary and presumably different in meaning, since they differ from each other either in the order of their phonemes or in the phonemes themselves.

If an aphasic becomes unable to decompose the word into its phonemic constituents, his control over its construction weakens, and perceptible damages in phonemes and their combinations easily follow. The gradual regression of the sound pattern in aphasics regularly reverses the order of children's phonemic acquisitions. This regression involves an inflation of homonyms and a decrease of vocabulary. If this twofold—phonemic and lexical—disablement progresses farther, the patient relapses into the initial phases of infants' linguistic development or even to their prelingual stage: he faces *aphasia universalis,* the total loss of the power to use or apprehend speech.

The separateness of the two functions—one distinctive and the other significative—is a peculiar feature of language as compared to other semiotic systems. There arises a conflict between these two levels of language when the aphasic deficient in contexture exhibits a tendency to abolish the hierarchy of linguistic units and to reduce their scale to a single level. The last level to remain is either a class of significative values, the *word,* as in the cases touched upon, or a class of distinctive values, the *phoneme.* In the latter case the patient is still able to identify, distinguish, and reproduce phonemes but loses the capacity to do the same with words. In an intermediate case, words are identified, distinguished, and reproduced; according to Goldstein's keen formulation, they "may be grouped as known but not understood." Here the word loses its normal significative function and assumes the purely distinctive function which normally pertains to the phoneme.

5   The varieties of aphasia are numerous and diverse, but all of them oscillate between the two polar types just described. Every form of aphasic disturbance consists in some impairment, whether severe or not, either of the faculty for selection and substitution or of that for combination and contexture. The former affliction involves a deterioration of metalinguistic operations, while the latter damages the capacity

for maintaining the hierarchy of linguistic units. The relation of similarity is suppressed in the former, the relation of contiguity in the latter type of aphasia. Metaphor is alien to the similarity disorder and metonymy to the contiguity disorder.

The development of a discourse may take place along two different semantic lines: one topic may lead to another either through their similarity or through their contiguity. The *metaphorical way* would be the most appropriate term for the first case and the *metonymical way* for the second, since they find their most condensed expression in metaphor and metonymy respectively. In aphasia one or the other of these two processes is reduced or totally blocked, an effect which makes the study of aphasia particularly illuminating for the linguist. In normal verbal behavior both processes are continually operative, but careful observation will reveal that, under the influence of a cultural pattern, personality, and verbal style, preference is given to one of the two processes over the other.

In a well-known psychological test, children are confronted with some noun and told to utter the first verbal response that comes into their heads. In this experiment two opposite linguistic predilections are invariably exhibited: the response is intended either as a substitute for or as a complement to the stimulus. In the latter case the stimulus and the response together form a proper syntactic construction, most usually a sentence. These two types of reaction have been labeled *substitutive* and *predicative*.

To the stimulus "hut" one response was "burnt out"; another, "is a poor little house." Both reactions are predicative; but the first creates a purely narrative context, while in the second there is a double connection with the subject "hut": on the one hand a positional (namely, syntactic) contiguity, and on the other a semantic similarity.

The same stimulus produced the following substitutive reactions: the tautology "hut"; the synonyms "cabin" and "hovel"; the antonym "palace"; and the metaphors "den" and "burrow." The capacity of two words to replace one another is an instance of positional similarity, and in addition all these responses are linked to the stimulus by semantic similarity (or contrast). Metonymical responses to the same stimulus, such as "thatch," "litter," or "poverty," combine and contrast the positional similarity with semantic contiguity.

In manipulating these two kinds of connection (similarity and contiguity) in both their aspects (positional and semantic)—selecting, combining, and ranking them—an individual exhibits his personal style, his verbal predilections and preferences.

In verbal art the interaction of these two elements becomes especially pronounced. Rich material for the study of this relationship is to be found in those verse patterns which require a compulsory *parallelism* between adjacent lines, for example, in Biblical poetry or in the West Finnic and to some extent the Russian oral traditions. This provides an objective criterion of what in the given speech community acts as a correspondence. Since on any verbal level—morphemic, lexical, syntactic, and phraseological —either of these two relations (similarity and contiguity) may appear—and each in either of two aspects—an impressive range of possible configurations is created. Either of the two gravitational poles may prevail. In Russian lyrical songs, for example, metaphorical constructions predominate, while in the heroic epics the metonymical way is preponderant.

In poetry there are various motives which determine the choice between these alternatives. The primacy of the metaphorical way in the literary schools of romanticism and symbolism has been generally acknowledged, but it is still insufficiently realized that it is the predominance of metonymy which underlies and actually predetermines the so-called "realistic" trend, which belongs to an intermediary stage between the decline of romanticism and the rise of symbolism and is opposed to both. Following the path of contiguous relationships, the realistic author metonymically digresses from the plot to the atmosphere and from the characters to the setting in space and time. He is fond of synecdochic details. In the scene of Anna Karenina's suicide artistic attention is focused on the heroine's handbag; and in *War and Peace* the synecdoches "hair on the upper lip" and "naked shoulders" are used to stand for the female characters to whom these features belong.

The alternating predominance of one or the other of these two processes is by no means confined to verbal art. The same oscillation occurs in sign systems other than language. A salient example from the history of painting is the manifestly metonymical orientation of cubism, where the object is transformed into a set of synecdoches; the surrealist painters responded with a patently metaphorical attitude. Ever since the productions of D. W. Griffith the art of the cinema, with its highly developed capacity for changing the angle, perspective, and focus of "shots," has broken with the tradition of the theater and arrayed an unprecedented variety of synecdochic "close-ups" and metonymical "setups" in general. In such motion pictures as the films of Charlie Chaplin and Eisenstein[13] these devices in turn were overlayed by a novel, metaphorical "montage" with its "lap dissolves"—the filmic similes.[14]

The bipolar structure of language (or other semiotic systems) and in aphasia the fixation on one of these poles to the exclusion of the other require systematic comparative study. The retention of either of these alternatives in the two types of aphasia must be confronted with the predominance of the same pole in certain styles, personal habits, current fashions, etc. A careful analysis and comparison of these phenomena with the whole syndrome of the corresponding type of aphasia is an imperative task for joint research by experts in psychopathology, psychology, linguistics, poetics, and semiotics, the general science of signs. The dichotomy here discussed appears to be of primal significance and consequence for the whole verbal behavior and for human behavior in general.

To obtain a glimpse into the comparative research suggested, an example may be cited from a Russian folk tale which employs parallelism as a comic device: "Thomas is a bachelor; Jeremiah is unmarried" (*Fomá khólost; Erjóma nezhenát*). Here the predicates in the two parallel clauses are associated by similarity: they are in fact synonymous. The subjects of both clauses are masculine proper names and hence morphologically similar, while on the other hand they designate two contiguous heroes of the same tale, created to perform identical actions and thus to justify the use of synonymous pairs of predicates. A somewhat modified version of the same construction occurs in a familiar wedding song in which each of the wedding guests is addressed in turn by his first name and patronymic: "Gleb is a bachelor; Ivanovich is unmarried." While both predicates here are again synonyms, the relationship

[13] Cf. his striking essay "Dickens, Griffith, and We": S. Eisenstein, Izbrannye stat'i, Moscow, 1956, 153 ff.
[14] I ventured a few sketchy remarks on the metonymical way in verbal art ("Pro realizm u mystectvi," *Vaplite*, Kharkov [1927], No. 2, pp. 163-170; "Randbemerkungen zur Prosa des Dichters Pasternak," *Slavische Rundschau* [1953], 7:357-374), in painting ("Futurism," *Iskusstvo*, Moscow, Aug. 2, 1919), and in motion pictures ("Úpadek filmu?" *Listy pro umění a kritiku*, Prague [1933], *1*:45-49), but the crucial problem of the two polar ways awaits a close investigation.

between the two subjects is changed: both are proper names designating the same man and are normally used contiguously as a mode of polite address.

In the quotation from the folk tale the two parallel clauses refer to two separate facts, the marital status of Thomas and the similar status of Jeremiah. In the verse from the wedding song, however, the two clauses are synonymous: they redundantly reiterate the celibacy of the same hero, splitting him into two verbal hypostases.

The Russian novelist Gleb Ivanovich Uspenskij (1840-1902) in the last years of his life suffered from a mental illness involving a speech disorder. His first name and patronymic, Gleb Ivanovich, traditionally combined in polite intercourse, for him split into two distinct names designating two separate beings: Gleb was endowed with all his virtues, while Ivanovich, the name relating the son to the father, naturally became the incarnation of all Uspenskij's vices. The linguistic aspect of this split personality is the patient's inability to use two symbols for the same thing, and it is thus a similarity disorder. Since the similarity disorder is bound up with the metonymical way, an examination of the literary manner Uspenskij has employed as a young writer takes on particular interest. And the study of Anatolij Kamegulov, who analyzed Uspenskij's style, bears out our theoretical expectations. He shows that Uspenskij had a particular penchant for metonymy, and especially for synecdoche, and that he carried it so far that "the reader is crushed by the multiplicity of detail unloaded on him in a limited verbal space, and is physically unable to grasp the whole, so that the portrait is often lost."[15]

To be sure, the metonymical style of Uspenskij is obviously prompted by the prevailing literary canon, late nineteenth-century realism; but in the personal habit of Gleb Ivanovich this tendency was carried to extremes and left its mark upon the verbal aspect of his mental illness, thereby demonstrating the primal significance of the cardinal dichotomy in language.

[15] A. Kamegulov, *Stil' Gleba Uspenskogo*, Leningrad, 1930, pp. 65, 145. One of such disintegrated portraits cited in the monograph: "From underneath an ancient straw cap with a black spot on its shield, there peeked two braids resembling the tusks of a wild boar; a chin grown fat and pendulous definitively spread over the greasy collars of the calico dicky and in a thick layer on the coarse collar of the canvas coat, firmly buttoned at the neck. From below this coat to the eyes of the observer there protruded massive hands with a ring, which had eaten into the fat finger, a cane with a copper top, a significant bulge of the stomach and the presence of very broad pants, almost of muslin quality, in the broad ends of which hid the toes of the boots."

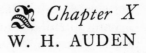
SQUARES AND OBLONGS

"There is a square; there is an oblong. The players take the square and place it upon the oblong. They place it very accurately; they make a perfect dwelling-place. Very little is left outside. The structure is now visible; what is inchoate is here stated; we are not so various or so mean; we have made oblongs and stood them upon squares. This is our consolation."[1]

Man belongs to two orders of being, the natural and the historical, the first of which may be subdivided into the inorganic and the organic. As a being composed of matter he is subject to the laws of physics and chemistry; as a biological organism he is involved in the cyclical organic process of birth, reproduction, and decay; as a conscious being who makes choices he is responsible for his history, social and personal. Consequently he is concerned with two classes of events, natural events and historical events, which form the subject matter of the sciences and the arts respectively.

Considered as a verbal system, the poem is a natural not a historical object. The laws of prosody and syntax are to it what the laws of physics and chemistry are to the physical universe. When he writes, the poet has to presuppose that the history of language is at an end, that the meaning and metrical value of the words he employs will not alter so that his poem becomes unintelligible or unmusical.

There is only one physical universe, but, in every language, a very large number of verbal universes are possible. The nature of any language, however, imposes certain limitations and preferences. Thus, in English, unrhymed five-foot iambics please the ear, unrhymed four-foot iambics do not.

[1] *The Waves*, Virginia Woolf.

The final poetic order of a poem is the outcome of a dialectical struggle between the feelings and the verbal system. As a society, the verbal system is actively coercive upon the feelings it is attempting to embody; what it cannot embody truthfully, it excludes. As a potential community, the feelings are passively resistant to all claims of the system to embody them which they do not recognize as just; they decline all unjust persuasions. As members of crowds, every feeling competes with every other, demanding inclusion and a dominant position to which it is not necessarily entitled, and every word demands that the system shall modify itself for its sake, that a special exception shall be made in its case.

To the degree that a poem is successful, society and community form one common order, and the system may justly love itself because the feelings which it embodies form a true community loving each other and it.

In a poem, as distinct from many other verbal societies, meaning and being are identical. Like an image in a mirror, a poem is a pseudo-person, i.e., it has uniqueness and addresses the reader face to face or person to person, but, like all natural beings and unlike historical beings, it cannot lie. One cannot say of a poem that it is true or false, for one does not have to consider anything but itself to discover whether or no it is a true order. If unfreedom or disorder are present, the poem itself reveals this on inspection. We may be, and frequently are, mistaken about a poem, but the cause is our own self-deception, not the poem.

In writing a poem, the poet can work in two ways. Starting with an intuitive idea of the kind of community he desires to call into being, he may work backwards in search of the system which will embody it most justly, or, starting with a certain system, he may work forward in search of the community which that system can most truthfully embody. In practice, he nearly always works simultaneously in both directions, modifying his conception of the ultimate nature of the community at the immediate suggestions of the system and modifying the system in response to his idea, as it becomes increasingly clear, of the future needs of the community.

Classical and Romantic are misleading terms for the two poetic parties, the Aristocratic and the Democratic, which have always existed, and to either of which every poet belongs, though he may switch his party allegiance during his poetic career or, on some specific issue, refuse to obey his Party Whip.

The Aristocratic Principle as regards the poetic subject: No material shall be made the subject of a poem which poetry cannot transform into its own universe. It defends poetry against didacticism and journalism.

The Democratic Principle as regards the poetic subject: No material shall be excluded from becoming the subject of a poem which can be poetically transformed. It defends poetry against limited or false notions of what is "poetic."

The Aristocratic Principle as regards poetic treatment: No irrelevant aspects of a given subject shall be expressed in the poem which treats it. It defends poetry against formlessness and diffuseness.

The Democratic Principle as regards poetic treatment: No relevant aspects of a given subject shall remain unexpressed in the poem which treats it. It defends poetry against academic aridity.

Any chosen metrical scheme is a law—for the poet and of the poem. Once he has chosen it, the poet is on his honor to find such words as can conform to its demands. He cannot scan "river" as an iamb or make it a three-syllable word.

A verbal system cannot be selected completely arbitrarily, nor can one say that any given system is absolutely necessary. The poet searches for the one which seems to him to impose the most just obligations on the feelings. Ought always implies Can, so that a system whose claims cannot be met must be scrapped, but the poet has to beware of accusing the system of injustice when the real fault is his incompetence and laziness.

As a natural object, the verbal system of a poem belongs to the organic rather than the inorganic order, i.e., instead of the mathematically exact symmetry of the inorganic, it is rhythmical, its symmetries are perceptible but unmeasurable. Seen from a certain distance, the features of the human face appear to be symmetrically arranged and constant in size and position, so that a face with a nose a foot long or a left eye only would appear monstrous. But, seen at close quarters, this regularity disappears, and the size and position of the features is different in every case. If a face could exist in which the symmetry was mathematically exact, it, too, would appear monstrous.

So with the metrical structure of a poem. If blank verse could be written so that every foot in every line was identical, all accented syllables carrying identically the same weight of accent and all unaccented syllables of exactly the same lightness, the poem would sound intolerable to the ear.

The process of poetic composition is a work of civilizing. A barbaric horde of emotions which cannot rule themselves are transformed into a just, loving, and self-ruling polis. Unless, however, there is already present in the initial horde a nucleus of self-rule, an idea, a phrase, the poet has no point from which to start. The degree of justice and self-rule possible in a poem is very much higher than in any historical political society. Every good poem is very nearly a Utopia.

In the earlier stages of composition, the poet has to act like a Greek tyrant; the decision to write this phrase rather than that must be largely his, for the demands of the poem are as yet inarticulate or contradictory. As composition proceeds, the poem begins to take over the job of ruling itself; the transeunt rule of the poet gets weaker and weaker until, in the final stages, he is like the elected representative of a democracy whose duty it is to listen to and execute the demands of the poem, which now knows exactly what it wishes to be. On completion, the poem rules itself immanently, and the poet is dismissed into private life.

The writing of a short poem is a more democratic process than the writing of a long one. As in a small political society, the demands of the material make themselves more directly heard and are more easily reconciled with each other. In a long poem, as in a large political society, direct rule by the material is impossible, and the poet is, at best, a wise and responsible representative who plans and legislates on its bewildered and grumbling behalf and, at worst, a dictator who establishes his empire by force.

All works of art are commissioned, in that the idea which stimulates an artist to create a given work "comes" to him. Among those works which are failures because uninspired, the number of self-commissioned works is probably greater than the number commissioned by patrons.

If works of art could be created by "inspiration" alone, i.e., automatically in a trance, artistic creation would be so boring or so unpleasant that only substantial rewards in money or social prestige could induce a man to become an artist.

The poet has to wrestle with the Muse as Jacob had to wrestle with the Angel at the ford, before She will bless him with truth. For those who are willing to believe everything She says, She has nothing but contempt, which She shows by telling them lies.

Artistic judgment is the capacity to distinguish between blind chance and providence.

"When I was writing the chorus in G minor, I suddenly dipped my pen into the medicine bottle instead of the ink; I made a blot, and when I dried it with sand [blotting paper was not invented then], it took the form of a natural, which instantly gave me the idea of the effect which the change from G minor to G major would make, and to this blot all the effect—if any—is due" (Rossini to Louis Engel).

All those whose success in life depends, neither upon a job which satisfies some specific and constant natural need like a farmer, nor upon inborn skill and acquired knowledge like a surgeon, but upon "inspiration," the lucky hazard of ideas, live "by their wits." Every "original" scientist or artist has something slightly shady about him like a gambler or a medium.

A poet is, before everything else, a person who is passionately in love with language. Whether this love is a sign of his poetic gift or the gift itself—falling in love is something which happens to a person, not something he chooses—it is impossible to say.

❧ Chapter XI
CHARLES W. MORRIS

MYSTICISM AND ITS LANGUAGE

Let us begin with words that have a familiar ring: "We generally think that 'A is A' is absolute, and that the proposition 'A is not A' or 'A is B' is unthinkable. We have never been able to break through these conditions of the understanding; they have been too imposing. But . . . words are words and no more. When words cease to correspond with facts it is time for us to part with words and return to facts."

It would certainly not be difficult to imagine Alfred Korzybski speaking thus against the "law of identity," insisting that the word is not the thing—all the while, with his characteristic gesture, dropping a matchbox from hand to hand. But in fact the words quoted are those of Daisetz Teitaro Suzuki, written in the 1920's and reprinted in his *Introduction to Zen Buddhism* in 1949.

In their attitude toward language, the general semanticist Korzybski and the Zen Buddhist Suzuki have indeed much in common. Both are aware of the inadequacies and pitfalls of conceptualization; both admonish man to master his symbols rather than being mastered by them; both believe that this attitude to language releases human spontaneity, wholeness, and sanity.

And yet there is a difference of emphasis between the general semanticist and the Zen Buddhist in the use of words which is of great interest and which deserves to be brought to the focus of our attention. The tendency of the follower of Korzybski (and indeed of most students of the theory of signs) is to favor the modes of expression of modern science. He sees the task of language to be an ever more adequate mapping of the world, and looks to science to supply this language. The general semanticist talks, or wishes to talk, as a scientist. And he gives the impression at times of believing that all men at all times should talk the same way.

The characteristic stress of the Zen Buddhist is quite different. There is certainly no general opposition to science or to scientific language in Zen; science is seen as performing its own unique and necessary function. Zen, however, insists that there is an important kind of experience (*satori*, Zen experience) of which the language of paradox and contradiction is the natural, appropriate, and necessary form of expression. As an example of this language Suzuki, in his *Introduction*, gives the following Zen utterance, an esteemed Gatha from the sixth century by Shan-hui:

> Empty-handed I go, and behold the spade is in my hands:
> I walk on foot, and yet on the back of an ox I am riding;
> When I pass over the bridge,
> Lo, the water floweth not, but the bridge doth flow.

Of such language, and the underlying experience which it expresses, Suzuki writes as follows: "If the system of logic that has been in circulation is found inadequate to explain away the *satori* experience and *mondo* that has grown up from it, the philosopher will have to invent a new system of thinking to fit the experience, and not conversely, that is, to disprove the empirical facts by means of abstract logic" (*Living by Zen*, p. 118). It is my belief that the "new logic" which Suzuki demands is furnished by the general theory of signs (semiotic), and that in terms of this theory we can get even today some insight into the nature of mysticism (at least in its Zen form) and its characteristic form of expression. Our problems are as follows: Why is it natural to speak at times in terms of paradox and contradiction? What experience calls for this mode of expression? What is the relation of the language of mysticism to the language of science? Mysticism as experience and as discourse has usually been approached theologically and philosophically; we shall attempt to view it as a complex sign process amenable to analysis in terms of a theory of signs.

As a preliminary to such analysis, it is necessary to remind ourselves that signs occur at various levels of complexity. In *Signs, Language, and Behavior* the topic is treated in detail. For present purposes it is sufficient to distinguish three main levels: pre-language signs, language signs, and post-language signs. As here viewed, a language is a system of signs which have a common core of signification to a number of interpreters, each of which can produce the signs; a language sign is any sign in a language. In the case of language signs the producer of the signs is an interpreter of the signs just as is the person or persons to whom the sign is addressed.

A pre-language sign is a sign which is not a language sign and which does not require the operation of language to gain its signification. The buzzer which for a dog signifies food at a certain place is such a pre-language sign. So are the signs to which a child responds before it has learned to talk.

A post-language sign is a sign which is not a language sign, but which requires the operation of language to gain its signification. An example is the reader's perception of a star, that is, the interpretation of a spot of light as a vast glowing body far away; this perception results from the fact that one has heard about or read about the astronomical theories developed in Western culture.

This distinction between pre-language sign and post-language sign is, I believe, of the utmost importance, and its elaboration may well provide one of the most important instruments of the science of signs. I am convinced that the notion of post-language sign is essential to the understanding of art, myths, magic, the totem, religion, prestige, race prejudice, and the complex types of perception. But neither the elaboration of the notion nor its diversity of application can be undertaken here. We must limit ourselves to the question of whether the conception of the post-language sign throws light upon the experience of the mystic and his language.

We need one further technical term. Let us introduce the term "interpretant" to name the effect on the interpreter which is necessary for something to be a sign. The interpretant corresponds to the term "idea" of everyday speech; here it will be assumed that an interpretant is, or at least involves, a neural process of such nature that when it is aroused the interpreter of the sign is disposed to react to certain kinds of things in certain kinds of ways.

The social genesis of language makes possible (as George H. Mead has shown in *Mind, Self, and Society*) a complex type of experience which he has called "taking the role of the other." Through language one can symbolize times and places other than the here and now of the speaker, and persons and things other than the speaker himself. Further, one can signify oneself as being those persons and things at other times and places, and thus call out in oneself the tendency to act as they would act. Through such role taking one can even react back upon oneself from the standpoint of another; it is in this way, Mead argued, that one becomes conscious of oneself as an object. For our purposes, however, the point to be stressed is that in this socially derived process of role taking one can become symbolically an object other than the self of the here and now: can symbolically be at a remote past before the present state of the world appeared and almost simultaneously be at a remote future when the present state of the world will have passed away; can symbolically roam the widest distances in space; can symbolically be a sun, a stone, a flower, a beetle, a drop of water, and the sea. And yet, all along, existentially one remains oneself, in one's own here and now.

Such complex role-taking processes seem to be essential to the mystical experience. To be sure, no one of them taken singly need have this quality: to imagine oneself on the moon looking down upon oneself on the earth may be interesting, but it is hardly mystical. Suppose, however, that the interpretants of these various symbolic processes are aroused simultaneously or nearly simultaneously. If the interpretants of signs are (or involve) neural processes, then (as Kenneth Burke has noticed in *The Rhetoric of Motives*) there is no reason why the interpretants of contradictory signs cannot be aroused simultaneously, though the corresponding reactions could not simultaneously be performed. In this way one can be symbolically both here and not here, in the past and in the future; can be both the fish that swims and the gull that dives. It is suggested that this simultaneous, or nearly simultaneous, arousal of the complex and often contradictory role-taking processes made possible by language constitutes an essential part of the mystical experience.

This does not mean that at the time of the experience the mystic is talking out loud—or even to himself. Here the notion of the post-language symbol comes into the account. For, as in the case of the perception of a star, an event within the body, a sound or gesture or posture, an object in the environment can become invested with the signification of these complex linguistic role-taking processes. The techniques of Yoga, the repetition of sounds such as *Aum* or *Namu-Amida-Butsu,* meditation before an image—these are examples of the ways in which post-language signs may be built up. When built up these signs tend to arouse the interpretants of a whole host of designative, appraisive, and prescriptive linguistic utterances which have occurred in their presence. Talking is necessary for their development but not for their subsequent operation. When talking ceases the post-language signs reverberate the meanings which language conferred upon them in their formation.

The mystic, having had his experience and "returned to himself," usually continues to talk. And the words which he utters bear the imprint both of his experience and of the conceptualizations dominant in the culture or the tradition in which he lives.

In so far as his words are wrung out of him by his experience they constitute what may be called the primary language of mysticism. This is much the same from culture to culture and from age to age. It everywhere employs a language of paradox and contradiction. If the symbolic interpretation which has been given of the mystical experience is at all correct, then this is the "natural" language to express and to evoke this experience. For if contradictory interpretants are aroused they of course tend to call out their corresponding contradictory signs. And if one desires to evoke an experience involving contradictory interpretants nothing is as effective as the use of contradictory signs. It is as appropriate for the mystic to talk the way he does as it is for a hungry man to think of food or for a scientist to seek to give his data quantitative form.

The secondary language of mysticism arises from the mystic's attempt to explicate for himself and for others his experience and his primary signs. And here the trouble begins. For the explication must be made in terms of some conceptual system, and this will vary from culture to culture and tradition to tradition. It is one of the unique merits of Zen to have recognized the relativity of these conceptual systems, and to refuse to commit itself finally to any one of them. Zen, when most fully itself, has no doctrine and no authoritative text.

Suzuki's writings are examples of the secondary language of mysticism, and of Zen's freedom in the use of symbols at this level.

In his earlier books he did not use terms from the Christian or Vedantist traditions; in *Living by Zen* symbols from both of these traditions are prominent. Suzuki is here true to words I once heard him utter: "When we recognize the inadequacy of all symbols— then we are free to use all symbols." This must be granted. But it should not cause us to forget the distinction between the primary language of mysticism and the various secondary languages used to discuss the primary language and its underlying experience.

Zen's refusal to commit itself to any one doctrinal interpretation of the "Zen experience" has but carried to its proper conclusion the widespread sense of the inadequacy of the secondary languages of mysticism. If the primary language of mysticism is characterized by paradox and contradiction, the secondary language is characterized by the use of negations. The mystic attempts to explain what he has experienced, tries to translate back into language the signification of the post-language signs which he has attained. But any propositions which he utters are felt to be partial and inadequate. And rightly so, since the complex network of symbolic processes which he is attempting to translate included contradictions. Positions in space and time were symbolized, but no single position; selves were symbolized, but also non-selves; minute things, but also vast things; good things, but also terrible things. So the whole of the experience is not characterizable in positive noncontradictory terms.

If one tries to remove the contradiction by saying that the mystic is *existentially* in the here and now and only *symbolically* not here and now (which indeed is what we have said), this may be true, but it is not a translation of the primary language or a description of the mystic's experience. Finally the mystic resorts to negations: that which he is trying to talk about is said to be nameless, to be neither temporal nor nontemporal, neither conscious nor nonconscious, neither this nor that. But since the primary experience was intensely positive, such negations are unsatisfactory symbols. And so the mystic in the end confesses the inadequacies of his secondary language and returns to his primary signs and experiences. This, as Zen alone has clearly realized, is as it should be. The primary language of mysticism cannot be "translated" into other terms. In attempting to remove its contradictions one is left with partial affirmations or mere negations.

The preceding comments do not pretend to be a full-fledged theory of mysticism; they aim merely to suggest the relevance of the theory of signs for such a theory. It may be well, however, to indicate several directions in which the foregoing argument might be expanded.

That the mystical experience, at least as found in Zen, does involve processes of symbolic role taking is suggested by the words of Shan-hui which were quoted. But it is also suggested by the secondary language of mysticism. Suzuki in many places alludes to the active "mentation" involved in *satori*. Thus he writes: "When all forms of mental activity are swept away clean from the field of consciousness, leaving the mind like the sky devoid of every speck of cloud, a mere broad expanse of blue, Dhyana is said to have reached its perfection. This may be called ecstasy or trance, but it is not Zen. In Zen there must be *satori:* there must be a general mental upheaval which destroys the old accumulations of intellection and lays down the foundation for a new life; there must be the awakening of a new sense which will review the old things from a hitherto undreamed-of angle of observation" (*Introduction to Zen Buddhism*, p. 96; cf. *Living by Zen*, pp. 193-194).

The recognition of the role of symbolic processes in the mystical experience may also help to explain why the mystic so consistently, and so confusedly, claims for his experience "truth" and "knowledge." Symbols are "of" something; they have references; post-language symbols carry the meanings of the linguistic propositions by which they were constituted. This suggests that the symbols of the mystic, or the symbolic aspects of the mystical experience, are knowledge about something. And yet these symbols lead to no specific predictions, and no scientifically relevant propositions may be deduced from them. This suggests that the mystic has no knowledge in the sense in which the scientist has knowledge.

The complexity of this situation is adumbrated by Suzuki as follows: "*Satori* may be regarded in one sense as a sort of knowledge, because it gives information regarding something. But there is a qualitative difference between *satori* and knowledge, they are essentially incommensurable. Knowledge gives only a partial idea of the thing known, and this from an external point of view, whereas *satori* is the knowledge of the whole thing, of the thing in its totality, not as an aggregate of parts, but as something indivisible, complete in itself" (*Living by Zen,* p. 151). I suggest that the mystic's use of the term "knowledge" covers the process of identification involved in symbolic role taking, while the scientist's use of the term is limited to the verified predictive content of symbols. Symbols, and so mental processes, are involved in both cases, but the use is different; in one case a complex congeries of symbolic processes is lived through consummatively, and in the other case specific symbols in propositional form function predictively.

Nevertheless, in the above quotation Suzuki does say that *satori* "gives information regarding something." What is this "something"? The mystic would tend to say, information about God, Tao, Brahman, Nirvana, the Infinite, that is, to talk as if the mystical experience had "an object." And yet Suzuki himself bears witness to the problem involved: *satori,* he writes, is "not one single experience to be differentiated from others" (*Living by Zen,* p. 152). This suggests that there is no single and unique object, one among others or one inclusive of all others, which is confronted in the mystical experience. Perhaps to think otherwise is to confuse the experience with talking about it, thus making it an "object" of other sign processes. Suzuki states that "it is the mind as a whole that has *satori;* it is an act of perception, no doubt, but it is a perception of the highest order" (*Introduction to Zen Buddhism,* p. 109). We have seen, however, that "perception" is a general term and applies to the levels of both pre-language and post-language signs. The (post-language) perception of a star brings forward no new sensory datum but only a higher-level process of symbolization; in the same way it is possible that the mystic "sees" no new object but perceives all familiar things in a new way. Much of the literature of Zen is certainly compatible with such an interpretation of mystical "intuition" or "perception."

Let us conclude by emphasizing the basic point of these fragmentary comments on mysticism and its language. It has been suggested that the mystical experience is not an emotional frenzy or the simple confrontation of a unique object, but rather the undergoing of a complex and contradictory set of linguistic role-taking processes which finally eventuate in post-language symbols carrying the meaning of this set of symbols.

Having undergone the process of symbolic identification with everything available to him, a person is a changed person; symbolically he is no longer merely one object among objects. As one object existing among other objects he is small and fragile, empty-handed, on foot, walking on a bridge. But having roamed afield symbolically, he rides the cosmic ox, and digs with the cosmic spade; and as the water, he sees the flowing bridge. The commonest things are henceforth perceived at both the old and the new levels: a spade is a spade, water is water, and a bridge a bridge; and yet they are more than they were, for they now are seen through symbolic eyes enlarged by cosmic wandering.

This experience is liberating. Einstein has testified to this, and has even spoken of it as "the sower of all true art and science." The psychologist A. H. Maslow has found it to be present in some degree in persons of maximum creativity and "psychological health."[1] It is available in varying degrees to all persons, regardless of their scientific and philosophical commitments. It is in no way incompatible with science, and it does not take the place of science. Nor can science take its place, or negate it. Semantically it is clean. Humanly it is finely, and finally, satisfying.

[1] "Self-Actualizing People," *Personality*, Symposium No. 1, 1950.

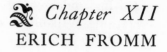

Chapter XII
ERICH FROMM

SYMBOLIC LANGUAGE OF DREAMS

One of the current definitions of a symbol is that it is "something that stands for something else." This definition is too general to be useful, unless we can be more specific with regard to the crucial question concerning the nature of the connection between symbol and that which it symbolizes. While there are many approaches to this question, I want to suggest the following differentiation between kinds of symbol as one most suited to guide us in our understanding of symbolic language as used in dreams.

We can differentiate between three kinds of symbols: the *conventional,* the *accidental,* and the *universal* symbol.

The *conventional* symbol is the best known of the three, since we employ it in everyday language. If we see the word "table" or hear the sound "table," the letters *t-a-b-l-e* stand for something else. They stand for the thing "table" that we see, touch, and use. What is the connection between the *word* "table" and the *thing* "table"? Is there any inherent relationship between them? Obviously not. The *thing* table has nothing to do with the *sound* table, and the only reason the word symbolizes the thing is the convention of calling this particular thing by a name. We learn this connection as children by the repeated experience of hearing the word in reference to the thing until a lasting association is formed so that we don't have to think to find the right word.

There are some words, however, in which the association is not only conventional. When we say "phooey," for instance, we make with our lips a movement of dispelling the air quickly. It is an expression of disgust in which our mouths participate. By this quick expulsion of air we imitate and thus express our intention

188

to expel something, to get it out of our system. In this case, as in some others, the symbol has an inherent connection with the feeling it symbolizes. But even if we assume that originally many or even all words had their origins in some such inherent connection between symbol and the symbolized, most words no longer have this meaning for us when we learn a language.

Words are not the only illustration for conventional symbols, although they are the most frequent and best-known ones. Pictures also can be conventional symbols. A flag, for instance, may stand for a specific country, and yet there is no intrinsic connection between the specific colors and the country for which they stand. They have been accepted as denoting that particular country, and we translate the visual impression of the flag into the concept of that country, again on conventional grounds. Some pictorial symbols are not entirely conventional; for example, the cross. The cross can be merely a conventional symbol of the Christian Church and in that respect no different from a flag. But the specific content of the cross referring to Jesus' death or, beyond that, to the interpenetration of the material and spiritual planes, puts the connection between the symbol and what it symbolizes beyond the level of mere conventional symbols.

The opposite to the conventional symbol is the *accidental* symbol, although they have one thing in common: there is no intrinsic relationship between the symbol and that which it symbolizes. Let us assume that someone has had a saddening experience in a certain city; when he hears the name of that city, he will easily connect the name with a mood of sadness, just as he would connect it with a mood of joy had his experience been a happy one. Quite obviously there is nothing in the nature of the city that is either sad or joyful. It is the individual experience connected with the city that makes it a symbol of a mood.

The same reaction could occur in connection with a house, a street, a certain dress, certain scenery, or anything once connected with a specific mood. We might find ourselves dreaming that we are in a certain city. In fact, there may be no particular mood connected with it in the dream; all we see is a street or even simply the name of the city. We ask ourselves why we happened to think of that city in our sleep and may discover that we had fallen asleep in a mood similar to the one symbolized by the city. The picture in the dream represents this mood, the city "stands for" the mood once experienced in it. The connection between the symbol and the experience symbolized is entirely accidental.

In contrast to the conventional symbol, the accidental symbol cannot be shared by anyone else except as we relate the events connected with the symbol. For this reason accidental symbols are rarely used in myths, fairy tales, or works of art written in symbolic language because they are not communicable unless the writer adds a lengthy comment to each symbol he uses. In dreams, however, accidental symbols are frequent, and Freud by his method of free association devised a method for understanding their meaning.

The *universal* symbol is one in which there is an intrinsic relationship between the symbol and that which it represents. Take, for instance, the symbol of fire. We are fascinated by certain qualities of fire in a fireplace. First of all, by its aliveness. It changes continuously, it moves all the time, and yet there is constancy in it. It remains the same without being the same. It gives the impression of power, of energy, of grace and lightness. It is as if it were dancing, and had an inexhaustible source of energy. When we use fire as a symbol, we describe the *inner experience* characterized by the same elements which we notice in the sensory experience of fire—the mood of energy, lightness, movement, grace, gaiety, sometimes one, sometimes another of these elements being predominant in the feeling.

Similar in some ways and different in others is the symbol of water—of the ocean or of the stream. Here, too, we find the blending of change and constant movement and yet of permanence. We also feel the quality of aliveness, continuity, and energy. But there is a difference; where fire is adventurous, quick, exciting, water is quiet, slow, and steady. Fire has an element of surprise; water an element of predictability. Water symbolizes the mood of aliveness, too, but one which is "heavier," "slower," and more comforting than exciting.

That a phenomenon of the physical world can be the adequate expression of an inner experience, that the world of things can be a symbol of the world of the mind, is not surprising. We all know that our body expresses our mind. Blood rushes to our head when we are furious, it rushes from it when we are afraid; our heart beats more quickly when we are angry, and the whole body has a different tonus if we are happy from the one it has when we are sad. We express our mood by our facial expression and our attitudes and feelings by movements and gestures so precise that others recognize them more accurately from our gestures than from our words. Indeed, the body is a symbol—and not an allegory—of the mind. Deeply and genuinely felt emotion, and even any genuinely felt thought, is expressed in our whole organism. In the case of the universal symbol, we find the same connection between mental and physical experience. Certain physical phenomena suggest by their very nature certain emotional and mental experiences, and we express emotional experiences in the language of physical experiences, that is to say, symbolically.

The universal symbol is the only one in which the relationship between the symbol and that which is symbolized is not coincidental but intrinsic. It is rooted in the experience of the affinity between an emotion or thought, on the one hand, and a sensory experience, on the other. It can be called universal because it is shared by all men, in contrast not only to the accidental symbol, which is by its very nature entirely personal, but also to the conventional symbol, which is restricted to a group of people sharing the same convention. The universal symbol is rooted in the properties of our body, our senses, and our mind, which are common to all men and, therefore, not restricted to individuals or to specific groups. Indeed, *the language of the universal symbol is the one common tongue developed by the human race, a language which it forgot before it succeeded in developing a universal conventional language.*

There is no need to speak of a racial inheritance in order to explain the universal character of symbols. Every human being sharing the essential features of bodily and mental equipment with the rest of mankind is capable of speaking and understanding the symbolic language that is based upon these common properties. Just as we do not need to learn to cry when we are sad or to get red in the face when we are angry, and just as these reactions are not restricted to any particular race or group of people, symbolic language does not have to be learned and is not restricted to any segment of the human race. Evidence for this is to be found in the fact that symbolic language as it is employed in myths and dreams is found in all cultures, in the so-called primitive as well as such developed cultures as those of Egypt and Greece. Furthermore, the symbols used in these various cultures are strikingly similar since they all go back to the basic sensory as well as emotional experiences shared by men of all cultures. Dreams of people living in the United States, India, or China today, as well as those which are reported to us from Greece, Palestine, or Egypt 3000 years ago, are essentially the same in contents and structure.

The foregoing statement needs qualification, however. Some symbols differ in meaning according to the difference in their realistic significance in various cultures. For instance, the function and consequently the meaning of the sun is different in northern countries and in tropical countries. In northern countries, where water is plentiful, all growth depends on sufficient sunshine. The sun is the warm, life-giving, protecting, loving power. In the Near East, where the heat of the sun is much more powerful, the sun is a dangerous and even threatening power from which man must protect himself, while water is felt to be the source of all life and the main condition for growth. We may speak of *dialects of universal symbolic language,* which are determined by those differences in natural conditions which cause certain symbols to have a different meaning in different regions of the earth.

Different from these "symbolic dialects" is the fact that many symbols have more than one meaning in accordance with various kinds of experiences which can be connected with one and the same natural phenomenon. Let us take the symbol of fire again. If we watch fire in the fireplace, which is a source of pleasure and comfort, it is expressive of a mood of aliveness, warmth, and pleasure. But if we see a building or forest on fire, it conveys to us an experience of threat and terror, of the powerlessness of man against the elements of nature. Fire, then, can be the symbolic representation of inner aliveness and happiness as well as of fear, powerlessness, or of one's own destructive tendencies. The same holds true of the symbol water. Water can be a most destructive force when it is whipped up by a storm or when a swollen river floods its banks. Therefore, it can be the symbolic expression of horror and chaos as well as of comfort and peace.

Another illustration of the same principle is a symbol of a valley. The valley enclosed between mountains can arouse in us the feeling of security and comfort, of protection against all dangers from the outside. But the protecting mountains can also mean isolating walls which do not permit us to get out of the valley and thus the valley can become a symbol of imprisonment. The particular meaning of the symbol in any given place can only be determined from the whole context in which the symbol appears, and in terms of the predominant experiences of the person using the symbol.

Accidental and universal symbols constitute the language which the dream employs. And almost all attempts to understand the nature of dreams were based on the common assumption that symbolic language gave expression to inner experiences in the form of sensory experiences happening in the physical world. There was also agreement in all great cultures throughout history that all dreams are meaningful and significant. Meaningful, because they contain a message which can be understood if one has the key for its translation. Significant, because we do not dream of anything that is trifling, even though the significant message might be hidden behind a seemingly trifling façade. But while there is agreement with regard to these main principles, we find a great deal of disagreement running through the centuries with regard to the essential meaning of dreams.

One school of thought, of which Plato and Freud are outstanding representatives, holds that dreams are expressions of the lowest and animal-like part of our soul, and that our irrational and evil strivings appear in our dreams, when the control of reason and conscience has gone to sleep. The opposite view, that dreams reveal our highest and most rational faculties, and even gifts of prediction which we do not have in our waking life, was held by many others from Biblical times to thinkers like Goethe and Emerson and psychoanalysts like C. G. Jung. From my own experiences in trying to understand dreams, I have come to the conclusion that dreams are not necessarily the expression either of our higher or of our lower self, but that there is no kind of mental activity, feeling, or thought which does not appear in dreams expressed in symbolic language. I believe that the only description of the nature of dreams which does not distort our interpretation by too narrow an expectation of the meaning of dreams is the broad definition that *dreaming is a meaningful and significant expression of any kind of mental activity under the condition of sleep.*

Obviously this definition is too broad to be of much help for the understanding of the nature of dreams unless we can say something more definite about the "condition of sleep" and the particular effect of this condition on our mental activity. If we can find out what the specific effect of sleeping is on our mental activity, we may discover a good deal more about the nature of dreaming.

Physiologically, sleep is a condition of chemical regeneration of the organism; energy is restored while no action takes place and even sensory perception is almost entirely shut off. Psychologically, sleep suspends the main function characteristic of waking life: man's reacting toward reality by perception and action. This difference between the biological functions of waking and of sleeping is, in fact, a difference between two states of existence.

The difference between the functions of sleeping and waking is more fundamental than any difference between various other kinds of activity, and accordingly the difference between the conceptual systems accompanying the two states is incomparably greater. In the waking state thoughts and feelings respond primarily to challenge—the task of mastering our environment, changing it, defending ourselves against it. Survival is the task of waking man; he is subject to the laws that govern reality. This means that he has to think in terms of time and space and that his thoughts are subject to the laws of time and space logic.

While we sleep we are not concerned with bending the outside world to our purposes. We are helpless, and sleep, therefore, has rightly been called the "brother of death." But we are also free, freer than when awake. We are free from the burden of work, from the task of attack or defense, from watching and mastering reality. We need not look at the outside world; we look at our inner world, are concerned exclusively with ourselves. When asleep we may be likened to angels, who are not subject to the laws of "reality." In sleep the realm of necessity has given way to the realm of freedom in which "I am" is the only system to which thoughts and feelings refer.

Mental activity during sleep has a logic different from that of waking existence. Sleep experience need not pay any attention to qualities that matter only when one copes with reality. If I feel, for instance, that a person is a coward, I may dream that he changed from a man into a chicken. This change is logical in terms of what I feel about the person, absurd only in terms of my orientation to outside reality (in terms of what I could *do*, realistically, to or with the person). Sleep experience is not lacking in logic but is subject to different logical rules, which are valid in that particular experiential state.

Sleep and waking life are the two poles of human existence. Waking life is taken up with the function of action, sleep is freed from it. Sleep is taken up with the function of self-experience. When we wake from our sleep, we move into the realm of action. We are then oriented in terms of this system, and our memory operates within it: we remember what can be recalled in space-time concepts. The sleep world has disappeared. Experiences we had in it—our dreams—are remembered with the greatest difficulty.[1] The situation has been represented symbolically in many a tale: at night ghosts and spirits, good and evil, occupy the scene, but when dawn arrives, they disappear, and nothing is left of all the intense experience.

From these considerations certain conclusions about the nature of the unconscious follow:

It is neither Jung's mythical realm of racially inherited experience nor Freud's seat of irrational libidinal forces. It is inner experience produced and molded by the specific conditions of sleep as against those of waking life. It must be understood in terms of the principle: "What we think and feel is influenced by what we do."

Consciousness is the mental activity in our state of being preoccupied with external reality—with acting. The *unconscious* is mental experience in a state of existence in which we have shut off communications with the outer world, are no longer preoccupied with action but with our self-experience. The unconscious is related to a special mode of life—that of nonactivity; and the characteristics of the unconscious follow from the nature of this mode of existence. The qualities of consciousness, on the other

---

[1] Cf. to the problem of memory function in its relation to dream activity the stimulating article by Dr. Ernest G. Schachtel, "On Memory and Childhood Amnesia," *Psychiatry*, February, 1947.

hand, are determined by the nature of action and by the survival function of the waking state of existence.

The "unconscious" is the unconscious only in relation to the "normal" state of activity. When we speak of "unconscious" we really say only that an experience is alien to that frame of mind which exists while and as we act; it is then felt as a ghostlike, intrusive element, hard to get hold of and hard to remember. But the day world is as unconscious in our sleep experience as the night world is in our waking experience. The term "unconscious" is customarily used solely from the standpoint of day experience; and thus it fails to denote that both conscious and unconscious are only different states of mind referring to different states of existence. This dilemma has been beautifully expressed by the old Chinese poet who said: "Last night I dreamed that I was a butterfly. I do not know now, am I a man who dreamed that he was a butterfly, or am I a butterfly who dreams now that I am a man?"

It will be argued that in the waking state of existence, too, thinking and feeling are not entirely subject to the limitations of time and space; that our creative imagination permits us to think about past and future objects as if they were present, and of distant objects as if they were before our eyes; that our waking feeling is not dependent on the physical presence of the object nor on its coexistence in time; that, therefore, the absence of the space-time system is not characteristic of sleep existence in contradistinction to waking existence, but of thinking and feeling in contradistinction to acting. This welcome objection permits me to clarify an essential point in my argument.

We must differentiate between the *contents* of thought processes and the *logical categories* employed in thinking. While it is true that the contents of our waking thoughts are not subject to limitations of space and time, the categories of logical thinking are those of the space-time nature. I can, for instance, think of my father and state that his attitude in a certain situation is identical with mine. This statement is logically correct. On the other hand, if I state "I am my father," the statement is "illogical" because it is not conceived in reference to the physical world. The sentence is logical, however, in a purely experiential realm: it expresses the experience of identity with my father. Logical thought processes in the waking state are subject to categories which are rooted in a special form of existence—the one in which we relate ourselves to reality in terms of action. In sleep existence, which is characterized by lack of even potential action, logical categories are employed which have reference only to my self-experience. The same holds true of feeling. When I feel, in the waking state, with regard to a person whom I have not seen for twenty years, I remain aware of the fact that the person is not present. If I dream about the person, my feeling deals with the person as if he or she were present. But to say "as if he were present" is to express the feeling in logical "waking life" concepts. In sleep existence there is no "as if"; the person *is* present.

In the foregoing pages the attempt has been made to describe the conditions of sleep and to draw from this description certain conclusions concerning the quality of dream activity. We must now proceed to study one specific element among the conditions of sleep which will prove to be of great significance to the understanding of dream processes. We have said that while we are asleep we are not occupied with managing outer reality. We do not perceive it and we do not influence it, nor are we subject to the influences of the outside world on us. From this it follows that the *effect of this separation from reality depends on the quality of reality itself.* If the influence from the outside world is essentially beneficial, the absence of this influence during sleep would tend to lower the value of our dream activity, so that it would be inferior to our mental activities during the daytime, when we are exposed to the beneficial influence of outside reality.

But are we right in assuming that the influence of reality is exclusively a beneficial one? May it not be that it is also harmful and that, therefore, the absence of its influence tends to bring forth qualities superior to those we have when we are awake?

In speaking of the reality outside ourselves, reference is not made primarily to the world of nature. Nature as such is neither good nor bad. It may be helpful to us or dangerous, and the absence of our perception of it relieves us, indeed, from our task of trying to master it or of defending ourselves against it; but it does not make us either more stupid or wiser, better or worse. It is different with the man-made world around us, with the culture in which we live. Its effect upon us is ambiguous, although we are prone to assume that it is entirely to our benefit.

Indeed, the evidence that cultural influences are beneficial to us seems almost overwhelming. The progress of the human race is based on the cooperation with all men, which was possible only in a social context, and by man's ability to communicate his ideas and practical achievements to his fellow men, and future generations. Man is what he is by his capacity for social organization, and the creation of culture, and this capacity differentiates him from the animal.

Is then the man-made reality outside ourselves not the most significant factor for the development of the best in us, and must we not expect that, when deprived of contact with the outside world, we regress temporarily to a primitive, animal-like, unreasonable state of mind? Much can be said in favor of such an assumption, and the view that such a regression is the essential feature of the state of sleep, and thus of dream activity, has been held by many students of dreaming from Plato to Freud. From this viewpoint dreams are expected to be expressions of the irrational, primitive strivings in us, and the fact that we forget our dreams so easily is amply explained by our being ashamed of those irrational and criminal impulses which we express when we were not under the control of society. Undoubtedly this interpretation of dreams is true, but the question is whether it is exclusively true or whether the negative elements in the influence of society do not account for the paradoxical fact that *we are not only less reasonable and less decent in our dreams but also more intelligent, wiser, and capable of better judgment when we are asleep than when we are awake.*

Indeed, culture has not only a beneficial but also a detrimental influence on our intellectual and moral functions. Human beings are dependent on each other, they need each other. But human history up to now has been influenced by one fact: material production was not sufficient to satisfy the legitimate needs of all men. The table was set for only a few of the many who wanted to sit down and eat. Those who were stronger tried to secure places for themselves, which meant that they had to prevent others from getting seats. Moreover, they used their power not only to secure their own positions but also to make use of and to exploit their fellow men, for their own material or psychic needs. Aside from a number of primitive communities, the history of mankind up to now is a history of the use of man by man. The power used to achieve these ends was often the power of the conqueror, the physical power that forced the majority to be satisfied with their lot. But physical power was not always available or sufficient. One had to have power over the minds of people in order to make them refrain from using their fists. This control over mind and feeling was a necessary element in retaining the privileges of the few. In this process, however, the minds of the few became as distorted as the minds of the many. The guard who watches a prisoner becomes almost as much a prisoner as the prisoner himself. The "elite" who have to control those who are not "chosen" become the prisoners of their own restrictive tendencies. Thus the human mind, of both rulers and ruled, becomes deflected from its essential human purpose, which is to feel and to think humanly, to use and to develop the powers of reason and love that are inherent in man and without the full development of which he is crippled.

In this process man's character becomes distorted and his heart hardens. Aims which are in contrast to the interests of his real human self become paramount. His powers of love are impoverished, and he is driven to want power over others. His inner security is lessened, and he is driven to seek compensation by passionate cravings for fame and prestige. He loses the sense of dignity and integrity and is forced to turn himself into a commodity, deriving his self-respect from his salability, from his success. All this makes for the fact that the man-made world of ideas is a mixture of his very best with all the lies and deceptions which are to hide and rationalize his inhumanity.

This holds true for a primitive tribe in which strict laws and customs influence the mind, but it is true also for modern society with its alleged freedom from rigid ritualism. In many ways the spread of literacy and of the media of mass communication has made the influence of cultural clichés as effective as it is in a small, highly restricted tribal culture. Modern man is exposed to an almost unceasing "noise," the noise of the radio, television, headlines, advertising, the movies, most of which do not enlighten our minds but stultify them. We are exposed to rationalizing lies which masquerade as truths, to plain nonsense which masquerades as common sense or as the higher wisdom of the specialist, to double talk, intellectual laziness, or to dishonesty which speaks in the name of "honor" or "realism," as the case may be. We feel superior to the superstitions of former generations and so-called primitive cultures, and we are constantly hammered at by the same kind of superstitious beliefs that set themselves up as the latest discoveries of "science." Is it surprising, then, that to be awake is not exclusively a blessing but also a curse? Is it surprising that in a state of sleep, when we are alone with ourselves, when we can look into ourselves without being bothered by the noise and nonsense that surround us in the daytime, we are better able to feel and to think our truest and most valuable feelings and thoughts?

This, then, is the conclusion at which we arrive: the state of sleep has an ambiguous function. In it the lack of contact with culture makes for the appearance both of our worst *and* of our best; therefore, in our dreaming, *we may be less intelligent, less wise, and less decent, but we may also be better and wiser than in our waking life.*

To conclude, it must be stressed again that the study of dreams is by no means primarily a tool to be used in psychotherapy for the understanding of neurotic phenomena. Dreams represent a language *sui generis,* a language with its own syntax and grammar, as it were, and the one universal language which the human race possesses. The study of dream language cannot be omitted if we wish to arrive at an understanding of language in its most general and universal aspects.

𝕏 Chapter XIII
LEO SPITZER

LANGUAGE OF POETRY

We may define language in its basic spoken form as a system of sounds and sound groups, produced by the delicate minimum movements of our articulatory apparatus, which are made to symbolize thoughts that have crystallized around certain points. Out of the incessant and turbid flow of life certain entities have been isolated and endowed with a relative acoustic fixity and duration with the result that predications about them can be made. Without acoustic fixations by words of concepts such as *night* and *day, atom, electricity,* acoustic fixations which can in turn be fixed in writing, the human individual would have to recapitulate for every new thought the whole bulk of thoughts of mankind on the subject. As Shelley says: language "rules a throng of thought and forms which else senseless and shapeless were."

Now such linguistic fixations, or words, as they are offered to the individual speaker of a language, are *to him* arbitrary, conventional, imposed by the chance of his being born into a particular speaking community. In general, no motivation of meaning of a particular sound group or word can be given by the speaker: in the terms of Plato no motivation for the words can be given by the nature of the things designated. Why does "horse" not mean "cat" or the reverse? Why is the horse called in Italian *cavallo* and in German *Pferd?* And even in the case of onomatopoeias and interjections, where an acoustic motivation of the words is possible, the particular speaker is bound to respect the convention of his speaking community: the rooster crows "cockadoodledoo" in English, *cocorico* in French, *kikeriki* in German, and still differently in other languages; if someone steps on your foot you will cry "ouch!" if you are an American, *au!* if German, *aïe!* if French. Nevertheless, the single speaker who uses *cavallo* in Italian, *Pferd* in German, "horse" in English can expect to be understood, or understood fairly well, by his fellow countrymen as if in consequence of a tacit convention or pact, as Plato called it. It is this unwritten but daily renewed linguistic contract with one's co-citizens, that daily plebiscite, which makes national cohesion possible, as is illustrated in reverse by the Biblical story of the confusion of tongues at the tower of Babel. The average member of a speaking community feels so much at home in his mother tongue that he would naïvely boast that *no other* language can express outward reality better than his. The anecdote of a Tyrolian German discussing with a Tyrolian Italian the merits of their respective languages is well known. The German brings the discussion to a close with the remark: "You call a *Pferd* a *cavallo* but it *is* a *Pferd*."

I have said that speakers of the same language understand each other *fairly* well, for in most cases the understanding is indeed not complete within the same community: cases of absolute unambiguity as the two mathematical (the geometric and the arithmetical) usages of the term "square" are rather rare and represent the maximum possibility of understanding through words. With the majority of words no such unanimity of understanding exists: the noun "square" itself has in the common language four or five different senses. In order to know what the word actually means in a certain situation we must know the context; if the context is zero, as happens to be the rule in newspaper headlines, we often fail to reach certainty. But even when the context is given, all the speakers do not always mean exactly the same when using a particular word. "Democracy" is different according to the Communist and the non-Communist creed; and surely not all speakers are agreed on what shade of color is "red" as opposed to "pink."

Understanding is then based only on that semantic kernel of the words on which all speakers of a language are agreed, while the semantic fringes are blurred. The founder of modern philosophy of language, Wilhelm von Humboldt, was right in saying that the speaking individual does not offer to his fellow speaker objective signs for the things expressed, nor does he compel him by his verbal utterance to represent to himself exactly the same thing as that meant by him, but is satisfied with, as it were, pressing down the homologous *key* of the other's respective mental keyboard, with establishing only the same link in the chain of associations of things with words, so that there are elicited corresponding, though not exactly identical, responses.

Yet irrespective of the variable ratio of understanding our words may find, we behave generally naïvely as though we were perfectly understood. And this illusion is one of the great sources of man's happiness: it gives him the feeling of being surrounded by a friendly world which shares with him all the associations he may have built up in his lifetime—for man fears nothing more than isolation in the universe. It is the enjoyment of the community of language which works at all public gatherings wherein the individual communes with the collective spirit. Great actors or orators give us a feeling of strength and elation because we realize that the maximum of expressivity does not interrupt the flow of understanding between them and us. And even in our most personal and intimate reactions we welcome the social character of the word that expresses *us* in terms of age-old experiences of the community: when we feel tender or sad we are likely to say to ourselves the word "tender" or "sad" and feel even tenderer or sadder—because we somehow have received a ratification, by the language of the community, of our personal state of mind. It is also their quality of social reassurance that keeps adages, "old saws," alive.

Language is then a system of arbitrary, conventional, ambiguous signs generally not felt as ambiguous by which the outward reality is interpreted for the speakers—and stylized: it is indeed an equally arbitrary stylization of reality when "cockadoodledoo" is assumed to be the cry of the cock and when the smallest part of an element, the atom, is called "the uncuttable one." Arbitrary stylization is present on all levels of language. It is present on the articulatory level—for out of the innumerable possibilities of phonetic articulation from whisper to shout our languages have chosen what Roman Jakobson has called "two-choice situations" (surds versus sonorous, aspirated versus unaspirated sounds, etc.). It is also present in word formation and morphology (flexion). We may assume, for example, that for primitive man every situation was unique and required a unique expression, a new kind of interjection or proper name, but that with his growing experience he became able to subsume a new situation under an older one and to express the former as a variant of the latter. His attention shifted from the unique to the regular, from the proper name to the common-noun stage. Latin *tatta* and *mamma* are originally exclamations of the babbling child, reserved for the father and the mother, *proper names* characterizing these unique persons in the family; but the common nouns *pater* and *mater,* offering the babbling syllables *pa-, ma-* but provided with the suffix *-ter,* testifies to a classification, the suffix being the linguistic expression of a regularity perceived in the world—indeed, a rhyme symbolizing a perceived analogy by equality of sound. And rhymes are stylizations of reality: they are found in Indo-European not only in endings but in stems: Latin *necto—plecto—flecto,* meaning "to plait, weave, bend," testify to a primitive symbolization of equality of meaning by equality of sound.

The most frequent suffixes are found in the paradigms of nouns and verbs; in primitive times the verbal expressions "I go" and "we go" may have appeared as quite different experiences, not as concrete variants of the abstract verb "to go." A remainder of such primitive thinking is the Romance so-called suppletive conjugation: French *je vais—nous allons,* Italian *vo—andiamo,* or the similar opposition in English "I go—I went." The so-called irregular verbs, generally the ones most frequently used in our languages, are remnants of a state of civilization in which the power of abstraction was not yet sufficiently strong to see, behind the actions of different persons, one common abstract denominator. Regular flexion is a means by which new concrete expressions of actions can be subsumed under one heading, "stylized" as variants of one basic pattern. The speakers of a language are not sensitive to the artistic rhyme quality of flexional endings; rhymes such as *nous allons—aimons—perdons—appercevons—sentons* are spurned by distinguished modern French poets precisely because the allure of rhyme rests for us on unexpected associations, on association in a poem of what seemed dissociated in outward reality. But this modern idiosyncrasy must not blind us to the fact that the origin of rhyme in modern poetry must be sought in the natural rhyme offered in all languages by the grammatical endings and the suffixes. In pagan antiquity (in which our poetic rhyme was unknown) the Greek and Roman rhetoricians used grammatical rhyme *in prose* in order to underline certain intellectual similarities or homologies, and it was the Christian Church father Augustine who first transferred the rhetorical prose rhyme of the ancients to a religious psalm composed in verse by him, thereby ushering in our Western (or Christian) poetic technique. This short history of the rhyme shows us in a paradigmatic example how the natural stylization present in the flexions and derivations of the language can be expanded artistically.

Stylization exists also in syntax. Expressions of the type of Italian *va pian piano*, "he is walking very slowly," offer a stylization of reality similar to the one we found in phonetics. In order to depict an unlimited stretch of time or length of distance the language has chosen only two links in the chain, which are called upon to represent the infinite extension (*piano piano piano piano* . . . etc., etc., has been abridged into *pian piano*).

In similar English twin formations such as "it rains and rains" or "zigzag" (which is an abbreviation of "[he went] zig and [he went] zag, and [he went] zig and [he went] zag and zig and zag . . ." *in infinitum*) we witness the representative or "stylizing" character of the number two: the number one is closed in itself, self-contained, unstructured; two (and even more three) offers an openness to the world, a possibility of structural expansion.

Finally, we find stylization of the outward world in the semantic development of our languages. Here we are generally faced with developments that took place a long time ago (though some new semantic developments may take place before our eyes). What seems arbitrary in the semantics of our languages, that is, without motivation accessible to all of their speakers, is, of course, the result of irreversible historical developments of thought which have come to act on the minds of our forebears and have not lost their grip on those of their posterity. This is what is called the power of language on thought, the power of the collective subconscious, as latent in the language, even in our enlightened modern civilization. Every language offers its speakers a ready-made *interpretation* of the world, truly a *Weltanschauung*, a *metaphysical* word-picture which, after having originated in the thinking of our ancestors, tends to impose itself ever anew on posterity. Thus our concept of the atom is basically the same as that of certain pre-Socratic Greek philosophers; or the modern biological and sociological technical term "environment" is Carlyle's coinage intended to translate Goethe's term *Umwelt,* which in turn is a translation from Newton's "circumambient medium" and Galileo's *l'ambiente,* themselves expressions ultimately harking back to Greek *to periechon* ("that which encompasses and embraces," meaning alternatively, the air, space, or the world spirit). Similarly the French term *milieu,* originally *milieu ambiant,* reflects the "circumambient medium" of Newton and through this the Greek term *periechon.* While in the cases of "atom" and "environment" the historical continuity of thought from Greek antiquity to modernity is of absolutely scientific nature (that is, the hypotheses underlying these expressions have never ceased to be scientific hypotheses), in other cases our enlightened modern thought tends to reject certain hypotheses which may have corresponded to earlier, more primitive thinking.

Take, for instance, a simple sentence in our modern Indo-European languages such as "I see him," in which the personal and transitive use of the verb is the same as in "I kill him," "I throw it away." This means that English and, I might say, Indo-European, presents the impressions made on our senses predominantly as human *activities,* brought about by our *will.* But the Eskimos in Greenland say, not "I see him" but "he appears to me," just as they say in the other cases just mentioned: "he dies to me," "it flies away from me." Thus the Indo-European speaker conceives as workings of his activities what the fatalistic Eskimo sees as events that happen to him. But in our Indo-European languages traces of the "happening" type of expressions for inner experiences are not msising: in Latin one said, for "I dreamed," "it dreamed itself to me"; and in English, "I remember," which has taken the place of a former "it remembers me," may still today alternate with the impersonal "it occurs to me"; German, the language of dreamers, has a series of impersonal expressions such as *es träumt, ahnt, schwant, deucht mir* along with *ich träume, ahne, denke,* all of which means that our Indo-European languages, some more, some less, still reflect an earlier cultural period where man conceived himself as more subject to action from outside than capable of action of his own, more sensorial than motoric. Indeed, "it occurs to me" is of the same impersonal type as that found in the meteorological expressions "it is raining, snowing," in which obviously man refrains from asserting any action on his part. When Lichtenberg opposed Descartes's statement "I think, therefore I am" by pointing out that the French philosopher had too lightly assumed the existence of a thinking ego on the basis of a speech habit which presents thinking as action on the part of the thinker, while he should have said "it thinks in me," he was reminding us, perhaps influenced by his native German, of that ancient irrational subsoil of the human ego which still lingers in us below the Cartesian pride of reason.

Now how should we explain the meteorological impersonal verbs with which we compared the type "it occurs to me"? Comparative linguistics teaches us that Greek impersonals such as ὕει ("it is raining") and βροντᾷ ("it is thundering") were originally simple *nouns* meaning "rain!" "thunder!"—that is, emotional exclamations stating nothing but the existence of meteorological phenomena. But as old as these remainders of purely phenomenalistic expression are expressions such as Ζεὺς ὕει, βροντᾷ ("Zeus is raining, thundering"), Zeus being an Indo-European God, *Dyaus-pitā* in Sanskrit, *Juppiter* in Latin, the Father-God of the bright shining day, who when he pleases can become the *Juppiter Tonans*. By these expressions an agent, a supernatural agent, is posited to whom the outward events can be retraced. With the sentence "Zeus is raining" man has attempted a first step toward science, to find causation in the cosmos, an explanation of the world by a myth. He has reached the first stage of science, which the positivistic philosopher Auguste Comte has called the theological stage. Many languages today still show the imprint of that religious stage. For example, in Hungarian one says for "it is raining": "the rainer is raining (*esik az eső*).

The repetition of the same stem ("rain-") in the sentence found in that relatively primitive way of expression produces a magic effect. It is well known that magic formulas indulge in such a device in order to keep the attention of the believer focused on the magic content, whereas the modern mind generally objects to such stem repetitions (whose ancient technical names are *adnominatio* or *paronomasia*) and acts according to a law of "semantic dissimilation." In popular French one says *il tombe de la pluie,* "rain is falling," not "rain is raining" (we can see this modern tendency at work not only in the case of the avoidance of the "inner nominative"—"rain is raining"—but also in that of the older, Biblical or magic inner accusative—"to live a life," "to dream a dream," ways of expression current in the Middle Ages but today, if used at all, accepted only when accompanied by a modifier: "to live a life of debauchery," "to dream a fateful dream").

The second stage of science according to Comte is the "metaphysical" one, in which occult natural forces or impersonal essences are assumed as causes. This stage is linguistically reflected by the "it" in our modern type of expression "it is raining," where "it" is a force outside of us, considered as an agent. The third stage of science is reached, according to Comte, in the modern era of positivism, when man no longer explains the world by anthropomorphic theology or vague metaphysics but by the sense-data accessible to him and by their controllable relationships. But one will notice that this stage has not yet penetrated into our common speech, which remains bound by theological or metaphysical tradition, "uncorrected" by science in the sense of Lichtenberg and Condillac (who thought that science and philosophy are nothing but corrections of common speech). We still do not say for "it is raining": "condensed atmospheric vapor is falling in drops," just as we still continue, in spite of Copernicus, to say "the sun rises," or "sets." In Neo-Greek the phrase "the sun is setting" is rendered by "the sun is enthroned like a king," in Rumanian by "the sun enters into sainthood." In both cases the splendor and glory of the natural phenomenon are interpreted in terms of the human-superhuman splendor characteristic of Byzantine art. Similarly, although it would seem possible only in primitive prelogical animistic thinking that sex could be attributed to inanimate things, the majority of European languages have up to today retained grammatical gender ("water" is feminine in French *eau* as it was in Latin *aqua;* "fire" is masculine in French *feu* as it was in Latin *ignis*). Language is then not satisfied with denoting factual contents, but forces the speakers to adopt certain metaphysical or religious interpretations of the world which the community may have learned to deny. These obsolete conceptions remain latent in the language: just as Aeneas when all hope was lost carried his father out of burning Troy on his shoulders, so we tend to espouse our forefathers' beliefs and words in any emergency—when we will react atavistically. Even atheists will then ejaculate, *"God!"*

and Voltaire has a libertine Swiss colonel pray in the stress of battle: "God, if you exist, save my soul, if I have one!"

The atavistic prelogical residue in our language, which may constitute a danger for the scientist unaware of the semantic fallacies of the latter (unaware, that is, of the "history of ideas" underlying our language), can however be used deliberately and with great aesthetic effect in literary art—in poetry.

When we hear in the refrain of a folk song inserted by Shakespeare into one of his plays the line "The rain it raineth every-day," we have the vague feeling that, although the factual content is no different from that of the conventional phrase "it rains every day," the form chosen presents the fact in a slightly new light. There is here posited an irrational power that raineth. "The rain rains" is indeed a quite unusual expression in modern English (though not in Hungarian, as we have said), suggestive, as it were, of another world than the one we are familiar with, indeed a magic world which for our enlightened mind has become a poetic world. In addition, certain linguistic and prosodic devices tend to enforce the impression that we have entered a world at the same time our own and not our own: the archaic ending *-eth* in "raineth," which evokes times immemorial; the iambic rhythm here suggesting the monotony of perpetually falling rain ("the raín it raíneth évery dáy"); the repetition of the stem "rain," which reinforces the impression of monotony. Here then the arbitrary character of our words has been annulled and a particular significance has been given to the acoustic impression, which has indeed become expressive of meaning. Thus words which had meaning only by convention have been made to express meaning in correspondence with their sound.

I have quoted a line of Shakespeare, which is surely not one of the most inspired, in order to show some basic elements required in the transformation of language by poetry. We found in that line a repristination of a mythological concept symbolized by linguistic devices destined to give motivation to the arbitrary words of the language—and that is precisely what poetry generally achieves: the production, by language-constructs differing from normal speech, of adumbrations of a metaphysical world in which the laws of science, causality, practicality, as we know them and need them in our workaday world, seem no longer to obtain and in which we vaguely come to visualize *other* laws.

Indeed, the account of the creation in Genesis (which conflicts with evolutionistic modern science) is couched in a poetic language whose spell still acts on all of us with undiminished force: "And God said: *Let there be light, and there was light.*" The power of this line, which the pagan rhetorician Longinus recognized as an example of what he called "the sublime," that is, the grandiose expressed simply, resides in the word-parallelisms of the two sentences, and in the use of the conjunction "and," as a result of which the command of God is presented as leading inevitably and naturally to its own fulfillment. In the Hebrew original the parallelism is even more complete because the same verb form serves for both the command and the fulfillment: *jĕhī aur vajĕhī aur.* That miracle of miracles, the creation of light, has become simple, self-evident *poetic* reality. Here the onomatopoeia restored by poetry is much more subtle and much more discreet than in the reproduction of the melody of rain in Shakespeare's refrain.

I must insist at this point on the fact that none of the "poetic" elements in the two short poetic texts are exclusively peculiar to poetry. We have found in them revivals of prescientific myths and prosodic devices or acoustic onomatopoeias, that is, stylizations of outward reality by language of a type customary in all our languages, stylizations which, however, give the "far from this world" impression only in the particular context in which they are used ("the rain rains" startles while the similar personification "the wind blows" does not; the repetition of the stem in "the rain rains" may seem astonishing while "it rains and rains" [with an iambic rhythm parallel to "the rain it raineth"] does not). In other words, poetry uses devices similar to those generally used by the (unpoetic) language at places in which these devices produce a poetic effect. Poetry does not step outside of the realm of language, but makes this appear, through its appeal to mythology and prosody, as a new, a nowhere land.

The effect in the two examples chosen was either sad or solemn. But poetic effect can also be gay. Take the short refrain in a satirical poem of ten stanzas about the corruptive effect of money by the seventeenth-century Spanish baroque poet Quevedo:

> Poderoso caballero
> es Don Dinero

In the refrain the "mythical" figure of a "Damsel Gold" is posited whose irresistible power is satirically described in the various stanzas. The recurrence of the two lines seems to underline the inevitability or fatality of the power of gold, and the fact that gold has been personified tends to widen the distance between the reader and the well-known phenomenon "gold." Damsel Gold moves in another world, in the world of abstraction, above our concrete world. On the other hand, the evoked image of a Spanish knight has for us some definite concrete connotations of familiarity by which the mythological distance is lessened: With the concept of the *caballero* are given power, courage, largesse, chivalresque behavior, all human traits appealing to our sympathy and consequently lighting up the atmosphere of doom which naturally hovers above the mythical figure. *Don Dinero* is then at the same time somewhat removed from and somewhat close to us, a fatal power, but humanized. Only poetry is able to create such a hybrid being. And the prosody to which the language of the refrain is subjected reinforces that hybrid or semi-mythological impression. It is the quite unexpressive word *dinero,* "money," that has been recomposed acoustically by the poet, indeed segmented into two parts: the "stem" *din-* and the "ending" *-ero;* the latter sound group, recurring at a short distance in the rhyme, helps solidify the allegorical equation *dinero = caballero,* and the first syllable *din-,* if taken together with the preceding *Don,* suggests the sound of gold coins carelessly dropped on a counter *(Don Din).* The poet has, by this ingenious phonetic find, imparted to the word a new acoustic quality. It is an achievement the more remarkable since it was by the addition of the pseudo-title *Don* to *dinero* that the personification *Dinero* was made possible. The new coinage *Don Dinero* thus comes to embody both the mythological and the concretely acoustic sides of the concept of gold. As the pseudo-title *Don* removes the concept of "gold" from us to the level of an abstraction, this very abstraction becomes acoustically perceptible to us in a manner the common noun "gold" could never have afforded.

In the poetic examples quoted we have always found prosody in the service of a myth. The questions now arise as to which of these two elements is more conducive to poetic effect and whether one of the two can be dispensed with without any lessening of this effect. I do not hesitate to answer that prosody in itself is able to

suggest a poetic or nowhere atmosphere in which laws different
from those of our world hold sway. Plato's myth of the androgyne,
surely poetic in itself, would seem to need that additional factor
of reality and convincingness which are given by verse in order
not to appear only as a fantasy.

It is only as a fantasy that we are able to accept Rabelais's myth
of the "unfrozen words," of words and noises uttered in a bloody
war in the arctic winter which unthaw in spring and of which
Pantagruel throws a handful on the deck of his ship—here "throaty
insults" and "bloody words," there "golden" and "green" and
"azure words." Portraying both the reality and the irreality of
human speech Rabelais leads us toward a new fictitious world by
expanding certain metaphorical patterns given in the language
(if there exist "golden words," green and azure words must also
exist; if we speak of "fixed phrases" why not imagine unfrozen
words? etc.), but this fictitious world itself is elusive: it lacks the
cement of prosody with which a Dante would make his transmundane imaginings real.

Prosody itself is generative of the mythical atmosphere (although
obviously prosody can be found also in service of triviality—
witness the jingles of modern advertising). I shall discuss here
stanza 4 of the poem "Consolation à M. Du Périer" by the
seventeenth-century neoclassic poet Malherbe, a stanza that has
been much admired by all French critics through the centuries
as it were instinctively, although the reasons for this admiration
can be easily defined by a critic versed in philology. In this case
I shall transcend in my commentary the one somewhat arbitrarily
detached master stanza in order to correlate it to the artistic
whole of the poem:

> Mais elle était du monde, où les plus belles choses
>   Ont le pire destin;
> Et rose elle a vécu ce que vivent les roses,
>   L'espace d'un matin.

The feminine pronoun *elle* refers to the daughter of M. Du Périer,
who died young, and the poem is a *"consolatio"* addressed to her
father, that is a neo-classic revival of an ancient genre of prose or,
more rarely, verse compositions by which stoic writers of antiquity
(men such as Plutarch or Seneca) were wont to show aggrieved
parents by ratiocination (by pointing out the inexorability of fate,

etc.) the futility of their emotion—a prosaic genre that with its appeal to reason in the presence of fate, lends itself rather to rhetoric than to poetry. How has Malherbe in the lines quoted— which for the French rank equal with Villon's *Mais où sont les neiges d'antan?* or Racine's *Dans l'orient désert quel devint mon ennui*—achieved poetic magic? Surely the identification of the maiden who died prematurely as a rose nipped in the bud has great poetic impact although it cannot be said to be original with Malherbe. The motif of the brief span of life given to rose and maiden is a *topos* of antiquity (Catullus' nuptial song; Ausonius' *De rosis*), treated also most frequently by Renaissance poets (Ariosto: *La verginella è simile alla rosa;* Ronsard: *Cueillez dès aujourd'hui les roses de la vie*). In the majority of Renaissance poems the adhortation "gather ye rose-buds while ye may" gave an erotic, epicurean flavor to the simile, but in his sonnet *Comme on voit sur la branche* . . . Ronsard expressed the melancholy of the death of the roselike being and presented a pagan rite celebrating the metamorphosis of the maiden's ashes into roses and her return to nature whence she came. But Malherbe, the stoic neoclassical poet, had no place in his moral system for a maiden who yields her beauty to an epicurean lover who has threatened her with the prospect of old age or death nor for a ritual of nature and beauty enjoyed by a lover who survives her death. He places her in the framework of the many other beautiful things of this earth that rapidly pass away. Her death must be subordinated to the inexorable law of nature as exemplified by many instances in the poem (parallels suggested by history: King Priam's, King Francis', and Malherbe's own losses, etc.).

It would seem that the basic rationalism of the genre of the *consolatio* and more particularly the attendant treatment of the loss of the young maiden by her father as "one case of loss among many in history" could lead only to the utterly prosaic and banal statement: "The beauty that was your daughter has passed away just as fatally as have many other things and persons." But here the verbal genius of Malherbe has enabled him to find a unique linguistic correspondence with the idea that it was universal fate that has stricken the maiden—and by this prosodic find all banality and prosaism has been transcended; indeed the law of fatality has been allowed to appear most forcefully precisely because it was only suggested. The age-old myth of the roselike existence of a maiden has thus reached a new flowering. Malherbe's find consists in the repetition of the word "rose," used first in the singular for the individual rose that was the maiden, then in the generic plural (ROSE *elle vécu ce que vivent* LES ROSES), and in the repetition of the verb *vivre,* first in the past (*elle a vécu* was the fate of Du Périer's daughter), then in the timeless present, both repetitions being enshrined in the verse in chiastic order. All of this suggests a mysterious, inescapable, fatally active law to which the individual fate of the maiden is subjected—the commonplace idea of the poem has here found an ideal rhythmic and verbal reflection. We feel: the rose must complete the destiny of a rose and what was a gift of nature must return to nature. Notice also that the first mention of the rose, the one in the singular, comes as a surprise to us: the establishment of an identification of the maiden with the flower (as in Heine's *Du bist wie eine Blume*) has been eschewed. The "quiet violence" of Malherbe's presentation of the maiden as a rose is a pure poetic gain. The postulation of reality, instead of the tentative approach given with a comparison, is highly poetic because it forces us to conceive new realities existing outside of our empirical world. This is indeed the poetic act *par excellence.*

Moreover, the first appearance of *rose,* grammatically to be defined as an apposition, occurs in the sentence without any determination of its logical relationship, which happens to be one of causality: *Because* she is a rose, as a rose she can live only as long as roses live—again a highly poetic device. The causal link that exists is suppressed in the wording but it is delicately suggested. To *suggest* but not to *define* is the business of the true poet, as Mallarmé has said. In addition, such an apposition without logical determination is a well-known elegance of Latin style. It appears again in stanza 3: "*et n'ai pas entrepris, injurieux ami, de soulager ta peine*" and is often found in Ronsard (in the sonnet *Comme on voit sure la branche: "La Pargue t'a tuée, et cendre tu reposes"*). Malherbe, as well as Ronsard of whom Boileau stated it, knew how to "*parler latin en français.*" The Latinizing construction gives the earnestness and solemnity of history to the passage. Finally, there is given to us in our line a second of respite by the ambiguous expression *ce que vivent les roses*—an *accusativus mensurae* indicating measure of time that does not truly measure, since *ce que* in itself could be a long as well as a short time, but as we come to the end of the line: *les roses,* we are prepared for the second alternative, which now crushes us with the dire finality of fate: *l'espace d'un matin.* Ausonius had written: *"Quam longa una dies, tam longa aetas rosarum."* Malherbe's paraphrase of the ancient verse omits the pedantic correspondence *quam longa . . . tam longa* and replaces it by the vague *ce que.* In addition, the rhyme *matin* with *destin* is conceived as if to seal the destiny of the rose: her *destiny* was to live one *morning*—and here a Biblical influence makes itself felt (the psalmist writes: *"Mane sicut herba transeat, mane floreat et transeat").* In this stanza, then, the great stoic rhetorician Malherbe has not indulged, as usually, in neoclassic ornate speech but reached powerful effect with utterly simple means; in other words he has reached the realm of the sublime as defined by Longinus.

The reader will, however, be astonished to learn that Malherbe has not reached such a summit of poetry immediately, by a flash of inspiration, but slowly and gradually, by patiently reworking a quite prosaic first draft. Stanza 4 read originally:

> Mais elle était du monde où les plus belles choses
> Font le moins de séjour,
> Et ne pouvoit Rosette être mieux que les roses
> Qui ne vivent qu'un jour—

We may suppose that it was relatively quite inconsequential technical considerations that have led Malherbe to reword the lines, with the perhaps unexpected result that a pedestrian text reached sublimity. Malherbe may have taken exception to the all too easy rhyme of a word with its compound: *jour—séjour,* a type of rhyme he himself censured when finding it in a poem of his pupil Racan. In addition the phrase *être mieux que (les roses),* "be better off than," may have appeared to him at second thought as one of the shallow idioms he would have been the first to chastise in poems of others: instead of suggesting a mysterious conformity of the maiden's fate with the universal fate of nature as in the final wording, the earlier variant *et ne pouvoit Rosette . . .* states an outright matter-of-fact equality. And finally, the name of the maiden *Rosette,* quite artificially concocted by Malherbe for the daughter of M. Du Périer (her name in real life was Marguerite!) only for the sake of a *précieux,* Petrarchistic pun, was bound to disappear because of the mature poet's opposition to the mawkish diminutives that had been overused by the school of the Pleiad and because the playful nuance of this name would have jarred with the solemn stoic character of the poem. We witness here an extraordinary case of, so to speak, "hesitant poetic alchemy," a transformation of the prosaic achieved not in one grandiose leap but piecemeal, by successive corrections which nevertheless were able to create one of the most perfect passages of French poetry—a case corroborating Valéry's oft-repeated admonishment to poets that it is not inspiration alone that creates. Ours is a memorable case to be cited against the current prejudice of critics reared in evolutionistic trends of thought that the rough draft of a poet, since closest to his original inspiration, must always betray more about the intrinsic meaning of his poem than later versions. It is Malherbe's final version of our stanza, on the contrary, that is truest to the intention of the whole poem in that it describes poetically the correspondence between individual and general human destiny.

If the line *rose elle a vécu ce que vivent les roses* translates a stoic vision into true poetry, we should expect to find the same experience similarly expressed in other passages of the poem. And indeed we find in stanza 9 *"Aime une ombre comme ombre, et des cendres éteintes éteins le souvenir"*—again two repetitions of word stems and chiasm, which in his case make oblivion appear inevitable.

Again, in stanza 17 the repetition of *deux fois:*

> De moi, déjà deux fois d'une pareille foudre
> Je me suis vu perclus:
> Et deux fois la raison m'a si bien fait résoudre
> Qu'il ne m'en souvient plus.

makes the "reasonable decision" in two cases of grievous loss appear as necessary, withdrawn from arbitrariness. And finally, in the last stanza:

> De murmurer contre elle [la Mort] et perdre patience
> Il est mal à propos;
> Vouloir ce que Dieu veut est la seule science
> Qui nous met en repos.

the stoic moral of renouncement (*sustine et abstine,* as Aulus Gellius formulated it in antiquity) has found an artistic embodiment in the parallelism of the two verbal forms *vouloir* [*ce que Dieu*] *veut,* indicative of the necessary parallelism between God's and our own desires. These lines are couched in a soldier-like austerity and simplicity, the image of that stoic soul that contracts itself because it knows of its own limitations and duties.

There is still a third element to be considered in our passage: the metric form of the quatrain, consisting in alternating alexandrines and six-syllable lines (a form which had been used before Malherbe in a translation of a psalm by Marot, who thus rendered the Hebrew *parallelismus verborum,* and which has been imitated by Victor Hugo in "A Villequier," a poem prompted by an incident similar to the one treated by Malherbe: the death of his grandchildren). Malherbe offers us, as it were, a rhythmic symbol for the contraction of the soul before the inevitable, its retreat into itself, the attitude he proposes as the only philosophy worthy of man; in reading the poem we are, so to speak, invited to practice the gymnastics of the soul of the stoic: after the expansion in the alexandrine the hexasyllable teaches restraint—diastole is followed by systole:

> De murmure contre elle et perdre patience
> *Il est mal à propos*
> Vouloir ce que Dieu veut est la seule science
> *Qui nous met en repos.*

The stringency of the universal law is often expressed in our poem in the short line, the line that enjoins restraint:

> 18. Mais, en un accident qui n'a point de remède
> *Il n'en faut point chercher.*

> 19. La cruelle qu'elle est [fate] se bouche les oreilles
> *Et nous laisse crier.*

> 20. Le pauvre en sa cabane où le chaume le couvre
> *Est sujet à ses lois.*

The philosophical necessity of renouncement is, as we have said before, symbolized by the lines in stanza 9:

> Aime une ombre comme ombre, et des cendres éteintes
> *Éteins le souvenir.*

Now we may point out the prosodic value of the foreshortened line in which the admonishment to "extinguish our memories" is expressed. It is as though the poetic form of such lines executed what its content preaches. Similarly, in stanza 17 the short line makes a compliance with the laws of the universe that seems truly above human power appear as easily accomplished; the psychological *tour de force* is, as it were, made acceptable by the metric device:

> Et deux fois la raison m'a si bien fait résoudre
> *Qu'il ne m'en souvient plus.*

Thus, to return now to our key couplet[4], the concluding line *L'espace d'un matin* is the exact metrical rendering of the idea expressed therein: the line is short—and brief is our life. In general, the dual principle on which the twenty-one stanzas of the poem are built is a reflection of the movement of the soul that longs to expand in grief but is continuously forced by reason to accept restraint—classical or stoic restraint. Thus a philosophical advice has found its prosodic counterpart; it has been symbolized by units of breath, it has been made kinesthetically perceptible. In other words, the abstract principle has been poetically relived by Malherbe.

French commentators generally repeat Sainte-Beuve's witticism: a second Malherbe should have arisen to curtail the excessive length of the poem of the first. But are these poor aestheticians not aware of the fact that this poem, a dirge which gains in momentum and solemnity with its length, just as a funeral cortege becomes the more impressive the longer the defile of marching mourners, is also a stoic exercise in self-restraint? The "gymnastics of the soul" imposed by the philosopher on the mourner has found its convincing poetic equivalent—which becomes more convincing through the self-possessed, if dreary, repetition.

Here then it was possible for poetry to evoke the rhythm of purely abstract thought. While it is relatively easy to compose poetry about love and spring, subject matters in themselves naturally poetic, the greatest challenge is offered to the poet when he proposes, as Lucretius and Dante have done, to sing of subject matter most rebellious to poetry, of abstract philosophical thought: "to make ideas sing" (in Valéry's words). I shall now choose a complete, if relatively small, poetic organism in order to show how, by means of delicate prosodic devices, a philosophical idea can be made poetry: the sonnet of the Idea by the French poet Du Bellay (published in 1549 in his collection of sonnets "L'Olive" as number 113). According to Plato the human soul is provided with wings wherewith to fly toward heaven, where dwells the divine idea of beauty, wisdom, and goodness: the true reality, of which all earthly beauty, wisdom, and goodness is only an imperfect copy. Let us see now how the Renaissance poet has converted this Platonic myth, which is itself a poetic description of man's constant aspiration toward the ideal, into *poetry:*

> Si nostre vie est moins qu'une journée
> En l'éternel, si l'an qui faict le tour
> Chasse noz jours sans espoir de retour,
> Si perissable est toute chose née,
>
> Que songes-tu, mon ame emprisonnée?
> Pourquoy te plaist l'obscur de nostre jour,
> Si pour voler en un plus cler sejour,
> Tu as au dos l'aele bien empanée?
>
> La est le bien que tout eprit desire,
> La le repos où tout le monde aspire,
> La est l'amour, la le plaisir encore,
>
> La, ô mon ame au plus hault ciel guidée,
> Tu y pouras recognoistre l'Idée
> De la beauté qu'en ce monde j'adore.

I believe that the aesthetic secret of the sonnet lies mainly in the fact that the motif of the soul's striving toward the Platonic idea is not only *stated* but *embodied* by rhythmical devices. We feel drawn by the poem into a movement of its own which, as we come to the end, is revealed to be the attractive force of the Idea. And since the words of the poem suggest an upward movement the reader is induced to imitate this movement in modulations of his own voice, by a musical intonation which indeed creates music out of the words. It would, I believe, be impossible for anyone to read the poem except by starting in a low register and gradually and steadily raising the pitch, until finally the Idea of beauty, *l'Idée de la beauté,* is revealed in the last two lines—the rise of pitch becoming symbolic of the flight of the soul toward higher and higher spheres and ultimately the empyrean. That other world which it is poetry's function to reveal has thus been suggested to us by quite sensuously perceptible linguistic or prosodic devices chosen by the poet, rhythm and pitch, which act on us, as it were contagiously. As for the sentence structure, the three hypothetic sentences of the first quatrain beginning with *Si* contain the reasons for man's discontent with this earth (the threefold "if" is indeed here a "since"), and the varying length of these three clauses reflects our restlessness (the *enjambement* in the second line cuts the three first lines into two unsymmetrical parts; only in line 4 are clause and line of equal length). The fact that the first stanza is filled with dependent clauses, the main clause following only in stanza 2, introduces a further rhythmical element portraying constraint. The soul, so to speak, is striving to free itself from the bonds of prison just as the dependent clauses make us fret to move impatiently toward the main clause *Que songes-tu.* . . . We come to realize our state of captivity in the prison of this world by the rhythm of the dependent clauses even before the word *emprisonnée* in the main clause spells out the nature of our existence. In the second stanza with its questions of benevolent admonishment *Que songes-tu* . . .? *Pourquoy te plaist* . . .? there is already contained a suggestion of liberation. To the idea of the prison are now opposed the ideas of "wing" and "flight," to "the darkness of the earthly day" *un plus cler séjour*. Stanza 2 must be spoken with higher pitch than the description of uneasiness in stanza 1. Liberation is at the doorstep of the prison cell with the mention of *l'aele bien empanée*—and liberation is *realized* with the first *la* of stanza 3, which everyone will naturally read with enormous energy (LA *est le bien que tout esprit désire*) as if the soul had already leaped toward its salvation and the sight of the goal were identical with the flight toward it. *Un plus cler séjour* has now indeed become a firmly established, well-determined goal. All the helpless repression of the soul described in stanza 1, all the still-doubting hope that was envisaged in stanza 2, is now transcended. In the *là* the elation manifests itself that goes with liberation, with the knowlege of the soul's destination. Inded the whole second half of the sonnet represents the fulfillment of the desires described in the first half, and the alternation between collective and individual suggested in the first part (stanza 1 is phrased in collective style: *nostre vie, noz jours, toute chose née*, while stanza 2 is entirely addressed to the individual soul: *mon ame),* will reappear symmetrically in the second part, this time lifted up to another climate (stanza 3: *tout esprit, tout le monde,* collectivistic, *vs.* stanza 4: *ô mon ame,* individualistic). Now the usual pattern of the sonnet: eight lines in the first, six in the second part, produces in our particular case an effect of *accelerando.* If the soul was relatively slow in freeing itself from the bonds of the prison, now in its flight heavenward it does what the French call *brûler les étapes!* The couplets in the tercets (*cc* d *ee* d), a French innovation in the Italianate form of the sonnet, give the impression of a double wing beat. And the five anaphoric *là*'s ("there . . . there . . .") are like rungs on a foreshortened ladder that leads toward heaven. Each *là* must be spoken according to the law of *acceleration* and on a higher note as a higher station in the spheres is reached with increasing swiftness. After the calmer measure of stanza 2 we find a new mood of impatience in stanzas 3 and 4, parallel to that of the first stanza, except that this time we feel that release will come. In lines 9 and 10 the initial *là*, as it were a bold plunge into space, is followed by a movement of steady calm: LA *est le bien que tout esprit désire,* LA *le repos où tout le monde aspire.* In line 11 the movement quickens and becomes *staccato* in breathless anticipation of an end to torture (in musical terms we could also speak of a *stretta*). Some pedestrian critics have censured the *encore* of line 11 as a *cheville,* a padding due to exigencies of rhyme; in reality this *encore* is a find worthy of a genius. I not only see in it a word added, in the manner of Latin *etiam* in lengthy enumerations, in order to point up the number of heavenly delights that await the soul, but hear in it the encouraging shout to the forespent athlete before his last bout: *encore!*—an encouragement to the soul to make the last effort before reaching the sky, an effort that will be rewarded by the infinite and unlimited enjoyment felt by the soul at the moment of the Epiphany of the Idea of beauty.

We have indeed come, as in a dream, to the empyrean, the tenth heaven—*la, ô mon ame, au plus hault ciel guidée*—without any previous allusion to the nine successive heavens that have been passed and that must have magically receded before the soul, like so many backdrops on a stage, melting one into the other. The five *là*'s do not mark the different spheres; they are only rungs which help us visualize the heavenly ladder. Neither was there any previous mention of a guide. Only now, by the wording so similar to that of Dante and doubtless inspired by him, do we realize that there must have been for this soul too a Beatrice *che guidò le penne de le mie ali a così alto volo*. And with the supernatural appearance of the Idea beauty and serenity at last prevail as they are depicted in a double line that is indeed one sweeping long line, corresponding to the triumph, elation, relaxation, fulfillment of the soul that has reached its goal: *(la, ô mon ame, au plus hault ciel guidée, tu y pouras recognoistre l'Idée de la beauté qu'en ce monde j'adore)*. The last two lines must be read as one because of the syntactic tie which exists between *l'Idée* and *de la beauté*. This is the metric device, well known to the ancients, called by them *synapheia*. The word *l'Idée*, of Greek origin and used by Du Bellay in its Greek double meaning of visual as well as mental perception, was still novel in France (the rhyme *idée—guidée* occurs in the sixteenth century before Du Bellay in the Platonist Maurice Scève's *Délie*). *Idée* has here the impact of a proper name of an allegory or of a goddess such as Pallas Athena. It marks the apex of the poem (the zenith, if the nadir was *notre vie* in line 1), and also the highest point reached by the voice of the reader, after which point the voice will immediately fall slightly when the soul, casting its glance back on the stretch of way it has wandered, is able to discern now on this earth, *ce monde*, reflections or copies of the archetype of the Idea of beauty. The final note of this "cyclical" poem, which leads us from earth to heaven and back to earth, is then no longer one of contempt for this earth but rather one of return to, and reconciliation with, our world, which appears now in a new light: no longer ephemeral as in the beginning but transformed by the poet's experience of heavenly beauty. The verb *j'adore* suggests a religious attitude sustained, confidently established, beyond all danger of the abyss—and it must be spoken with calm emotion that should stay with us even after we have finished the reading of the poem.

To resume the observations hitherto made, the philosophical idea of the striving of the soul toward the eternal archetype of beauty has been rendered by our poet in a sensuous manner, by rhythm and pitch, as they symbolize the force of attraction felt by the soul. And Du Bellay has achieved this effect without violating the traditionally given metric form of the sonnet, only by introducing into the normal decasyllables a particular rhythm suggestive of the *idea* of the sonnet.

Now our direct observation about Du Bellay's rhythmic organization of the traditional sonnet pattern in the service of an idea (in the service of the idea of the Idea)—this observation is verifiable by any reader, must carry the *consensus omnium* simply because it can be ratified by the generally human kinesthetic sense and it is as factual and real a trait as any observation in the natural sciences based on sensuous perception. As long as French will live our poem will produce out of itself the same kinesthetic reaction; and even if French should die, our poem, brought by miracle to a faraway island together with a dictionary and an elementary grammar of French, would elicit the same musical response in an elite of philologists of that island who would be able to decipher it. If the *consensus omnium* cannot immediately be reached by an average public today this is greatly due to the lack of training at school of our general public in kinesthetic matters. In order to facilitate for the layman apperception of the acoustic symbolism I have pointed out in the Du Bellay poem, one should emphasize, as in the beginning of this chapter, the existence and nature of similar phenomena of expressivity in the *common language*. A phenomenon of expressivity is given in our languages only when content and form meet, when there is an acoustic parallelism between *significatum* and *significans*. To add to my previous examples an observation made by Maurice Grammont, the word *ticktack*, often the first word learned by babies in many countries, is an expressive way of designating a watch, in which the name, corresponding acoustically to the object so named, produces aesthetic pleasure in the child whereas the word *tactic*, in which the sound-meaning correspondence is missing, is completely unexpressive. Similarly in our poem an impression of acoustic-ideological correspondence was produced by Du Bellay's particular devices in sonnet 113. For an example of a poem with the same content as ours without an acoustic form that matches it—an analogy to the case of *tactic* in the general language—one has but to turn to the sonnet in Du Bellay's *"L'Olive"* preceding ours, number 112. Here we are shown the Christian God in His providence choosing among the different Ideas representing the souls of man the most beautiful ones, which then will be attracted toward Him in a purifying flight toward heaven:

> Dedans le clos des occultes Idées,
> Au grand troupeau des ames immortelles

Le prevoyant a choisi les plus belles,
Pour estre à luy par luymesme guidées.

Lors peu à peu devers le ciel guindées
Dessus l'engin de leurs divines aeles
Vollent au seing des beautez eternelles,
Ou elle' sont de tout vice emondées.

One finds here the upward movement of purification, the wings
that carry the souls toward heaven, the guidance by divine powers
—but the acoustic correspondence is missing. It is even as though,
because the union of sense and sound failed to materialize, the
metaphoric expression of the sense, uninspired by rhythm, became
tedious and contorted. What should we make of the "engine" of
the divine wings which is wound up (*guindée*) like a pulley on a
ship?

Are we able now to retrace any previous stages of the master
sonnet number 113 which would allow us to follow the gradual
development from a lesser poetic to a highly poetic level, as it was
possible for us to do for stanza 4 of Malherbe's poem? In the case
of the sonnet of the Idea the pre-stage is not represented by a first
draft of Du Bellay's, but by an Italian model which was pointed
out by Vianey in "*Le pétrarquisme en France*" (1909). Our sonnet
seems to be, at first glance, a rather close paraphrase of an Italian
original, of a sonnet written by the Petrarchist Bernardino Daniello which Du Bellay may have read in an anthology published
in 1545 by a Venetian printer:

Se 'l viver nostro è breve oscuro giorno
Press' a l'eterno, e pien d'affanni e mali;
E più veloci assai che venti o strali,
Ne vedi ir gli anni e più non far ritorno:

Alma, che fai? che non ti miri intorno
Sepolta in cieco error tra le mortali
Noiose cure? e poi ti son date ali
Da volar a l'eterno alto soggiorno,

Scuotile, trista, ch' è ben tempo homai,
Fuor del visco mondan ch' è si tenace,
E le dispiega al ciel per dritta via:

Ivi è quel sommo ben ch' ogni huom desia;
Ivi 'l vero riposo; ivi la pace
Ch' indarno tu quagiù cercando vai.

What interests us here in connection with the relationship between language and poetry is the case of two poems having an identical content, and to a great extent identical wording, while differing vastly in form: thus it is not the mythological content alone that conditions great poetry. Daniello's poem is a relatively mediocre treatment of a subject matter to which Du Bellay alone has given perfect form. If Daniello has, by the syntactical concatenation of his stanzas 1-3 with the culmination in the imperative *scuotile*, "try thy wings" (line 9), aptly expressed the desire of the soul to free itself from the *visco mondan*, the worldly mire, he has not found an adequate rhythmic expression for the wings naturally given to the soul. The whole third stanza, in which there is administered to the soul a didactic admonishment about breaking its chains, has been boldly omitted by Du Bellay, who, after having reminded the soul of its wings, immediately sets before her the heavenly goal. It was the sudden revelation of a goal which gave all its dramatic intensity to the first *là*. With Du Bellay the soul needs no exhortation to follow the straight way (*la dritta via*) to heaven; with him the straight way is given immediately with the mention of the wings and all earthly mire is left far behind. While the three *ivi*, "there," of Daniello refer only to *ciel*, already mentioned as the goal in line 8, the *là*'s of Du Bellay anticipate, indeed evoke that high goal before it is explicitly designated (only later, in line 12, do we learn that it is toward the empyrean, *le plus hault ciel*, that the soul has proceeded). For with Du Bellay the soul congenitally knows its goal, with no need to have its course mapped. And, of course, Daniello, more a preacher than a poet, was concerned with teaching us quietly, in a predicatorial trichotomy, that heaven is the seat of the highest good, of repose and peace which are not found on this earth, whereas the true lyricist Du Bellay evokes in his five *là* segments the impatience of the soul to reach heaven. Indeed, while the *ivi* of Daniello refer to the transmundane world envisaged as a totality, each *là* of Du Bellay seems to point as it were to another level of the heavenly spheres. Neither is it chance that the Frenchman, in line with his more sensuous talent, enumerates as two additional *là*-members love and joy and introduces as the climax the Epiphany of the Idea with all its emotional and dramatic impact. Finally, once Du Bellay had glimpsed the Idea in the tenth heaven, he was not, like the Italian, tempted to cast a last bitter glance toward the vanity of the earth but was able at last to recognize also on this earth the adumbrations of the Idea of beauty, the tie between the two worlds. By Du Bellay Platonism has not been preached to us, it has been lived for us; the force of attraction of the Platonic idea has been rhythmically impersonated. With very slight changes Du Bellay has been able to create a poem totally different from that of the Italian, different in content as well as form—the typical achievement of a classic which produces great results with a minimum amount of material effort.

In order to follow here the poetization of language in the sonnet to its ultimate source we may ask ourselves about the "source" of the sonnet of Bernardino Daniello on which in turn Du Bellay's sonnet is based. Is it Plato's dialogue *Phaidros?* In that dialogue we find indeed the simile of the wings applied to the soul. The soul (of the gods and of man) is compared there with a chariot, the charioteer and the two horses of which are winged. In the case of the gods the two horses, equally inspired by virtue, draw by their common effort the chariot toward the soul's true goal while in the case of man one horse is wicked and tends to draw the chariot down toward an alien goal. The wings given to the soul have the function of "lifting what is naturally heavy" in it toward the heights of the divine, toward the contemplation of divine nature consisting in beauty, wisdom, and goodness—but there is also given to the soul of man the possibility to ruin or loose its wings and to fall heavily to earth. The truly winged human soul is that of the philosopher. When he encounters on this earth a reflection of divine beauty, divine frenzy or enthusiasm seizes him, a frenzy due to his remembrance of the Idea which man had once glimpsed, before his fall, when he was still allied with the gods. The common people are right then, says Plato, in calling the philosopher a fool. For the philosopher, when recognizing the exemplar of beauty in earthly beauty, starts, as it were, to take flight, with fresh wings and impatient to fly (Plato is using here thrice in the same sentence the stem of the verb, "to fly"), but, alas, can only look upward like a bird, blind to the things of this earth. "Every human soul must have indeed once contemplated the true reality, otherwise it could not have become a living being." To remember that vision of true reality is given to only a few elect human beings and this only in the state of ecstasy. It is thus such a state of ecstasy of a philosopher who "recognizes" the Idea of beauty that is described in Du Bellay's sonnet: a state of beatific vision, with its cyclic character as defined by Shakespeare. ("The poet's eye, in a fine frenzy rolling/doth glance from heaven to earth, from earth to heaven").

But there are several details in the sonnets of Daniello and Du Bellay which cannot come from the *Phaidros*—for instance, the idea of the transient nature of things earthly, or again the identification of the highest good with peace and repose, to say nothing of such stylistic elements as the "if"="since" clauses or the three-fold (fivefold) anaphora with "there." All these features come from Boethius, *De Consolatione Philosophiae*, that fifth-century dialogue between Dame Philosophy and Boethius, the Roman high official and scholar (who may or may not have been a Christian), to whom while he was suffering in a dark jail Philosophy, that is, a stoic or Christian version of Platonism, brings her light. The dialogue, in prose, is interspersed with various poems intended to sum up the philosophical discussion at its different stages, from which I quote the following hymn. Boethius offers us here a picture, conceived in terms of Ptolemaic science, of the whole astronomical and natural cosmos as ruled over by God, and then follow the lines:

> Sunt etenim pennae volucres mihi,
> quae celsa conscendant poli;
> quas sibi cum velox mens induit,
> terras perosa despicit . . .

> *His* regum sceptrum dominus tenet
> orbisque habenas temperat
> et volucrem currum stabilis regit
> rerum coruscus arbiter.

> *Huc* te si reducem referat via,
> quam nunc requiris immemor,
> *haec*, dices, memini, patria est mihi,
> *hinc* ortus, *hic* sistam gradum.

> Quodsi terrarum placeat tibi
> noctem relictam versere,
> quos miseri torvos populi timent,
> cernes tyrannos exsules.

These lines show a fivefold anaphora of demonstratives (*hic-huc-haec-hinc-hic*), and also the Platonic conception of remembrance ἀνάμνσις.=*memini*), here rhetorically emphasized by repetition of the prefix *re-* (*reducem, referat, requiris*). Now the rhetorical device of anaphoric pronouns is well known to any reader of Ovid or Martial, the rhetorical Augustan poets, while more purely lyrical poets such as Catullus or Tibullus seem to shun this device. One may remember such passages as in *Tristia* where the "ravages of time" are described:

> *Hoc* [sc. tempus] temperat dentem terram renovantis aratri,
> *hoc* rigidas silices, *hoc* adamanta terit,
> *hoc* etiam saevas paulatim mitigat iras,
> *hoc* minuit luctus maestaque corda levat.

Instead of saying "time blunts the edge of the plowshare, wears away the flint-stone and the steel, mitigates wrath, diminishes sorrow and cheers up the sad heart," the rhetorical lyricist prefers to hammer into our minds the fact of the *identity* of the cause (*hoc*) behind those different developments, an overstressing which is lost on our modern imagination. Once we have understood this identity tediousness is the immediate consequence. The series of anaphoras in Boethius is not basically different from that of Ovid. Boethius too wishes to impress on us a single idea that the the the true homeland of man's soul is the beyond (*haec patria est mihi*). His five demonstratives used as it were to show us the way to our destination are no less didactic than are in a medieval painting the fingers of different sages or saints all pointing toward heaven—so many "pictorial anaphoras." In a late Latin text such as Boethius, which for 1000 years has been interpreted as a monument of Christian faith in the beyond, the particular set of anaphoras came to be felt as a supreme expression of the human yearning for the other world—and to Renaissance sensibilities it seemed to point to a world in which the synthesis of Christianity and Platonism was real. We witness here the wondrous vitality of a formal (prosodic) pattern once it has concluded a significant alliance with a great concept, in other words, once sound and meaning have met to form a perfect expressive unit. The *hoc* anaphora applied by Ovid to time has been read through the centuries by students of the classics without striking any response comparable to that of the *hic haec huc* linked in Boethius with Platonic-Christian other-worldliness, a device which has come to a unique revival 1000 years after Boethius—with Du Bellay, who adds to the device that ascensional movement which was latent in the Platonic idea.

Now the case of an observation of a particular artistic device directly inferred from the evidence of a text later being revealed, by investigation of sources, as *distinctive* of that text—perhaps as *unique* in world literature—this case is not isolated. The critic would not have been struck by a certain detail in a text were it not singularly convincing in this, and only this, context, did it not appear as though consubstantial with that text, did it not impress us as a *locus classicus* undiluted into a *locus communis*. If our investigation of the literary sources of the sonnet of the Idea has been ultimately disappointing and anticlimactic, it has at least served to prove beyond doubt the uniqueness, if not in content, at least in poetic form, of that sonnet.

If we look back at the prosodic devices found in the poetic texts discussed in this chapter (word parallelism, onomatopoeization, rhyme, anaphora, etc.), we are struck by the variety of phenomena which can however be reduced to the one basic phenomenon: symbolic *repetition of sound elements,* connotative of identities or homologies in outward reality, which is already given in language as such but is expanded in poetry. It is, as we said before, the "number two" which allows the poet to interpret the world poetically by introducing ideas of patterns or structures which will become the more poetic the more these verbally indicated patterns or structures differ from the structures which have become usual in our current thought or in the grammar of our languages. The poet must thank his Creator, of whom he proudly bears the name ποιητής "Maker"), for having created *omnia in mensura et pondere et numero*. It is not by chance that Professor Anna Hatcher has chosen precisely this Biblical motto for a study of the Old French poem on St. Alexius (published in *Traditio* VII), in which the numerical patterns, expressive of inner development of the protagonist and extending throughout a poem of more than 500 lines, are carefully studied. We may ask ourselves whether in this case (and in the more complicated one of the *Divina Commedia*) we have truly to do with prosody or rather with thematic composition. It is perhaps not an undue word use to call the thematic architecture of a poem a "prosody of thought."

We have found that the poetic effect in all examples offered was at bottom due to that basic phenomenon inherent in human language, *expressivity*, which has been extended and intensified by

the poets so as to produce in us the illusion of an "as if"—a world
in which the myths of yore come true. The desire for illusion, for
surcease from the laws of causality is indeed deep-rooted in all of
us. On the lowest level, in an age of mass civilization and of
timidity of imagination, this desire will send many to the comic
strips, which give them the disinterested enjoyment of a world
which, while freed from the modern implications of determinism
and transfigured by the comic spirit or the spirit of adventure, can
still somehow be felt to be *their own world* (and many will turn to
the world of the Shmoos, those word-born beings that have developed out of the Yiddish word for "profit, illicit gain" into prototypes of that abundance and goodness of the earth which is freely
given to all men). On the highest level, the more boldly imaginative reader will enjoy Dante's crushing or elevating picture of an
entirely imaginary world with a physics and a biology quite
aberrant from our own, wherein it is love that moves the sun and
the stars and where the disembodied souls live in the presence of
God, while miraculously retaining their earthly physical appearance and emotions.

But, we might ask, must man, in order to free himself by poetry
from the prison of his actual environment, always take refuge in the
poetry of past ages which necessarily embodies obsolete mythological and cosmological conceptions? Could modern man never turn
to poetry that would express modern scientific truth with all its
metaphysical implications, endowed with that artistic beauty and
that realistic evidence which in Dante compels belief? Is the life-
giving power of poetry reserved only for sublime folly which
makes real what the poet believes he knows; is it denied to the
sober wisdom of truth that truly knows? The fact that there has
not yet appeared a modern Dante who would make modern
science sing (who would, that is, make science appear as belonging
both to our own and to a transmundane world) is, however, easily
enough explained: the burden of age-old myths still weighs too
heavy on our words to allow them to express the mythology of our
time. The greatest modern historian, Arnold Toynbee (the greatest
because the most poetic, because he has sensed most keenly the
necessity for modern historiography to free us from the doom of
history) often has recourse to poetic myth—but his poetic myths
are revivals of ancient myths (for instance, his myth of the birth of

a new civilization that represents an answer of a human community to the challenge of the Devil who has invaded the world of God). It is my personal feeling that the concepts of the moral world, of God and Devil, will not be abandoned altogether in the centuries to come but will gradually be rephrased and shaded in consonance with our modern scientific knowledge of the physical world. After all, Dante's poetic codification of medieval science and its synthesis with Christian theology came 1500 years after the poetic codification by Lucretius of pagan untheological science. We should then restrain our modern impatience and wait for another 1500 years for the poetic language to mature that would furnish adequate instruments for the expression of the scientific world-picture of Einstein and Curie and of the religious implications this may have. The mills of language grind slow, but they grind exceedingly fine.

I hope that I have been able to show that language, far from being only a banal means of communication and self-expression and even of orientation in this world (a way that leads toward science and is "perfected by science"), offers us also a means for freeing us from this world thanks to its metaphysical and poetic implications. Language, the raw material of poetry, is distinguished from the raw materials of the other arts in that it is already in itself a refined human artistic activity, an *energeia* which embodies meaning in sound produced by the most immaterial and elusive instruments of the human body (our breath playing on delicate keyboards behind the screen of our face). And this same material-immaterial activity, *language,* the main vehicle for the communication of meaning in the business of this world, is able to transform itself into the rainbow bridge which leads mankind toward other worlds where meaning rules absolute.

❧ Chapter XIV
HUNTINGTON CAIRNS

LANGUAGE OF JURISPRUDENCE

Legal speculation endeavors to depict in language the structure and occurrences of the external world as they are related to the phenomena of the law. That enterprise is surrounded by numerous dangers. "Symbolism is very fallible," Whitehead has observed, "in the sense that it may induce actions, feelings, emotions, and beliefs about things which are mere notions without that exemplification in the world which the symbolism leads us to suppose." At the least, language is the medium through which legal thinkers communicate with one another and record the knowledge they discover. There is the related circumstance that language has a connection with legal reality. Thus the relations between words and meaning, and between words and things, are matters that legal speculation must face in its effort to reach a valid understanding of the nature and role of law.

Language is a subject which has been little explored by legal thought. Law, in the intimate connections it has always maintained with formal logic, has skirted the problem of language but it has rarely been interested in the relation of the language of the law to that discipline. No doubt the charges that contemporary jurisprudence has brought against formal logic are justified. In one aspect the relationship between law and logic has hindered the development of legal thought. Lawyers too often have adopted without question the methods and conclusions reached in logical analysis. This has led to superficiality and the construction of inadequately grounded systems, as in Fortescue's attempted adaptation of English law to Aristotle's doctrine of the four causes. In another respect, it has led to what the Germans call *Begriffsjurisprudenz,* or the abuse of abstractions in legal thought. Long before Jhering, Holmes, and others denounced the practice of sacrificing desirable results for logical consistency, the practice has been condemned by Blackstone. Unfortunately, the first rudiments of science the Norman conquerors imbibed, he remarked, "were those of Aristotle's philosophy, conveyed through the medium of his Arab Commentators, which were brought from the East by the Saracens into Palestine and Spain, and translated into Barbarous Latin." The law of those times was "therefore frittered into logical distinctions, and drawn out into metaphysical subtleties, with a skill most amazingly artificial, but which serves no other purpose than to show the vast powers of the human intellect, however vainly or preposterously employed."

No doubt lawyers and judges have tended to abuse logic, and probably also the confining form of the classical logic assisted in that activity. Perhaps the generalization of the classical logic to include both invariance and transformation will some day help to meet the problems presented by so unstable a system as the law. In any event, notwithstanding its abuses, logical technique when properly applied is a necessary tool in legal analysis. The alternative is the chaos of contradiction.

At the root of the sound employment of logical method is the problem of symbolism. Logical technique is the manipulation of symbols according to certain standards. If we wish to understand that technique we must first understand the nature of the symbols we employ.

From the point of view of legal theory, the chief problem with respect to language is its characteristic as a bearer of meaning. This is a complicated matter and extends from the idea of signs to the nature of the relationship which exists between language and the structure of the world. Contemporary thought has been marked by the large attention it has given to language, and the conclusion is general that it is one of the most fundamental and difficult of all the problems of philosophy. For the most part, the issues which have been raised have been distributed as follows: To psychology has been given the task of ascertaining what actually occurs in our minds when we use language with the intention of meaning something by it; to epistemology has been assigned the problem of defining the relation that subsists between thoughts, words, or sentences and that which they refer to or mean; to the special sciences, such as law, has been given the problem of using sentences formulated from the position of the subject matter of their own domains, so as to convey truth rather than falsehood; finally, there is the purely logical question: What relation must one fact (such as a sentence) have to another in order to be *capable* of being a symbol for that other? All these issues bear upon one another, and they all converge upon the problem raised for legal theory, namely, the capacities of ordinary language to meet the tasks of the law. No doubt, ultimately all the questions are subsumed by the problem of what may be inferred with respect to the structure of the world, including the social realm, from the structure of language. The language problem is thus so complex that it seems impossible to attack it except in a piecemeal fashion. This means, for the present at any rate, that the results of analysis are tentative and partial. If the results are valid they should eventually form a consistent whole, but much work remains to be accomplished before that position will be reached.

Plato's attempt in the *Cratylus* to analyze the problem of the possibility of significant false statements is an illustration of the close relationship between law and the issues raised by the study of language. Cratylus, in the course of maintaining the paradox that it is impossible to speak falsely because one cannot utter the thing that is not, is forced by Socrates to argue that a bad law is no law. Since we do not know with certainty the order of the Platonic Dialogues, it is impossible to say if the idea first presented itself to Plato at this time. Although in the *Cratylus* the idea is an inference from a false proposition there is no doubt that Plato accepted the notion that a bad law is no law as a valid one. It is advanced also in the *Hippias Major* and in the somewhat doubtful *Minos*. In Cicero's hands the doctrine became associated with the law of nature. Cicero realized that the naked formula that a bad law is no law was insufficient; in order to remove the formula from the realm of caprice he saw that a standard was necessary. He therefore argued that, while a set of words, as embodied in a statute, might have the formal character of law, the words did not possess the real character of law if what they expressed was contrary to the law of nature. This idea was current in the Middle Ages and is a part of our law today. The standard against which the law is to be measured has varied, but the substance of the doctrine has never been lost to sight. The early Bolognese author of the *Petri Exceptiones Legis Romain* rejected all laws which were contrary to *aequitas,* and Bracton laid it down in his treatment of the coronation of the English kings that an authority contrary to justice and equity was no authority. The doctrine of unconstitutional statutes and the laws invalid because contrary to a "higher law" is a sophisticated, contemporary expression of the ancient Platonic theory.

Legal thinking with respect to the problem of language, when looked at historically, has raised three general questions. It has endeavored to mark out the ideal forms of expression for the conveyance of legal meaning; it has considered the nature of a professional language; and it has reflected to some extent upon the connections between words and things. These are matters about which much uncertainty seems to prevail, and the opinions which have been advanced are conjectural rather than the result of inferences from sufficient grounds.

Speculation on the proper modes of legal statement has oscillated between two extreme views. It has been assumed that the end of language in the domain of the law is either truth or power. The issue was first sharply raised in Plato's dialogue the *Gorgias.* Socrates extracted from *Gorgias* the famous definition of rhetoric as the art of persuasion as exemplified in the law courts and assemblies, and whose subject matter is the just and the unjust. But if the aim of rhetoric is merely to persuade, then the business of the rhetorician is not to instruct a law court but only to make it believe. Thus, the rhetorician is able to persuade juries to acquit the guilty. Plato does not attempt, at the level of legal discourse, to resolve the issue which has been raised. His discussion of legal procedure is no more than an example to illustrate and sharpen the moral question involved. Socrates' first argument in rebuttal is that the power to do wrong is not real power; thereafter, the argument leads to the heart of Plato's general theory of value and the State.

With Aristotle rhetoric entered upon its modern phase; in his writings, it has been said, a science was at once begun and finished. He recognized the legitimacy of the issue as it had been framed by Plato, but he put the moral question aside. He thought that we should in fairness fight our case with no help beyond the bare facts; that nothing should matter except the proof of those facts.

However, judges and juries are moved by the art of language, and it thus has a real importance; but it is not as important as people think. Language as an art form is fanciful and meant to charm the hearer; no one would think of using fine language when teaching geometry. Aristotle admits that rhetoric may be abused, but he argues that that does not make out a case against its proper use to discover the facts. In dialectic, the dialectician may deliberately use fallacious arguments; in that case he is known as a sophist. No such distinction exists in rhetoric. The man who uses false arguments and the man who uses sound ones are both known as rhetoricians. Aristotle's point is that rhetoric possesses a definite subject matter that can be treated systematically. Any subject, except virtue itself, which is studied in that manner yields a power that may be used unjustly to do great harm. The short answer to the problem of the abuse of knowledge is that science must run that risk. The result of a mathematical investigation can be either beneficial or harmful, e.g., it can provide us with electric energy or with an automatic pistol for the murderer.

Aristotle thereupon proceeds to study the various arguments and styles that are most likely to affect different classes of hearers. He concludes that the chief excellences of style are clearness and propriety. Those ideals were taken up by subsequent students of the subject and have persisted to the present day. Their presence in Roman law (if not in practice, at least as ideals) is evident from the writings of Cicero and Quintilian. They are expounded with admirable insight by Montesquieu in his remarks on the style proper to legislative drafting, and they are reaffirmed in the goals of "lucidity, simplicity and system" proclaimed by Sir Henry Maine, himself the author of one of the greatest of legal prose classics.

In practice, of course, the style of legal prose varies from age to age, as does the style of prose generally. Coke and Hale thought that legal prose, as it displayed itself in pleading and legislative drafting, reached perfection during the reign of Edward III; it was, they thought, neither obscure, prolix, nor uncertain, but, on the contrary, it was concise and clear. The same qualities are also found in the nonlegal English prose of that period, as represented by Wyclif, Mandeville, Trevisa, and Chaucer, provided those writers are not following too closely foreign originals. On the other hand, Coke and Hale complain sharply of the prolixity and obscurity of the legal prose of their own times. However, by their period two styles were current in English literature—one ornate and the other plain. The ornate style had come in with Lyly's *Euphues* and was to stamp the later Elizabethan and Jacobean literature with variegation and gorgeousness, as we can see, to take legal examples, in the mature prose of Francis Bacon and the writings of Selden. The plain style reached perfection, or something like it, in Hooker's *Laws of Ecclesiastical Polity*. It was carried on by Jonson, Latimer, Bunyan, and, to take an example from legal philosophy, Hobbes. For the most part, literary historians are content to let the great revolutions in style speak for themselves, without searching for precise causes. The law for the critic has been that flux rules all, perhaps because men become tired of any style, however perfect and appropriate.

Law, however, is perhaps not as equivocal as art, and it may be possible to discern a general drift and to account for it in some degree. If there is a law of legal prose it may be described as a movement from terseness to prolixity. Once legal prose occupies itself with minute details its course is not reversed until the legal system itself is radically modified. From the exactness, brevity, and simplicity of the Twelve Tables to the wordiness of the *Novels* of Justinian, from the 1321 words of the Declaration of Independence to the 12,962 words of the order of the Office of Price Stabilization establishing the ceiling price of manually operated foghorns and other manufactured items, legal prose seems in the grip of an iron law. Literary prose changes from the ornate to the plain, and back again, as men become tired of one or the other; more often the two streams run parallel. Official legal prose, however, seems an illustration of Herbert Spencer's evolutionary law of a development from homogeneity to heterogeneity; it appears to be an instance of unilinear evolution, perhaps the only known example.

Whether or not the course of legal prose can be used to rehabilitate discarded evolutionary theories need not detain us. The fact that legal prose does tend toward prolixity has, however, been noted by the legal historians; but they differ in the selection of the causal factor held responsible for the result. Holdsworth is of the view that legal prose of the English medieval period, as evidenced by the statutes, is more concise and more intelligible than the prose of the succeeding periods. He attributes this to the circumstance that the statutes were drafted by the best lawyers of the day, and also to the fact that the prevailing style of legal draftsmanship was good. He points out that the prose of the conveyances of the period has not been equaled in conciseness or clarity by that of any later period.

However, in the sixteenth century the drafting of statutes began to pass out of the hands of experts. Private members and petitioners for private acts, rather than the executive government, began to assume responsibility for legislative draftsmanship. In addition, the style of legal draftsmanship, in the drawing of pleadings, conveyances, and other documents, was tending to become more verbose, and thus even the statutes which the lawyers drew exhibited the same quality. All these tendencies were aggravated in the eighteenth century. An additional factor entered the picture when conveyancers were employed to draft acts. Since they were paid according to the length of their conveyances, they naturally employed the same style which gained them their living. An illustration of the writing of the period is the title of the Act of 1744:

An Act to continue the several laws therein mentioned for preventing theft and rapine on the Northern borders of England; for the more effectual punishing wicked and evil disposed persons going armed in disguise, and doing injuries and violences to the persons and properties of his Majesty's subjects, and for the more speedy bringing of the offenders to justice; for continuing two clauses to prevent the cutting or breaking down the bank of any river or sea bank, and to prevent the malicious cutting of hop binds; and for the more effectual punishment of persons maliciously setting on fire any mine, pit, or delph of coal, or cannel coal; and of persons unlawfully hunting or taking any red or fallow deer in forests or chaces, or beating or wounding the keepers or other officers in forests, chaces, or parks; and for granting a liberty to carry sugars of the growth, produce, or manufacture of any of his Majesty's sugar colonies in America, from the said colonies directly to foreign parts in ships built in Great Britain, and navigated according to law; and to explain two Acts relating to the prosecution of offenders for embezzling naval stores or stores of war; and to prevent the retailing of wine within either of the Universities in that part of Great Britain called England, without licence.

It was writing of this sort which drew from Bentham his tract entitled *Nomography or the Art of Inditing Laws.* He accused legal draftsmen of ambiguity, obscurity, and overbulkiness, of using different words to mean the same thing, of attaching different meanings to the same word, of redundancy, long-windedness, and of putting distinct subjects in the same sentence, of not helping the reader with the ordinary aids of composition (such as the division of the discourse into parts of moderate length, the use of concise titles, and the employment of numbered paragraphs), and, finally, of general disorderliness. He concluded: "The English lawyer, more especially in his character of parliamentary composer, would, if he were not the most crafty, be the most inept and unintelligent, as well as unintelligible of scribblers. Yet no bellman's verses, no metrical effusion of an advertising oil-shop, were ever so much below the level of genuine poetry, as when, taken for all in all, are the productions of an official statute-drawer below the level of the plainest common sense."

Bentham attributed the evils he enumerated to the knavery or folly of lawyers generally. Holdsworth rejects this diagnosis as superficial. His own opinion is that the principal cause for these evils was the excessive individuality of the statutes passed by the legislature; and that it was this individuality which prevented coordination between them in respect of either their form or their substance and caused an immense amount of repetition in statutes in which many similar provisions were necessary.

Lord Bryce, on the other hand, sees an important political principle in the "tedious minuteness" of contemporary English and American statutes. He points out that the verbosity of the later imperial Roman legislation is surpassed by that of the modern English and American statutes. However, the imperial legislation had a prominent virtue: it went much less into detail and did not seek to exhaust possible cases and to provide for every one of them. Bryce denies that this is due to greater art on the part of the Roman draftsmen, but attributes it rather to the range of power allowed to Roman officials and judges, and to the faint recognition of the rights of the individual subject. Our modern prolixity is "a laudable recognition and expression of that respect for personal liberty and jealousy of the executive which have distinguished the English race on both sides of the Atlantic." Thus, the apparent relative excellence of the later imperial legislation in form is in reality an evil in substance, for it is due, not to any superiority of legal skill, but to the existence of an autocracy which did not care to limit the discretion of its subordinate officers.

These arguments suggest the reflection that while there is indubitably good and bad legal draftsmanship it has so far proved impossible to prescribe, either generally or in detail, what constitutes good draftsmanship in itself. Undoubtedly, there is a best way to do everything, and no doubt also there is a style appropriate to all the objectives of legal discourse. It might seem, as Aristotle thought, that clarity of expression is one ideal that might with safety be suggested. But Roman law found it desirable in certain situations to use expressions which no one understood, and modern draftsmen have apparently found it impossible to avoid using such indefinite words as "reasonable," "fair," "proper," "competent," and "just." The truth is that statutes are enacted with many aims in view and they thus, of necessity, will exhibit a variegated prose. They may be deliberately obscure in order to allow greater discretion to enforcement officials, or because the legislature cannot make up its mind what the law ought to be and prefers to allow the courts to settle the question in its precise ramifications. Sometimes, as in modern decrees and statutes, particularly in authoritarian systems, there will be much hortatory rhetoric, which would offend Montesquieu but be in accord with the standards urged by Plato in the *Laws*. The considerations that enter into the draftsmanship of many statutes are so complex that it is impossible to prescribe any particular style for their expression, just as it is impossible to tell poets how to write love poems. We may have views on whether the draftsmanship of a particular statute is good or bad, just as we may judge individual love poems; but we cannot, with any finality, tell the draftsmen or the poets in advance how to write their compositions.

A professional language, for the purposes of this inquiry, may be defined as the special language which the experts in a particular field habitually use in talking to one another. Language is used for two general purposes which can be sharply distinguished, but which in law frequently overlap. Its first use may be called scientific, and its aim is to convey precise information with respect to some state of affairs. An example of this use is: "The action of debt lies in four classes of cases." Its second use is emotive, and it is designed to produce in the reader certain attitudes and emotions. The Preamble of the Institutes of Justinian and the bulk of the statements in the Declaration of Independence are examples of this use of language. This is not to say that all art must be banished when language is employed for scientific purposes. Coke, in working out the theory of defamation in *Bittridge's Case,*[1] and Blackstone,[2] in expounding the law of evidence, are as precise, perhaps, in their statements as the language admits, but at the same time their prose contains an undeniable element of art. Their main intent, however, is to state as exactly as may be that which is the case. The things to which they refer are, they believe, actually related in the way in which they refer to them. In that sense, such art as their prose contains is accidental and even unnecessary; their aim as lawyers would have been fully accomplished if it were altogether missing. The main object of Shakespeare's description of the death of Falstaff, on the other hand, is not to convey information but to produce an emotional effect in the reader. If he had failed in that he would have failed as a poet, which is to say, in his whole purpose. The use of language, however, in the scientific sense raises the problem of whether ordinary language is accurate enough for the purpose.

For legal purposes ordinary language may be defective in two senses. In the first sense, English and the other European languages seem to possess in the eyes of logicians inherent logical defects which are responsible for improper inferences about the nature of the world. If this view is correct, one of the tasks of legal theory is that of determining that its own characterization of the structure of the legal realm does not have its roots in the faults of language.

At the outset it should be noted that professional philologists do not share the apprehensions of the logicians. Thus Jespersen[3] attempts to show that, apart from Chinese, which has been described as pure applied logic, there is perhaps no language in the

---

[1] (1602) 2 Coke's Rep. (Fraser ed.) 311.

[2] 3 Bl. Comm. 370-371.

[3] Growth and Structure of the English Language, 1923, p. 12. The language factor may be involved in the circumstance that stuttering is unknown among the Chinese, while Great Britain stands at the forefront of European nations in its prevalence. On the other hand, four out of five stutterers are men, stuttering does not exist among primitive peoples and such relatively advanced groups as the Shoshone and Bannock Indians of southeastern Idaho, and stutterers who are sexually stimulated cease to falter.

civilized world which stands so high as English when judged by
the standard of logic. Against this view is Russell's widely influential argument that most propositions can be cast in the sub-
ject-copula-predicate form; every fact, therefore, has a similar
form, namely, a substance possessing a quality; thus monism is
the correct interpretation, since the fact that there were several
substances (if it were a fact) would not have the requisite form.[4]
It can probably be shown that the subject-predicate notion has
played a role in legal thought comparable to the one it has assumed in philosophy. An example is the various attempts which
have been made to classify legal phenomena. In that enterprise
Austin's[5] declared aim was to develop a general jurisprudence
founded upon "necessary principles, notions and distinctions," i.e.,
those which a developed system of law must possess. The exposi-
tion of those principles, notions, and distinctions is dependent,
in Austin's view, upon "certain leading terms which we must
necessarily employ." One of these necessary terms in his classificatory scheme was that of "thing" in the sense of a permanent
object perceptible through the senses, not a person.

But is this idea one which the facts or logical analysis requires?
At bottom it is a physical conception whose lineage may be traced
to one of the Aristotelian notions of substance, or οὐσία, as the
concrete, individual thing. But Justinian's classification of private
law into the three branches, the law of persons, the law of *res,* and
the law of actions, managed to dispense with the notion. The *ius
rerum* of Justinian is based on an entirely different idea from
Austin's Law of Things. Justinian's *ius rerum* is the law of patri-
monial rights, the discussion of all those rights known to the law
which are held to have a value capable of being estimated in
money. A *res* was thus an element in wealth, an asset. At bottom it

---

[4] Bertrand Russell, "Logical Atomism," in *Muirhead* (ed.) *Contemporary British
Philosophers,* First Series, 1924, p. 368; *idem, The Analysis of Matter,* 1927, p. 242:
"Philosophers have, as a rule, failed to notice more than two types of sentences,
exemplified by the two statements 'this is yellow' and 'buttercups are yellow.'
They mistakenly supposed that these two were one and the same type, and also
that all propositions were of this type. The former error was exposed by Frege and
Peano; the latter was found to make the explanation of order impossible. Consequently the traditional view that all propositions ascribe a predicate to a subject
collapsed, and with it the metaphysical systems which were based upon it, consciously or unconsciously. This did away with the objections to pluralism as a
metaphysic." However, this does not mean that there is no connection between the
categories of language and the structure of reality.

[5] *Jurisprudence* 4th ed., 1879, pp. 368, 1108.

was an economic conception. Even in this instance Roman law did not escape the subject-predicate logic. It still believed that the essence of a fact consisted in the circumstance that some thing had some quality. It escaped the net of Austin's conception of a material thing, but it was still thinking in terms of substance. Leibnitz was perhaps the first to suggest the present-day idea that property might be a relation. He did this, while still a boy, in the thesis which earned him the degree of master of philosophy. About this time he was also, according to his later statement, freeing himself from the Aristotle of scholasticism and absorbing some of the current mathematical thought. Whether he owed his property conception to that study it is impossible to determine.

Ordinary language may also be defective in the sense that it is vague; that is to say, it may be uncertain whether or not a word or statement applies to a given object or situation. "The scope of words is wide," said Homer, "words may tend this way or that way." The notion of vagueness lies at the heart of the problem of the settlement of disputes. The adjustment of conflicting claims is not the whole of law but it occupies a large area of that domain; and its whole focus is upon the important conception of vagueness. The idea of vagueness has been defined by Charles Peirce as follows: "A proposition is vague when there are possible states of things concerning which it is intrinsically uncertain whether, had they been contemplated by the speaker, he would have regarded them as excluded or allowed by the proposition. By intrinsically uncertain we mean not uncertain in consequence of any ignorance of the interpreter; but because the speaker's habits of language were indeterminate." The view of contemporary logic that all material terms are vague has its counterpart in the modern rule of law that the words used in a statute are always of uncertain meaning.

Languages, in addition to the defect of vagueness, suffer from the unavoidable circumstance that there are more things in the world than there are words to describe them. The shades of color known to artists and optics vastly outnumber the words available to name them. No doubt also a general paucity of words has prompted the great mystics to resort to the symbolism of love for descriptions of their profoundest experiences. The professional languages that have been devised by the law at different times, as well as the languages of art, science, religion, and philosophy, are attempts to meet the problems of vagueness and incompleteness.

Two tendencies are at work today as a result of the need that is felt for accuracy and an adequate terminology. The first is the likelihood that scientists will confine themselves to a limited number of languages for the expression of the results of their researches. Before World War II it was evident that some languages had succumbed in the race of scientific world competition. A research worker who confined himself to French, German, and English had at his command all that was important for his work. If significant material appeared in other languages it was promptly translated. It now seems not unlikely that the Western scientist will find himself forced to acquire Russian, probably, unless he has exceptional linguistic gifts, at the expense of some European language. Certainly most present-day Western legal scholars, educated before World War II, find themselves handicapped by their inability to examine, except through the medium of translations, the legal conceptions which are developing in the Slavic area.

The second tendency is the movement toward mathematical symbolization which has been felt in many fields including the law.

If we but look about us [writes Valéry], we will see speech dwindling in importance in every field where accuracy is on the increase. Undoubtedly common speech will always be used to teach the manufactured languages, and adjust their strong and accurate mechanisms to minds as yet unspecialized. But by contrast, speech has become more and more a means for the first rough approximations, and is being ousted as systems of purer notation develop, each one more adapted to one special use. . . . Knowledge has found the way to make laws plain to the eye, readable at sight, and now the world of experience is in a way *duplicated* by a visible world of curves, planes and diagrams that transpose properties into figures, whose inflections our eye can follow and thus feel, by their fluctuation, the mutability of a magnitude. *Graphs* attain a continuity that words cannot, and they are plainer and more exact. Words doubtless call the graphs into being, give them meaning and interpret them, but words no longer consumate the act of the mind's possession. A kind of picture writing is growing up to connect qualities and quantities, a language whose grammar is a body of preliminary conventions (scales, axes, quadratures, etc.), and whose logic is the dependence of figures or parts of figures, their properties in situation.

The advantages of an exact symbolism are obvious: it permits us to achieve clarity of meaning, to concentrate upon what is essential in the assertion, to isolate the constant from the variable features, and to carry on much analysis without thinking about it. There is an indication that Descartes's dream of the establishment of a "universal science of order and measurement" may in the future be something of an actuality. But a completely analytic language which would reveal at once the logical structure of the facts asserted or derived is still only a dream even in the heaven of symbolic logic. The language devised in the *Principia Mathematica* is intended to be such a language. However, it has an unfortunate weakness. As Russell remarks, it is a language which has only syntax and no vocabulary whatsoever.

In the special languages they have utilized or constructed from time to time it is clear that lawyers have not been unaware of these problems. The Roman classical jurists developed a professional form of speech which departed from common usage in many respects. Its idea was simplicity and exactitude, and it therefore eschewed rhetoric, neologism, metaphors, unusual words, archaisms, and emotion; things were called only by their technical names. The history of the common law exhibits analogous ideas. For various reasons English was a long time in securing a foothold. However, the story that William the Conqueror forbade the use of the native tongue in the courts of law is regarded as a fabrication. Latin was the written language of the law during the twelfth and thirteenth centuries, and legal records were kept in Latin until the year 1731. In France Latin persisted as the language of the law until 1539, when it was abolished at the instigation of Francis I. There is speculation that the learned clerks in the England of the thirteenth century may have thought and spoken in Latin, and that Bracton may have thought about law in Latin. But French for a time seemed as if it would have the final victory; it was the language of the upper classes, and the common law originally was the law of the upper classes. The formal records of the king's courts were kept in Latin, but the cases were "pleaded, shewed, and judged" in French.

This practice left an indelible mark upon the legal vocabulary of Anglo-American law. The English which eventually supplanted French was an English, as Maitland has observed, in which every cardinal word was of French origin: action, agreement, appeal, arson, assault, attorneys, battery, bill, burglary, claim, clerks, condition, contract, conviction, counsel, count, court, covenant, crime, damage, debt, declaration, defendant, demand, descent, devise, easement, evidence, execution, felony, grant, guarantee, guardian, heir, indictment, infant, judges, judgment, jurors, justices, larceny, lien, marriage, master, misdemeanor, money, note, obligation, pardon, parties, partner, payment, plaintiff, pleadings, pledge, possession, property, purchase, reprieve, robbery, sentence, servant, slander, suit, tort, treason, trespass, verdict, ward.

Various deductions have been drawn from this history. Roger North thought that the rules of English law were not expressible properly in English. Selden believed that law French was a technical language equal in precision to that employed by the civilian. Bacon, if we may judge by his practice, held the opinion that English was an unreliable medium and that Latin was the language most meet for legal thought. Maitland was distressed because a German jurist was able to expound the doctrines of Roman law in genuinely German words, whereas an English or American lawyer who attempted to write a page and use only genuinely English words would find himself doomed to silence. Nevertheless the exactness and technicality of law French as a professional language filled Maitland with admiration. "Think for a moment," he wrote, "of 'an heir in tail rebutted from his formedon by a lineal warranty with descended assets.' Precise ideas are here expressed in precise terms, every one of which is French: the geometer or the chemist could hardly wish for terms that are more exact or less liable to have their edges worn away by the vulgar." This technical language, he supposed, made for precise thought and exact logic and thus, according to Holdsworth, played no small part in securing the permanence and sovereignty of the common law; moreover, it made the common law strong to resist foreign influences.

Thus law French, according to these accounts, came close to Cardozo's ideal of a table of logarithms for the law. As a judge Cardozo envied the peace of mind of the mechanical engineer who knew that the towers and piers and cables of his bridges had the inevitableness of truth. He sighed for a legal table of logarithms, the index of the power to which a precedent must be raised to produce the formula of justice. However, views such as those of Maitland and Holdsworth are no doubt exaggerated. Law French to the professional philologist is a "curious mongrel language." In the thirteenth century Anglo-Norman became more and more inconsistent and irregular, and many authors confessed their uncertain knowledge of the language. However, the official Anglo-Norman of legal documents and reports of cases, which began at a later date, is fairly consistent in its irregularities and preserves a certain tradition. Anglo-Norman versification has been praised by philologists much as law French has been praised by legal historians. It has been imagined that the Anglo-Norman poet put together certain features of the English metrical system, especially English rhythm, with the French system and subjected the result to intricate rules of the caesura. This opinion, however, has proved untenable. No doubt the English lawyer had more learning and theory than the Anglo-Norman poet, even when the poet belonged to the clergy; this perhaps gave him more command over law French than the poet was able to achieve over his medium. But all Western languages, as contemporary logic has shown, are radically deficient in the logical properties for which law French has been praised.

If the legal vocabulary in its refined phases has fallen short of those characteristics which a developed professional language should possess, it nevertheless has had the power to influence other domains of thought. Maine has pointed out that, after the separation of Western and Eastern philosophical interests, it was jurisprudence, and jurisprudence only, for the cultivated citizen of Africa, Spain, Gaul, and Northern Italy, which stood in the place of poetry and history, of philosophy and science. Western thought, in its earliest efforts after the transfer of the seat of empire to Byzantium, took its departure from the language of Roman law, which was a Latin that had preserved much of the purity of the Augustan age. The effects were eventually far reaching. The phraseology of Roman law was employed by political theory to state the new relations between sovereign and subject necessitated by the decay of the feudal system and the appearance of the Reformation. Ethics up to the time of Kant, that is to say, when it was occupied with the theory of human conduct, and before it became ontological, was saturated with Roman law. The difference between the theological systems of Eastern and Western Christianity Maine accounts for on the ground that, in passing from the East to the West, theological speculation passed from the

assumptions of Greek metaphysics to the assumptions of Roman
law. The physical sciences and metaphysics show little influence of
Roman law. Maine in fact makes the point that no Greek-speaking
people has ever felt itself seriously perplexed by the issue of
determinism and free will. He argues that the problem of free
will arises when we contemplate a metaphysical conception under
a legal aspect. How came it to be a question whether invariable
sequence was identical with necessary connection? Maine's answer
is that the tendency of Roman law was to look upon legal consequences as united to legal causes by an inexorable necessity. Much
of our thinking in political speculation, ethics, theology, and such
fields proceeds analogically, and it would be curious if the situation
described by Maine had not been the case. For Roman jurisprudence was a basic subject of instruction; it embraced one of
the primary sets of ideas in terms of which the world was understood by the thought of all periods until almost the beginning of
the nineteenth century.

These views on the character of legal speech bring us to the
great tasks of juridical inquiry: (1) the explanation of legal
phenomena and (2) the determination of the best techniques for
the utilization of law as an instrument in the social order. The
object of the first inquiry is understanding, and the investigation
is satisfied if that goal is reached. Its method is the separation of
the essential from the accidental, and the presentation of the
results in a systematic form. The purpose of the second task is
the establishment of a valid legal order, one which permits the
kind of social relations which allow the best life for the community. Both problems presuppose the operation of principle in
human society and, in this view, they appear more closely related
than recent speculation indicates. We have been told that the
second problem alone should engage the attention of the serious
student. Modern empiricism has put both classical metaphysics
and its legal philosophical counterpart on the defensive. All that
has been charged against the abstract efforts to understand the
world—that the inquiry is senseless, because the questions thus
raised admit of no solution; that the scientific approach is the only
one that can lead to knowledge; that abstract analysis is no further
advanced than in the days of the Greeks—has also been urged
against philosophical jurisprudence. This has led to an emphasis

on the actual working of law in society and to a neglect of the questions which philosophy suggests underlie that inquiry. The technical objections to abstract inquiry for the most part have been shown themselves to involve metaphysical assumptions which stand in need of analysis. In any event, how law works is either arbitrary or a matter of principle; and, if the latter turns out to be the case, then the distinction between the two questions is not, in Bacon's simile, an actual line of cleavage but a vein in a continuous block of marble. Both questions, moreover, seem in the light of recent discussions to depend to a large extent for their answers on problems which have arisen in linguistic analysis. In other words, if the structure of language is a reflection of the structure of the world, a clue to the conditions of the legal order may be hidden in its mysteries.

From the juristic point of view there appear to be two basic problems of language: to discover the means by which we may overcome the vagueness of the language of the law and to understand to what extent language, in the legal process, symbolizes the external world. Much of the business of lawyers, administrative officials, and judges is devoted to ascertaining the meaning of sentences having to do with legal matters. The law, in this respect, stands ahead even of philosophy and theology in the elaborateness of the techniques which have been devised to assist in the task. It falls far short, however, of the goal achieved by formal logic and mathematics. The rules and methods which those two subjects have devised for the development of implications achieve a rigorousness and certainty which is beyond the capacities of ordinary speech. Nevertheless, the techniques already worked out in the legal process are an indication of the possibility of further improvement. They show that by formulating in advance the rules that will be applied in particular instances meaning can be attributed to hopelessly obscure or contradictory sentences. The application of rules may not yield the meaning that was intended; but it arrives at an intelligibility which notice was duly given would be the case, assuming the occurrence of the sentences in the legally defined realms of discourse. Thus a man who makes a will is on notice that if he uses technical terms they are liable to be construed in their technical sense, and a legislator is on notice that where general words follow the naming of particular classes of persons or objects, the general words will be held to be applicable only to persons or objects of the same general nature or class as those named.

Legal propositions, like propositions of the other realms of discourse, are generally, though not in all quarters, taken as referring to something or as possessing meaning. It is important to know in what sense legal propositions perform this function. Contemporary thought has given great attention to the problem of symbolism; the focus has been on language generally, on the special languages of metaphysics and poetry, and on the symbol in art, logic, mathematics, science, and religion. It is possible that the position already reached in linguistic study explains meaning and reference in the legal proposition; but it may also be that the language of the law is as special as that of other disciplines and requires its own interpretation. Whatever the result, the answer has an immediate bearing on legal theory. It will point either to the arbitrary and conventional nature of legal discourse or to a connection between the legal proposition and the objects and relations of the external world. This inquiry appears to be prior to any attempt to explain legal phenomena at the level of their operation in society, or to any effort to develop law as an effective instrument of social control. We may never, in our inspection of legal phenomena, be able to achieve an explanation that passes beyond that of recurrence. But that position is dependent upon our view of symbolism, which, in turn, rests upon the nature of legal discourse. The signs and symbols of legal language refer to relations as basic as those marked out by painting and mathematics. But propositions expressed in language raise a special question. Language has properties which bear directly upon the truth or falsity of propositions, and the question of validity is thus inextricably bound up with the nature of language.

At this point it will be helpful to glance at three attempts to clarify the idea of language. They display, as well as may be, the growth of complexity in linguistic studies; they also lay bare the points of controversy about which the subject now revolves. In 1900 Henry Sweet[6] defined language as "the expression of thought by means of speech-sounds." This definition, like most modern ones, owes much to Locke's[7] theory of language, which held that

---

[6] *The History of Language,* 1900, 1.
[7] *Essay Concerning Human Understanding,* 1690, Bk. III, c. 1.

man had by nature his organs so fashioned as to be fit to frame articulate sounds called words, and also the further endowment of being able to use these words as signs of internal conceptions, of making them stand as marks for the ideas within his own mind. Definitions of this type are criticized on the ground that they improperly contrast language and ideas on the one side with animal cries and emotions on the other; they lead to a metaphysical dualism which conceives speech only as an external physical manifestation of inner psychical processes. In 1921 Sapir[8] proposed the following reformulation, which was subjected to the same criticism: "Language is a purely human and non-instinctive method of communicating ideas, emotions, and desires by means of a system of voluntarily produced symbols." Finally, in 1946 Charles Morris,[9] as part of a systematic analysis from the point of view of contemporary semantics, arrived at the following: "A language is a set of plurisituational signs with interpersonal significata common to members of an interpreter-family, the signs being producible by members of the interpreter-family and combinable in some ways but not in others to form compound signs." Notwithstanding the apparent technical precision of this definition, Morris suggests that the term "language" is so vague and ambiguous in usage that perhaps it should not be employed at all in scientific studies.

Whatever the merits or defects of these definitions they succeed, nevertheless, in raising a question which has important consequences: Does man differ in kind from the animals by virtue of language? From Aristotle to the present day there has been much influential opinion, in Humboldt's words, that "man is man by virtue of language alone"; however, Humboldt adds, "in order to discover language, he would already have to be man." Grotius made this proposition one of the assumptions of his theory of law. The argument generally advanced in support of the assertion is that human sounds differ from animal sounds in that the former are the bearers of meaning, while those of the latter are not bearers of meaning in the sense in which meaning is applied to human speech. This argument is the burden of many current theories of semantics. What is essentially the same argument, but derived from biology and social theory, has been well expressed by Briffault:

[8] *Language*, 1921, p. 7.
[9] *Signs, Language and Behavior*, 1946, p. 36.

There is no true equivalent of human society in the animal world, and there is nothing corresponding to the medium by which, in human society, individual minds act upon one another. We dwell in a world of conceptual thought; the various situations to which we react do not present themselves to us as feelings merely, but as ideas. It is not to sensations alone that we respond, but to the significance, or value, which those sensations bear in terms of ideas, sentiments, opinions, thoughts, and the complex associations which are linked with those ideas and sentiments. If those conceptual meanings were eliminated from our minds our behavior in relation to any given situation or set of conditions would be entirely different from what it is, and would be similar to the behavior of animals. That conceptual mentality depends upon the symbolism of language; without language it would not exist.

He then adduces, in support of the argument, empirical evidence in the form of reports of experiments and observations on wild children, and the results of analyses of the mental condition of imbeciles and deaf-mutes.

Against this traditional position is the argument introduced by Darwin that "there is no fundamental difference between man and the higher mammals in their mental faculties," a view widely shared by contemporary biologists and anthropologists. In linguistic theory the Darwinian results have been strikingly expressed by Anatole France. "What is human language," he asks, "but the cry of the beasts of the forests or the mountains, complicated and corrupted by arrogant anthropoids. . . . The professors think to define the absolute with the aid of cries that they have inherited from the pithecanthropoid monkeys, marsupials, and reptiles, their ancestors. It is a colossal joke!" Thus, on this theory, the sentence "The spirit possesses God in proportion as it participates in the absolute" becomes, when reduced to the sounds of the forests, and the sighs with which savages once expressed their joys and wants and fears, "The breath is seated by the shining one in the bushel of the part it takes in what is altogether loosed."

At this stage of linguistic study it is impossible to resolve on the basis of empirical data the issue thus raised, since there is a lack both of the necessary data and of agreement on the interpretation of certain fundamental characteristics of speech. There have been careful attempts to show, on the basis of modern linguistic analysis, that all the functions of human speech are present in at least a rudimentary form in the cries of animals and birds; but the evidence admittedly is scanty, and is certainly inadequate to overcome the present results of general analysis. The lack of agreement in language research arises in the effort to determine the purpose of language. Any answer to this question will be in part arbitrary, that is to say, a matter of definition dictated to an extent by the ends the writer may have in view. Thus, for the purposes of some forms of positivism, language serves three purposes: to indicate facts, to express the state of the speaker, to alter the state of the hearer. From the idealistic position, meaning is the *sine qua non* of language, and the sounds are merely the bearer of that quality. Meaning in this view has three functions: to represent one element of experience through another, to indicate, and to evoke. These positivistic and idealistic conceptions overlap, but they are not equivalent. The latter, however, is in accord with linguistic studies generally, and appears to offer a more fruitful approach for legal theory, since it emphasizes the symbolic aspect of language. This is a characteristic of language that legal theory must analyze in order to discover whether its assertions are merely conventional or are indicative of something objective.

Thus, if meaning is the central fact of language, we are entitled to say that whatever the author of the sentence reconstituted by Anatole France may have meant, he did not mean what France's reconstituted sentence says. The two sentences are not synonymous assertions, and the reduction of the first to the second is thus erroneous. Further, the reductive sentence begs the question. It is human language, and is therefore not the sounds of the forest. It also possibly possesses a meaning. An anthropologist recording it from the lips of a primitive spokesman certainly would not hesitate to put it into meaningful form of some sort.

Not only is meaning in the sense of a reference to an external situation an apparently more fruitful conception for legal theory, but it appears to be inescapably an aspect of the legal process itself. From this point of view linguistic analysis has reduced meaning to a triadic relation: (1) an object, (2) that to which it points, and (3) an observer conscious of the relation. This theory is an effort to meet the subjectivity which says that meaning is what man makes it. Thus to a court in the United States the advocacy of communism by a public school teacher is an abhorrent practice, while to a court of the Soviet Union it is an element in the good life. This is properly taken as an instance of relativity and not of subjectivity. The doctrine of communism will be viewed differently by different judges; but conscious perception is not itself an element in the relationship between communism and good or evil. Subjectivity arises because of the conventional element present in language. When the Supreme Court defines "income" as the gain derived from capital, from labor, or from both combined, it is to a certain extent giving "income" a stipulated meaning. But convention is not entirely arbitrary; there is always an end in view which guides the choice of the elements to be emphasized. At bottom, however, there is the ultimate circumstance of communication; and communication in its final aspect is not conventional since it is a product of a general experience in which symbols are understood in common. "The elements of language," Sapir writes, "the symbols that ticket off experience, must therefore be associated with whole groups, delimited classes, of experience rather than with the single experiences themselves. Only so is communication possible, for the single experience lodges in an individual consciousness and is, strictly speaking, incommunicable. To be communicated it needs to be referred to a class which is tacitly accepted by the community as an identity." The Supreme Court's definition of income, while it may not describe a social occurrence with the precision desired by an economist, has nevertheless an accuracy adequate to guide taxpayers and administrative officials along a general path.

An additional element in this theory is the doctrine of context, which is directed specifically at the nominalistic view which conceives of verbal meaning as the denotation of words and considers it to be primary. The argument is that complete definiteness of denotation is seldom attained for any word by itself. An utterance, Malinowski wrote, "becomes only intelligible when it is placed within its *context of situation.*" In order to clarify the idea of context Urban has reintroduced the scholastic doctrine of *suppositio,* but has defined it more widely to assert: the meaning of the word is determined by its *suppositio,* i.e., to understand a word we must understand what it supposes. Thus, if the Supreme Court says, "The police power is an attribute of sovereignty and exists without any reservation in the Constitution," the proposition has meaning only if certain suppositions are taken for granted.

Among other things it supposes certain inherent powers in government, and the reality of sovereignty. The utterance also assumes a universe of discourse, i.e., a systematic context in which the proposition alone has meaning. The Supreme Court's proposition is put forward in the universe of discourse of the federal system and is not intended to be applicable to the government of the Bantus or Odysseus' island of the Phaeacians. Thus the context of the objective situation gives definite meaning to our words, but that objective situation is always a limited one. The limiting factors are the suppositions, although they may possess a generality that allows the proposition to hold anywhere. "Two plus two equals four" is true anywhere in the universe if the suppositions on which it is founded are granted. Mill's notion that two and two might equal five on some other planet would be valid only if the suppositions were changed. The universe of legal discourse, however, does not possess the generality of logic and mathematics; it is a universe that is narrowly limited.

That the verbal theory of meaning is totally inadequate to account for the operations of the legal process is evident by inspection of most court decisions. Moreover, the courts themselves are now generally in agreement with the linguistic position that every linguistic expression is ambiguous. Let us take as an example a statute which seems on its face ·to present no difficulties. The "finality clause" of a standard government form of contract reads:

> Except as otherwise specifically provided in this contract, all disputes concerning questions of fact arising under this contract shall be decided by the contracting officer subject to written appeal by the contractor within 30 days to the head of the department concerned or his authorized representative, whose decision shall be final and conclusive upon the parties thereto. In the meantime the contractor shall diligently proceed with the work as directed.

It would seem that one of the meanings of the provision is that an administrative decision of a claim is final and conclusive upon the parties, and the Supreme Court has so held.[10] Although this result is in accord with what appears to be the plain meaning of the words, the Court did not rely upon that ground alone. It based its decision, in part, upon the principle that parties competent to make contracts are also competent to make agreements of the kind

[10] U.S. *v.* Moorman, 338, U.S. 457 (1950).

represented by the clause. It also pointed out that such contractual provisions have long been used by the government, and that neither their creation nor their enforcement has ever been condemned by Congress. Thus the Court took the words as part of a contextual setting and measured their meaning by a system of values. In a subsequent case, which followed almost immediately, the Court held that the words did not mean what they said, but that an administrative decision could be set aside by the courts if fraud were alleged and proved.[11] Two justices dissented, holding that an administrative decision should be reversed where it is plainly out of bounds, whether because of fraud, perverseness, captiousness, incompetency, or just palpable wrongness. A third justice would have allowed the impeachment of a decision not only for fraud but also for a gross mistake necessarily implying bad faith. Thus meaning involves reference to a universe of discourse which is conditioned by its presuppositions. Moreover, as Urban points out, the supposition, when closely examined, is found to involve always a reference, direct or indirect, to values. So far as the legal process is concerned this is particularly evident in the interpretation of the present statute. However, if the linguistic analysis is accurate, it is true for the legal process without exception. If the linguistic analysis is inaccurate, it may nevertheless still be a valid proposition for the legal universe of discourse.

Law is as omnipresent in society as art and religion, and like these it has its own universe of discourse. It has developed its own language techniques for reporting and interpreting the world which occupies its attention. Those techniques are learned as arduously as are those of other activities—poetry and science—which give accounts of aspects of the nature of things. The special vocabulary of the law is both conventional and the product of long periods of growth. The phrase "date of finality" in a tax statute will be given a unique definition for the purpose of the statute, but the word "tax" itself has an etymology of ancient origin. With technical languages which attempt to give an account of fundamental matters there is always the question of the sense in which they perform their task, and their relationship to one another. There is also the subsidiary problem of an "ideal language."

[11] U.S. *v.* Wunderlich, 96 L. ed. 113 (1951).

This latter issue seems impossible of realization. The type of ideal language here considered should be distinguished from the ideal language of logicians, on the one hand, and international languages on the other. In logically perfect languages every simple object would be designated by one word and no more; things that are not simple would be expressed by a combination of words. Such a language would, however, be useless for the purposes of the law since communication would be impossible. Each speaker, inasmuch as his experience differs from that of all other speakers, would have a vocabulary that was essentially private and that could not enter into the vocabulary of other persons. The logically perfect language sacrifices communication for precision. An international language would make the converse sacrifice. Descartes, who, in 1629, was among the first to suggest the idea of such a language, proposed the construction of an artificial language to be used as an international medium of communication. Although the ideal of the inventor of Volapük was "to one human race, one language," present-day hopes are more limited. The artificial language is held to be no more than an auxiliary to the national languages when it is not possible to communicate in them; their primary objective is communication at the level of natural languages as spoken by foreigners. Thus an ideal of the Italian mathematician Peano was the elimination of grammar, and his *Latino sine flexione* was constructed on that basis; it used only the ablative of Latin nouns and one simple form of each verb. His argument was that in the sentence "Two boys came yesterday" number and tense are duplicated. It would be just as clear to say "Two boy come yesterday." But the law requires of language both precision and communication; its needs require that neither be sacrificed.

Mill has stated as well as may be the requisites of a language which attempts, in part, the task confronting the law. Every general name in the language should have a meaning, steadily fixed and precisely determined. It should also possess a name wherever one is needed, wherever there is anything to be designated by it, which it is of importance to express. Finally, in addition to a terminology there should also be a nomenclature. These ideals are more suited for the type of philosophical language Mill had in mind than they are for the law's language, which must always be prepared for material application.

To begin with, the terminology of Anglo-American law, which takes its origin in Roman law, exhibits extraordinary precision. Whenever the law is professionalized, whether in classical, medieval, or modern times, one result is a vocabulary of great accuracy. If we take the English professional experience as typical, from the earliest times to the present day the language of the common law has been kept under continual vigilance. Its subtlety has been refined by generations of men with a desire for perfection and with an acuteness of perception. In the course of the centuries English law has produced five great works—those of Glanvil, Bracton, Littleton, Coke, and Blackstone—which rank in the exactitude of their language with the classic studies in physics and natural science. Glanvil's work, the first treatise on the common law, lets many important terms go without precise definition *(knight service, frank-almoign, serjeanty, socage, burgage)* and borrows others without accurate distinction from the Roman system *(mutuum, commodatum, depositum, pignus);* but the unsettled state of the law in the twelfth century may perhaps be pleaded in mitigation. The general accuracy of the treatise is attested by the use subsequent commentators made of it. The remaining works are all the product of immense labor in which care was given to the terminology. Blackstone's *Commentaries* had the benefit of being repeated thirteen years as lectures before they were put with the utmost scrupulousness into their final shape in book form. To these preeminent works must be added the studies by other commentators and historians, and the writings of a host of able judges, lawyers, textbook authors, and analysts who have labored to make the English legal vocabulary the extraordinary instrument it is. As a technical language permitting analysis of a highly abstract kind, and at the same time capable of application to the concrete affairs of the world, it is surpassed by none.

The requirement that a language should provide a name wherever one is needed is a test that the legal vocabulary has always met. The introduction of new terms to cover new situations has been the customary procedure of writers upon English law since the earliest times. It is also a process that will doubtless never cease, as the words and terms that have newly come into use testify: percentage depletion, pretrial hearing, collapsible corporation, unfair labor practice, zoning, juridical review, letter of commitment, collective bargaining, grant-in-aid, short-term capital gain, displaced person, classified information, communist front organization. Similarly, the requirement of a nomenclature in addition to a terminology is a problem that has concerned legal thinkers, particularly the analytical jurists and the writers of the great systematic textbooks. In a field such as the law, which must be flexible, the nomenclature is as adequate as can be expected. It cannot hope to be as fixed as that of natural science subjects, such as botany and geology, whose objects have a permanence necessarily denied to those of the law.

Nevertheless, for all the accuracy of its vocabulary there seems to be a constant failure of communication within the realm of legal discourse. No doubt much of this failure may be attributed to faulty draftsmanship. Even if we put this element aside, however, the inability of a legal spokesman to convey his meaning to a legal hearer appears an ineradicable factor in the law's processes. The lack of power of a legislature to put into words the meaning it intends, the same lack of power on the part of judges to talk to one another and to the bar, and the inability of lawyers to express their clients' meanings in the papers they prepare for them is responsible for much litigation. This failure seems to be due to two causes which it appears impossible to eliminate.

There is, first of all, the necessary disparity between words and that for which they stand. Logical positivism has argued that it is possible to manipulate a symbolism divorced altogether from meaning. This is true in the sense that the mathematician need not keep the meanings of his symbols before him while he is developing them. It does not follow, however, that the symbols themselves are devoid of all meaning. However attenuated their reference may be, they point to something in the external world, as is evidenced by the circumstance that mathematical results are in fact applied to that world. It is possible to write a meaningless sentence, such as *Bahura moput sen;* but we cannot manipulate it in any way unless we know the parts of speech which compose it, and in that case we have then assigned a meaning to it. All words are ambiguous because they have a plurality of references. The phrase "pumpkin pie" suggests different associations to all who hear it. A legislature that used the phrase in a pure food act without a description of a pumpkin pie's contents would, in the absence of judicial legislation or administrative interpretation, have passed an unworkable statute. Modern chemistry would have no difficulty in producing an object that looked, smelled, and tasted like a pumpkin pie, but contained no part of a pumpkin. It is the business of the legal vocabulary to reduce the plurality of references of words to as limited a compass as possible; but the limitations of language are such that the task can never be completely accomplished.

In the second place, even if the meaning is defined with the greatest precision the problem of values will always remain. There appeared to be no difficulty with the verbal meaning of the statute quoted above with respect to administrative finality in the interpretation of government contracts. The words themselves pointed to a clearly identifiable process within the administrative setup. There was no ambiguity in what they said in that respect; but the Court held the verbal meaning not to be the legal meaning when the statute was measured against the Court's universe of values.

We may therefore say that until the universe of legal discourse becomes a determinative one a failure of communication is an inescapable concomitant of the legal order. That the legal vocabulary can ever achieve complete determinacy is of course most unlikely. Perhaps the best that can be hoped for is the situation defined by Ogden and Richards: "A language transaction or a communication may be defined as a use of symbols in such a way that acts of reference occur in a hearer which are similar in all relevant respects to those which are symbolized by them in the speaker."[12] Part of the business of the law is to separate the relevant from the irrelevant. Its language achieves great accuracy by expressly stipulating the relevant. But in the background a universe of values is always present, and no matter how exact the stipulation the unforeseeable complexities of human life will force a recourse to that universe for meanings beyond the literal.

The language of the law is thus a relatively highly developed system of symbolic discourse. It has a vast store of labels at its command which enable it to take possession of the objects of which it is speaking. In the present state of our knowledge it is

[12] *The Meaning of Meaning*, 5th ed., 1938, p. 205.

impossible to determine how these symbols or labels are devised. The problem is both psychological and metaphysical, and while the theories are numerous the answers are inconclusive. If mental states are the primary objects of knowledge, and the external world is deduced from them, the answer will be one thing; if reality is a system of relations and values it will be another; if knowledge is limited to a classification of sense impressions it will be yet another; if, however, the mind does something to the data when it applies a label to them we will have still another.

Such disputes, which are endless in philosophy and scientific discussion today, have their counterparts in the law. Are juristic conceptions deductions from assumed premises? This was the view of the nineteenth-century philosophical school. Or are juristic conceptions derived from the study of historical sources, as the historical school insisted? The modern functionalists agree that both methods should be abandoned in favor of one which formulates concepts from a study of the actual workings of the legal process, but which corrects them from an evaluative point of view. The metaphysical and psychological elements involved in the formation of concepts have not, for the most part, occupied the attention of jurists. Instead of asking themselves *how* they devised concepts, in the sense of the extent to which the mind may be a factor, they have concentrated upon developing a system of concepts which have appeared to them valid. Since the question of how concepts are formed has not been answered by any of the disciplines that have investigated it, it would seem that jurists are not, in this respect, lagging behind the accomplishments of colleagues in neighboring domains.

The problem of what it is symbols refer to is as controversial as the problem of their formation. Symbols in current theories may be representative of the world, they may copy it, symbolic schemes may be isomorphic, or they may stand for necessary relations in objects. For example, does the symbol "absolute rigidity," which is extensively used in physics, refer to an objective reality? Again, the responses to these questions are determined by the presuppositions of those who attempt to reply. And again, the legal books abound with the same type of question. Does the phrase "corporate entity" refer to a real object or to something fictitious? Is a legal fiction a real or an imaginary object? Is an unincorporated association a person? In what sense can a New York corporation be said to be present in Maryland? Until the day of a general resolution of such problems the legal order is faced with devising answers in terms of its own universe of discourse. The language of the law appears to possess characteristics of uniqueness which do not yield to the positions reached by analyses of other word systems.

In the realm of the language of the law symbols make six references: to (1) structures, (2) the nonfactual, (3) eventualities, (4) reiterations, (5) juristic laws, (6) actualities.

1. By "structures" are meant the standing systems of legal relations. Examples are the arrangements of the United States Constitution, family and property law, corporations, labor unions, and governments. It is this group that raises the question of reification. Thus, in the medieval period of English law the king was thought of as a natural man; there is little said of him in the Year Books that was not meant to be strictly and literally true of a man. But the Tudor assault on feudal ideas brought a new problem to the fore: Should the royal prerogatives be assigned to a natural man? The Tudor lawyers solved the problem by personifying the kingly office and asserting that it was a corporation sole, immortal, omnipresent, infallible. Bacon objected to the analogy on the ground that it was not exact—the crown went by descent, but corporations take by succession. Nevertheless, the analogy stuck, and although many statutes were required to clarify it, Holdsworth attributes to it the modern position of the king as representative of the state and the visible and intelligible embodiment of the unity of Great Britain and her Dominions beyond the seas.

Analogy is never demonstrative, and the resulting reification may therefore be valid or invalid. Thus Mr. Felix Cohen objects to the courts asking themselves the question: Where is a corporation? In Tauza *v.* Susquehanna Coal Company a Pennsylvania corporation was sued in New York. "The essential thing," said Judge Cardozo in determining whether or not it could properly be sued, "is that the corporation should have come into the state." The Court is here plainly thinking analogously in terms of a natural person. Mr. Cohen argues against such hypostatization, and suggests that such cases should be decided in terms of the economic, social, and ethical issues involved. It is probably just as impossible to abolish reification from the legal process as it is from the analyses of physicists. The solution no doubt, as Mr. Cohen suggests, is Russell's maxim: Wherever possible, logical constructions are to be substituted for inferred entities. Since true conclusions may follow from false premises, courts no doubt reach valid results from the use of reified entities. They would, however, be on sounder logical ground if they thought of corporations, kingship, property, contract, and other such objects in relational rather than substantive terms. Their practice, however, for the most part is otherwise, and some legal symbols therefore refer to a logically illegitimate class of entities in the sense that the legal order speaks of them as if they were things.

2. The "nonfactual" are those propositions outside the realm of fact to which the legal order attaches consequences. If a seller warrants a horse to be sound and it is in fact unsound the purchaser can nevertheless recover on the warranty. However, if a statute on its face requires an infant to give written notice the courts will not enforce it; similarly, if a statute requires an affidavit to state that the judge "will not afford the defendant a fair trial," it will be disregarded as beyond human knowledge. The so-called "legal fiction" falls within the category of the nonfactual. It is an instrument to assist the operations of the legal order or to achieve one of its ends.

Thus the proposition "the Island of Minorca is in London, in the parish of St. Mary Le Bow, in the Ward of Cheap" is factually false but was legally effective in Fabrigas *v.* Mostyn.[13] In that case the plaintiff, a resident of Minorca, brought an action against the governor of Minorca for assault and false imprisonment. The proposition was allowed by the court in London for practical and technical reasons. Sometimes in such places as Minorca there were no established courts of justice; further, it was believed that the

---

[13] Fabrigas *v.* Mostyn (1773), 20 S.T. 81. Literary men as well as lawyers have difficulties in the presence of legal fictions. Thus Mr. Pickwick exclaimed, after being told that there were half a dozen men ready to go bail for him for a fee of half a crown: "What! Am I to understand that these men earn a livelihood by waiting about here to perjure themselves before the judges of the land, at the rate of half a crown a crime! . . ." "Why, I don't exactly know about perjury, my dear sir," replied the little gentleman. "Harsh words, my dear sir, very harsh words indeed. It's a legal fiction, my dear sir, nothing more." *Pickwick Papers,* c. XL. See also William Empson's poem "Legal Fiction" written on the maxim that the owner of the soil also owns to the heavens and to the center of the earth. *Poems,* 1935, 23.

governor was in the nature of a viceroy and ought not to be tried in the colonial courts where he might be imprisoned; and finally, the charge against the governor was really that he had abused the authority of the king's letters patent; but to try that issue would be to try the seigniory, which earlier cases had held could be done only in English courts.

Again, the law was that if A conveyed land to B and later attempted to convey the same property to C, who paid full value for it, C got no title. The modern recording acts attempt to meet this situation. They provide that if B does not record his deed C gets good title. If B does record the conveyance C is presumed to have constructive notice of the transfer although he may in fact have had no actual notice. The fiction of constructive notice is not, however, the simple instrument it may appear. Thus, if A did not own the land he purported to sell B, the fact that B recorded the deed would not give the recordation the force of constructive notice. That is to say, if A, after the purported transfer to B and the recording of B's deed, should acquire good title to the land, A could convey good title to C. Propositions of the kind "C had notice of the conveyance to B," when in fact he did not, are therefore not existentially false statements. The meaning of such a proposition is that in the realm of legal discourse, if certain relations obtain, the proposition will be given effect. The issue turns, not on whether what the proposition asserts is factually true, but on whether certain consequences shall follow from what it says.

3. "Eventualities" are those occurrences which have not yet happened but which, in a legal context, may happen. "Sovereignty" in the Austinian sense, "justice" in the sense of Plato's *Republic,* while they may never have been realized on this earth, are eventualities in this sense. If the American states were to repeal their present laws against primogeniture, then primogeniture would remain an eventuality until the first estate created it. Existing objects are latent with eventuality; they are subject, that is to say, to be classified in many ways. Thus in Trollope's *The Eustace Diamonds* the story turned in large part on whether or not the diamond necklace was an heirloom. If it were an heirloom it could be claimed by the Trustees of the Estate; if it were not, it was the property of Lady Eustace as a gift from her husband.

Chapter XXV of the novel prints the solicitor's opinion in full, with the citation of some actual authorities. In such cases the law has not infrequently recognized the stipulated character of its decisions and has avoided letting them turn on such questions as: What is the real nature of an heirloom? In 1700 Lord Somers was told that it was *"quasi absurdum et impossibile"* that a court dissolved one day could be treated as existing the following day and united to another court. "We are not now discoursing upon a subject of philosophy," he said, "nor speaking of the natural existence of things. There indeed, it would be absurd to say, that what was dissolved and annihilated one day should yet have such an existence as to be united to anything the day following: but we are speaking upon a legal subject, touching the construction of a law, where fictions, and relations, and conclusions have place."

4. "Reiterations" are those relations in repetitive situations to which the law gives legal effect. Examples are specific crimes, election processes, property conveyances, torts, judicial and administrative procedures, and contract arrangements. It is to this and to the following class that the bulk of legal symbols refer.

5. "Juristic laws" are law or laws in the strict legal sense and also such general laws as may be discovered by legal theory. Examples are the legal principle that certain promissory notes are negotiable, and Maine's generalization that the movement of progressive societies has hitherto been a movement from status to contract.

6. "Actualities" are the particularities of "structures," "the nonfactual," "eventualities," "reiterations" and "juristic laws." Examples of actualities are the words which compose the United States Constitution, the horse that is warranted, the diamond necklace in *The Eustace Diamonds,* and the murder weapon in a homicide.

Behind these six categories lies Descartes's ideal of science as a subject whose essence remains unchanged no matter what objects it handles. No categorical scheme of any one science can embrace more than a fraction of the complexities of nature. The more it seeks inclusiveness the further it removes itself from the data. A subject which has law as the object of its understanding must keep the actual operations of legal systems constantly before it and must not, as is legitimate in mathematical physics, attempt extensive forecasts of events. Its primary aim is to explain the existent, and while it should allow for the possible, the understanding of what is presents difficulties sufficient to absorb most of its energies. Even such an apparently simple task as the enumeration of the possible forms of government failed in the hands of Aristotle, as the subsequent course of history disclosed. While conceptual schemes are in essence approximately isolated systems, they are not arbitrary, and should meet two important conditions. A system must be logically complete, and it must, at the same time, have applicability. Thus, analytical and historical jurisprudence in the nineteenth century were both in part deductions from Roman law; but for the remainder of their material the first looked to English sources and the second to Germanic. As systems for handling law generally, both failed to achieve the wholeness which is a prerequisite of all such conceptual schemes. On the other hand, the nineteenth-century philosophical school, while it may have developed its ideas with a consistent wholeness, put them eventually into such an attenuated form that it became impossible to apply them in any meaningful sense. No doubt, also, the aim of science is to seek the simplest formulations of complex facts. For a subject such as legal theory this is scarcely more than a counsel of perfection. Maine long ago pointed out a circumstance of which contemporary thought has lost sight. There are, Maine observed, only two subjects of inquiry, with the possible exception of physics, which are able to give employment to all the resources of the mind: One is metaphysics, which knows no limits so long as the mind is satisfied to work on itself; the other is law, which is as extensive as society.[14] We appear to have only a dim discernment of the complex factors which lie at the basis of legal phenomena, and to assume that we know the categorical scheme in which all that happens can be formulated is to make the mistake of past ages. Whitehead, in suggesting this criticism of natural philosophy, has formulated the motto for the life of every legal theorist: Seek simplicity and distrust it.[15]

These three conditions are applicable to any scientific theory. But a system of categorical symbols for the law has two special

[14] Thomas Arnold, as an educator, took an even more exalted view of law. Its study, he said, was "glorious, transcending that of any earthly thing." Stanley, *Life and Correspondence of Thomas Arnold*, 13th ed., 1882, p. 81.
[15] *The Concept of Nature*, 1920, p. 163.

conditions to meet. In the first place, a scheme must make a choice between two possibilities. It may attempt to isolate the factors which constitute law as it must appear in any system, or it may seek to classify the notions on which particular legal systems are founded. Philosophical jurisprudence set itself the first task, and analytical and historical jurisprudence the second. In the end the philosophical approach failed—notwithstanding the generality of the premises with which it initiated its inquiry—since it let itself become limited, by clinging timidly, to Roman, Germanic, and English notions. But the impulse behind this approach was a sound one. To select for study the concepts which animate any particular system of law has results which may be beneficial: it may suggest practical improvements. However, that study will be conditioned by the partial nature of the materials before it; the degree of generality of its conclusions will be a function of a local situation. If we want to arrive at ideas about law of a higher order we must see it as a whole, we must approach it as comprehensively as law displays itself in society, which is to say, universally. This is not an untried method. It was the method, but for society in all its aspects, which was at the bottom of Plato's *Republic;* and it was also the dominating conception of Comte when he showed, for modern times, the effective wholeness of society.

In the second place, a set of categories designed to meet the tasks of a general theory of law must escape from the presuppositions of particular systems of law. Discussion of legal problems in terms of property, crime, tort, personality, and so on, is to go far toward solving the problems in accordance with the *suppositio* of the common law, or of civil systems; but there is no assurance that the problem is solved otherwise than on a transitory basis or, indeed, that there is a genuine problem at all. We see the drawbacks, in their most evident form, of operating with common or civil law notions in the imposition of these ideas on totally unrelated foreign systems, such as the law of primitive communities. The attempt, still prevalent, to force the English language, through the medium of pedantic grammars, into a Latin mold, is a comparable case. Chwistek puts the case of a peasant who has been placed in chains because he has taken some oak from a woods. The peasant maintained that the oak belonged to no one since God planted it.

The resolution of his claim depends upon the decision whether reality should be formalized by means of one or another concept of property, i.e., upon the solution of the problem of formalizing reality in this case. Naïve application of the principle of contradiction is not sufficient in this situation. It cannot be said that the piece of oak either belongs to the landowner or does not belong to him. It is the property of the landowner in the eyes of the landowner; it is not the property of the landowner in the eyes of the peasant. To say, as dialectic requires, that it is and it is not, is to say too little, as has been observed. Such a statement would only confirm that the concept of property is not applicable in this situation. Moreover in such a statement the unquestionable fact would be ignored that two different concepts are employed, i.e., the term is being used in two fundamentally different senses.

Legal theory needs a set of categories that permits it to operate with a pattern of reality that does not impose a local *suppositio* on a general situation.

These then are the symbols of the law, and within their intricacies lies perhaps the solution of many problems which juristic analysis has heretofore failed to meet. The theory of symbolism is a newly developing subject and it has so far uncovered more questions than it has answered. However, it has succeeded in showing how fundamental are the relations between language and the scheme of things. To the mystical vision of Heraclitus and his followers the visible world was a manifold, partly true and partly false, but embodying a *Logos,* a truth which passes through every phase and form. The *Logos* is disclosed through speech, and the structure of man's speech reflects the structure of the world.[16] So empirically minded a philosopher as Russell has reaffirmed the doctrine today, and it finds curious expression in the following passage by Proust: Flaubert was "a man who by his entirely new and personal use of the *passé défini,* the *passé indéfini* of the present participle, of certain pronouns and prepositions, has almost as much renewed our vision of things as Kant did with his Categories, his theories of Knowledge, and of the Reality of the external world." In linguistics, the argument is that language is inescapably a series of assertions. Thus, in the vast majority of modern languages there is some sort of formal barrier between the two terms of the assertion. On the one side is the noun, which is associated with its most common subject of discourse, that is to

[16] Plato, *Cratylus, passim.* Cornford, *From Religion to Philosophy,* 1912, p. 192.

say, a noun or thing. On the other side is the verb, which is associated with concepts of activity. No language, it is stated, fails wholly to distinguish between noun and verb. All this suggests a reexamination of such matters as the Aristotelian logic and the Kantian Categories, which took their departure from linguistic forms. It suggests also that the subject-predicate logic may not be as outmoded as the proponents of the relational logic have urged.[17]

Possibly through symbolism legal theory may find hypotheses of which it stands in need. Contemporary legal thought is living on a capital of ideas accumulated through many centuries. A surprising number of those ideas have a vitality adequate to any condition so far encountered, but the relations of the present-day world demand from the law new approaches of a fundamental kind. The principal requirement is an understanding that while the universe of legal discourse is clearly marked the solution of many of its tasks lies beyond that realm. Symbolism by increasing the clarity of our thinking may be helpful.

[17] Cf. Russell, *op. cit.* While Russell rejects the subject-predicate idea as deduced from language, he argues nevertheless that "there remain certain linguistic distinctions which *may* have metaphysical importance. There are proper names, adjectives, verbs, prepositions, and conjunctions. It is natural to hold that, in an ideal language, proper names would indicate substances, adjectives would indicate the properties by means of which substances are collected into classes, verbs and prepositions would indicate relations, and conjunctions would indicate the relations between propositions by means of which we build up what are called 'truth-functions.' If there really are these categories in the world, it is desirable that language should symbolize them, and metaphysical errors are likely to result if language performs this task inaccurately. For my part, I believe that there are such categories, except, perhaps, conjunctions."

Chapter XV

HAROLD D. LASSWELL

LANGUAGE OF POLITICS

When language is specialized to the purposes of politics it becomes the language of decision. It states, justifies, and seeks to influence decision. In our civilization we think of decisions as the voice of courts, administrative and executive agencies, legislatures, constitutional conventions, and electorates. Any specific decision may be accompanied by justifications, as when the Supreme Court gives currency to the opinions of the justices. We take for granted that decisions are the outcome of influencing activities that include the presentation of evidence and argument before judicial tribunals, the conduct of hearings and debates in legislative bodies, and advocacy before the general public carried on by political parties, pressure groups, and individuals. Decisions can be classified for many purposes into three groups: those which are authorized but not controlling; those which are controlling and not authorized; those which are both authorized and controlling. A legislative body may be authorized by a constitutional document to act in certain matters which in practice it is unable to touch, since the executive has invaded its field of formal competence. When power is effective though unauthorized, we may speak of it as naked power. Finally, law is power which is both authoritative and controlling.

As language is fashioned into an instrument of power it is continually affected by expectations about how the response of the audience will affect power relations. The impact of political considerations on the flow of communications in a given body politic may occur at any link in the endless chain of communication. At each link there may be deliberate or unconscious omissions, modifications, and additions which can be attributed to the influence of perspectives relating to power. When it is a matter of omission, we speak of censorship. Propaganda is concerned with the affirmative handling of modifications and additions. For convenience we may diagram the principal characteristics of the process of communication in any body politic, and explore the three main functions performed by communication.

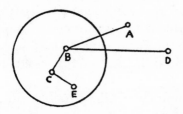

The large circle encloses the territory of any politically organized society. Small circle *A* stands for any member of the community situated abroad and sending back messages about the foreign environment. This is the first great task of communication: *surveillance* of the environment. Surveillance may be carried out by diplomats, press correspondents, secret agents, or even tourists. The term does not assume that the flow of reports from abroad are true, but only that they purport to say something about the setting in which the body politic is living. Small circle *B* stands for any recipient of messages from *A*. It may be that *B* will respond promptly by initiating an act with repercussions upon the foreign environment, as when the Secretary of State issues instructions which are eventually transmitted as an official offer to *D*, who is any foreign recipient of communications originating in the great circle. The Secretary of State may not feel able to respond to the changed situation abroad without having the advice of the President, or even the Cabinet, the Congress, and the public at large. In this case the *concerting of response,* which is the second major function of communication, becomes a more complicated matter. *C* represents all within the body politic to whom *B*'s messages are relayed. *C* may initiate a response that fuses with the general reaction of the entire body politic to the foreign environment. Finally, we note that *C* may communicate with *E*, transmitting the political and social traditions of the state. This is the third or *educational* function of communication.

Political considerations may affect the nature of the messages sent by A to B. The primary observations which A has an opportunity to make may be restricted by the measures taken by the foreign elite to prevent outside scrutiny. It may be that A adapts his reports in the hope of stimulating his country to adopt more vigorous mobilization policies. If B finds such a message inopportune, he may withhold, modify, or add to it before transmitting anything to C. Perhaps A will send a conciliatory offer of negotiation to D, and succeed in restraining C from demanding a more assertive line. At the same time C may sense the fact that the world situation is insecure and modify his educational communications accordingly.

When we examine the chain of communication from the point of view of content, we are made aware of the special role that is played by key symbols and clichés. Some of the key symbols refer to the participants in the arena of politics, naming groups and individuals. These are the "symbols of identification," and they are by no means static. The President of the United States, for example, has almost ceased to speak of the nation as the "Union," as was done after the triumph of the North in the Civil War. The most frequent term is "American." Significant shifts in power are indicated, and to some extent implemented, by the appearance of new symbols of identification, such as the "British Empire" or the "British Commonwealth." The choice of one symbol above another provides clues to the orientation of the communicator, and perhaps of his audience, as when anti-British newspapers in the United States play up the "Empire" and ignore the "Commonwealth."

Key symbols also include references to political demands, such as "collective security" or "disarmament," which figured largely in the political vocabulary of the interwar years. In addition to the symbols of demand are the symbols of expectation, whose function is to indicate matter-of-fact assumptions about past, present, and future. "Inevitable war" is such a symbol.

We distinguish clichés from key symbols in terms of length. The cliché is a brief and quotable statement. Many clichés elaborate a symbol of identification: "land of the free and home of the brave." Others expand symbols of demand: "kick the rascals out." And there are clichés of expectation: "prosperity is just around the corner." The clichés of demand are the slogans of politics, in the sense that they are brief statements addressed to large audiences for the guidance of their political acts: "Arise, ye prisoners of starvation."

What is the peculiar significance of key symbols and clichés? Why do they play such a prominent role in public communication? For one thing they economize communication in the interest of action. Key terms and hackneyed statements provide a special language of cues which may mobilize an entire population under appropriate circumstances for political action.

Not the least of the functions performed by key symbols and clichés is that of providing a unifying experience for all members of the body politic, irrespective of their position in the social structure. Key words and expressions enter into the experience of young and old, layman or expert, philosopher or politician. Such symbols provide a common denominator between those who specialize on political "doctrine," or upon the political "formula," and the nonspecialists who know only the folklore, the "miranda," of the community. We speak of political doctrine as the propositions which formulate the philosophy of the state. The widely disseminated cliché "life, liberty and the pursuit of happiness" comes from one of the most successful documents in which the philosophy of the founding fathers was expressed. We speak of the political formula as embracing the authoritative prescriptions of the community (the laws). Some of the most widely circulated clichés come from the formula, even as the phrasing of the formula may incorporate clichés from the community at large or the doctrines of the ruling philosophy. "Due process of law" is a cliché which is found in the Constitution and is repeated in much wider circles than the courtroom. Popular lore, which we call miranda (following Charles E. Merrian), abounds in key symbols, clichés, and other embellishments. No one can think of "Yankee Doodle," for instance, without recalling a host of politically pertinent perspectives.

Frequently the role of the key symbol or the cliché has little to do with any complex intellectual configuration but serves almost exclusively as a focal point of sentiment, thus contributing to civic cohesion. The physical stimuli used in transmitting symbols may perform this function as a result of generalization (in the sense of descriptive psychology). Charles W. Morris calls this

the "ikon" function, which may be illustrated by the veneration
in which fundamental documents are held, such as the copy of the
United States Constitution displayed at the Library of Congress
in Washington.

The interpenetration of technical and lay language is indispensable to solidarity, since some differentiation of training and
outlook is to be taken for granted in all societies. It is possible
to generalize Macaulay's famous comment upon the political sect
to cover any society: "Every political sect has its esoteric and its
exoteric school, its abstract doctrines for the initiated, its visible
symbols, its imposing forms, its mythological fables for the vulgar.
It has its altars and its deified heroes, its relics and pilgrimages, its
canonized martyrs and confessors, its festivals and its legendary
miracles."[1]

Doctrine, formula, and miranda are parts of any political
"myth." When the myth is invoked by the ruling class of the body
politic, we call it "ideology." A challenging myth is "counter-
ideology."

So much confusion has been confounded by translating Plato's
conception of myth as a "noble lie" that it is worth emphasizing
the fictional rather than the duplicitious nature of the "invention"
which Plato put forward in the *Republic*. A fiction is not appro-
priately made subject to the sole test of factuality, since much of
its significance is figurative. When the adults of a community
become exercised over the factuality of a prevailing myth, we are
seeing evidence of disintegration. Many levels of "reality critique"
can exist harmoniously in the same family, or in the same body
politic, since there is a progression from childhood to maturity in
the discrimination of meanings. The myth unifies experience and
inspires dedication to the goal values of the community. From
the myth comes the basic vocabulary of politics, including a storehouse of metaphor and allusion. The myth is an inexhaustible
treasure for the creative artist, and a tie that binds the community
in space and through history. It must not be supposed that the
myth is wholly static, even in a folk culture living in a permanent
habitat. And this applies with special force to the political societies of our rapidly changing age. The continuity of the body
politic is endangered when the task of reinterpreting the myth

[1] "Hallam," *Edinburgh Review*, September, 1828.

does not keep pace with the ever expanding perspectives of the community. The interpretation of the myth is, and must be, a perpetual process. From the point of view of solidarity, one responsibility of the reinterpreters is to see that disruptive conflicts are avoided between "literalists" and "symbolists," the former of whom insist upon the factuality of any portion of the myth, while the latter argue in favor of a more figurative conception.

The complex function of myth, and of the specialist on myth, is nowhere exhibited with greater clarity than in litigation. In our civilization the parties to a controversy are represented by counsel who are learned in the law, and judged by their peers, or by judges who are also learned in the law. In the appellate courts the lay element drops out, and the lawyers talk to one another. The proceedings are conducted in a framework which is provided by the authoritative statements prescribed by constitutions (written and unwritten) as amplified by statutes, ordinances, decrees, and judgments. Within this context the "plot" unfolds. Stripped to the barest outline, the pattern of communication in a court is as follows:

Litigant: "I identify myself as a party to this controversy. I submit the following claims, which I justify as follows. I reject any counterclaims on the following grounds."

Court: "I am authorized to take jurisdiction of this controversy, and to proceed as follows. I accept (or reject) the appropriateness of the proposed identification of the litigants as 'parties'; and I accept (or reject) the claims and justifications which are put forward; I (may) add other justifications of the claims which I accept (or reject)."

By describing himself as "a lawful heir" the litigant is introducing himself as a party, but in so doing he is seeking to predetermine the outcome. Hence, at some point in the proceedings the court must decide whether to agree that the litigant has correctly identified himself. Even when the identification appropriate to the litigant has been settled, the claims to property (or some other value) may be rejected or modified.

The technique of justifying a claim is to choose a statement from an authoritative source and to affirm that the specific claim can be more readily derived from this statement than can any counterclaim. It may also be necessary to affirm that the chosen statement has more prescriptive weight than other statements which may be invoked on behalf of a counterclaim. Factual statements are offered (or, more precisely, fact-form statements) in order to legitimize the application of justifying statements to the litigants and to relevant circumstances.

A recurring symbol in litigation, of course, is "law," which is a key symbol of the myth. When we look into the role of "law" as a key symbol it is at once apparent how diverse are the many significations which are attached to it. As we shall suggest, one of the principal functions of such a symbol is "creative ambiguity," which under favorable conditions enables it to perform an integrative role. It is in the name of the "law" that the defeated litigant is expected to acquiesce in the final outcome of the controversy. Something more than the naked force of the community can maintain obedience when the "law" appeals to a conscience that demands compliance. We speak of creative ambiguity because the meaning of "law" is usually ambiguous, and it is capable of being handled as a creative means of advancing and defending the fundamental values of society.

The following type-sentence, uttered by the counsel of a litigant addressing a court, may be used to pose our essential questions: "The law is so and so." To the layman, perhaps, this is an unambiguous sentence. Not so to the analyst of communication. Is the reference to the past, in the sense that past appellate court opinions are being summarized for the benefit of the court? Is the reference to the future, so that the statement is a prediction of what the highest appellate court might say on appeal? Is the meaning a direct demand upon the court to agree that the legal doctrine is as stated? Is the counselor stating his considered private view of the law, or is he acting as an advocate who is trying to influence the outcome by presenting a statement which he privately regards as false (or doubtful), but which he thinks the court will regard as plausible? Or, if the court will not accept the statement as fully plausible, will it be accepted as sufficiently plausible to warrant enough extended consideration to satisfy the client of the counsel that counsel is putting up a strong effort in his behalf? Is counsel attempting to draw the proceedings toward a protracted argument over a point which will give the court an opportunity to turn him down, hence demonstrating independence, and clearing the way to accede on the principal issue? Is the intention of the counsel to draw the opposing attorneys into exaggerated preoccupation with one set of justifications in the hope that the impact of a final argument upon another point will receive great weight? Since meaning is a matter of context, the significance of the symbol "law" can be comprehensively understood only when the context is known. And the perspectives indicated in these questions are only a part of the context in which the symbol "law" may be invoked in a type-sentence.

There is no feasible method of revealing the entire configuration in terms of which any detail can be definitely construed. However, there are some sources of ambiguity which can be dealt with. It is possible to discriminate between statements which are "normatively ambiguous" and those which are relatively explicit in so far as their manifest content is taken into account. If we remind ourselves of the nature of sentences which are comparatively unambiguous, we will be reminded of the frequency with which the symbol "law" is utilized in statements which are normatively ambiguous. Consider, for example, the following: "I have said that the law is so and so; but the time has come to change it, and I ask you to do so, and I predict that you will be sustained by the highest court in the land." Further: "I believe the law to have been thus and so, and I regard it as undesirable that this should continue to be thus and so." To employ the terms introduced above, some sources of misinterpretation are reduced when the manifest content of a statement clearly indicates whether the maker of the statement approves or disapproves of something, or whether he is determined to act in a certain way. Demand statements follow the pattern of saying, "I believe...," "I support...," "I will do the folfowing...." The intentions of the speaker are often masked by the use of expectation statements rather than demands, as when the counsel says, "The law is so and so," meaning that he wants the law to be thus and so.

In a complex civilization the creative ambiguity of legal language when employed in litigation can contribute to harmonious adjustment of the body politic to new circumstances. The rapid tempo of change is bringing new situations into existence to which old pronouncements can be made to apply, if at all, by imaginative acts of interpretation. Creativeness is lost if the court allows itself to be trapped into "narrow technicality." The effect of technicality is to undermine the disposition to conform, not because the litigant loses, but because he loses ignobly. The loss is imposed in the name of a trifle, and not in relation to the fundamental purposes of the community. Courts may lose creativeness by seeming arbitrariness, neglecting to spell out a plausible link between the tradition embodied in doctrine and the deprivation which is currently inflicted upon the litigant.

From a formal point of view the interplay of argument before the court is a "syntactic" process, to apply the term proposed by Charles W. Morris to cover the analysis of the internal meaning of a family of propositions. Such a family of propositions is provided by the authoritative statements within which the litigants are assumed to talk. Although the operation is nominally syntactic, it is apparent on inquiry that a much larger context is brought into view. One of the simplest devices to enlarge the context is the introduction of a question of semantics. Typically "semantics" has to do with meanings outside the family of propositions, and investigation is therefore essential. A semantic question usually arises when the interpretation of a word is alleged to depend upon the way in which it was used at the time the authoritative source was constituted.[2]

Let us take an example which is not wholly hypothetical, but which we shall discuss with no regard to the way in which the matter was disposed of. Assume that Congress passes a statute purporting to regulate interstate commerce and providing for the protection of migratory birds. Nobody doubts that Congress is authorized under the Constitution to regulate interstate commerce. But the statute may be attacked on the ground that the word "commerce" was always used to refer to the exchange of goods and services among human beings, and that the flight of birds is not a human activity. It cannot therefore be assumed that the framers of the Constitution intended to charge the federal government with authority to regulate wild life. Once the issue is raised, it is necessary to go beyond syntactic analysis to the study of the evidence about eighteenth-century semantics.

The context may be enlarged in another way. Suppose it is

[2] Concerning points of terminology, see Allen Walker Read, "An Account of the Word 'Semantics,'" in *Word*, August, 1948, pp. 78-97.

argued that the fundamental aims of the Constitution should govern interpretation. To some extent the goal values of the American people were made articulate in the Preamble to the Constitution, and in the debates of the Philadelphia Convention, and of the ratifying bodies in the several states. In addition to such explicit statements, we may examine the frame of government as a whole and consider the intentions which must be assumed in order to account for these provisions. Having regard to these sources, let us assume that a basic intention of the framers was to contribute to the formation of a more perfect union capable of protecting the resources of the American people by doing on a grand scale what lies beyond the effective scope of the states when they act individually. If the depletion of wild life, a natural resource, endangers the welfare of the nation, and if separate state action is not in fact able to cope with the problem by conserving this resource, the Court may sustain the regulation of migratory birds as coming within the purview of the intentions of the founding fathers.

If the context is enlarged in this manner, many different sorts of data and of interpretative comment are made relevant. Any knowledge of factors which deplete migratory birds must come from specialists who have studied the matter. Information about the trend in wild-life destruction must come from qualified observers. The projection into the future of the fate of the birds is a more complex matter than continuing recent trends into the future (extrapolation). It is necessary to take into acount the future magnitude of the factors which have been found to affect the life of birds. Perhaps the prediction is that the rate of destruction will accelerate as industrialization increases. In considering the basic *goals* of the framers, it is apparent that the limits of syntactic analysis and of semantic inquiry are soon crossed. Attention must also be given to scientific knowledge about *conditions, trends,* and *projections.* The appropriateness of the goals of the past to the objectives of the present enters into the picture and modifies the outcome.

That a varied context of value goals may be taken into account by courts has often been shown in explicit terms. A court may say in so many words that the problem of "consistency with past intentions" is laid aside, and that other aims are being discussed

"Morality" may be referred to and a given alternative attacked as an "outrage of conscience." The goal of "enlightenment" may be introduced when we are told that an informed citizenship is essential. We hear of the importance of encouraging "skill," not only in connection with patents, but in the provision of vocational opportunity. "Well-being," in the sense of bodily and psychic health, may be named; and "wealth" frequently comes into the picture in reference to production and consumption effects. "Respect" is another value, as when defamatory statements or acts of discrimination are involved. Concern may be expressed for civil loyalty and for congenial human relationships, both of which involve "affection" as a value. Besides "power" in the sense of consistency with authoritative intentions, other power considerations may be thought of, such as national security.

Most of the adaptations in the language of litigation to which we have been referring are deliberately made. But the language of politics also reveals that many changes do not come from conscious intention. This applies especially to peculiarities of style. If we gain a deeper understanding of the factors affecting style, we may find a means of discerning some of the deeper currents of historic change.

When we speak of style in the language of politics we are not concerned with style in the sense of "fine writing," but solely with the arrangement of the elements of any act of communication. The elements of communication are "symbols" and "signs," the former being the interpretations and the latter the physical stimuli by which the interpretations are mediated between the communicator and the audience. If I use the word "law," the signs are the black marks on paper; the symbols are the subjective events of intention and of audience interpretation.

Style can be described in many ways. It is obvious that styles vary in brevity or prolixity, and in repetition or variation of elements. Some other style characteristics are likely to prove especially significant for the understanding of political developments. We may, for example, classify style according to the modifications which are made on the basis of expectations concerning the reply. When communication elements are changed in order to enhance the contrast with the reply, we speak of "effect-contrasting." When the modification is according to the reply which is anticipated, this is "effect-modeling."

It seems probable that effect-contrast is the principal trait of styles in a non-democracy. The absolute monarch, for instance, tends to communicate in a manner which the subject cannot reciprocate, as when the monarch remains erect and the subject bows to the ground. An elaborate pattern of gesture and symbol is involved when the subject approaches the moment of an audience, in awaiting the attention of the ruler, and in withdrawing from the presence. What is said and done by the superior is in contrast with the replies permitted to the loyal subject.

In democratic communication, on the other hand, manners are simplified and speech is comparatively direct and clear. The typical pattern of communication is the greeting and the handclasp between equals, which can be described in style terms as "effect-modeling."

Clues to the finer structure of style can be obtained by examining personalities who deviate in the paranoid or the over-dependent direction from the norm of equality. The paranoid deviate typically manifests his attitude by looking down upon others, and by adopting a "condescending" or supercilious tone. The over-dependent person replies humbly, showing every sign of abnegation in the presence of the other.

The connections between conflict and style are worth investigating in detail. A leading hypothesis is that at the phase of acute conflict effect-contrasts are the dominant pattern. When two warriors are shouting demands to surrender, and believe that each has a good chance to win, the function of defiance is to prepare the way for receiving an eventual surrender. Hence the defiance is an effect-contrast, though the act is expected to be consummated in the future rather than the present. When ruling groups begin to distrust their own power position, they typically resort to the magnifying of effect-contrasts in the hope of sustaining obedience. The officer who doubts the obedience of his men may meet the situation by raising his voice, adopting a truculent tone, and putting on a pugnacious swagger. If courts doubt that their verdict will be accepted, the ritualism of the oath may be inflated, and all ceremonies connected with the entire proceedings may be complicated.

Besides questions of style the study of political language may succeed in throwing some light upon the invention, diffusion, and restriction of ideologies. This is a matter of great importance for

the study of world politics and history, since a basic problem is to
account for the rise and spread of successful myths and the decline
and disappearance of the unsuccessful. Our historical epoch has
witnessed at least two world-revolutionary patterns in the name of
which the peace of the world has been, or is being, shaken. Is it
likely that communism will become universal and unite the globe
in a single state?

Comparative history and politics provide some guidance on this
issue. It can be pointed out, for example, that the French pattern
of world revolution did not succeed in cementing a world state,
even though many of the symbols of the French pattern were
adopted elsewhere. One mechanism by which the power pattern
prevailing in Europe at the time of the Revolution was protected
was "partial incorporation" (and "partial rejection"). Some foreign
monarchs learned to speak in the name of the nation rather than in
dynastic or class terms. At the same time the demand to surrender
to France as the country of the Revolution, or to join the commonwealth of republics, was rejected.

A typical category of adjustment in which partial incorporation
(or rejection) occurs is "symbol-splitting." This operation sepa-
rates a "plus" symbol (an ideological lamb) from a "minus" symbol
(which is thereupon treated as an ideological goat). The separation
of "national" from "international" socialism, of "social fascists"
from "socialists," and of "democracy" from "bourgeois democracy"
offers concrete examples. It is probable that symbol-splitting is
most likely to occur in reference to symbols which are present
in rival ideologies. Hence the study of symbol-overlap provides a
key to many changes in the language of politics, and a means of
predicting the course of some developments. The struggle between
the Soviet and the non-Soviet world to keep possession of certain
terms, while decontaminating these symbols, is a conspicuous phase
of contemporary world politics.

Cliché-splitting (together with argument-splitting) is an example
of the same basic mechanism. In litigation both sides as a rule are
seeking to justify their claims in the name of the same set of
authoritative prescriptions. Hence the drawing of distinctions is
a famous trait of legal disputation. In the general arena of politics
cliché-splitting is sometimes carried on with much brilliance. An
ingenious instance of a favorable cliché reference followed by a

devastatingly unfavorable one is afforded by the following verse
of A. Boyce Gibson on a contemporary theme:

> Collective farms may have their charms,
> A man's a man for a' that.[3]

When a great historical crisis is examined in detail, the analyst
is made aware of the extraordinary amount of ingenuity with
which the symbol-splitting technique can be utilized as a means of
preventing or postponing the division of the community in two
antagonistic and segregated camps. On a simpler level a skilled
speaker is usually able to prevent his audience from lining up
against him when he adversely criticizes a "plus symbol," if he
takes care to identify himself with at least part of the plus term,
while splitting off another label to be the scapegoat. When Robert
Dale Owen was crusading against the influence of the clerical profession, for instance, he separated the "priests," treated as the positive symbol of the clergy, from "priestcraft," which he adversely
criticized.[4] The frequency of ambivalent attitudes among people
has impressed every close observer of human beings. The same
symbol is partly plus and partly minus, and one or the other pole
may gain the upper hand, possibly to be followed by oscillations in
the other direction. The modern psychiatric study of the child has,
if anything, increased the stress put upon ambivalent attitudes,
tracing the sequence of such examples back to the split symbol
of the "good" mother who indulges the infant and the "bad"
mother who imposes deprivations. These early prototypes provide
the underlying structure of the predispositions which evolve
through interaction with succeeding environments.

As matters stand today we are only beginning to comprehend
the richness of the language of politics and law, and to discern
the unconscious as well as the conscious dimensions of the problem.
It is becoming clear how language is refashioned when it is employed as an instrument of power. Ultimately our task is to discover how language can become a more efficient means of subordinating power values to the shaping and sharing of the other
values of human life. We must devote more attention to the "mys-

[3] *Meanjin Papers*, Summer, 1946, Brisbane, Australia.
[4] "An Address on the Influence of the Clerical Profession" (as delivered in the
Hall of Science, New York), London, J. Watson, 15, City Road, Finsbury, 1840.

tery" of insight, and to the balance between figurative and literal elements in the interpretation of myth. When Plato proposed his myth, the "single bold flight of invention" (Cornford), he believed that the guardians ought to be able to accept it "if possible." In striving to clarify the goals and institutions of a free commonwealth, we are determined to make it possible, and persuasive, for the scholar and man of action, the layman and the expert, the philosopher and the scientist to hold a common perspective concerning the fundamental values of human dignity.

♜ Chapter XVI
FRANCIS FERGUSSON

LANGUAGE OF THE THEATER

I It is impossible to speak with scientific authority of *the* language of the theater. Everyone knows that the theater speaks many languages: English and Chinese and Russian and French, to say nothing of the dead languages, and the tongues of tribes which are hardly known beyond their islands or jungle hide-outs. And if one enlarges the notion of "language" to include nonverbal means of communication, as one must when studying the theater, then the topic becomes still more unmanageable. Thinking only of the English-speaking theater, one sees at once that it has used music and dance and spectacle, as well as words, to convey its meaning, and also the traditional allegory of *Everyman,* the "symbolic stage of the Elizabethans," the conventions of Restoration comedy, and a number of other systems of signs and symbols which may be regarded as languages. Any one actual theater would require a lifetime's study and practice to explore fully the properties of its "language."

But there is comfort to be derived from these considerations. All that one can do, in studying the language of the theater, is to consult one's own knowledge and experience; and where there would be so much to know, the difference between the knowledge of savants and our knowledge is comparatively small. Mr. Allardyce Nicoll is learned in the history of the theater; yet we do not naturally turn to him to find out what the theater *is,* as a means of communication. We think of our own experience of the theater and ask ourselves what the theater as we have known it is trying to communicate.

I suppose that when we say "theater" we are always thinking of one or more performers before an audience. This does not define any particular theater, or even the art of drama which is usually taken to be the theater. For musicians, lecturers, dancers, teachers, storytellers at dinner parties, and many others perform before an audience. And even when a parent lectures his offspring he may be uneasily aware of an element of "theater" in his performance. In short, "theater" in this very general sense is a notion which shades off at the edges. It appears to refer to a protean medium of communication underlying the more exact languages and present in a more or less rudimentary or instinctive way in the entire life of man in society. It is theater in this sense which all may know; and it is this which one must consult in attempting to see what could be meant by the language of the theater.

Everyone who has felt stage fright is aware of the peculiar and disturbing power of this "language." The house is darkened, the audience falls silent; soon the curtain will open. The performer, waiting in the wings, is seized by the ancient excitement: the irrational sense of guilt, the butterflies in the belly, and then— if he is experienced—the lightness and concentration which mean that the organism is summoning its energies for an important effort, an ordeal which may be sweet or bitter. Experienced performers like stage fright, for they know that without it the performance would be dead. They need its energies, and they have a technique for pouring them into the form, the meaning, which they must impose upon the other humans assembled in the darkness, on pain of a peculiarly disheartening sense of failure.

Man is not the only animal who feels that public performance is an important and perilous means of communication. Gallinaceous birds begin to strut and spread their feathers in preparation for their wooing dances before an audience of hens. Cats seem to suffer something like stage fright as they prepare to imitate, in play, the fight or the hunt: round-eyed, switching the tips of their tails, they seem to feel as absurdly threatened and important as a prima donna in her dressing room. But at this point the analogy with human theater ends. The birds and animals have only one thing to "say" about the nature and destiny of their species, while man is notoriously so flexible and intelligent that he cannot rest content with one version of his life on earth, or one language for communicating it. Since Babel he has shown infinite fertility in the invention and communication of images of himself. For this reason the human performer, waiting in the wings, may feel more hopeless terror than the kitten waiting to perform his little war dance. If he has imagination, if he is about to face a rootless modern crowd with the intention of offering it some meaning beyond the clichés of the entertainment industry, he may feel in advance the metaphysical chill of a breakdown in communications.

Of course the failure of a performance is never total. For the actor faces his audience with *some* prepared meaning; and as soon as the curtain is open and the performance has declared itself, the worst is over. We glimpse the unusable potentialities of the theatric medium only in the moment before we start; thereafter we accept a limited meaning, and a limited version of the language of the theater. In short, there is an important distinction between the language of the theater, as we might try to think of it "in itself," and any *actual* theatric language, which is always limited.

I suppose this distinction applies to any language. We say we know English; yet who has ever explored and controlled all of its potentialities? The great writers know the language better than we do. As we study Shakespeare or Joyce we become aware of properties, resources for conveying meaning, which we did not know the language possessed. Moreover, when we learn to read Joyce or Shakespeare we learn to perceive their meaning, the object which their language is designed to show us. It is impossible, in practice, to separate the language from its object or meaning, for the language is alive only in so far as it does convey a meaning. The reverse is probably not true: we can, I think, perceive or know things which we cannot talk about in any language. But any *actual* use of language—English or the theater—is limited in meaning (by the object it is trying to convey and also) by the author's sense of the properties of the language itself; and the perception of the meaning and the control of the language are cognate.

This brings me back to the point with which I began. We may all know that "theater," as an indispensable and protean means of communication, exists, for we have all felt its powers and perils at various moments in our own experience. But, like other languages, the language of the theater is used in different ways, and for different purposes, by many masters, ancient and modern, domestic and foreign. It is they who have explored its properties; and it is clear that one's conception of this language, one's estimate of what it can and cannot do, will depend upon one's knowledge of their practice. So we proceed with a few general observations which, at best, can be no more than suggestive.

2   Because the theatric medium, or language, is so universal and protean, it has been assessed in many ways during the long life of our Western tradition. We judge the theater by what we get out of it, and we are likely to assume that the actual living theater at any moment—Broadway or Hollywood, for example—exhibits its essentials. No wonder there are many who would deny that it is a language at all and are content to think it meaningless: at best distraction, at worst inexplicable dumb show and noise.

But let us return to the performer before his audience, at the crucial moment before the performance begins. I have suggested that his stage fright may be due to his sense of the unmanageable and therefore alarming potentialities of the medium he is about to try to use. This "medium" is, of course, the performer himself —not only his physical appearance but his inner being, which he suddenly (and rightly) feels to be cruelly perceptible to many waiting fellow creatures. The stage acts like a kind of X-ray; it invites us to contemplate the man who boldly appears there. We see what his dress, his walk, his voice, his mannerisms add up to, just as we get a tune when we grasp the coherence of the separate notes. It is the same kind of active perception, or imaginative grasp—the work of the "histrionic sensibility" as I like to call it— which guides us in daily action, the basis of the practical (and often unformulated) judgments whereby we find our way through the human jungle. But the stage invokes this kind of perception with a certain terrifying formality. It bids us gather, pause, and look. The performer, caught in this focus, will "say" things which he does not mean, and bring an unexpected roar of laughter from the house, unless he somehow limits and controls his actual inner life. By the focus of his own spirit he controls the focus of his audience. And thus his medium is his being, his problem to control it through concentration, and by its shifting stage-life to speak to his audience.

It seemes probable that the theater developed out of primitive ritual, which celebrated constant aspects of human nature and destiny; and that the performers, mimes or dancers or chanting chorus, were its medium, rather than words. The greatest dramatists and connoisseurs of the theater build on this ancient and primitive basis; they think of the theater as *playing* before an audience. Their more general meaning arises from the complex relationships between the many stage-lives which they set in motion before us. They appeal to the histrionic sensibility; and the greatest among them (a Sophocles, a Shakespeare) presents by this means a singularly complex and many-sided image of the human—both his potentialities for good or ill and the comic or pathetic or terrible actuality of his life, as it shifts moment by moment. This they can do because they use, not merely the bodies or voices or concepts, but the beings of the performers: the human himself in the eye of the audience.

But I am of course talking about the *ideal* language of the theater, which some may sense but no one may use fully. The actual theaters of our tradition always accept drastic limitations: a traditional object, or meaning, and a reduced version of the performer's medium. For though the performers are the basis of the theater, the theater also uses words and concepts; it shares in the whole life of its surrounding culture. And the attempt to limit and control the theater often amounts to reducing it to one of the more exact languages—as though the stage were a mere illustrative adjunct of philosophy or social theory.

The French theater of the seventeenth century, for example, is defined by certain rules, conventions, standards of taste, which are apparently derived from a mathematical ideal of clarity and distinctness. What Molière communicates has an extraordinary clarity and distinctness. What Racine communicates is not the same thing, but it too approaches the static finality of the clear and distinct idea. I do not know of any theater which can rival this one in elegant exactitude. Yet how much it excludes; how limited is its use of the medium; how narrow (though deep) its meaning is. It does not have room for "unaccommodated man," the "bare, forked animal" of Lear.

Those whose sense of the theatre is akin to that of the neoclassic and rationalistic French seventeenth century will estimate the language of the theater by its success in emulating the more re-fined, even the technical, languages of our civilization. But those who know only the stages of the modern world are likely to form totally different notions of its properties.

I have suggested that the theater at its best uses the performer on his stage for the disinterested purposes of contemplation, to share the perennially absorbing vision of man. But this medium may be used for other purposes, and the mass theaters of our time do not contemplate. The performer may neglect or deny the in-telligence altogether and reach the audience by a sort of sensuous or willful contagion. It is this property of the theatric medium which the modern world characteristically exploits: Hollywood in one way and the totalitarian regimes of eastern Europe in an-other way. Hollywood tends to titillate the sensuality of the twelve-year-old least common denominator of the world's population, while keeping the intellectual content as vapid and noncommittal as possible. Its aim is pleasure with no dangerous consequences; and we see how it has succeeded in drawing countless millions to its screens. Its only rival is the totalitarian theater of Russia and the late-lamented Nazi Germany. This theater also does not con-template, but, unlike Hollywood, it propounds a simple notion as a basis of political action. Its aim seems to be power rather than pleasure, the formation of the dynamic mass-man of its philosophy: "the soul of Deerslayer attached to a ten-ton tank," as this creature has been defined. It thus does impose a primitive ethic, speaking to the will rather than to the self-pity or eroticism of the crowd. But in Moscow as in Hollywood the language of the theater is pitifully truncated, a lingua franca with no "words" for what has been called humane.

It was, I suppose, Plato's sense of these dangerous possibilities in the language of the theater which caused him to despair of it altogether. Perhaps he was struck by the degeneration of the Athenian stage in his time; certainly there is no evidence that he would have felt the force in Matthew Arnold's remark that Sopho-cles saw life steady and saw it whole. And since Plato there have been many who wished to censor or abolish the theater, as the Russians in our time cut it down, in order to make it serve their philosophy. This is natural, and perhaps inevitable when the language of the theater degenerates, losing all sense of its wider potentialities and higher function.

In the West we do not, as yet, censor the theater as the Russians do. Hollywood emasculates it for its own venal ends; but the flabbiness is not imposed from without. We could not, as yet, agree on a principle of censorship, and the degeneration of our theater is due to bewilderment and not dogma. We do not know what we mean to say by the language of the theater; and from this circumstance, I suppose, comes our contemporary doctrine of art for art's sake, in its many forms. When this doctrine is applied to the theater, it consists in saying that the drama means nothing but itself, just as "pure" music or painting is supposed to do. This of course would amount to denying that the theater is a language at all: a stage work would not *mean* but *be*. This doctrine, in various modifications, has served some of our best contemporary artists, even artists of the theater; but I do not pause over it because it seems to me that it is only a partial truth—a suggestive heresy like Plato's—and that it does not adequately describe the common experience of the theater. We want it to mean something; we "read" it as referring beyond itself to something which we may confirm from our experience, or memory, or other sources outside the stage work itself.

When I speak of the language of the theater I am thinking of it at its best, as we may learn to understand it through the study of a Sophocles or a Shakespeare. And I am endeavoring to follow the lead of those inquirers who have seen that it may convey a central and catholic vision of man in a way which no other "language" can. Aristotle (a philosopher and not a man of the theater) tried to indicate this power by assimilating the theater to *his* art, saying that poetry (by which he meant drama) was more "philosophical" than history. Hamlet said that the aim of playing was to hold the mirror up to nature—thus making a similar point more directly. Henry James remarked that the Comédie Française, with its repertory of classics living perennially in performance, served the French as a "school of manners"—by which he meant that it transmitted the image of man, the masterpiece of many moralists and artists, which formed the nation's life, generation after generation. I do not maintain that Aristotle, Shakespeare, and James meant exactly the same thing. Each of them was thinking of a particular theater; and the Greek, Elizabethan, and French theaters are not identical, but only analogous. Each of them, as their admirers saw, seeks to present a central and inclusive view of human nature and destiny; the views are not identical, nor are the "languages" by which they are conveyed. But they all suggest what one might mean by the analogical concept of *the* language of the theater at its best, its ideal properties and function.

3   I have remarked that the language of the theater at its best, as the greatest masters use it, is in a sense *primitive*. But I do not mean that it is rudimentary like the products of Hollywood or Moscow. The popular theaters of our time are not so much primitive as degenerate, for they work with clichés of thought and feeling which come, not from anyone's primary experience, but from the derivative ingenuities of propagandists and advertising men.

The primitiveness of the theater, at its best, is based upon the ancient sense of the human engaged in significant performance, or playing, before an audience. This playing communicates something prior to words and in this sense is a primitive language. The awareness below words seems to touch memory: our own individual remembered feeling, which reveals so much more than momentary actuality about what we really are. The language of the theater, through the playing of actors who use their remembered feelings, speaks to us on this basis, as one may confirm if one thinks of what a Nazimova could do without words at all. Moreover, the play as a whole—Shakespeare's "sad stories of the death of Kings," or even Lorca's contemporary folk theater, with its many echoes of old Spanish music, tales, and customs—seems singularly fitted to communicate racial memory at a level below words, or even, perhaps, myths and traditional stories. That is why the very primitiveness of the theater enables it to be more philosophical than history, and to serve as a school of manners: it speaks of a residuum of human lore, individual or communal or both, which the exact languages cannot communicate.

But, like all languages, the language of the theater must be loved, practiced, cultivated, if it is to be a living language. And, again like all languages, it cannot be adequately translated into any other language. That is why, when we try to discuss a particular play—i.e., to handle its meaning in words and concepts—we are obliged to "interpret" it.

The whole notion of interpretation is in bad odor in our time.

The mind naturally demands literal truth and univocal concepts. We are inclined to feel that only languages which are capable of communicating "truth" in this sense mean anything at all. That is why we are impatient with the study of literature, especially literature of the past, which obviously requires some sort of interpretation; and it is why we so easily relegate the theater, at its best, to the warehouse, along with the biographies of dead worthies in whom no one is interested and monographs on the diseases of the horse which were superannuated fifty years ago. Perhaps it is not too much to say that the ancient distinction between the Letter and the Spirit, which underlay the transmission of humane and religious culture from the ancient to the modern world, is discredited, and that the loss of this lore, this technique or habit of interpretation, of reading *through* the literal word, or fact, or concept, to a meaning or spiritual content beneath them, at least partly accounts for the loss of a vital relation to our tradition.

However that may be, there is an analogy between the traditional interpretation of Scripture, or of the pagan Classics, which consisted in seeking the Spirit beneath the Letter, and the proper "reading" of the language of the theater as a living language. When St. Paul read the Old Testament, when Dante read St. Paul—or, for that matter, Virgil or Statius—they paid strict attention to the Letter of the ancient author first; but then they tried to penetrate to the life of which the Letter, in their view, was a sign. The Letter, the sign, showed its mortal limitations of time and place; but the Spirit was supposed to be still of significance to the reader. And the devout attempted to apprehend the "Spirit" by assimilating their inner lives, at least at the moment of actual reading, to the inner life of the ancient writer. A good actor "reads" his part in an analogous way. He masters the Letter first: the words, deeds, situations of his character. But when he has really mastered the part, he imitates with his own being the "action" or *"moto spiritale"* from which the fictive character's words and deeds spring. It is this "action"—the mimicked life—which the audience is invited to see. And it is the lives of the characters, in their temporal succession and shifting relationships, which constitute the language of the theater and communicate to the audience the "life" of the play.

If these observations are fairly just, perhaps we must say that there is an element of "theater," of mimetic response, of significant make-believe, in all understanding of poetry in the widest sense. This would show us again that the notion of the language of the treater shades off at the edges and that, in a significant sense, it is to be found off-stage as well as on a real stage. Plato certainly employs it in the dialogues and thereby places his dialectic, his analysis of words and concepts, *within* the more primitive and all-inclusive medium. Thus he gives us not only the dialectic but a sense of its *provenance* and of the unformulated reality it seeks to grasp. And so Dante *dramatizes* the thinking of his Pilgrim in the central cantos of the *Purgatorio,* showing at once the validity and the limitations of doctrine as a means of guiding and nourishing the soul. Thus, if one thinks of the language of the theater as usable off-stage also—as, essentially, the medium of communication which appeals to our primitive sense of the human, the histrionic or mimetic grasp before predication—then this language may be called fundamental in our civilization. At least it would seem to be a source of our humane culture, as distinguished from our specialized and technical vocabularies.

It follows that there are many things which the language of the theater cannot do. It does not serve any of the purposes of the exact languages, which have a mathematical ideal of clarity and precision. It has been of no use in scientific investigation, or in the applications of science which have given us such power over the physical world. It cannot satisfy our appetite for literal facts and univocal concepts; and the pseudo-scientific jargons, which purport to give us the truth about human nature "as" the conditioned reflex, the weakened sales resistance, or the bell-shaped curve, satisfy this appetite far better than the language of the theater can ever do.

The ideal object which the ideal language of the theater is fitted to indicate, or *mean,* is human nature and destiny, not rationalizing man, or economic man, or mass-man, but the mysterious creature, who may be viewed in many complementary perspectives. But in our centrifugal period few even wish to contemplate the central mysteries, or to cultivate the languages in which they may best be spoken of. We do not cultivate the language of the theater at its best, in its most fundamental uses; and any language reveals its life only when warmed by our attention.

The reader is invited to consider one of the masterpieces of this language, a play of Shakespeare's, for instance. It lies dumb in its unopened book, or, when someone tries to get it onto the stage, it babbles foolishly in the ear of one of our reluctant Broadway reviewers. But assume that every bit of its play, its make-believe, is significant, and that the whole has a perennial life to communicate to its admirers. Then you may find that, like Dante's Siren, it will tell you as much as you are fitted to take in:

I gazed upon her; and, as the sun comforteth the cold limbs which night weighs down, so my look made ready her tongue, and then set her full straight in short time, and her pallid face even as love wills did color.[1]

[1] *Purgatorio*, Canto XIX, 11. 10-15, The Temple Classics, J. M. Dent & Sons , Ltd., London.

ꙮ Chapter XVII
MARGARET NAUMBURG

ART AS SYMBOLIC SPEECH

Art as symbolic speech is of growing importance today as a form of creative expression. Man's long-standing use of symbols as a means of communication, although ancient in origin, is less understood, in recent times, than his use of symbols in mathematics and logic.

We have through the explorations of anthropology and archaeology come to know more about man's symbolic art. We have also become aware of the importance of symbolic images as derived from the unconscious through the development of psychoanalysis. This broadened understanding of the scope of man's capacity to express in visual symbols has led to a number of contradictory interpretations as to the value and meaning of both ancient and modern symbolic art. For a more comprehensive grasp of such art, the differing translations of the meaning and function of symbolic creation, as understood by the creative artist, the aesthetic critic, or the psychoanalyst, need to be examined.

Art as symbolic speech has played a major role in both the conscious and the unconscious cultural expression of man throughout the ages. In order to become more clearly aware, from the vantage point of today, of the myriad ways by which universal picturization has been for man a means of profound communication, it is necessary to reassess the diverse and often contradictory estimates of such symbolic expression in our own time as well as in ages past.

Symbolic art was brought to the attention of the public by the surrealists. From the time when they took over the area of the unconscious as the base of their creative direction, the line between art and non-art became less certain, so that today we have a continuous discussion by the art critic, the public, and some psychoanalysts as to what really constitutes "art." The snowballing of interest in the symbols of modern art has reached a point where the attitudes of those who oppose or defend abstract and symbolic art need to be seen in a fresh perspective.

A generation ago it was far simpler for self-styled authorities to sift the sheep from the goats who had grazed in the fields of the arts. But there are changes taking place today, in many of our artists, which sometimes baffle the public as well as the critics and psychologists. Painters and sculptors, well trained in the disciplined use of form and color, have frequently, after completing their apprenticeship on imitative levels, broken with their more conventional past and begun to create a new world, based not on the external objectification of form but on personal response to inner experience.

For many modern artists this has involved a renewal of contact with the unconscious and its symbolic modes of expression. While psychoanalysis has undoubtedly influenced modern art as a means of rediscovering the unconscious factors in man's psyche, other influences have also affected its evolution. These include comprehension of ancient and primitive art through the explorations of archaeology and anthropology; such a range of creative expression was until recent times generally unknown to Western man.

We can no longer, as in that period of "art for art's sake," consider the art of today as something to be valued apart from other aspects of living. The artist, like the man in the street, is at present reacting to the stress and threats of this "age of anxiety." We need therefore to consider how and why the modern artist's attempts to express his inner world in symbolic projections have been interpreted by some critics as a direct expression of modern man's response to life and by others as an escape from the realities of present-day existence. Only in this context can we begin to sift what is objectively valid from what may be personally weighted by the subjective preferences of the interpreter, be he art critic or psychologist.

Before we can consider the nature and function of art in its symbolic aspects, we need to be fully aware of the way in which the modern concept of art has been modified by the developments of anthropology and archaeology. We therefore include the cave paintings of prehistoric man, the ritual objects of ancient Egyptian and Indian civilization, as well as the recovered Mayan temples and Cretan palaces, in our efforts to estimate the meaning of man's existence on this planet. In the dizzy realization that the span of man's creative expression is so unending and so complex, we unwittingly impose our own recent and personal concept of "art" upon those faraway expressions of man's imaged response to life. In such attempts to evaluate what our Western culture regards as the significant graphic and plastic productions of the past, as "art," we have not taken into account the profoundly different motivation of the peoples of those remote epochs toward their own creative expression. Because ours is an age in which art lacks religious dynamism, we have failed to comprehend the basic motivation of those imaged projections of prehistoric and ancient man. We continue to call such graphic or sculptured expression "art," but to the man of those times his plastic creations served another purpose; for early and ancient man sought through such projections to relate himself to the cosmos and search out the meaning of existence. It has therefore remained impossible for many interpreters today to bridge the motivational gap between the visual expressions of our own day and those of earlier periods. Critics must first be completely aware that what the man today offers to the public as art is a means for personal distinction as well as personal expression. Earlier cultures, which produced anonymous carvings of strange gods and mythical creatures, did so as a gesture of religious dedication, which is not to be confused with "art" in our modern sense. Only when we are able to relinquish, temporarily, our specialized focus on "art" can we relate ourselves to so different a view of life as is found in certain ancient and primitive cultures.

But whatever interpretation of imaged expression we may give to our "art," we must realize that modern man still draws from his unconscious today, as did men of past cultures. Evidence of this is clear in the identical primordial symbols which are found in various parts of the world in the form of rediscovered paintings and modeled shapes. Later we will consider the psychodynamics underlying the unity of expression shown throughout the world in the symbolic products of all men.

An astute analysis of how modern man imposed his conception of "art" upon all the imaged projections of prehistory and ancient

historic civilizations is given by Malraux in *The Voices of Silence*.[1]
He traces how the modern concept of "art" has been continually
imposed upon the creative expression of other cultures preceding
our own—cultures which were motivated by other values. Writes
Malraux:

The Middle Ages were as unaware of what we mean by the word
"art" as were Greece and Egypt, who had no word for it. For this
concept to come into being, works of art need to be isolated from
their functions [which, as described by Malraux, were religious]. . . .
When, with the Renaissance Christendom selected, from amongst the
various forms created for the service of other gods, its most congenial
method of expression, there began to emerge that specific "value" to
which we give the name of art, and which was, in due time, to equal
those supreme values in whose service it had arisen. . . . Thus when art
became an end in itself our whole aesthetic outlook underwent a
transformation.[2]

Our interest in considering art as a form of symbolic speech is
not, primarily, concerned with the emphasis that modern art has
projected onto all imaged projections, but rather with the exploration of the universal roots of such expression in terms of both its
recurrent symbols and its recurrent use of similar technics. In
order to make this comparison between method and motivation
in the use of imaged projections in both ancient and modern
times, it might, therefore, be well to begin by summarizing some of
the mechanisms most frequently employed in modern symbolic art.

The surrealists introduced a cultivation and permissive release
of unconscious content in their art. The publicizing of psychoanalysis undoubtedly influenced the development of such expression by the responsive artist. Such trends included a growing
interest in and emphasis on the irrational in fantasy and dream
images; increased use of distortion and archaic forms of expression;
substitution of a part for the whole, the use of transparency, and
the development of multiple instead of unified focus. These and a
number of other methods found in the expression of modern symbolic art have received contradictory interpretations as to their
meaning from both art crtics and psychoanalysts.

Siegfried Giedion, the well-known Swiss architect and art critic,

[1] André Malraux, *The Voices of Silence* (tr. by Stuart Gilbert), Doubleday, New York, 1953.
[2] *Ibid.*, p. 53.

has clearly analyzed the similarity in the technical and psychological attitudes toward creation in the modern artist, the primitive, and the child:

... Truthful witnesses, both in the fields of science and of art, show us that the purely rationalistic outlook is drawing to an end. We can also recognize today strong affinities with prehistoric art, which are based on the continuity of human experience. Things that have for a long time remained buried beneath the surface of daily life are awakening again. When we are moved by similar tendencies, age-old reiterated experiences come again to the fore. This is the key to the means of expression in modern art.

Similar methods appear today and at the dawn of art, among others: *abstraction, representations of movement, transparency, simultaneity*. . . .[3]

Going back as far as possible in the realm of art only makes sense when one probes into fundamentals; when one searches *not to find external likeness, but to compare modes of representation*.[4]

What is most important in Giedion's formulation is his recognition that in modern art similar tendencies in one culture have evoked again the age-old experiences of man and his concomitant methods of expressing them. Giedion is also careful to compare the similarities of inner motivation rather than external likenesses in such imaged projections. His emphasis rests on the positive quality and significance of forms in modern expression as well as in prehistoric art.

To Giedion's list of similarities in the modes of presentation there might be added such devices as condensation, distortion, and stylization as well as the expression of nonrational and timeless concepts. To such means of projecting inner images the public is now more responsive since they have been so fully explored and authenticated in the developments of pschoanalysis.

The French psychologist G. H. Luquet has also offered a far-reaching analysis, in his *Art Primitif* and in *Art and Religion of Fossil Man*, of the motivation of expression in the art of the child and primitive man which is important to our further comprehension of the technical methods of projection employed in modern art. He points out the way in which both child and primitive draw elements which they consider essential, drop out others which may not concern them, and then include aspects which are

[3] Siegfried Giedion, "Transparency: primitive and Modern," *Art News*, Summer, 1952.
[4] *Ibid.*, p. 49.

known to be there but are not visible. The goal then of both child and primitive, as analyzed by Luquet, is not "objective realism" but what he calls "mental realism." This is an extremely important and interesting observation which, since it is broadly applicable to much of what has of late been developed in the greater sophistication of modern symbolic art, deserves to be fully quoted:

The intellectual realism of primitive art is the opposite of visual realism, differing in two ways; in one aspect, the design contains elements of the model that are not visible, but which the artist considers indispensable; and contrarywise he neglects elements of the model which are evident to sight, but which lack interest for the artist. . . .[5]

A [drawn] image is to the adult [meaning modern man] a likeness when it reproduces *what the eye sees*, while for the primitive it is similar [to the object] when it translates *what his spirit knows*. In explaining at one and the same time, the shared features and the distinctions between the two types of "figured art" we call the first "visual realism" and the second "mental [or intellectual] realism. . . .[6]

It is well understood that when a child is left to express himself spontaneously, he does not draw directly from nature, but uses stylization or memory; usually . . . the design drawn does not reproduce the real object before his eyes and which he does not even look at, but he makes a representation of what is contained within his spirit, what I have called the "internal model." . . . An internal model [also found among primitives] gives proof of spontaneous choice made by the spirit from among the visual data of perception. . . . Only those elements which the artist considers essential are retained and reproduced in the design.[7]

[5] G. H. Luquet, *L'Art Primitif*, G. Doin & Cie., Paris, 1930, p. 68.
[6] *Ibid.*, p. 67.
[7] *Ibid.*, p. 69. Translation of these passages is by the writer. The original:

"Le réalisme intellectuel de l'art primitif s'oppose donc au réalisme visuel de deux façons contraires d'une part, le dessin contient des éléments du modèle qui ne se voient pas, mais que l'artiste juge indispensable; inversement il néglige des éléments du modèle qui sautent aux yeux, mais qui sont pour l'artiste dénués d'intérêt. . . .

"Une image est ressemblante pour l'adulte quand elle reproduit *ce que son oeil en voit*, pour le primitif lorsqu'elle traduit *ce que son esprit en sait*. On exprimera à la fois le caractère commun et le caractère distinctif de ces deux sortes d'art figuré en appelant le premier un réalisme *visuel*, le second *un réalisme intellectuel*.

"Il est bien connu que l'enfant laissé à sa spontanéité dessine non d'après nature, mais 'de chic' ou de mémoire; bien plus, lorsqu'on l'invite à dessiner d'après nature ou d'après des modèles dessinés, son dessin ne reproduit pas l'objet réel qu'il a sous les yeux et que souvent il ne regard même pas, mais la représentation qu'il en a dans l'esprit, ce que j'ai appelé le *modèle interne*. . . . Le modèle interne temoigne d'une sélection spontanément affectuée par l'esprit parmi les données visuelles de la perception. . . . Seuls sont retenus et reproduits dans le dessin les éléments que l'artiste juge essentiels."

. . . There are two main kinds of resemblance and, since realism aims at likeness, two kinds of realism; *visual realism,* which calls solely for the representation of the characters of the model that can be seen from a given point, and *intellectual* [or mental] *realism,* which consists in the full representation of all the features which the model possesses, which "are there." Drawing is in the first instance a fixed visual impression, and in the second instance a definition expressed by lines instead of words.[8]

In elaborating the differences between "visual realism" and "intellectual (or mental) realism" Luquet explains that the designer "in order to portray the characters of a model . . . is obliged to choose, whether consciously or otherwise [this term 'otherwise' can be identified with our emphasis, today, on 'unconscious' as opposed to conscious expression] between the two courses of representing that which he sees of it or that which he knows of it."[9]

In the same discussion Luquet makes another point of special interest to us, when he shows that the primitive artist, "will come up against this inevitable difficulty that although the model can *successively* represent diverse aspects *alternately* hiding or showing such and such a feature, the characteristics figured in the design can be shown but simultaneously."[10]

This analysis by Luquet of the methods employed in primitive and child art are confirmed by the well-known British art critic Roger Fry, who, in analyzing what he terms the "highly conceptualized vision" in children's drawings, is describing exactly what Luquet has defined as "mental realism." And like Luquet, Fry remarks that "conceptualized imagery, so vigorously expressed in children's drawings, obtains also in almost all early art."[11]

Since Luquet emphasizes that his term "mental realism" includes perception by man's spirit, and since Fry's term "conceptualized vision" sounds almost too intellectual as a way of describing a child's vision, would not a term like "intuitive actualization" come closer to being an accurate description of such psychological selection, made by both child and primitive in their art projections?

Prior to the psychoanalytic approach to symbolism, a group of mid-nineteenth-century investigators uncovered the meaning of

[8] G. H. Luquet, *The Art and Religion of Fossil Man* (tr. by J. Townsend Russell, Jr.), Yale University Press, New Haven, 1930, p. 71.
[9] *Ibid.,* p. 70.
[10] *Ibid.,* p. 70.
[11] Roger Fry, *Last Lectures,* Macmillan, New York, 1939, p. 51.

sexual symbols in pagan and Christian art and ritual.

Since these primarily British investigators revealed to a puritanical England, half a century before Freud, that sex symbols transferred from pagan cults were hidden within all Christian art and ritual, they deserve consideration. That these writers lacked understanding of the psychological reasons for the reiteration of sex symbols in so many cultures is evident in their attempt to analyze the symbols. It was not possible at that time to comprehend the psychological motivation which produced such omnipresent sexual symbolism in ritual and religion until a clearer understanding of the mechanisms of unconscious projection had been reached.

Two British investigators, Payne Knight[12] and Thomas Inman, M.D., are representatives of this pre-Freudian exploration of sexual symbols in pagan and Christian art. Inman, in one of his briefer books on ancient pagan and modern symbolism,[13] includes symbolic designs derived from such ancient cultures as the Babylonian, Syrian, Hebrew, Hindu, Egyptian, Greek, Roman, and early Christian. Writing in the middle of the nineteenth century, he exposes his own prudish Victorianism in the way he handles the forbidden topic of sex for his readers. Inman writes:

In the following pages the author has felt himself obliged to make use of words which are probably only known to those who are more or less "scholars." He has to treat of parts of the human body, and acts which occur habitually in the world, which in modern times are never referred to in polite society but which, in the period when the Old Testament was written, were spoken of as freely as we now talk of our hands and feet. In those days, everything which was common was spoken of without shame, and that which occurred throughout creation, and was seen by everyone was as much the subject of conversation as eating and drinking is now. The Hebrew writers were extremely coarse in their diction, and although this has been softened down by subsequent redactors, much which is in our modern judgement improper still remains. For example, where we simply indicate the sex, the Jewish historians used the word which was given to the symbol by which male and female are known; for example, in Gen. 1:27 and V. 2 and in a host of places, the masculine and feminine are spoken of as *zachar* and *nekebah,* which are best translated as "borers" and "bored."[14]

[12] Richard Payne Knight, *An Inquiry into the Worship of Priapus,* privately printed, London, 1865.
[13] Thomas Inman, *Ancient Pagan and Modern Christian Symbolism,* Peter Eckler, (New York, 4th ed., 1922).
[14] *Ibid.,* p. 30.

In tracing the hidden sexual symbols of ancient Hindu and Egyptian art, Inman explains to the then uninitiated public that the symbol of the eye represents "androgyne creator," shown by the "outer oval as female," and the eyeball as "the circle" representing "the male lodged therein—i.e., the androgyne creator."[15] He refers, also, to the significance of "the archway . . . or door, which is symbolic of the female, like the *vesica piscis,* the oval or the circle."[16]

In showing illustrations of the androgyne Brahma, Inman explains that "It represent Brahma supreme, who in the act of creation made himself double, i.e., male and female. In the original, the central part of the figure is occupied by the triad and the unit, but far too grossly shown for reproduction here. They are replaced with the *crux ansata.*"[17]

Should the reader think of this as merely a sign of Victorian squeamishness, it is worth while to mention that even today some of the physiological diagrams of male and female figures which are employed for medical and Red Cross teaching must still be drawn with the sexual organs of the male omitted.

The pointed oval form, as a universal symbol of the female, known in Christian art as the *vesica piscis,* often surrounds the images of the Virgin or various saints. Inman, in order to describe this form, explains its symbolic truth as referring to "the feminine element in creation." This symbol, he says, could be found in "designs which naughty youths so frequently chalk upon walls to the disgust of the proper part of the community."[18]

Inman reviews the manner in which pagan symbols have permeated Christian worship and therefore convinced him that Christian doctrine "is simply horrible—blasphemous and heathenish." He writes: "*I cannot help regarding the sexual element as the key which opens almost every lock of symbolism,* and however much we may dislike the idea that modern religionists have adopted emblems of an obscene worship, we cannot deny the fact that it is so, and we may hope that with a knowledge of their impurity we shall cease to have a faith based upon a trinity and virgin—a lingam and a yoni."[19]

15 *Ibid.,* p. 7.
16 *Ibid.,* p. 8.
17 *Ibid.,* p. 9.
18 *Ibid.,* p. 47.
19 *Ibid.,* p. 101. Italics mine.

We shall presently cite some of Inman's illustrations to compare with the sex symbols of a still extant primitive culture and those of contemporary mental patients.

One of the first French psychiatrists to note the sexual symbols in the drawings of his "insane" patients was Max Simon, who was also shocked by such "obscene drawings" and ordered the patient to cease making them.[20]

In the fifty years following these nineteenth-century investigators of sexual symbolism the expansion of psychoanalysis led the general public as well as the artist to become increasingly aware that the unconscious speaks in symbolic images. Thus, the discoveries of psychoanalysis concerning the dynamics of the unconscious, as well as the uncovering of the symbolic art of prehistoric cultures and ancient civilizations, have given a new perspective to the meaning and value of unconscious elements in the symbolic aspects of art.

We know now from modern as well as ancient examples that distortion, for instance, may be due not to ignorance or pathology but to purposeful emphasis. We can also recognize that simultaneity of focus in a head by Picasso or primitive man, while differing from external appearances, may nevertheless intensify an inner meaning. Acceptance of such direct and simultaneous expression of multiple aspects of human or other form is conclusive confirmation of the significance of recurrent symbolic imagery in man's art. For in such projections, whether made by the primitive, the child, or the modern artist, there are, in the choice and arrangement of these non-literal but none the less universally valid formulations, certain deep psychological laws at work.

Giedion has pointed out how modern artists, from their own psychological need, rediscovered technics that were used by primitive and ancient man. Luquet has analyzed similar technics in the art of primitives and children but has showed no awareness of their applicability to the technics of the modern artist. Several other viewpoints concerning the interpretation of art deserve consideration.

In a recent lecture Dr. Franz Alexander discusses the trends and significance of contemporary art from the viewpoint of psychoanalysis. In considering the characteristics of modern painting

[20] Max P. Simon, "Les écrits et les dessins des aliénés," *Arch. anthrop. crim.*, Paris (1888), *3*:318-355.

as non-objective or abstract, Alexander's summary of its outstanding features agrees with that of Giedion and Malraux in stating that it deals with distortion, "the fantastic, the mystical" and reacts toward "dreamlike symbolism."

Another feature, states Alexander, is the tendency to use primitive perspective or to mix different perspectives, presenting an object from all sides at the same time. . . . All these characteristics from the point of view of psychology, can be interpreted as the manifestation of a central trend: withdrawal from the world as perceived through the sense organs, and substituting for it a newly created, different kind of world. . . . We see, then, that the denial of the real world of objects is a well-nigh universal characteristic of contemporary art. It is not merely a reinterpretation of the world . . . this is universal in every art . . . but a fundamental transformation combined with an aggressive denial of the objects in the form they are commonly perceived.[21]

We must remember that, as a Freudian, Alexander considers the goal of integration for the human psyche of the artist, as well as other men, to depend on an acceptance of what he emphasizes as the "reality" of the world of the senses; this concept of deterministic psychoanalysis demands a rational control of the irrational or mystical aspects of the emotional life of man.

To confirm his point that healthy art depends on an acceptance of the actual external world, Alexander cites the impressionist movement. Since impressionist pictures, as Alexander understands them, deal with the outer world of landscapes and people, he therefore assumes that impressionist methods depict the concrete reality of existence. But their contemporaries, who rejected the impressionists, criticized them for not presenting what the public of that time considered as reality; and that same audience scorned the vision of the impressionists as presented in their scientific fragmentation of color. The impressionists of yesterday, like the abstractionists of today, were attacked by their contemporaries as failing to represent the reality of the visible external world.

The well-known British art critic Laurence Binyon, while recognizing the role of the senses in creativity, includes another factor. In his book *The Spirit of Man in Asian Art* he writes: "Art has

---

[21] Franz Alexander, "The Psychoanalyst Looks at Contemporary Art." This article is a chapter from Dr. Alexander's forthcoming book, *The Western Mind in Transition.* It is based on an address delivered to the Society for Contemporary American Art, Chicago Art Institute, March 4, 1952. Also published in *Explorations in Psychoanalysis,* Julian Press, New York, 1953.

no existence apart from the bodily senses. And yet it is a spiritual activity. It is concerned solely with appearances, yet in its own way, no less than philosophy or science, it seeks for and discovers something behind appearances. . . . You cannot separate the spirit from the body. Art is a perpetual witness to that. It is the meeting place of spirit and sense, which so many have tried to set in opposition and divorce from one another."[22]

When the analyst makes the senses the means of measuring what he calls "reality," does he not ignore the "something behind appearances" which intensifies reality? This added factor includes "mental realism" as defined by Luquet, as well as the inner contemplation of the Eastern artist or the Christian mystic; all these approaches lead to a non-literal presentation which has the quality of a reality that includes but reaches beyond the physical senses.

Psychoanalysis has made both the artist and the general public increasingly aware of the fact that man's unconscious thinks and feels in symbolic images. It has shown most clearly that intellectualization and the exaggerated verbalism of our culture have been imposed on the deeper and more primitive levels of our unconscious mode of imaged expression. That the primary method of unconscious projection in man deals with pictorial images was first explained by Sigmund Freud in relation to his study of dreams. What he states concerning the impulse of some patients to express their dreams in pictures rather than words applies not only to neurotics but also to normal people. In his *General Introduction to Psychoanalysis* Freud wrote: ". . . All dream experiences are predominantly pictures. Part of the difficulty of dream telling comes from the fact that we have to transpose pictures into words. 'I could draw it,' the dreamer says frequently, 'but I don't know how to say it.' "[23]

Although Freud did not pursue the use of drawing in psychoanalytic treatment, it has in recent years become recognized as a fruitful mode of exploring the imaged projections of the unconscious. Analytically oriented art therapy has become possible as a consequence of Freud's achievement in recording the psychological mechanisms of unconscious response in man. So fundamental

[22] Laurence Binyon, *The Spirit of Man in Asian Art,* Harvard University Press, Cambridge, 1936, p. 214.
[23] Sigmund Freud, *General Introduction to Psychoanalysis* (tr. by G. Stanley Hall), Boni & Liveright, New York, 1920, p. 69.

have been his revelations of human motivation that not only psychologists but the general public have adopted the analytic concepts of projection, sublimation, identification, condensation, etc., as a current expression of the way man thinks and speaks today. Although the layman may not understand the deeper significance of these psychological mechanisms, he has come to accept the validity of the unconscious in his life. At the same time, the contemporary artist has made his own use of the dynamism of the unconscious and its symbolic content as revealed by psychoanalysis.

Malraux, in considering the irrational and dream element in modern art, refers to the "diabolical destructive principle" found "in the demons of Babylon, of the early Church and the Freudian subconscious," which, according to him, "all have the same visage. And the more ground the new devils gain in Europe, the more her art tends to draw on earlier cultures which, too, were plagued by their contemporary demons."[24] To make his point that a faith reaching beyond personal artistic expression is the source of great art Malraux cites Goya, who, he states, "foreshadows all modern art: nevertheless painting in his eyes is not the supreme value; its task is to cry aloud the anguish of man forsaken by God. The seemingly picturesque elements are linked up . . . as the great Christian art was linked with faith . . . with certain deep-rooted collective emotions, which modern art has chosen to ignore. . . . The fantastic in his work does not stem from albums of Italian *capricci,* but from the underworld of man's fears."[25]

This is a valuable pronouncement, even though Malraux assumes that the way for modern man to rejuvenate his art is through a return to Christian faith. Assuredly there is need at this moment for man to recover faith and belief in himself and his significant relation to the cosmos. For today man is sunk in the maze of his own materialistic and nationalistic shibboleths. Such creative renewal can no longer be linked to the narrowness of any specific creed, be it the dogma of a religion or of a particular psychology. Malraux and psychoanalysts who look forward to curbing the irrational element in man will never revivify art by their ordered prescriptions. Neither approach shows sufficient faith in

[24] Malraux, *op. cit.,* p. 54.
[25] *Ibid.,* p. 99.

the transformative power of man's unconscious. While the unconscious contains destructive and fearful forces which some religionists and some psychoanalysts warn against, the unconscious is also the source of that generative power which makes it possible for art to become a means of integration and renewal to the human psyche.

Sexual symbolism in primitive and non-Christian art has been often misunderstood and distorted. To the primitive, sex symbols were not something to be decried or feared. They represented for him a positive and universal life-giving force in the cosmos and in man. In much anthropological research this attitude of primitive peoples is evident.

There is a tendency among certain art critics and artists today to dismiss what is known of the art projections of psychotics or the "insane" as being entirely meaningless. Malraux formulates this point of view when he states that while the "insane" artist holds an "inner monologue" with himself in which he "speaks solely and for himself," "the genuine artist holds a dialogue with the world."

Such an interpretation of "insane" or psychotic art by Malraux is related to the non-dynamic psychology of an earlier epoch. Pre-analytic psychology usually judged psychotic art as meaningless. The recent findings of psychoanalysis have modified such a view. It is now recognized that the symbolic projections of mental patients are all meaningful whether immediately comprehensible or not.

Through improved technics, psychoanalysis has become increasingly aware of the unconscious mental processes of psychotics. Freud originally considered psychotics untreatable; because of modified technics a growing number of schizophrenic and manic-depressive patients are now being successfully treated by psychoanalysts. This means that behavior once considered totally bizarre and senseless expressions of psychotics is now perceived to be symbolic communication from the unconscious which it is possible to decipher. It is therefore inaccurate to dismiss the projections of a psychotic as being without meaning. Psychiatry now recognizes that no gesture, no facial expression, no jumbled phrase or strange design projected by a psychotic is meaningless. All such projections are charged with specific symbolic significance, whether they are comprehensible or not to another person. For it is now known that disturbed patients are not merely talking to themselves but attempting to communicate with others by little understood means.

The kind of symbolism chosen by man in his visual projections from prehistory until the present period has certain strikingly similar elements. The archaic patterns projected from the unconscious imagery of man today are rooted in the same human responses as those which motivated man in primitive times; for age-old patterns of symbolic response remain active and observable today.

We have seen what well-known art critics and psychologists have noted that whenever inner experiences have been projected by man, at different stages of cultural development, into nonrealistic images, their creators tend to use similar technics. We have realized that such technical methods of expression, discovered spontaneously in different epochs, are found to include the use of abstraction as a means of expressing inner realizations; the use of simultaneity of focus rather than perspective; the intensification of the dynamics of movement by means of distorted line; and the use of "transparency" or overlaid images to depict what the mind knows to exist, rather than what the eye actually sees.

The recurrent use of universal symbols relating to the creative principle in the cosmos and in the individual life of man, as personified in the imaged projection of sexual symbols, is significant. It is not surprising that in man's efforts to express his relation to the universe and to his own experience we find the same life symbols, in the unconscious of contemporary as of primitive and ancient man.

While we find the use of sexual and other human symbols throughout the ages of man's creative projections, we are not in a position to know, but only to speculate about, what such symbolic expression may have meant to early man in primitive or ancient cultures that have now passed away. From artifacts and ritual objects as from stone tablets and papyri, archaeologists and anthropologists have helped to reconstruct forgotten and long-buried cultures. But the findings of modern man as to the meaning of the symbolic remains of ancient societies are based on the ideas, beliefs, and prejudices of our own different culture. We can only speculate about but do not really know the total purpose of remote priapic or mystery rites. Important as is the insight gained from the psychoanalytic approach to symbolism, especially to sexual symbols, it cannot reproduce all aspects of the ancient significance of such symbols to primitive man or to ancient cultures not rooted in the Western tradition. It is therefore of considerable interest to supplement the psychoanalytic approach to sexual symbols with that of a still surviving primitive culture like that of the Maori.

In a little-known but fascinating volume on *Maori Symbolism,* a living Maori, Hohepa Te Rake by name, has described and interpreted the meaning of the culture and sacred legends of his people. This record was taken down by a court reporter, Miss Ettie A. Rout, in New Zealand and its contents were approved by this high-ranking Maori. As stated to the reporter, Miss Rout, this Maori leader came to the conclusion that since Western scientists had been able to uncover the inner meaning of some Maori symbolism, and because his own Maori culture is dying, it was his obligation and duty to explain the true meanings of the long-withheld, secret teachings of the Maori tradition. What he has revealed in this book has been delineated by means of various modes of symbolic expression, such as movement, gesture, carving, and tattooing.

In the interpretation of Maori symbolism, Miss Rout explains: "When we speak of Maori art it must be understood that we speak of Maori Symbolism. There was no art apart from Symbolism . . . that is, there was no such thing as Art for Art's sake. The carving was not sculpture in the European sense at all; it was writing and expression of ideas and principles. . . . The twin ideals of Ancient Maori life were Beauty and Duty, but Beauty must be expressed through the performance of the Duty of cultivation. On this Religion of Cultivation and its Symbolism the whole of Maori Life and Art was based."[26]

According to Hohepa Te Rake, the male and female life symbols are hidden within the arabesque carvings on the rafters of the sacred Maori houses; they were always present but partially disguised. ". . . It was the duty," he explains, "of the artist to conceal as well as reveal: the Sacred Symbol was to be the foundation

[26] Etti A. Rout, *Maori Symbolism,* Harcourt, Brace, New York, (Kegan Paul, Trench, Trubner, London), 1926, pp. xxx-xxxi.

of the pattern. . . . Usually only half is represented: or half the
male and half the female (symbol) are combined. . . ."[27]

In order to show how the Maori employed their sacred life
symbols in their carvings as a means of communication, three
examples have been chosen to compare with a similar form in

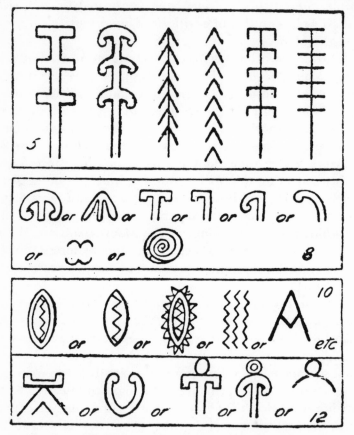

Figure 1. *Maori Sacred Life Symbols: Male and Female*[28]

Christian iconography. Figure 1 illustrates the separate patterns
of the male and female life symbols. Figure 2 shows the fusion of
the masculine and feminine symbols in what was known as the
"Sacred Heart" pattern. Figure 3 shows the well-known form
of a Jade Tiki; "the whole carving," according to Miss Rout,[29]
"is phallic writing."

[27] *Ibid.*, p. 199.
[28] *Ibid.*, p. 20.
[29] *Ibid.*, p. 295.

. . . To the Maori nobility the Sacred Heart Design signifies the combination of the male and female life-symbols, and this combination can be traced in many decorations.[30]

Maori jade Tiki . . . are symbolic ornaments representing the Immortality of the Race and the means of achieving it. They are composed entirely of the male and female life symbols and sacred beaks carved in the form of the phallus. . . . The hand-carving of a jade Tiki

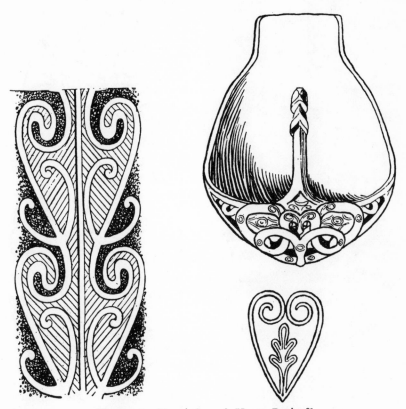

Figure 2. *Maori Sacred Heart Design*[31]

occupies many generations . . . in fact, it is supposed never to be "finished": each generation added a little to these sacred heirlooms. . . . The *eyebrows* and *eyelids* are sometimes formed of two sacred male Life-Symbols, but usually of two sacred Beaks. . . . On this plate it should be noted that the lower part of the jade Tiki is a representation of the three-toed feet and legs as disguise for labia and external female genitalia.[32]

[30] *Ibid.,* p. 213.
[31] *Ibid.,* p. 52.
[32] *Ibid.,* p. xxix.

The closed eyes represent the labia, the male life-symbol forms the nostrils, the *mouth* is the *Sacred Heart* (i.e., external female genitalia in conjunction with the male organs) and the protruding tongue is the *membrum virile*—the tongue's significance in all Maori carvings. There are three toes and three fingers . . . this Trinity in form is

Figure 3a. *Maori Jade Tiki,* the Maker of Man[33]

Figure 3. *Outline Form of Jade Tiki:* for identification of male and female life symbols[33]

based on the Male Life-Symbol, but the significance is to express the threefold life of man, Intelligent, Moral and Physical. The spirals on this carving represent the male testes.[34]

In the Maori designs of sacred life symbols in Figure 1, the first, second, and fourth rows of symbols are clearly representative

[33] *Ibid.*, p. 226, 227.
[34] *Ibid.*, pp. 300-301.

of the male principle and the third row of the female principle. The oval or elliptical forms, in row three, are a universal symbol familiar not only in primitive but in both Eastern and Western cultures. When this oval form appears in Christian art as a surround of the Virgin or the Christ figure it is known as the *vesica piscis.*

Figure 4. *Virgin Showing Divine Impregnation:* medieval Christian iconography[35]

Figure 4 is an interesting example of the way in which this same symbol has been used in Christian iconography. In this design the male and female principle in Christian symbolism is clearly illustrated. Here the ovoid form of the *vesica piscis,* representing the vagina, contains the configuration of the Christ child. The divine impregnation of the Virgin by the creative principle is illustrated through the descent of the sun's rays from the dove, as symbol of the Holy Ghost.

For comparison with the use of sex symbols in Maori art and Christian iconography two symbolic designs of a young woman produced during art therapy are significant. In Figure 5 is shown

[35] Inman, *op. cit.,* p. 92.

one of a series of small patterns rapidly produced by an emotionally disturbed college girl. She did not, while making them, recognize the meaning of these imaged projections. Only later was she surprised to see that she had made a drawing of "an Infant Contained Within the Vaginal Form of the Mother."

Figure 5.   *Chalk Drawing of an Infant Contained Within the Vaginal Form of the Mother:* drawn by young woman patient during art therapy[36]

Figure 6 is an unconscious projection made by the same college girl some months later, during art therapy treatment. This design is similar in form and meaning to the combination of male and female symbols in the Maori "Sacred Heart" pattern (Figure 2). The patient recognized that this conjunction of male and female symbols expressed her own acceptance of femininity.

[36] Reproduced by permission of the publisher from Margaret Naumburg, *Psychoneurotic Art: Its Function in Psychotherapy*, Grune and Stratton, New York, 1953.

Figure 6. *Painting Expressive of the Unified Male and Female Principle:* painted by the same young woman patient who made Figure 5

The comparison in the use of sexual symbols in the culture patterns of Maori, medieval Christian, and modern man has been shown to suggest the universal use of such forms to express similar meanings.

In order to illustrate how similar symbolic content has been expressed by similar technic in the art of primitive and modern man two examples of the use of transparency are shown. The first, Figure 7, is an elephant cave painting made by primitive man. The second, Figure 8, is a chalk drawing of "Four Generations" made by a woman patient during art therapy treatment. In both

Figure 7. *Elephant   Cave   Painting   of
Primitive   Man*[37]

pictures the same technic of transparency has been employed in order to emphasize the non-visible internal organ of the heart. We do not know and can only speculate as to the meaning of the elephant in the cave painting of primitive man; but we do know from the comments of the disturbed patient, a woman of fifty-five, that she drew the transparency of red hearts in the three figures of women to represent the emotional bond connecting the three generations of women to the great-grandchild of the woman at the left. The patient identifies herself with the second woman to the left.

The technic of "transparency" was selected as an example of a method much used in primitive and child art and favored also today by many modern artists—a technic aptly defined by Luquet

[37] G. H. Luquet, *The Art and Religion of Fossil Man,* p. 91.

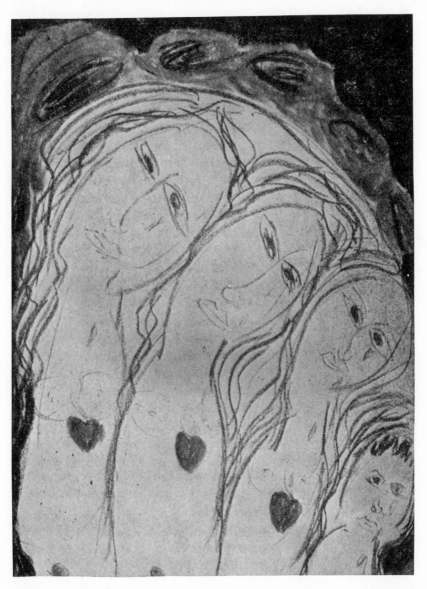

Figure 8. *"Four Generations":* chalk drawing by a woman patient during art therapy

as a method of translating what "the spirit knows" rather than "what the eye sees." Not only Luquet but Binyon and Fry also emphasized the importance of the total response of the spirit of man combined with his sensory perceptions as the source of his creative expression.

Armed with the knowledge that man's unconscious speaks today as well as yesterday in archaic pictorial images, the investigator of symbolism has at his disposal fresh psychological tools for deciphering many as yet little understood aspects of human behavior and expression.

✿ Chapter *XVIII*
JEAN P. de MENASCE

A PHILOSOPHY OF TRANSLATION

ON TRANSLATING POETRY

I   There is a contribution to be made to literary criticism from the approach of the linguist who has been interested in the problem of translation, and in the more general problem of symbolism from a philosophical point of view. The notes that follow represent an attempt at such a contribution.

The use of language, as distinct from the structure of language, evidently provides us with a scale, ranging from the crudest sort of baby speech or of "pidgin" (a pure intercourse language by which the speaker is trying so hard to make himself understood that he imagines he is using the words of the hearer whereas he is really using his own) to the most technically abstract language of symbolic logic. Both extreme types are highly simplified. On the one hand there is the simplification of the concrete situation—here and now, this or that—and on the other the simplification of rigorous abstraction, with a one-to-one correspondence between each word and each reality. Both speakers are aiming at preventing any misunderstanding on the part of the hearer. The no-man's-land we recognize as existing in most types of speech is abolished. The immediately practical and the supremely intellectual have this directness in common.

Now I need not insist on the shades language is likely to take on according to the various spheres of human interests which require to be expressed in words. I will only note that the "remoteness" both the scientist and the man in the street are prone to blame on the language of the jurist, the historian, the psychologist, or the art critic is not "a matter of words." It is not as though all language, falling short of the rigor of symbolic logic, were nothing but speech that had missed the mark, to be ranked with the expression of pure emotion, devoid of knowledge. The word follows the thought and whatever obscurity or clarity the word may possess does not, *per se,* contaminate, or communicate itself to, the mode of knowledge peculiar to that particular subject matter. Given an adequate range of culture, it is not because we use words wrongly, or because we use the wrong words, that we have difficulties with difficult subjects, but because the matter itself is obscure and requires more than one approach through induction and abstraction. This is a philosophical problem primarily, and one to which I shall return.

One implication of the view I am sketching is that "poetry" is not such as it is because it is using poetic language; on the contrary, poetic language is the language required by poetry, set up, invented by poetry, however much it may be put to other uses. French school boys, a generation ago, used to memorize the names of the departments of France, with their *chefs-lieux* and their *sous-préfectures,* by means of a sort of rhymed doggerel. In the fourteenth century the elements of formal logic were put into rimed verse, even by so genuine a poet as Ramón Lull. This is merely a borrowing of the poetic form, not for its poetic value but for the accidental property it has of being easily memorized.

One of the tasks of literary criticism is no doubt to discover and describe, to analyze, the fundamental poetic experience that lies at the root of a particular work of art. It belongs to the philosopher to give a thoroughgoing explanation of that experience, not in this or that case in particular, but with respect to human activity as a whole. The philosopher of aesthetics is not immediately concerned with art criticism, but his contribution to the theory of beauty and of human creativeness is nonetheless vital to the art critic. Again, it is obvious that, as the artist is concerned with a far-reaching and deeply human experience, the critic is also required to enjoy, at least to some extent, a breadth of human experience without which he is likely to remain, for all his learning, merely a blind pedant.

But, giving philosophy and human experience their indispensable share, it remains, I think, to consider also the *nature* and *use* of the material poetry is made up of, to study the very language of poetry in its specific quality, thereby getting a glimpse into the creation or reshaping of that peculiar product of the human person, sensible and intellectual, social and individual, active and contemplative. We may study, apart from other concerns, the art of using a system of significant sounds to compose the poetic experience. This involves not merely the analysis of the structure of that system but the description of what is actually produced in the world of language when language is put to that use. It would be interesting to compare *discovery* in science and *creation* in art, remembering that the artist is expressing something that is *in him,* and that in art the *material* becomes part of the work achieved.

For it cannot be forgotten that poetry, as an eminent example of what we call "style," is a mode of composition that is not indifferent to, or separable from, the emotion or the experience it is meant to convey. I am not at all talking about the sincerity of the poet, the equation of his real feelings to what he is trying to say. I am trying to point out a contrast: on the one hand, the language of science or philosophy, or the language of everyday life, is chiefly required to be as transparent a garment as will fit the thought; it is a scaffolding we gladly remove once the archway has been built; its perfection is to state what has to be stated in words so used that we forget words have been used. The art of poetry, on the other hand, cannot allow us to dissociate the words from what they express; however lucid and direct, they are *part* of the message conveyed; they contribute to the expression of the poetic emotion in a special sense, as if they were not merely signs but things, and cannot be dismissed as supernumerary.

As Jacques Maritain has shown in his study of signs, there is a sense in which they may "contain" what they mean. They are, and are not, the things meant. For a "primitive"—more justly for any man living under the spell of imagination, of images—they are. They are not, if our intelligence allows us to distinguish between the sign and the things signified. But a primitive mentality is not a stage of humanity that is superseded and forgotten; it is something that remains, and, in a way, rightly so, in the mind of the civilized man.

When we come to what the old logicians called "practical signs," signs primarily intimating action, the case for identifying imaginatively sign and reality is even stronger: the intimation comes to be conceived of as efficient, not only, as in the Christian doctrine of the sacraments, through a special dispensation of God, but in its own right. Language thus becomes efficient as well as significant. You may call this a magical use of language, but the phrase is vague and requires distinctions with which I am not now concerned. It is, however, close to the poetic use, because in both cases the sign is envisaged as something adhering to the reality, and almost as being part of it. When any aspect or type of reality is thought of as positively requiring an expressive instrument through which it may be apprehended, the artist becomes a magian or a magician. This is the permanent temptation of a line of genuinely great poetry, ranging from Novalis to Rilke. The poem is an incantation—in Patmore's words, "the song that is the thing it sings."

Now the ordinary approach to this problem consists in studying the "musical" quality of language, the color, weight, rhythm, of the sounds and forms of speech, purely as sounds, purely as music. But the question is why that particular ensemble of musical phrasing should be suitable to the meaningful expression of poetic emotion: why language is at all lovely, or why, in a given language, one mode of linguistic expression should be more beautiful, and thus more suitable for the expression of the beautiful.

It is at first sight obvious that that peculiar quality is not purely musical, cannot indeed be so in view of the fact that one set of sounds in a given language is as beautiful as it is unpleasant in another language. Words do not stand universally to their meaning and intelligible content in the same ratio as a tune stands to a poem that has been set to music. You get the same pleasure out of *Don Giovanni* whether it is sung in Italian or in German; you get pleasure out of *Pelléas et Mélisande* only when sung in French, because here the music follows the unique accentuation of the French phrase. But talking of poetry as such, as the field of language in which the expressed is, so to speak, adhesive to the mode of expression, my contention is that there is something to account for that property of language in its very nature, not only in its particular uses, and that there is, notwithstanding, in the poetic experience, with its urge toward expression, a measure of creative freedom and, fundamentally, something so universally human that it accounts for the fact that even poetry can be translated.

What do I understand by the poetic experience which I am assuming throughout underlies poetry? Since much as been made of the real resemblance between the poetic and the mystical experience, it will not be superfluous to make a few remarks in order to clear up the obvious confusions. Speaking as a theologian— the psychologist, as such, is not competent to deal with the supernatural—I should say that the chief difference between them is that the experience of the mystic is that of *receiving,* of "suffering" —*pati divina*—a divine "touch" or "motion"; that of the poet, even though it *may* be termed a "revelation," is a revelation of beauty, and not, directly, of divine *love.* The vision of the mystic is ineffable; even to call it a vision is saying too much. But if he has to express it—out of the abundance of his heart—then it is likely his language will be that of images and will fit into poetry. St. John of the Cross is a case in point. When he has to express his particular experience, for the sake of *checking* with the Revelation made to mankind, he is at a loss to find words and phrases and realizes, as no poet does, the inadequacy of language. He will borrow from Scripture, from theology, from philosophical concepts and imagery, but at times the most profane imagery will suit his purpose best. That is what makes the study of the mystics so difficult: they are expressing similar states in many different ways and are using, sometimes, philosophical or theological patterns in a free way, for the want of something better, just as the poet may be using philosophy, not as his underlying inspiration, but as "motifs," elements, brought in *ad hoc.*

To return to the language of poetry, the beauty of the poem, like all beauty, a *"splendor formae,"* a *radiation,* implies that there must be some "matter" upon which the radiations are supported, say a substratum for them. Now the material of poetry, being words, is in its own right loaded with intelligibility, with meaning, and it seems that the use of words in poetry—as opposed to prose —implies, not only a choice of words and syntactic structure heavily loaded with meaning, but also giving them new meanings, new references, in their very use. The novelty may be slight, but novelty there must be if the poetry is not to be a mere repetitious construction of words. This process, which might be called the poetic "keying" of language, functions both on the plane of meaning *and* on the plane of the purely musical, *phonetic* aspect of language.

As regards meaning, it is quite obvious that poetry makes use of "suggestive" words—words having, in addition to their meaning, an aura of immediate references given them by previous usage, by tradition, both poetic and prosaic, and therefore closely bound up with the particular context in time and space. The stock suggestions of a word have to be considered in their full historic value. This holds good not only for Chinese poetry, where literary allusions make it practically impossible to *understand*—much less to enjoy—the meaning of a poem without reference to a whole *corpus* of *topoi*, evoked by a single word or perhaps a mere assonance. It is true of any poetry, and the "surprise" we may have felt in 1923, at the appearance of *The Waste Land*, with its numerous "quotations," only shows that we had fallen into considering poetry as a narrowly individualistic use of language—which made *vers libre*, for instance, such thin reading before it became, in its turn, a "context." Even great poetry, with its supratemporal quality, cannot dispense with a context. But the essential context is so deeply human that it allows the poetry to escape the limitations of its temporal—*zeitbedingt*—references.

Incidentally, let it be said that the uniqueness of the work of art is not due to the uniqueness of the *experience*. The experience of love is a common one; the uniqueness is in the creation, through and in the experience, of a *something* made of a specific material, endowed with a new significance. We may feel like Rembrandt, but we may no longer paint like him.

Quite apart from the literary references, the nature of words as signs of something intelligible gives poetry a much wider range of reference than does the material of any other art (including music); indeed, poetry may suggest color and sound and shape and motion without having to make use of any combination or fusion of techniques. In the opera, or in polychromic statuary, music and the drama, sculpture and painting combine to make up for their inherent limitations. Poetry rules over the materials of all the arts, merely by being able to name them all, to conjure them up, to use them as so many wave-lengths for the outburst of the poetic intuition, without endangering the unity of its own proper and quasi-universal medium, language.

The poetry of a particular poet or of a particular period can indeed be studied with regard to the most prominent type of sense references. Some poets are visual, others kinematic; with others the material chosen is the more secret workings of their inner senses, imagination, and memory. I do not mean they are expressing these in poetry; I mean they are using this kind of inner life as their favorite or typical set of images in order to express their poetic intuition of something beyond. Poetry of this kind may even express something superficial, whereas "extravert" poetry may really be pointing to something deep and *inner*. The material qualifies, but does not determine, the profundity of the intuition.

Let us now leave the sphere of meaning for the world of sounds. The recent work of linguists may here be of use to the literary critic when dealing with the poetic, i.e., with the *creative,* use of language. It is obvious that a sound or group of sounds is not *musically* beautiful in a given language unless it fits into the phonemic structure of that language. French, Polish, or Portuguese nasals sound unpleasant to an Italian or a Hungarian, and clusters of sibilants in the Slavonic languages are distasteful to an Arab or a Persian. It is a fact that the sounds of a language are not mere sounds but are, from the outset, connected with meanings, and differentiate meanings according to rules which are proper to each language. Sound occurrences are not atomic and isolated; they arise from meaningful oppositions and distinctions; they have not only *phonetic* but *phonemic* (or *phonological*) value. When children invent a secret language the result is not chaos but a systematic body of opposed and related sounds, either inspired from their mother tongue or sharply departing from it according to certain rules. The language of poetry—as opposed to that of prose—runs on the same lines: the choice of certain harmonies of sound (or meaningful disharmonies), the insistence on a meter which is both more stressed and more regular than that of prose (for prose knows meter, too)—all this stamps language in its vocabulary, in its rhythm, in its syntax and what not with a new quality that cannot but be associated with its sound-value.

That poetry at times departs from its ordinary use of those materials is a sign of its creativeness but does not disprove the existence of poetic speech. Indeed, it is in the nature of poetry that it should balance, oscillate, between a conservative (say classic) and a revolutionary (say romantic) use of language, that the language material should be brought to a state of intensity or to a state of disruption, that the poetic—like any other tongue—should now take in loan words from the legal, the philosophic, the technical languages, and now exert strong, intolerant censorship. The alternation between austerity and abundance is part of the same process of giving *"un sens plus pur aux mots de la tribu."* Poetry makes its language, and poetic language in its turn makes poetry. And this is true on the level of sound just as on the higher levels.

It might at first sight be supposed that this creative function which we assign to poetry with respect to language should altogether preclude the translation of poetry. That poetry can be translated—into poetry, of course—is proved by the existence of some capital translations. This fact does not merely evidence a tour de force; it shows that the poetic experience has been so perfectly transmitted by poetry, that it has, in a sense, been made so accessible to the translator, that he may, so to speak, re-create it in another language. It also means that there exists an affinity between the poetic language of different idioms, qua *poetic.* Just how far that affinity depends on the unity of poetic experience or on the play of history by which poetic fashion spreads from one country to another, from one culture to another, remains to be examined in each case. A history of verse translation in Europe is a rewarding theme for a man gifted both with a sharp *Sprachgefühl* and with still keener feelers for the depths of human experience. So little work has been done on those lines that we are in the happy condition of being able to welcome almost anything on that topic.

LANGUAGE CATEGORIES AND CONCEPTUAL CATEGORIES

2   The language of poetry is, we found, a "state" of language that is inclined to express the beautiful. Should it be correct to say that the beautiful is convertible with being, and with the true and with the good, then, surely, there would always be in the expression of reality—i.e., of the beautiful—something essentially poetic. This is a philosophical doctrine on which one may be allowed to suspend one's judgment. (If it were true, linguistics would be indissolubly linked up with aesthetics. But my own remarks suggested that this was not the

case, and that the *emotion* with respect to the beautiful was not common to all models of expression).

It was suggested that there was, previous to expression, a poetic experience—and this word should be taken as meaning an emotional process, characterized *not* by its being in any way un-noetic, including indeed the knowledge of something, but by the knowledge's being given *in* the very emotion and without the mediation of a discursive process. This is a feature of *experience* as such, in this particular, technical sense of the word, and is common to the poetic and to the mystical, which need not imply more than a *similarity* of psychological conditions between the poet and the mystic. The fundamental difference is to be judged not by the psychological pattern of the process but by the content of the experience: in one case the beautiful, in the other the divine touch.

Now in the present discussion we are concerned with another aspect of language: language as expressing essentially and primarily knowledge given through universals, through concepts, and not as "tasted" or "felt" in emotion, whether poetic or religious. This is not saying that the language expressing truth has no emotional connotation and is wholly abstracted from the reality of emotion. It merely means that the primary and immediate function of such modes of expression as are noetic is to deal with reality in so far as it is known, though, of course, the known may and must evoke love, and the pursuit of the loved. Again, the content of the *known* may be an emotion, but the emotion does not enter into the knowledge as an ingredient. The psychologist is not *per se* a poet. (Indeed, much of the success of psychoanalytical treatment comes from directing the attention of a patient who is overconcerned emotionally with his emotions to a more objective and almost scientific way of considering those emotions. This may also suggest one of the snags of analysis: the patient thinks he is cured because he knows the nature of his trouble—a Socratic attitude, with all the benefits of irony, but exposed to the old Aristotelian objections.)

It is perfectly clear, also, that there are other languages than the purely poetic and the purely noetic; the language of order, commandment, is primarily concerned not with a giving notice of reality but with provoking action. This has not been studied half enough, or rather it has been considered as a by-product of noetic language, not as something specific, as it tends to become. Fundamentally, there is no difference between the word "Look!" and an arrow or an exclamation mark pictured on a street signal, or the blast of a siren: they are "practical," actional signs bringing about an automatic response, which may have been acquired by way of intellectual knowledge but does not essentially require it. Training is not always "learning." It is significant on the other hand that this should ever have come to be considered by some as typical of the very process of human knowledge. Here again, but at the other extreme, we are asked to believe that there is only *one mode* of expression, and even only one mode of knowledge. The emotion of poetry is no longer everything; language is essentially *practical*. Though I am arguing against these extreme theories, I quite see their point; if they overemphasize the emotional and practical aspect of man's knowledge, and of man's language, it is because they are rightly impressed with the importance, in man's life, of emotion and of action. But they run the danger of "reducing" the *noetic* values of human life, or explaining them away, instead of interpreting them in the full human context. But they are, quite rightly, reacting against an over-intellectualistic interpretation of man. However, I submit that *language,* being meaningful sound, is connected in an essential way with the thinking activity of man, though the range of its uses is more extensive than intellectual knowledge. Language is shaped by man as a whole. *"Le style, c'est l'homme";* but the reverse is not true: the possibilities of language do not exactly cover man's manifold activities; even his intellectual life is not exhausted by his use of language.

The point I would like to emphasize is that man's noetic life is developed by means of the concept, of the universal, abstracted from the world of sense data and probing into the nature or essence of things. The progress of science is toward greater precision, a closer correspondence between tentative generalizations and the reality, as experience and speculation show it to be. The process implies, when dealing with physical reality, constant readjustment of notions, the goal being an adequate analysis of all the complexities of reality. But the process, however elaborate, never transcends that degree of abstraction that operates *per genus et differentiam* and by quantitative measurement. The process of analysis, synthesis, and measure, if it is to be true to reality, must operate with universals that must correspond universally to the reality they mean. If we find that a notion hitherto used as a unit actually covers a number of different things, that very notion will have to be given a new meaning: either narrower, to cover only a special field of its older province, or broader, with a variety of subdivisions of which its older meaning is only one.

Now let us see what happens in the making of nonscientific or *unspecialized* language; it corresponds originally to some rough-and-ready distinctions we make in our universe—and this will no doubt be colored by one or other of the most vital aspects of human life. A good example is that of the division of nouns into classes: Indo-European masculine, feminine, and neuter are probably descendants of an older couple made up of *animate* and *inanimate;* when a person, male or female, is envisaged as a *thing,* it becomes neuter either because it is *not yet* a person, or for some other reason. (Thus: *das Kind* or *das Fräulein,* but *die Frau.*) Epicene words in old Greek have been shown, when feminine, to have a broader, more general connotation, and when masculine to refer to a given occurrence. Generic and abstract words are mostly feminine. In languages with a more elaborate system of noun classes, such as the Bantu languages, the division of things in the universe is not according to sex but according to size, shape, animal species, and so strong is the sense of the distinction of things as exemplified in those classes that the particular class-prefix of the important word is attached to all the other words in the sentence. Another example is that of languages in which a great many concrete words are used for all the particular situations concerning one of the vital things in a given society. In classical Arabic, dictionaries list hundreds of verbs referring to the camel's behavior. In some North American Indian languages, there are special verbs meaning "to see" according to the relative positions of the seer and the seen. The same process may give rise to what seems linguistic austerity, rather than abundance, in a language such as Hottentot, where an epithet, taken in itself, *ipso facto* refers to the *cow;* when you use the word "beautiful" you need specify only if you are speaking of a woman or a house, not if you are referring to a beautiful cow. This means that, as far as adjectives go, the word is divided into two classes, cows and non-cows.

The various relations in which a being may stand to others, as given in declensions, may be as neatly distinguished as in the old Indo-European system, preserved only in a few living languages, or almost entirely deficient as in English or French; but that means that another system of distinctions has taken its place: possession is no longer expressed by a genitive suffix, but by a preposition. One kind of simplification has been compensated for by another way of expressing difference. If the verb has the same form for all persons, singular and plural, then the use of the pronoun is indispensable, diacritical, not merely rhetorical.

All I wish to say is that languages have developed divisions of their own, classes of beings, types of action, types of properties and relations, that are made according to certain patterns—juridical, social, physical, or biological—the crudeness of which is preserved in the language notwithstanding the fact that technical language has meanwhile developed under the pressure of scientific analysis. Furthermore, even technical language preserves, in some form, in its very foundations, and even when it is using Greek words rather than Latin, the linguistic material previously shaped by non-scientific expression, while going beyond its original limitations, now felt to be detrimental to the progress of analysis and precision. Science is able to create new language, not primarily by a critique of language but by a new awareness of reality for which it requires new terms; but the new terms are old terms, or combinations of old terms, endowed with a new *power*. When science is lagging, it is not owing to the inability of the scientist to deal with words, but owing to a momentary failure in coping with reality. Only a very naïve scientist would imagine that by changing his vocabulary he is going to improve his methods of research.

When we come to philosophy these trite truths seem to carry insufficient weight with the majority of our contemporaries. They realize, however obscurely, that philosophical abstraction is not on the same level as that of science. This is exemplified in the words which the philosopher uses: they are, first, much more imaginative than those of the scientist; but, otherwise, the philosopher claims that he is using notions that range beyond the categories of the scientist—that are, in a sense, more technically *refined*, if more difficult to *define*. The philosopher has to deal with a sphere of reality which is both transcendent and immanent;

in his language, too, he boasts of this catholicity and does not blush to take recourse to an imagery derived from the lowest order of concrete, material being. The transcendence of his highest object makes him painfully aware of the inadequacy of his highest concepts and of the necessity to complement one analogy with another. His use of imagery, however, is entirely different from the poet's: an analogy, to be of any use to him, will have to undergo a process of purification, of intellectual "refining," that leaves him with a notion as technical as any the scientist brings in, but he is, so to speak, more humbly aware of its own inadequacy as regards the fullness of being. That is also the reason why the vocabulary of philosophy is so much more conservative than that of science: the notions being higher and fewer, the progress of philosophy follows an entirely different *tempo*. Further, the obvious fact that there are several—I do not say many—philosophies, whereas there is only one science, points to limitations due both to the depth of the object and to the frailty of the philosophers. That the difference of emphasis or of starting point, and the blindness to one or the other of the aspects of being, should strongly mark their language is a matter of course. But the difficulty of equating these languages, of *translating* one philosophy into another, shows that it is not a matter of language. Indeed, when two philosophies come to grips, the question is not how the one is going to annex the other, as a chemist may annex a newly discovered element into his system, or a historian new facts, but how the one is going to assimilate the other, absorbing all that is vital in it and rejecting ruthlessly error and one-sidedness. The criterion, here, is the tendency in any one philosophy to account for being in its totality.

The image I have just used is, in a sense, misleading. If philosophers quarreled because they did not mean the same thing while using the same word, it would indeed be a matter of words, and the quarrel would have no point. It is because they disagree about each other's account of reality, of a reality that can be grasped only through analogical, supra-scientific notions, that they find themselves disagreeing in language, as a consequence of the case. When a Thomist disagrees with a *Vedantin*, both parties may well have to spend some time in clearing up differences of vocabulary; the fact that they can do so, that they can agree to a certain number of equations, owing to their common view of some particular reality, leaves them more free to perceive their fundamental opposition—an opposition that would be evinced just as well through the Latin of Spinoza as through the Sanskrit of Śankara.

Can these remarks be of any use to a student of language? They may, perhaps, help him to restate some useful truths: that philosophy has its own technique, philosophical, not aesthetic, of criticizing language; that philosophy has something to say about the aesthetics of language; that the philosophy of language can on no account be philosophy *tout court*.

ON THE CATHOLICITY OF REVELATION

3 In further illustration of the way in which language is stretched to accommodate cultural or intellectual needs, I should like to recall some striking examples of linguistic "acculturation." First, of course, one language borrows from another the elements it requires, because they are originally lacking. This is the case, say, of one "technical" tongue's invading wholesale another idiom. The language of technology is largely English, both in French and in the Eastern tongues that are rapidly being tuned to a technical civilization; so also is the language of sports. In the Middle Ages the language of astronomy was imported from the Arabic-speaking countries and has since then remained close to its origins. But the importation, however massive, of a vocabulary has never changed the structure of a language. Turkish has about one-third Arabic and one-third Persian words, and English has, more than German, retained its Latin-French vocabulary, without either of them losing its specific character. On the other hand, in some cases the borrowing has been, so to speak, arbitrary, i.e., uncalled for by any specific lack or demand on the part of the borrower. One of the paradoxes of human progress lies in the fact that the Egyptians, having invented the alphabet, never chose to make use of it to the full by entirely breaking away from their elaborate ideographic system of writing. They used both together at the same time (think of an automobile worked both by engine and by horse). The Persians, after the Moslem conquest, gave up, little by little, a quantity of Persian words in favor of Arabic words, many of which were really no better than the old ones. Much later, hardly two decades ago, an attempt was made to reverse this process by expelling all Arabic words from modern Persian; the failure to do so, in spite of an Academy backed by law and police, is explained by the hold of the classical literature, chiefly of poetry, even on the common people. To revert to pure Iranian was to sever the modern tongue from its best roots. The experiment was tried in Turkey with somewhat greater success, but in both countries there has been, in recent years, a return to the "mixed language" of the classics. Germany, at the time when, like most other European countries, it was under the sway of French manners and arts, had largely borrowed French words that were given German forms, many of which were to be gradually eliminated in the course of a few generations. The same was true of Hebrew in the first centuries of our era: Greek and Latin words, chiefly juridical and technical, crept in and remained in use as long as the conditions which had led to their introduction prevailed, i.e., until the Jews were swallowed up into the Arab-Moslem culture. From that moment, we can follow the influx of a fast developing language, Arabic, on a cognate tongue, Hebrew, no longer as a process of borrowing *words* but in a more subtle way. Hebrew is forming perfectly good new words from original Hebrew roots, "to match" similar formations in Arabic. How this can take place between languages considerably farther apart than are Arabic and Hebrew is an important aspect of the process I have been accounting for.

The examples I find most striking are not instances of "imperialism" or cultural conquest. The Romans in England, the Arabs in Spain, the Italians and the French in Europe, the British in Africa and Asia, thanks to the prestige of their civilization or their military success, introduced new linguistic goods of a fairly simple nature. It is easy to adopt new words when you have already adopted new things; but what of a language bringing new notions, a new world of thought and life, not of things? The history of the propagation of Buddhism in Asia and of Christianity the world over is the most palpable illustration of the freedom of the spirit in respect to its linguistic instruments. Again, "freedom" here implies not that the mind does not require language but that it is not bound by the limitations of any given language, that it is free—not to do away with words, but to choose, or create, or transmute them, so as to adapt them to its own purposes.

The original language or languages of Buddhism were Indo-European dialects of the Indic group. In its northern expansion Buddhism encountered languages as different as Tibetan and Chinese, Mongol and Sogdian and Tocharian, Uygur and Saka, and later Corean and Japanese. In moving south it met with the Dravidian languages (Tamil chiefly) and southeast, with Siamese, Cambodgian, and Malay. In Chinese there were several generations of translators busy rendering Pali and Sanskrit texts into a language that was made to reproduce the original, word for word: an artificial language, to be sure, a language of scholars and erudites—but those learned texts were the very basis of the preaching of Buddhism even to the ignorant and unlettered. When Buddhism vanished from India proper, its center of gravity shifted northward to Burma, China, and Tibet and southward to Ceylon. Had the doctrine changed? It had evolved, no doubt, but the question whether northern or Mahayana Buddhism is an entirely new departure from southern, Hinayana Buddhism—whatever the answer—has nothing to do with specifically Chinese or Tibetan modes of thought. Northern, devotional Buddhism is much more akin to other forms of *Indian* religiosity, such as Bhakti, than to Chinese Tao or Confucianism. What was modified through the introduction of Buddhism into China was the Chinese language, not, primarily, Buddhist thought; or, shall we say, the transformations which Buddhism underwent in China had nothing to do with the peculiarities of the Chinese language. There grew up a Chinese-Buddhist religious vocabulary, so tightly corresponding to each other that modern scholars are able to retranslate into Sanskrit Chinese translations of Indian texts that have long been lost in the original. No doubt the Chinese terms did not, from the outset, exactly correspond to the original; but by the time the doctrine had been expounded and commentaries and super-commentaries piled up, the Chinese and Tibetan words had been given Buddhist meanings and their new citizenship was being everywhere recognized. European scholars who know classical Chinese have to change the key when they pass on to the study of Buddhist texts. In the field of Tibetan, Western scholarship started with Buddhist texts, and it is only recently that ancient documents giving the everyday language of the Tibetans in the age of Buddhist expansion have enabled us to measure the transposition the language had undergone under the influence—and for the requirements—of Buddhism.

The enormous size of the Buddhist canon of scripture accounts for the importance of this bookish translation-language in the spread of Buddhism to the East; the style of the theological sutras, being highly technical, called for a technical translation medium. The case is different with Christianity. The style of the Gospel is that of everyday life; the technical Jewish Old Testament vocabulary had already passed—with all the required transformation—into Greek. The Greek *koine* is not only a vulgar dialect of a literary tongue—so is Pali; it is being wielded by polyglots who are more conversant with Aramaic and Hebrew. This situation has its complexities: e.g., when Luke, whose language is Greek, translates his Aramaic source, he chooses to maintain the exotic note, remaining more literal than the Greek translator of the Aramaic of Matthew; when the latter writes "poor in spirit" rather than "poor" (as in Luke) he is, probably, "explaining" the Hebrew *anawim* by a gloss, justified as it may be. When John speaks of *Logos* he is introducing a notion from everyday Greek that has also its long history in Greek philosophy, and in Philonic, or pre-Philonic, thought, suffused with Judaism—a word that has an etymological equivalent in the Aramaic *memra*, but with as many different connotations and harmonies. This old word, with a cluster of meanings in two languages, is intended to describe an entirely new reality. The context alone, not of the words and phrases but of the other realities, new and old, involved, gives the right interpretation: believers, some literal-minded, some allegorically inclined, hostile critics, Jewish, pagan, and Moslem, theologians and philologists will dispute for centuries, and contribute —on the human side—to clear the ambiguities of the word in the light of an objective account of the whole teaching, which is much more than words. Even then the strife continues, not only on account of those who disbelieve in the Reality behind the word but because there is no purely human guarantee that the interpretation of a word covering a divinely revealed notion is absolutely right—unless that very interpretation be, in some other divine way, made equally certain. Any scriptural religion requires a tradition and a magisterium, not for adding to scripture but for insuring that it is interpreted correctly. This is not saying that the words used in Scripture have neither genealogy nor history; it is just saying that they may mean *more* than is given in their history. The paradox of Revelation is that they *always* mean more.

I have been suggesting that this paradox does not belong exclusively to the language of Revelation but is inscribed in the very nature of human speech, as the instrument of a mind that is always going beyond the limitations of its mode of expression. In the case of a revealed notion, limitations are encountered not only at the level of language but deeper, at the level of thought. It is in the nature of concepts, borrowed as they are from our knowledge of finite reality, that they should be transformed and refined if they are to reach to an infinite reality. Whether that is possible, whether we can think of God in judgments affirming a positive content, whether only the negative is legitimate, whether conceptual knowledge should be entirely discarded and replaced by pure feeling: these are metaphysical and theological questions that have to be dealt with on their proper ground. The approach to them from the side of linguistics is likely only to bring in confusion. What language gives us, in this connection, is the level-mark of human thought. Language registers and hoards up its attainments, registering, at the same time, the level of its own flexibility and achievement as an instrument of expression. The philosopher is right in starting with a nominal definition and in reviewing the "meanings" of a word. He is, in so doing, "feeling" the range of possibilities of his material, like a pianist getting acquainted with each note of his keyboard before he starts using his piano. That is the advantage of the philosophical approach to the study of the history of ideas. In ages less sophisticated and perhaps more creative, people made bold to seize upon a respectably established world and force into it their own meaning, irrespective of other people's feelings; the fearful consequences ensuing may well be compared to the position of a man who has got promptly married to a woman he thinks pleasant, and suddenly finds himself burdened with the girl's whole family. Exogamy has its advantages, too, other than those of the preconcerted *mariage de convenance*.

In the linguistic history of Christianity we are always coming across a process of slow and delicate selection in counterpoint with more brutal impositions. As was the case with poetry, playing with the old and succumbing to the new, we find the Christian sometimes winning over an old word, sometimes enforcing a new one that will have, for a time, to suffer as an "alien." Bible translation is a suggestive illustration. Should one use native words, that sound familiar and homely, to bring out the fact that Revelation knows neither Greek nor Jew, or are they too closely involved in a pre- or an anti-Christian context? Even the *anti* may chance to bring out some illuminating contrast. A loan word, however foreign it may sound at first, has the glow of virginity. Its success depends on the irradiation of the Christian faith on the totality of life. This is the contemporary procedure in mission countries where the language is so superficially known as to arouse the suspicions of the timid European translator. He has to play for safety. Islam did this in the grand manner. The religious vocabulary of the various Moslem languages is Arabic. But then Islam had a theory of scriptural inspiration by which the Koranic *text* was the revelation. The language itself was the revelation, not only beautiful and true but *inimitable*. If Moslem scholastics were, at one moment, of divided opinions as to whether the Koran was created or uncreated, there was, almost from the beginning, the notion that the language could not be surpassed in perfection. Even now, many Moslem theologians hold it a sin to have the Koran transated into other languages. Where official translations exist, published by Moslems, they are mostly accompanied by the Arabic text. Such doctrines have never prevented Islam from pursuing its apostolic march. But Islam has rightly been called the religion of a Book, Christianity being the religion of a Person, who was called the Word but wrote no book and whose teaching is best transmitted by the living, spoken word.

At the other end of the scale, we are reminded of a religious text used daily in ritual, written in a language long dead and in a style so difficult as to require both a translation and a commentary, neither of which, however official they may be, is really adequate. I am referring to the Gathas of Zoroaster. Perhaps one of the reasons for the downfall of Zoroastrianism is this unwanted esoteric feature. The obscurities were there even for the initiate, and modern scholars are not always better off. Thus Zoroastrianism was never able to win over countries other than that where it first flourished, and has to take its revenge on comparative linguists.

And now to conclude. The remarks point to a conception of language as artifact, reflecting both the intellectual and the social nature of man. Language in so far as it is the instrument of our intellect partakes in its universality and is apt to express the highest knowledge of man as well as the most obscure emotional experiences. As an expression of meaning it reflects in its own way the fundamental function of mind: to assimilate the intelligible, to correlate and symbolize it in an inner, unspoken word. In so far as it is social, it follows the rules of human sociability, of convention and freedom, of stability and creativeness, of exuberance and silence. It has its status in the natural law of human relations besides being subject to the laws of technique and art.

𝕏 *Chapter XIX*
RUTH NANDA ANSHEN

LANGUAGE AS COMMUNICATION

Language may be compared with the spear of Amfortas in the legend of the Holy Grail. The wounds which language inflicts upon the thought of man can be healed only by language itself.

The authors of this volume have attempted to show that, while the words which language possesses are human, they have an intrinsic power by which, finally, they appear to transcend themselves. From language as idea to language as communication the word develops into new forms. In such manner it is able to purge itself of those fallacies and illusions to which the common usage of language inevitably subjects the word. The mind of man can proceed from the common speech of daily life to the language of metaphysics, religion, art, science, physics, mathematics, law, or logic. But the power and validity of the symbolic form, the inevitability of symbolic thought, can never be avoided. Every idea, as Flaubert reminds us, is not only perceived by a single, initial intuition, but is at the same time inseparable from its symbol. It is indeed the *universalium in re.*

The effort has been made in this book to point to that linguistic reality, as Shelley has done, which reveals that language "rules a throng of thought and forms which else senseless and shapeless were," thus making communication between man and man possible. Spoken language may be defined as a system of sound and sound groups, produced by the delicate minimum movements of man's articulatory apparatus, which are made to symbolize thoughts crystallized around certain points. These points may be termed acoustic fixations, which can then achieve a permanent form in writing. Were this impossible man would be compelled to recapitulate at the birth of each new thought the entire mass of thoughts humanity has ever conceived. Even science has been described by the eighteenth-century philosopher Condillac as only *"une langue bien faite"* out of previously accumulated knowledge.

But it is an error to believe that language depends, for its communicability, upon mere doing—even doing well. The historic fallacy of this hypothesis has been demonstrated by the noble errors of Francis Bacon, whose chief interest was not at all religious truth and the eternal destiny of man. For this is a matter of faith, of supernatural revelation extending beyond the realm of reason. Bacon was rather concerned with the progress of knowledge, and with the communication of this knowledge. He was concerned with achieving well-being, not blessedness. He pragmatized knowledge and language. He was concerned with the accomplishments of the present and the promises of the future. He perfected skeptical criticism. With superb acumen he classified what he considered to be the categories of human errors, the fallacies and idols of man's mind. No one has more successfully laid bare their roots and their origins, natural as well as social, specific as well as general. And no one has demonstrated less confidence in the spontaneous and unfettered exercise of reason and of language.

Bacon was the preeminent precursor of experimentalism, leading to the multiple techniques of communication of our time. He insisted that human, theoretical reason and language not only are perverted and diseased but are in themselves fallacious and unstable. And he proposed the cure: not to attempt to employ reason and language where they cannot be employed and for purposes for which they are unsuited. Man is endowed with reason and language, he declared, not for the sake of speculation or of spinning out theories about things that are beyond the realm of reason and language but for the sake of action. For the essence of man is action, not thought. But Bacon was not aware that such values and ideas cannot be divorced from the words which express them and which lead to concrete doing.

The changing contents of words, their ability to conceal or reveal their essential meaning, record the history of civilization. And language thus becomes the mirror of the aspirations of those who are liberated or oppressed. The mimetic impulse in man is released. And he is thus able, unfettered, to impart the universal meaning of his communication or, enslaved, is able only to utter words which have been emptied of their universal content. True communication, in its spiritual and moral power, becomes impossible, for example, in a totalitarian political state. For in such a state language degenerates into a power instrument. It becomes a means of storing knowledge in order to manipulate people in war and peace. This is one of the inescapable results of the pragmatization of thought. This is one of the profound fallacies of believing that it is in action alone, in practice, in "experience" that man finds the foundations of knowledge, of the only knowledge that is available and important to him, the only knowledge which he can communicate. For the pragmatist, theoretical reason and language are chimerical, fanciful. Without discipline and control, they run wildly astray. The firm and unequivocal ground of "experience" is their anchor to reality. Thus man must not permit them to wander at will. He must shackle them by precise rules of procedure. He must restrict and restrain them to their only valid and legitimate use, the empirical and pragmatic method of communicating intelligible knowledge. Bacon's *Novum Organum* is the apotheosis of "experience"—the only avenue for the transmission of ideas, for the communication of thought. It offers man the fruitful certitude of well-ordered "experience" as against the sterile "uncertainty" of reason and of the abstract *logos*. The disenchantment and disillusionment of the work of Agrippa received the reply of Bacon *On the Advancement of Learning*.

This pragmatic philosophy of language as mere communication emptied of its attribute of communion ignores the pristine astonishment of man when in the history of the world the human mind first began to philosophize and to communicate ideas. The mind discovered that language was in truth already in existence. It was already fitted out with all the wealth of forms and notions, and, as Kant has taught us, "a great part, perhaps the greatest part, of the office of reason consists in dismembering the notions which it already finds in itself." It finds, for example, the cases of declension in the substantive, adjective, pronoun, the voices, tenses, and modes of the verb, and the plenitude of ready-made notions of object and relations. All the categories which represent the most important relations, the fundamental notions of all thought, as being, becoming, thinking, feeling, desiring, motion, energy, activity, lie within the human mind as part of the ontological structure and entelechy of man's nature. In this way language as the garment of thought becomes communicable because all men participate in its universal essence. Language becomes universally intelligible. And by means of this universality the subject is, so to speak, sheathed in the statement. This universality is illustrated by the fact that a given race of men as a historical entity is indifferent to the morphology of language and that language can no more be comprehended on the hypothesis of race than it can be understood on the hypothesis of the laws of physics or mathematics. A given language may be and often is independent of a specific culture area, the English language itself presenting a conspicuous example of the phenomenon that it is not spoken or written by a unified race.

Universality is the essence of language, thus making possible the presence of the symbol in relation to every object. Language made concrete by symbolic imagery is thus able to evoke something further than its immediate meaning, and style gains a second voice from its overtones. There is an effort so to impart proportion as to indicate values; and the discovered communicability, the "speakingness" of relationships, is thereby more felt. Indeed, the deciding of the communicable relation between thing and thing, between act and act, is in itself a great part of man's linguistic expression.

It is this very necessity of proportion, this striving of language toward univocality in meaning, which serves the needs of communication. However, such total absolute stability can be purchased only at the price of incommunicability. Then language ceases to be spoken. Normal linguistic situations cannot, even should not, achieve absolute univocality or equilibrium. If law, religion, symbolic logic, or scientific discourse professes to attain it, such equilibrium could exist only by inhibiting spontaneity and change. In this way the Aristotelian system, a system which had grown rigid and sterile, was finally abnegated since those conditions no longer exist in which this system was conceived and to which it was intended to apply.

The use of normal language as communication, whether in religion or law or in the natural sciences, whether in Latin, Sanskrit, or Coptic, will ceaselessly require constant definition and exegesis. Since the daily, common vernacular is lacking in precision, such sciences as mathematics and logic demand formulas and specific symbols for their intelligibility and communicability.

In spite of the fact that languages themselves spring from different centers of development, the course of this development is, fundamentally, so similar in all the arenas of human culture that the agreement of the basic forms and the structure of the sentences in all stages of development, on the basis of which communication becomes possible, is explicable only by a common essence in mankind for forming language, by an all-pervading spirit which everywhere guides the development of language according to the identical laws of bloom and decline. In other words, all conscious human thought and therefore *experience* becomes possible because of language.

This enlargement of the meaning of language and of experience was not perceived by Bacon. He seemed incapable of knowing that pure empiricism, language as mere function, bereft of meaning, only leads man astray. It can no more lead to *experience* than to experiment. An experiment, indeed, is a question we put to nature. It presupposes a language in which man is able to formulate his questions. For experiment is not the foundation of theory or hypothesis. It is merely a means of testing the hypothesis, of confirming or refuting it. Since no phenomena can possibly exist which do not imply *concepts,* science itself cannot be said to result from an accumulation of phenomena. But Bacon was committed to the pursuit of "the order of things and not that of ideas." Therefore he was destined to fail in his attempt to reform the mind of man.

Descartes, however, did comprehend the necessity of going beyond common sense and classification—which Bacon aimed at just as intently as Aristotle did. Descartes was committed to the pursuit of "the order of ideas, not that of things." Although, however, this made possible the success of the Cartesian revolution for 300 years in Western thought, it too was doomed finally to end in sterility and meaninglessness since it separated in its own unique way the original unity and harmony of spirit and nature, man and God, idea and expression. While defining the *cogito,* it neglected the *sum,* the "I am." It is this question of the *ergo sum* which constitutes the compelling, existentialist plight of modern man. For him language as communion no longer exists since this would presuppose the presence of the Infinite in the finite. But in our time the Infinite is no longer accepted as contained within the finite. The Infinite has, so to speak, evaporated and man now finds himself suffering from the most serious malady of the soul, that objectivation which threatens him with degenerating into a mere *thing*, and making communication itself impossible, in spite of all the technological devices it possesses, since the subtle essence of communion, out of which ultimate intelligibility and communicability are born, is no longer present.

When we say that the finite has become emptied of the Infinite, we mean, in other words, that the concept of truth, the adequation of name and thing, is lacking, And this lack prevents thought from withstanding if not overcoming the demoralizing and mutilating effects of a formalized, instrumentalized language. It is to Plotinus and Plato we must turn rather than to positivism for preserving the idea of truth, which means the correspondence of language to reality. Neither the existentialist philosophy nor literature is committed today to the expression of the *meaning* of things and of life, to the voice of all that is silent and mute, to bestowing upon nature a medium for comprehending her joys and sorrows—in other words, to the knowledge of reality by its rightful *name*.

The tongue of nature is absent. The word, the cry, the gesture of mankind which in truth do possess an inherent quality and meaning are in our time mere events, mere happenings. And so we must ask ourselves, what is denoted by the proper name? What is the *self* which demands self-realization and which must, as Socrates insisted, know itself before it can be communicated to others? Herein lies the meaning of freedom, a freedom which cannot be renounced since man does not possess the choice of avoiding choice.

It is the self which is finally revealed through, among other ways, language. From this point of view language may be said to be the most important form of human communication. Although communication does exist among other forms of life, among some mammals, birds, or insects, they do not speak. With the existence of man, nature itself begins to give evidence of a psychosocial phenomenon. The property of conceptual thought which is inherently human, with its objective correlate in the form of true speech, assured man of the possibility of creating history, of giving birth to a world, and the method of the cumulative transmission of experience.

In this way language remained a continuum. Phoneme mingled with morpheme, morpheme with construct, and construct with discourse. Thus the continuum reaches from the one who speaks to the one who hears and finally to the entire speech community. There are four ways of communication: man speaks to God, to himself, to one other, to many others, in the past, present or future. The community thus possesses a historical descent linguistically and is itself a linguistic ancestor. Through spoken and still more adequately through written language, man can achieve what is possible for no other organism. He is able to transmit the results of experience to later generations and to do so cumulatively.

It is not, however, to be assumed that language alone makes the culture. Yet this possibility to transmit the knowledge of a culture constitutes a second mechanism of inheritance in addition to that of genetics. But an entire speech community laboring for generations is required in order to make the specific form of language a self-perpetuating system, able to maintain itself in that dynamic equilibrium, that vital rhythmic movement between rigidity and fluidity, which bestows status upon the language. This human mechanism is thus able to transmit a system of knowledge, ideas and attitudes, not a mere system of material units as in a physical inheritance.

In this morphology of language in relation to the problem of communication it is necessary to note in what way modern languages have tended to separate abstract thought. We are struck by national or racial differences of thought when we read modern philosophy in English, German, French, or Italian. And this, of course, constitutes a question not only of semantics but of philosophies of life. Mathematics is now the only universal language, although only a pseudo language. This is an interesting antithesis to medieval Latin, which tended to concentrate on what men of various races and lands could think together. It is like drinking at the springs of Castalia to recognize the character of this universal language which inheres, for example, in Dante's Florentine speech, and the localization of this "Florentine" speech appeared to emphasize universality, since it cut across the modern division of nationality. In our time in order to comprehend German, French,

Language: Its Meaning and Function

348 *Language: Its Meaning and Function*

American, Islamic, or Far Eastern languages in their literary or philosophic expression, we must first understand the minds of these respective peoples. However, although Dante was an Italian and, to boot, a patriot, he was first and foremost a European.

The problem of communication in our time is exceedingly complex since words have associations, and the groups of words *in* association have associations. This constitutes a sort of local self-consciousness since such words are the growth and fruit of a *particular* civilization. Thus it is difficult for modern languages to divest themselves of their isolated characteristics. But in Dante the transcendent nature of his ideas, the passionate conflict of old feelings with new, the effort and triumph of new renunciation, even greater than any renunciation at the grave, because it was a renunciation that persisted beyond the grave, as we see in the *Vita Nuova*, reveals how exquisitely Dante expresses the recrudescence of an ancient passion in a new idea, a new emotion, a new situation which comprehends, enlarges, and bestows meaning upon experience. "Gazing on her, so I became within, as did Glaucus, on tasting of the grass which made him sea-fellow of the other gods. To transcend humanity may not be told in words, wherefore let the instance suffice for him for whom that experience is reserved by Grace." In such manner we see that the language of Dante is the perfection of a common language and therefore universally comprehensible and communicable.

In a *living* language man has always tried to make his understanding, his consciousness, explicable and communicable. Out of our everyday language, which has often been denounced as a "horse-dealer's tongue," there has developed on the one hand the rational symbolism of mathematics and on the other hand poetry. In the living language both elements are contained: the poetic and the rational. But the living language of mankind is neither tarnished poetry nor a blurred substitute for mathematical symbolism. On the contrary, neither the one nor the other would or could exist without the nourishing stem of the language of our everyday life, with all its complexity, obscurity, crudeness, and ambiguity.

Wilhelm von Humboldt was right when he stated that the speaking individual does not offer to his fellow speaker objective signs for the things expressed. He does not compel him by his verbal utterance to represent to himself exactly the same thing as that meant by him, but is content with, so to speak, pressing down the homologous key of the other's respective mental keyboard, with establishing only the same link in the chain of associations of things with words, so that there are elicited corresponding, though not exactly identical, responses. And yet we behave naïvely as though we were understood in spite of the variable ratio of understanding our words may find. This profound illusion is one of the sources of man's deepest security. Through this illusion he gains the assurance, often false, of being surrounded by a friendly world, participating in it, a world which shares with him all the associations he may have experienced throughout his life. For there is nothing more terrifying to man than isolation in the universe, separation from that cosmic collectivity of which he is a legitimate and indispensable part. In this valid relationship man becomes at one with God and therefore with himself. "The glory of man," declares Valéry, in his essay on *Eureka*, "and something more than his glory, is to waste his powers on the void . . . thus it would seem that the history of thought (and thus of language) can be summarized in these words: *It is absurd by what it seeks; great by what it finds.*" And it was Pascal's unique genius which confirmed that "the slightest *movement* affects the whole of nature in its absolute fulness and perfection," implying that the "slightest movement," a spoken word, will act creatively if meaning and communicability are present. From this it would appear that a failure of moral responsibility toward the universe could not possibly issue in an act of creation, nor would action produce stars that are both beautiful and hallowed without the *word* as a "magic recipe"—one might even say as an incantatory magic.

The fundamental premise of this chapter lies in the assumption that without a basic *communion* between man and nature or man and man there can be no communication, except of course on a merely externalized, technological or scientific plane. And such communion must issue from a central unity and not from a parallelogram of forces colliding inadvertently from multiple and unpredicted directions.

For the "desire" for language is rooted in man's nature, a desire which urges that the final object of this desire be truly desirable and capable of being known, communicated. Man can never be content, as all other forms of life presumably are, to pursue ends solely because they are dictated by the momentum of his vital impulsions and interests. The ambiguity of the term "desirable," upon which John Stuart Mill foundered, is an illustration of the problem involved. A sound is audible if it can be heard, and the test of its audibility is the fact that someone does hear it. Is the criterion of the desirability of anything, in like manner, the fact that there happens to exist somewhere the desire for that thing? To answer in the affirmative is a betrayal of language. This is not what men intend to say when they assert that something is desirable. They mean to utter the belief that, whether or not there happens to exist any desire for the desirable thing, it *is* desirable and men ought to desire it because it is good and intrinsically worthy of their effort. The belief may indeed be an error, but the utterance of this belief is a judgment, an evaluation about something present, objective and discoverable and therefore communicable, and independent of and even transcending the caprices and contingencies of our *de facto* preferences or aversions. Such quality of the mind appears to be the most significant characteristic of man, namely, that he is able to give utterance to persuasions of this order, and that only such ultimate goals as are believed to be bathed in the luminous splendor of a transparent objectivity which at the same moment embraces the subject can evoke the full measure and deep plenitude of his devotion.

It is in no way the part of wisdom to assert that such persuasions are born in the mind solely because man is inevitably deceived and cheated by language. The position that the verbal expression of judgments of value has betrayed him into a misconception of the objectivity of values on the analogy of the objectivity of fact misinterprets the reality. The deep and often hidden wisdom that language incorporates and often symbolizes may not be so readily abrogated. Furthermore, we are not permitted to judge the meaning and validity of discourse in terms of prior restrictions upon what words must mean, as derivatives of some special hypothesis or theory.

Were a beast, a voracious lion, pursuing his prey, to attempt to justify his goal by uttering a judgment of objective value, we would be compelled to accept the word of the lion. But at the same time we would be compelled to penetrate beneath the linguistic stratagem of the beast and to expose the vital interest it might wish to conceal. The lion has no need of language since the horizon of his universe does not extend beyond the peripheries of nature's concrete, physical law. The energies of the beast are utilized in the service of its imperative and compelling wants and desires.

The ontological thirst and hunger that are the appetitive ends of all effort, that which is good, reasonable, desirable, common to mankind and therefore communicable to men, this thirst and this hunger belong to man alone.

Language as communication compels us to take cognizance of the existentialist position in modern thought. This position makes evident an inherent frailty and ineptitude of the philosophy of existentialism whether found in Kierkegaard or Heidegger, two of its most salient examples—an ineptitude to include the essence of mankind within the existence of each man. In other words, the divine substance is denied; there is an astonishing renunciation of any measure of grandeur of which the human race might be capable. This philosophy means that existence actuates nothing, that there can be act without potency, man without human nature. The principle of language, especially of language as communication which is implicit in the thought of Kierkegaard and Heidegger, excludes the possibility of communion with transcendent being, thereby excluding the genuine experience of communication both as a concept and as an expression of existence.

The existentialist theory of man possesses an intrinsic phenomenological weakness. It is unable to *account* for human communication. For the existentialist as for the positivist, language is not; it must be made. For the existentialist, the ordinary mode of being with others is impersonal, debased, and authentic communication between persons becomes impossible. Even Jaspers, who struggled with this concept, was unable to avoid the implications and conclusions of his existentialist hypothesis, namely, that the more authentic a man becomes, the more isolated and unintelligible he seems to be.

The rejection of universal concepts and judgments renders an ultimately intelligible and communicable solution impossible. In order that a man find within himself enough coherence and power to re-create language, he must first be fixed; in other words, he must be named. Unless this takes place language and its words become things, objects. And then when two individual human beings meet each other, each tries to absorb the other as a thing, as an object, into his world. In this way conflict is engendered and communion is put to flight. Common ends are nonexistent inevitably and a priori. Commitment to love, to friendship becomes thereby an impossibility, a *non sequitur*. Words become exogamic, a mere social process excluding the human person. Transcendent and fixed or universal meanings are repudiated and communication is exteriorized depending on the mere social act and hoping to derive therefrom a meaning which it is actually intended to bestow. The existentialist forgets that words are germs of being. He forgets that words are promises. He is unable to regard language as an actual involvement in the life that it supports and re-creates at every moment.

Moral solipsism is the price to be paid for this isolation of the human person from the human community. For if meaning is not contained within the word a priori, then the quest for truth becomes futile and it is an act of absurdity to search for a deeply buried treasure which may be unearthed. There is nothing anywhere, nothing that awaits us, nothing in the world or above the world, nothing with which we are able to confront the words and phrases which we shape. But if language is to be synonymous with life, with the work and blood of each living soul, then the profound and discreet virtue that is ever present in truth and man's love for it cannot be abandoned, and integrity between man and man cannot be betrayed.

To speak means to commit oneself. Thus the meaning of this morality is evident. As in the ethical system of Kant, man achieves the universal in his own flesh. And when man communicates with his fellow man, he casts himself into a universal order, although it may at first be unknown and foreign, for which he is responsible. He himself *becomes* universal and through experiencing this *communion* with the cosmos he escapes from his cosmic loneliness which his physical existence imposes on him, and he is at last able to *communicate* with his fellow creatures. This is man's sole requirement, to actualize with humility and with caution, through his very existence, the universality and the essence of which he is fundamentally constituted. In other words, man must *love* since he *is* love; in this lies his promise and fulfillment as man; in this there is, suddenly and mysteriously, power and presence, and the nothingness is dissipated since man is able to return to himself and thus to the path of mankind.

Cognition itself demands reevaluation. The act of cognition has been reduced by modern epistemology to the presence of a mere datum. The ontologic substance has evaporated from modern logic, which is manipulated by technicians who are unaware of the meaning of symbols and who have abrogated the signifying functions of concepts and judgments. The intentional structure of ideas has been ignored, thus making it impossible to achieve descriptive formulas which may adequately embrace the higher levels of intuitive and rational communication. The soul of man is lost or at best oscillates from the individual to the universal, from the historical to the eternal, revealing the contradictory and anguished desire that preserves the dignity of the human person while at the same moment it is enslaved by a rigorous and implacable social order, deceiving man treacherously into the belief that his fulfillment lies in the sacrifice wherein he destroys himself in order that the universal may be preserved. Thus the mind of man becomes imprisoned within an impenetrable surface, and the metaphysical assumption, the question of the way in which man is able to know the content of another mind, becomes at once without any possible resolution.

The word "communication" has many uses; there are various levels of communication, and these levels may differ in the signs employed, the modes of meaning and interpretation, the manner in which the many aspects of the discourse are interrelated, and finally the quality of communion which is gained. The highest communion compels us to accept a form of existence which possesses a transcendent finality. It is an order postulated as well as intuited since man must be saved from despair by the hope for permanence and fixity concealed within the mobile life of words. For man has equally an ethical and a teleological necessity to believe in the Absolute, to believe in the existence of God. This is at once man's exigence and his prayer.

However, there is another order of communication: material communication most accessible to the quantitative methods of modern, natural science. Such communication functions by means of natural signs: the exploitation of the tone of one's voice, gestures, facial expressions. These do not evoke conceptual meanings but rather induce active modes of response such as fear or hatred and are strategic devices in wielding techniques of mass propaganda and advertising, and in evoking mass responses of an active nature. Then there is the telegram which can be read with a "key." But such devices are incapable of transmitting the awareness of one human being for another, of communicating the mystery of human personality, for this form of communication does not presuppose communion.

Abstract, intelligible discourse is another form of communication, in which ontologic necessity is substituted for psychic association. Basic assertions must then be analyzed and formulated in a universal structure. Innuendo, suggestion, and even coercion give place to persuasion and logical analysis. Empathy surrenders to agreement or disagreement, and man believes that out of the confused obscurity of unconscious conflict the entire problem of communication is lifted into a luminous arcanum suffused with the light of reason. Inference appears to be no longer necessary since man has gained access to the mind of his neighbor. But then the question arises as to the possibility of access to the inner consciousness of one's neighbor apart from inference. Herein lies the difficult problem of the sign, the symbol, and the *signatum* discussed in some of the preceding chapters of this volume.

It must be conceded that there exists no single, univocal concept embracing every form of communication. And yet we may concede that philosophic communication is the most fundamental and far-reaching, for the final issue is indeed being itself, upon the recognition of which depends authentic cultural communion. For not only thought but reality itself is determined by the structure of language, and there are many questions concerning being which may be not only clarified but even solved by an adequate interpretation of the linguistic symbols of the human race.

Language as communication commits man unequivocally—whether silent or expressed. It commits him to the reality that finally the differentiations of cultures may be compared with the multiplicity of dialects throughout civilization. The essential content of the language of the spirit is the same for all mankind. The only difference is that of the words employed, words expressing the same basic ideals and aspirations, frequently even in the same idioms. Even God is God also as word for all mankind and as such is a promise and a germ of being.

Verbal and visual language is universally intelligible and is fundamental alike to all civilizations of the world. Man must know that this is the only path that can lead to higher and deeper degrees of cooperation, organization, and unity—to higher and deeper degrees of collective conscience, consciousness, and individual dignity. For language is the distinctive mark of man. Even intuition is postulated upon the presupposition that consciousness and knowledge must penetrate their object and melt together with it. And as long as there remains any distance between the object itself and the thought of the object, we cannot reach or speak of truth. But consciousness and knowledge depend finally neither upon identification nor upon reproduction, as empiricism and sensationalism have demanded. They depend upon objectivation —the pristine function of language. For it is then that we may pass from the passive acceptance of single sense-data to a fresh, constructive, and spontaneous insight into the universe. Language thus becomes indispensable not only for the construction of the world of thought but also for the construction of the world of perception, both of which constitute the ultimate nexus of an intelligible communion, spiritual and moral, between man and man.

Language is an *energeia,* an activity, not only of communication and self-expression but of orientation in the universe. It is the spirit made flesh; it is the proof of the existence of God in accordance with the exigence that language bears within itself and imparts to us. This is the theology, the *word* God and the *fact* of God. And it is only by faith and by works that the meaning of this word, which was in the beginning and will be to the end of time, may be re-created. For the violent muteness, the desperate isolation, of man finally breaks through in language, and it is the creation of ever widening horizons of human communication which is now coming to embrace all mankind that we are summoned by an unbending necessity to nourish and to honor.

This is the unique beholding of our epoch: the vision of communication through communion. We need not seek the Word. The Word is given with man. The Word is found by Time.

BIOGRAPHICAL NOTE

RUTH NANDA ANSHEN   Editor, Science of Culture Series; World Perspectives

W. H. AUDEN   Poet

RICHARD P. BLACKMUR   Professor of Literature, Princeton University

GEORGE BOAS   Professor of the History of Philosophy, Johns Hopkins University

HUNTINGTON CAIRNS   Secretary and General Counsel, National Gallery of Art, Washington, D.C.

FRANCIS FERGUSSON   University Professor of Comparative Literature, Rutger University

ERICH FROMM   Psychiatrist

KURT GOLDSTEIN   Former Director of the Neurological Institute and Institute for Research of Brain-Injured Soldiers, Frankfurt, Germany; Visiting Professor of Psychology, Brandeis University

ROMAN JAKOBSON   S. H. Cross Professor of Slavic Languages and Literatures, Harvard University

HAROLD D. LASSWELL   Professor of Law and Political Science, Yale University

JACQUES MARITAIN   Former Professor of Philosophy, Princeton University

JEAN P. DE MENASCE   Professor of Iranian Religions, Ecole Des Hautes Etudes, Paris, France

CHARLES W. MORRIS   Fellow, Center for Advanced Study in the Behavioral Sciences, Stanford, California

MARGARET NAUMBURG   Psychologist

SWAMI NIKHILANANDA   Leader of the Ramakrishna-Vivekananda Center, New York: Member of the Columbia University Seminar on Interreligious Relations

LEO SPITZER   Professor of Linguistics, Johns Hopkins University

PAUL TILLICH   University Professor of Philosophical Theology, Harvard University

N. H. TUR-SINAI   Former Bialik Professor of Hebrew Philology, Hebrew University, Jerusalem